All the pages in this book were created—and are printed here—in Japanese RIGHT-to-LEFT format. No artwork has been reversed or altered, so you can read the stories the way the creators meant for them to be read.

FLIP IT!

S0-BCN-998

RIGHT TO LEFT?!

Traditional Japanese manga starts at the upper right-hand corner, and moves right-to-left as it goes down the page. Follow this guide for an easy understanding.

For more information and sneak previews, visit cmxmanga.com. Call 1-800-COMIC BOOK for the nearest comics shop or head to your local book store.

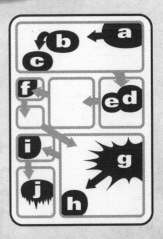

Jim Lee
    Editorial Director
John Nee
    VP—Business Development
Hank Kanalz
    VP—General Manager, WildStorm
Paul Levitz
    President & Publisher
Georg Brewer
    VP—Design & DC Direct Creative
Richard Bruning
    Senior VP—Creative Director
Patrick Caldon
    Executive VP—Finance & Operations
Chris Caramalis
    VP—Finance
John Cunningham
    VP—Marketing
Terri Cunningham
    VP—Managing Editor
Alison Gill
    VP—Manufacturing
Paula Lowitt
    Senior VP—Business & Legal Affairs
Gregory Noveck
    Senior VP—Creative Affairs
Sue Pohja
    VP—Book Trade Sales
Cheryl Rubin
    Senior VP—Brand Management
Jeff Trojan
    VP—Business Development, DC Direct
Bob Wayne
    VP—Sales

KAMIKAZE KAITO JEANNE © 1998 by Arina Tanemura.
All Rights Reserved. First published in Japan in 1998 by
SHUEISHA Inc., Tokyo.

KAMIKAZE KAITO JEANNE Volume 1, published by
WildStorm Productions, an imprint of DC Comics, 888
Prospect St. #240, La Jolla, CA 92037. English Translation
© 2005. All Rights Reserved. English translation rights in
U.S.A. and Canada arranged by SHUEISHA Inc. The stories,
characters, and incidents mentioned in this magazine are
entirely fictional. Printed on recyclable paper. WildStorm
does not read or accept unsolicited submissions of ideas,
stories or artwork. Printed in Canada. THIRD PRINTING.

DC Comics, a Warner Bros. Entertainment Company.

Sheldon Drzka – Translation and Adaptation
Saida Temofonte – Lettering
Larry Berry – Design
Ben Abernathy – Editor

ISBN:1-4012-0555-0
ISBN-13: 978-1-4012-0555-3

WHILE JEANNE SAVES SOULS, WHO WILL RESCUE MARON'S? AVAILABLE NOW!

Kamikaze KAITO Jeanne

Volume 2

By Arina Tanemura. The battle against demon-possessed paintings continues as Kaito Jeanne and Sinbad's competition heats up! Meanwhile, life at school grows complicated for Maron, as she must deal with her growing feelings for Chiaki and her guilt over being kissed by Sinbad—not realizing they're one and the same! And Chiaki hides a dark secret that could shatter everything. **Collect this entire series—all 7 seven volumes are currently available!**

KAMIKAZE KAITO JEANNE © 1998 by Arina Tanemura/SHUEISHA Inc.

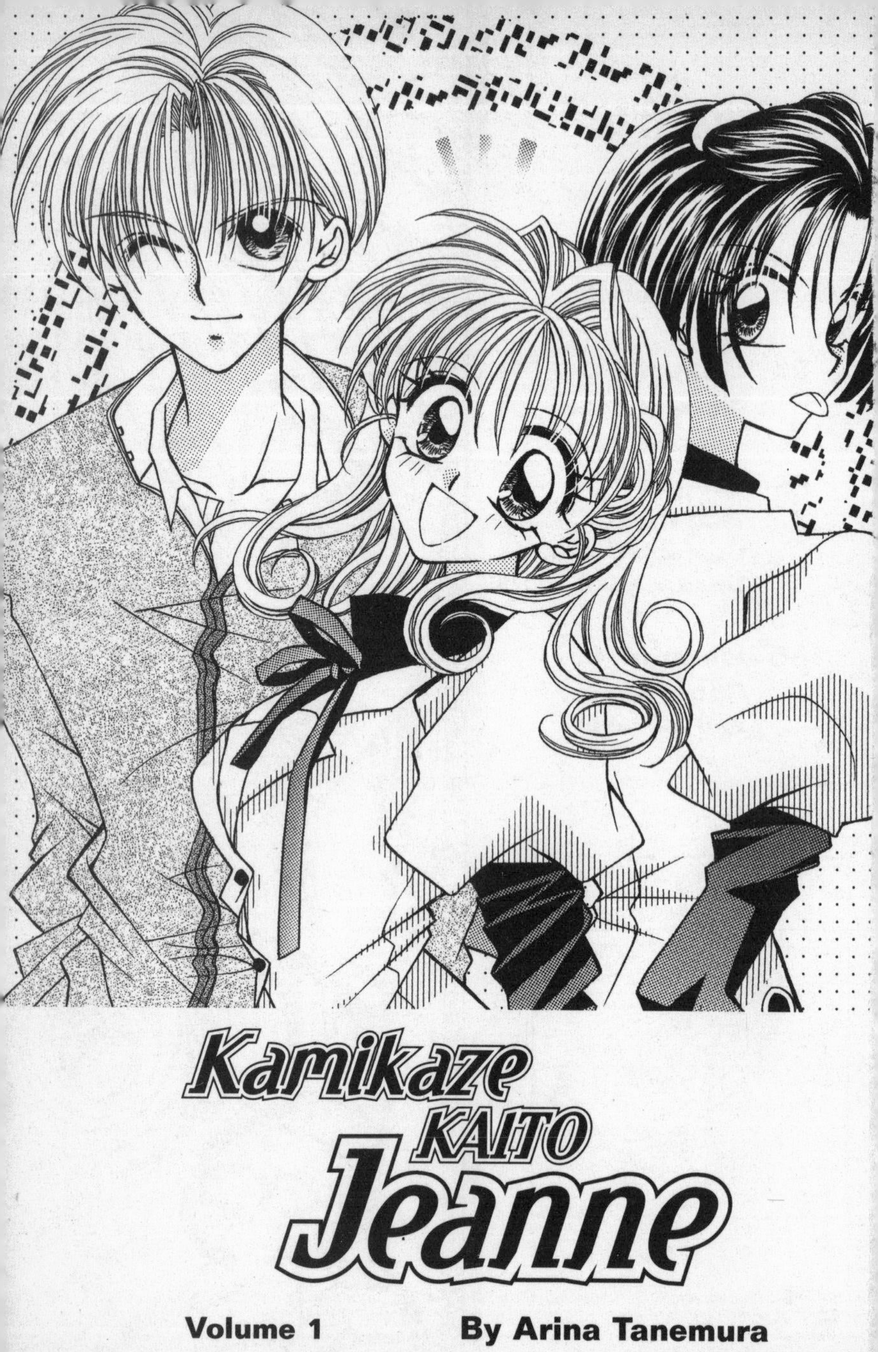

Kamikaze KAITO Jeanne

Volume 1 **By Arina Tanemura**

CONTENTS

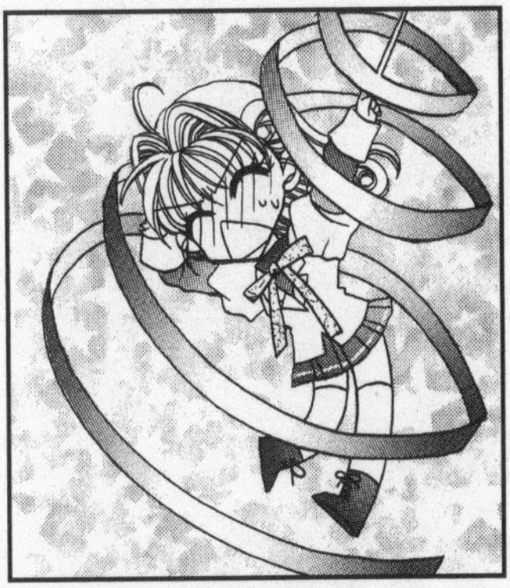

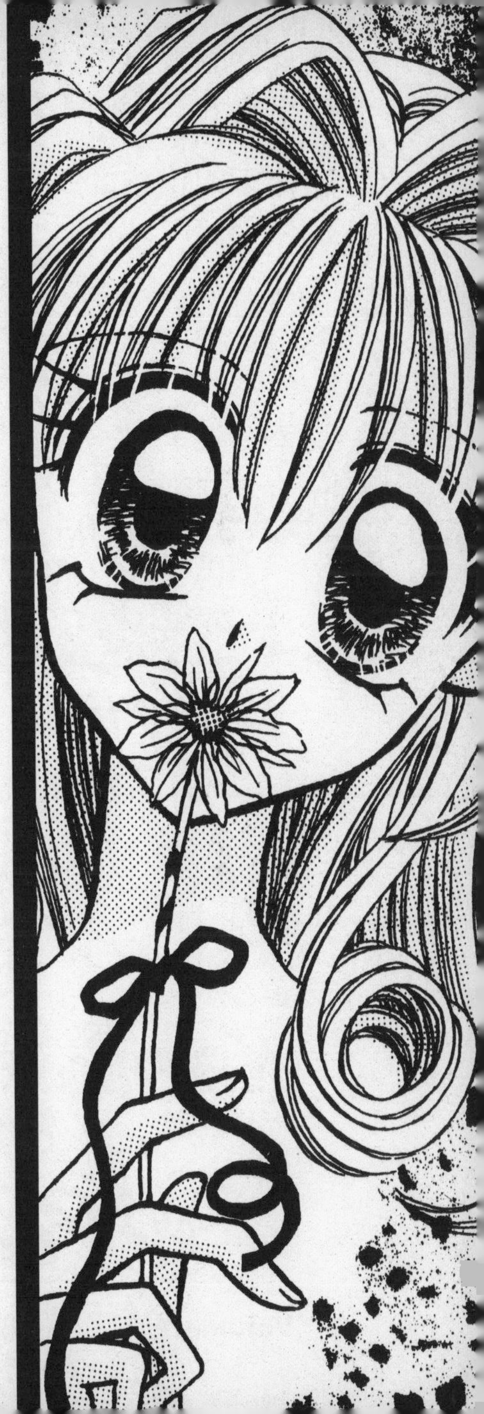

Chapter 1 THE BACKLIT MADAMOISELLE

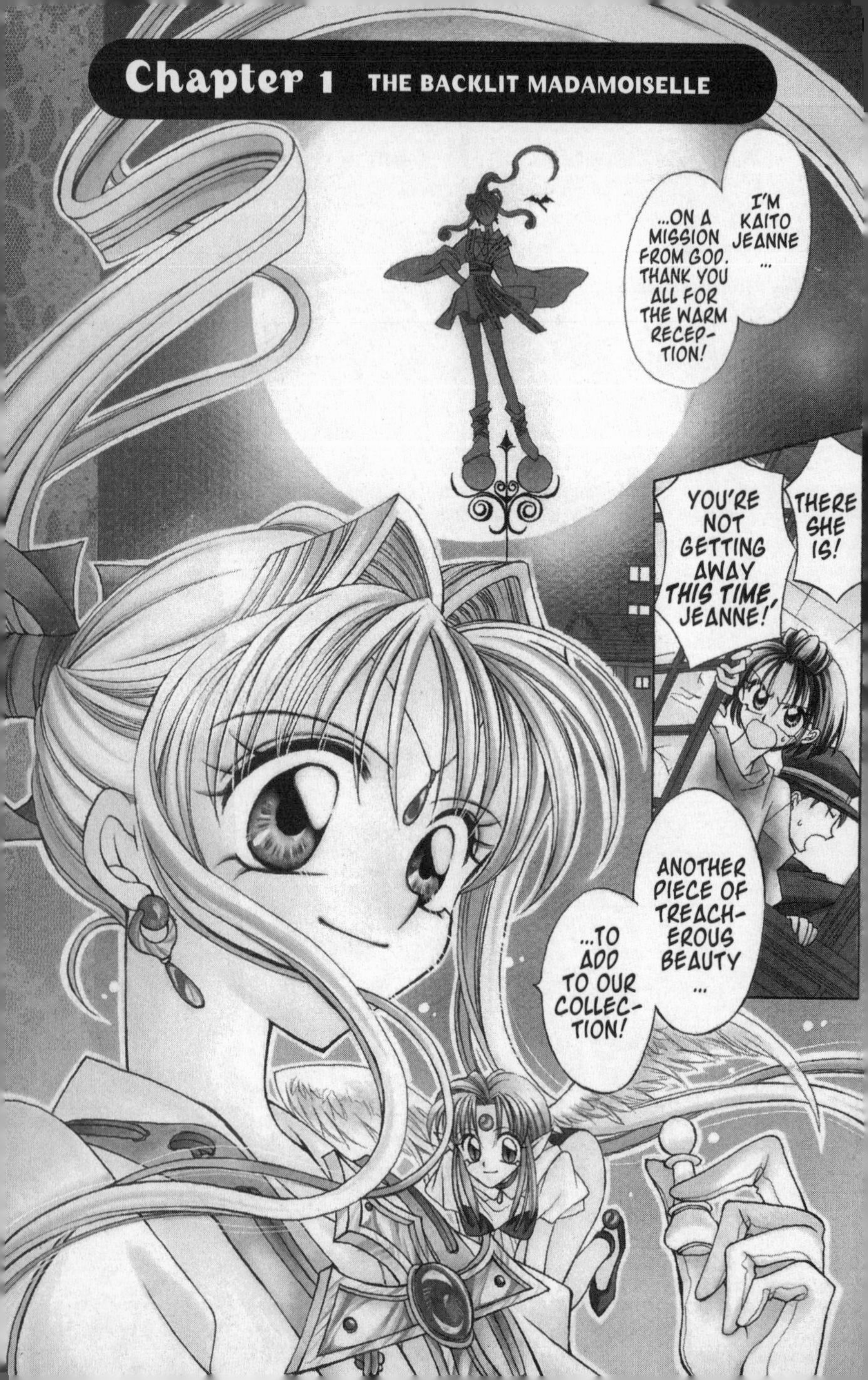
I'M KAITO JEANNE ...
...ON A MISSION FROM GOD. THANK YOU ALL FOR THE WARM RECEPTION!
THERE SHE IS!
YOU'RE NOT GETTING AWAY THIS TIME, JEANNE!
ANOTHER PIECE OF TREACHEROUS BEAUTY ...
...TO ADD TO OUR COLLECTION!

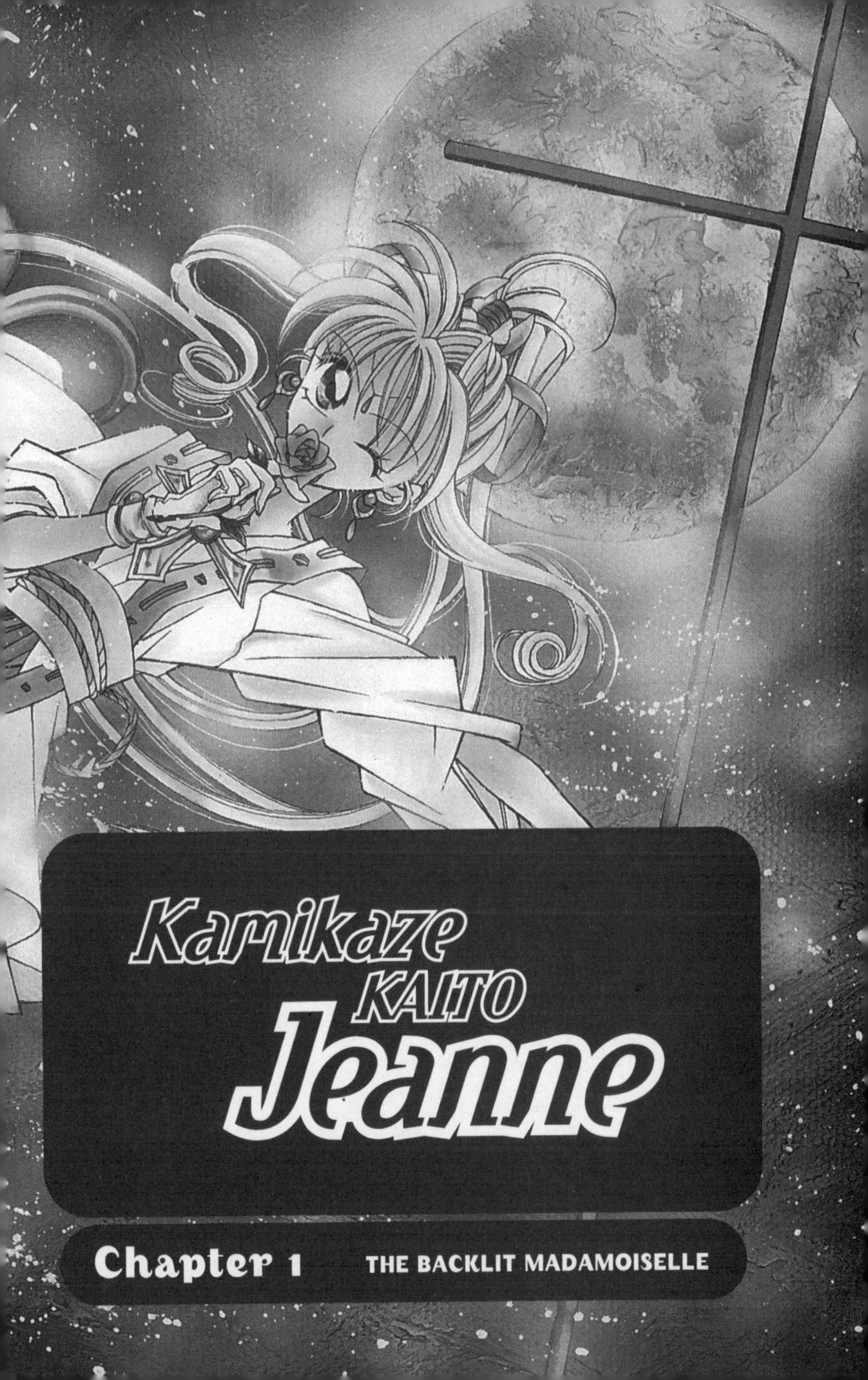
Kamikaze KAITO Jeanne
Chapter 1
THE BACKLIT MADAMOISELLE

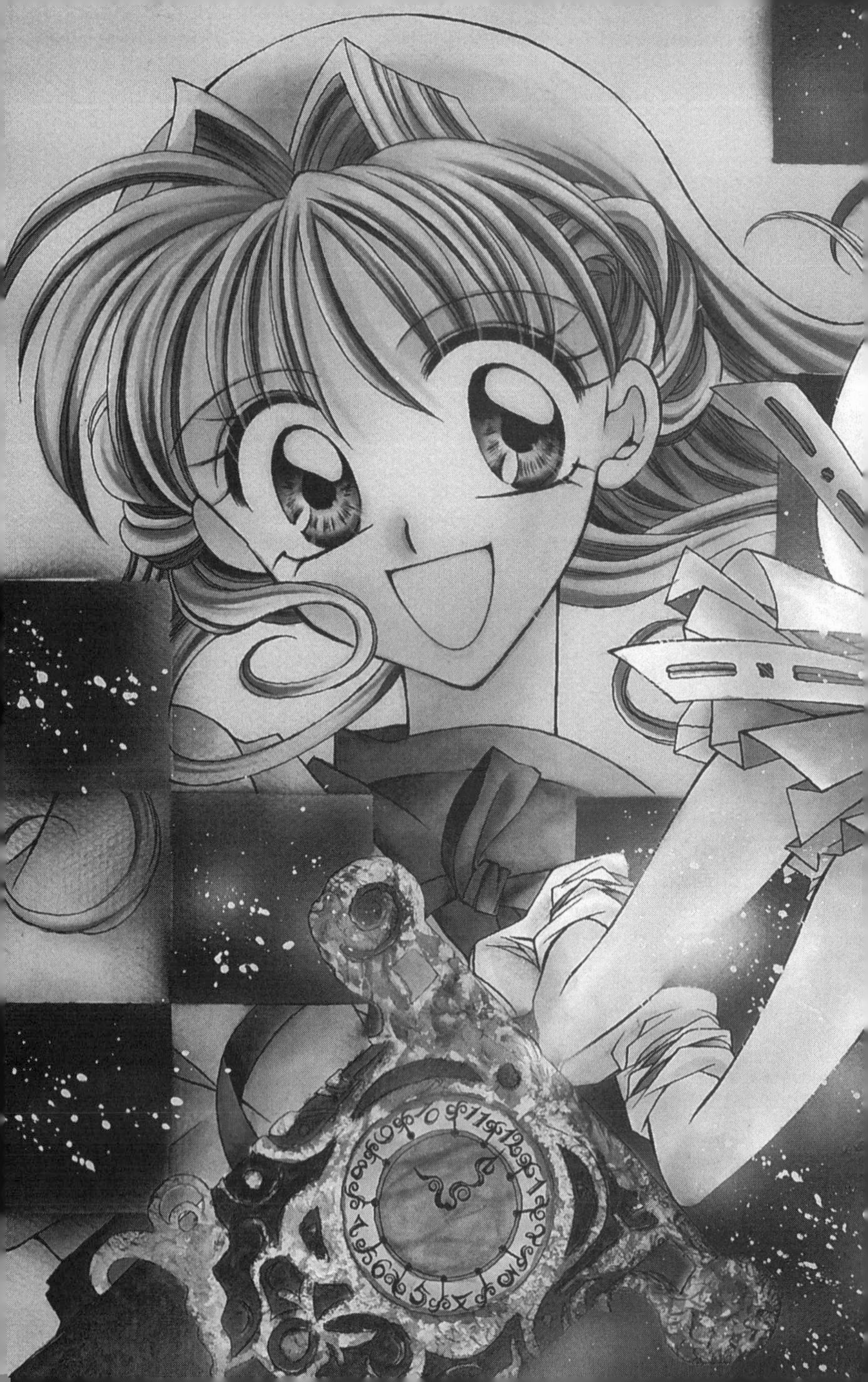

TITLE DRAWING AND STORY COMMENTS

ABOUT THE FIRST STORY, "THE BACKLIT MADAMOISELLE."

My editor thought of all the taglines used for the opening page of each story. I love 'em all! "Suddenly, from out of nowhere, appears the beautiful Kaito Jeanne, on a mission to steal **your** heart tonight!"

Well, here's the historical first episode, the first time I ever made a 50-page story, and was it **hard!**

This serial adventure was decided on just before I finished my last one, "AE-O-N" (and I had just two months to do it!), so I felt pretty rushed when I started it. However, I'm happy with the way the cover drawing turned out (I'm used to working in black and white for manga stories, so I'll avoid a "color commentary" about the cover). Anyway, her cover pose and the whole layout of the cover aren't bad, I guess. Some (or maybe a lot of) people may have figured it out, but "Jeanne" has appeared once before, in a story I created before going pro. It started one day some time ago when I received a fan letter that said, "Arina-sensei, you're my goddess!" At first, I thought something like, "What the...?! Yeah, I **wish!**" But, then, I turned it over in my mind, thinking that in my stories, I do create characters and a world, so in a sense, I am kind of like a god.

———————→ CONTINUED>>>   →

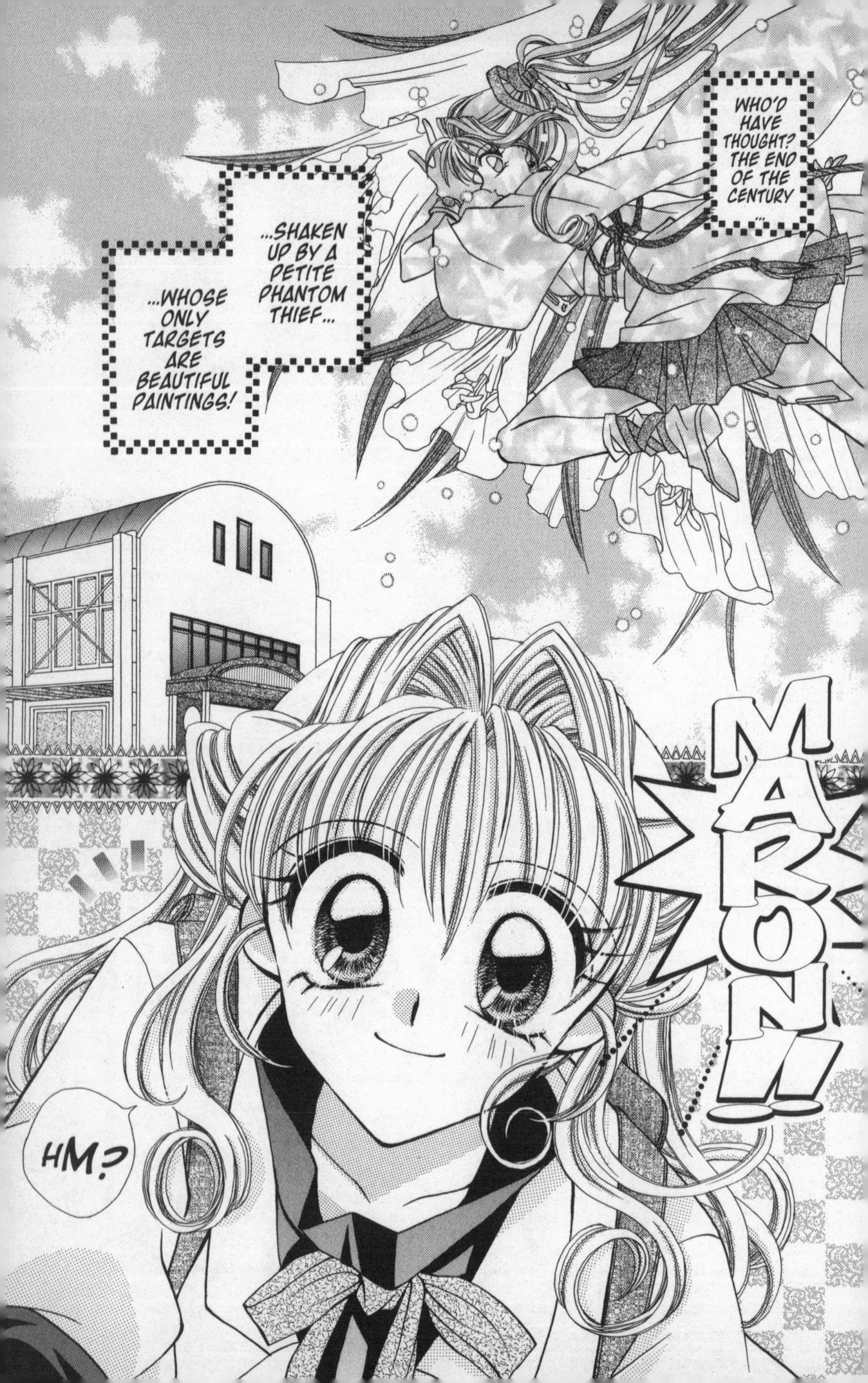
WHO'D HAVE THOUGHT? THE END OF THE CENTURY...
...SHAKEN UP BY A PETITE PHANTOM THIEF...
...WHOSE ONLY TARGETS ARE BEAUTIFUL PAINTINGS!
MARON!
HM?

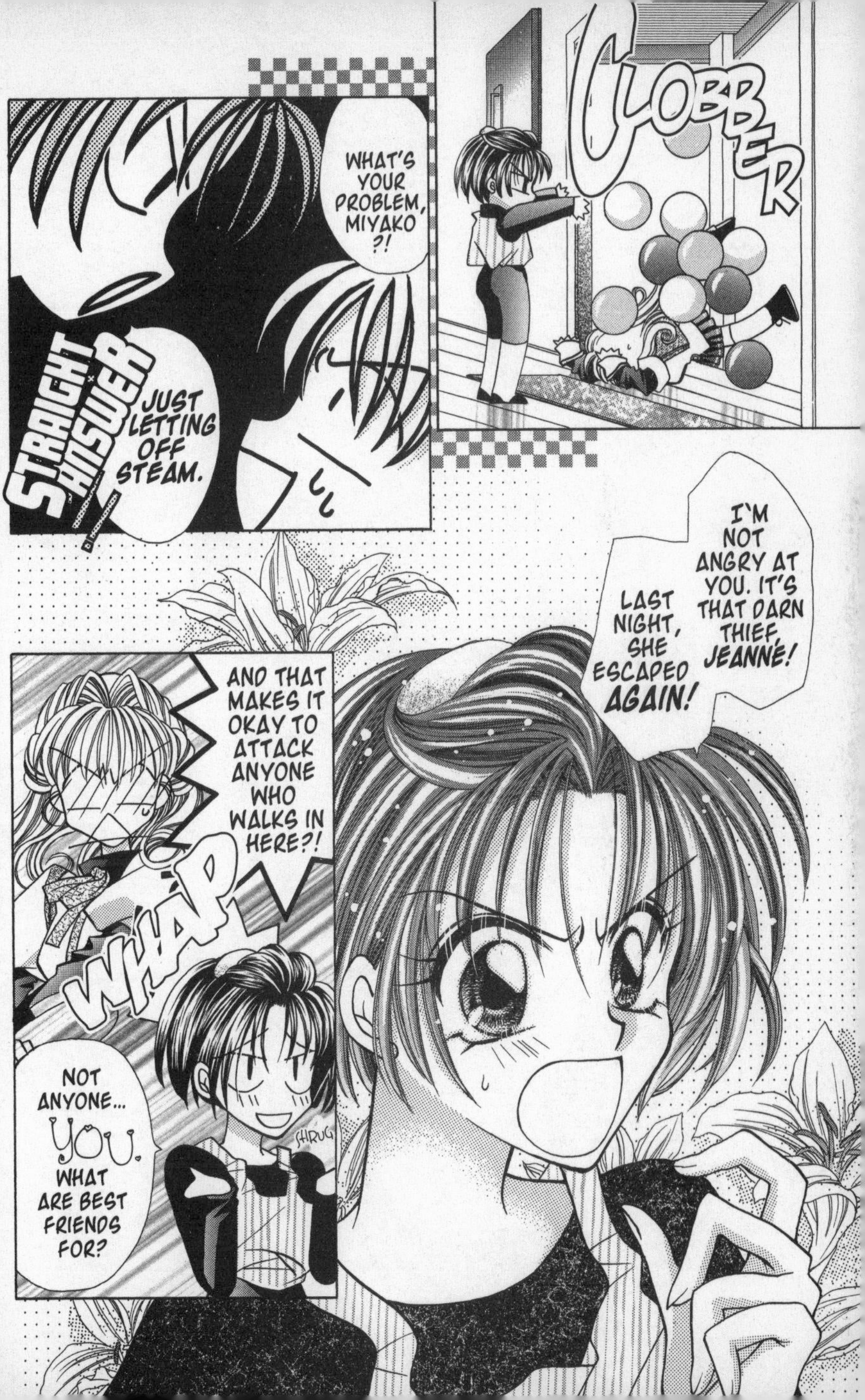
CLOBBER
WHAT'S YOUR PROBLEM, MIYAKO?!
STRAIGHT ANSWER
JUST LETTING OFF STEAM.
I'M NOT ANGRY AT YOU. IT'S THAT DARN THIEF, JEANNE!
LAST NIGHT, SHE ESCAPED AGAIN!
AND THAT MAKES IT OKAY TO ATTACK ANYONE WHO WALKS IN HERE?!
WHAP
NOT ANYONE... YOU. WHAT ARE BEST FRIENDS FOR?
SHRUG

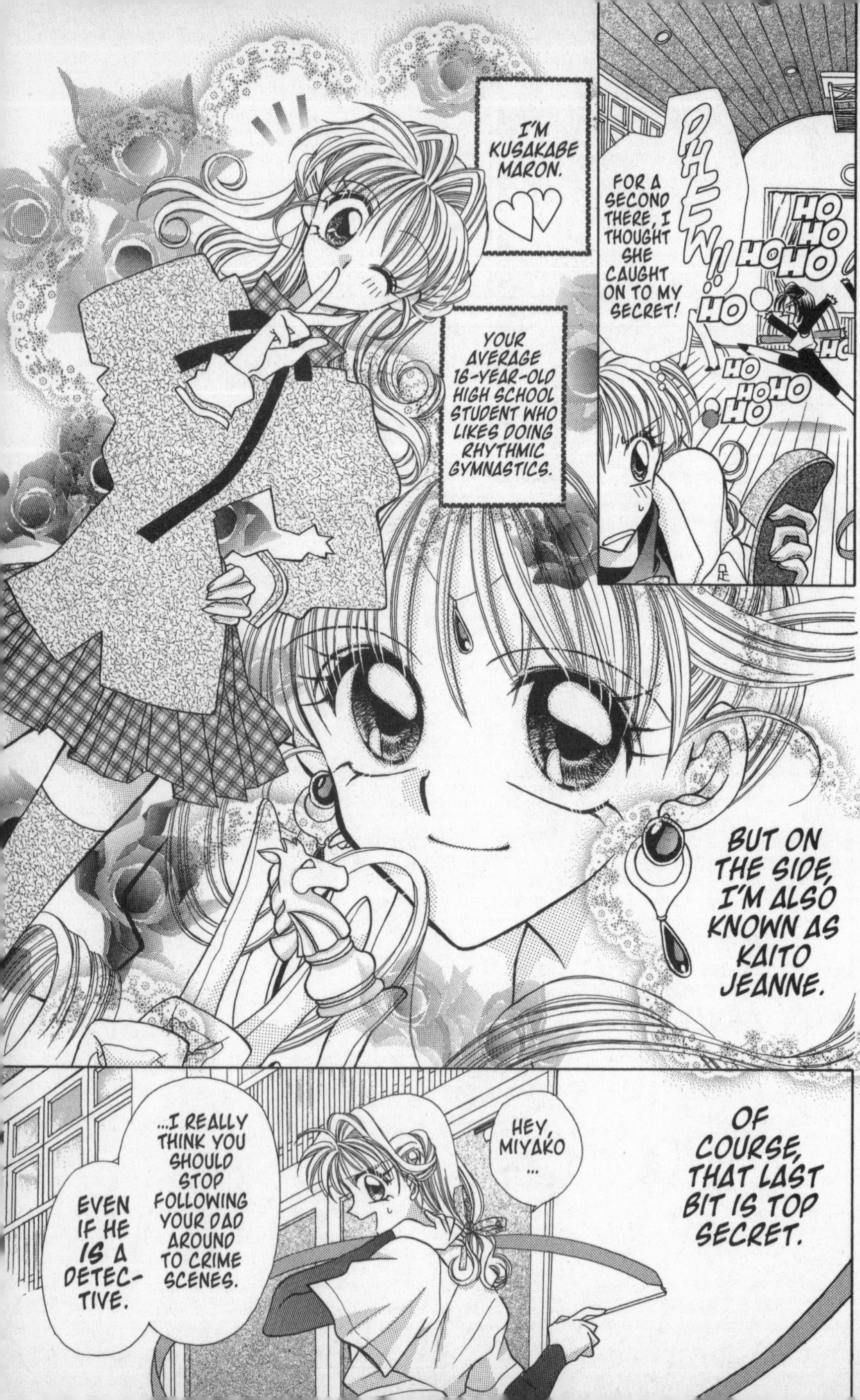
PHEW!!
FOR A SECOND THERE, I THOUGHT SHE CAUGHT ON TO MY SECRET!
HO HO HO HO
HO
HO
HO HO HO HO
I'M KUSAKABE MARON.
YOUR AVERAGE 16-YEAR-OLD HIGH SCHOOL STUDENT WHO LIKES DOING RHYTHMIC GYMNASTICS.
BUT ON THE SIDE, I'M ALSO KNOWN AS KAITO JEANNE.
OF COURSE, THAT LAST BIT IS TOP SECRET.
HEY, MIYAKO ...
...I REALLY THINK YOU SHOULD STOP FOLLOWING YOUR DAD AROUND TO CRIME SCENES.
EVEN IF HE *IS* A DETECTIVE.

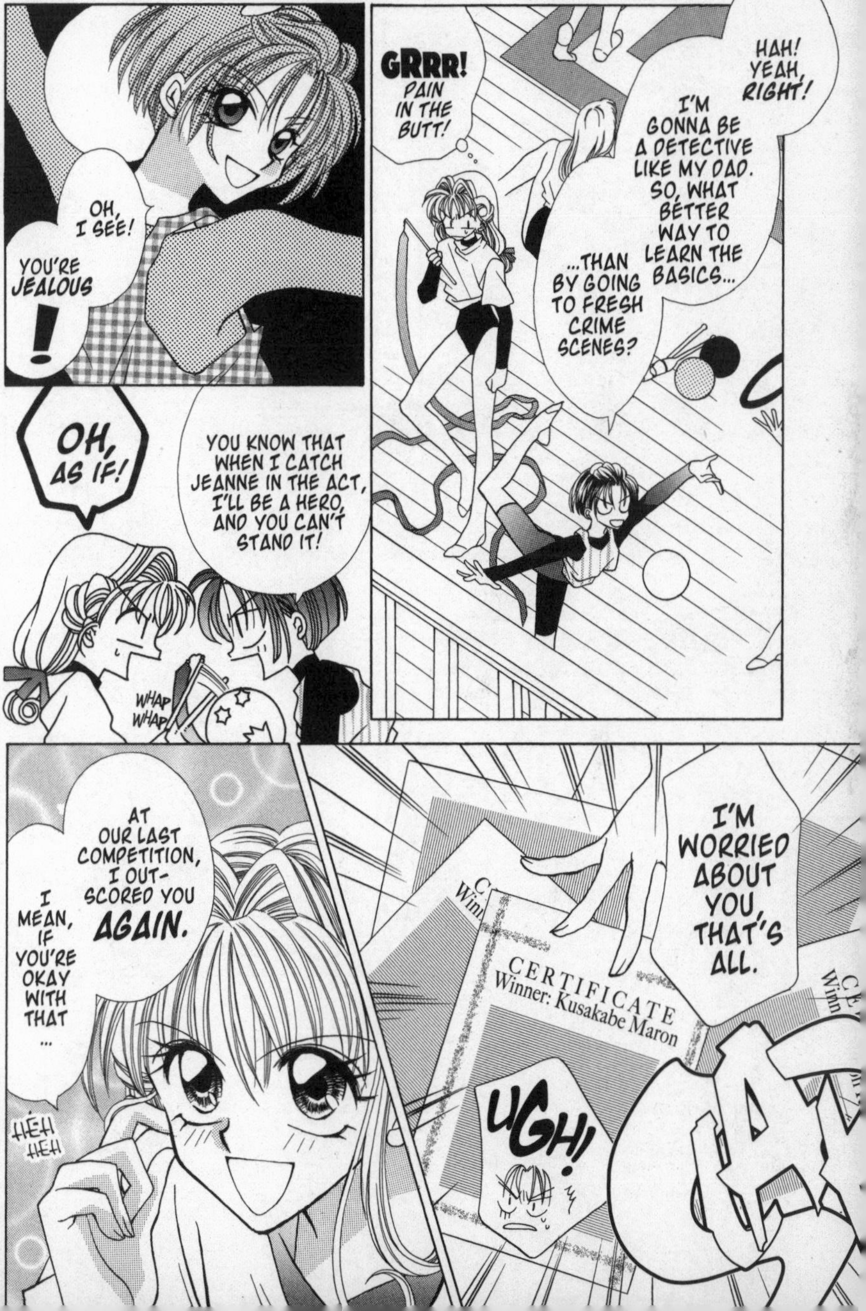
HAH! YEAH, RIGHT!
I'M GONNA BE A DETECTIVE LIKE MY DAD. SO, WHAT BETTER WAY TO LEARN THE BASICS...
...THAN BY GOING TO FRESH CRIME SCENES?
GRRR! PAIN IN THE BUTT!
OH, I SEE!
YOU'RE JEALOUS!
YOU KNOW THAT WHEN I CATCH JEANNE IN THE ACT, I'LL BE A HERO, AND YOU CAN'T STAND IT!
OH, AS IF!
WHAP WHAP
I'M WORRIED ABOUT YOU, THAT'S ALL.
CERTIFICATE
Winner: Kusakabe Maron
UGH!
AT OUR LAST COMPETITION, I OUT-SCORED YOU AGAIN.
I MEAN, IF YOU'RE OKAY WITH THAT ...
HEH HEH

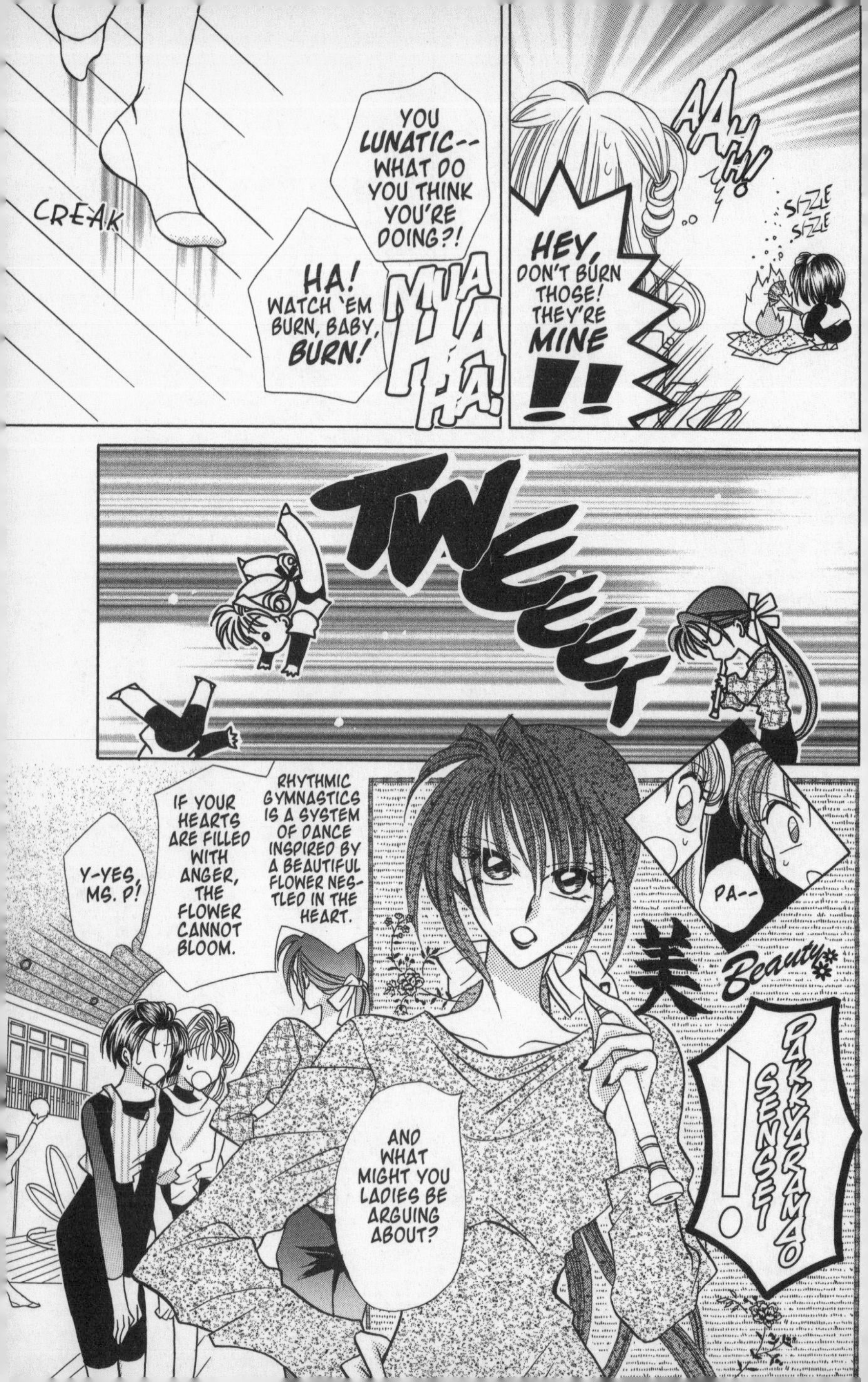
AAHH!
SIZZLE SIZZLE
HEY, DON'T BURN THOSE! THEY'RE MINE!!
YOU LUNATIC-- WHAT DO YOU THINK YOU'RE DOING?!
MUA HA HA!
HA! WATCH 'EM BURN, BABY, BURN!
CREAK
TWEEEET
PA--
美
Beauty
PAKKYARAMAO SENSEI!
RHYTHMIC GYMNASTICS IS A SYSTEM OF DANCE INSPIRED BY A BEAUTIFUL FLOWER NESTLED IN THE HEART.
IF YOUR HEARTS ARE FILLED WITH ANGER, THE FLOWER CANNOT BLOOM.
Y-YES, MS. P!
AND WHAT MIGHT YOU LADIES BE ARGUING ABOUT?

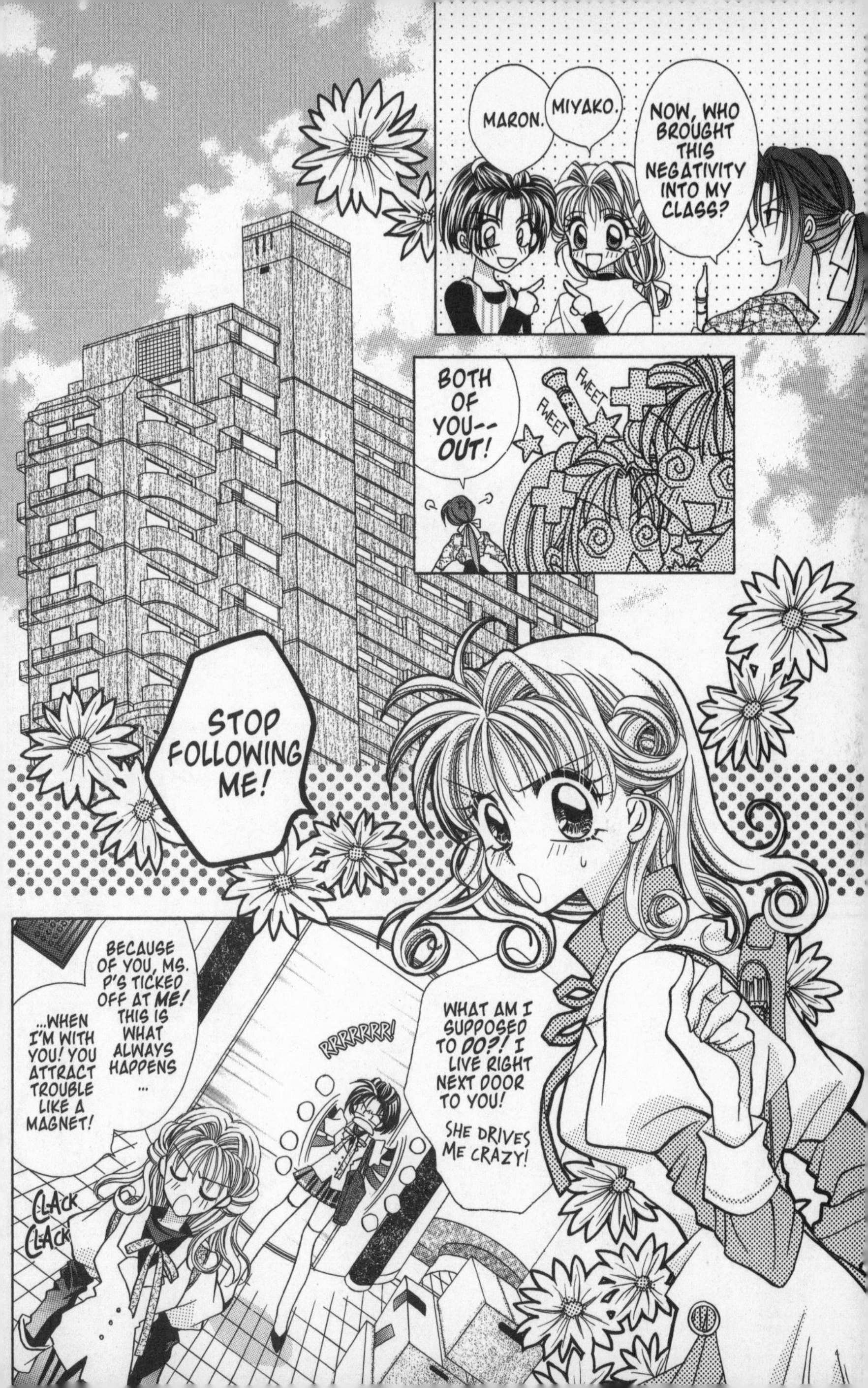
NOW, WHO BROUGHT THIS NEGATIVITY INTO MY CLASS?
MIYAKO.
MARON.
FWEET
FWEET
BOTH OF YOU--OUT!
STOP FOLLOWING ME!
WHAT AM I SUPPOSED TO DO?! I LIVE RIGHT NEXT DOOR TO YOU!
SHE DRIVES ME CRAZY!
RRRRRRR!
BECAUSE OF YOU, MS. P'S TICKED OFF AT ME! THIS IS WHAT ALWAYS HAPPENS...
...WHEN I'M WITH YOU! YOU ATTRACT TROUBLE LIKE A MAGNET!
CLACK
CLACK

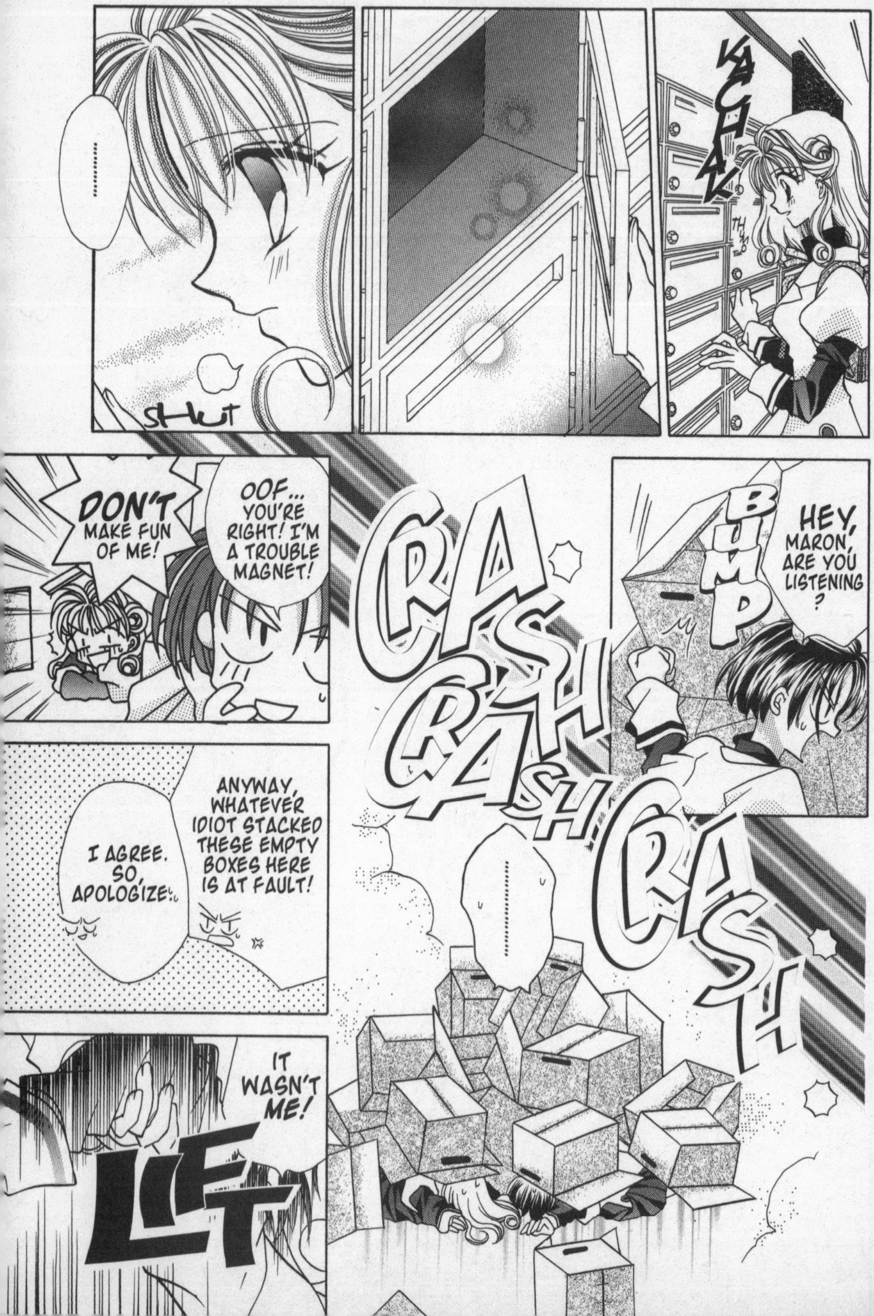
KACHA
......
SHUT
BUMP
HEY, MARON, ARE YOU LISTENING?
CRASH
CRASH
CRASH
CRASH
......
OOF... YOU'RE RIGHT! I'M A TROUBLE MAGNET!
DON'T MAKE FUN OF ME!
ANYWAY, WHATEVER IDIOT STACKED THESE EMPTY BOXES HERE IS AT FAULT!
I AGREE. SO, APOLOGIZE.
IT WASN'T ME!
LIFT

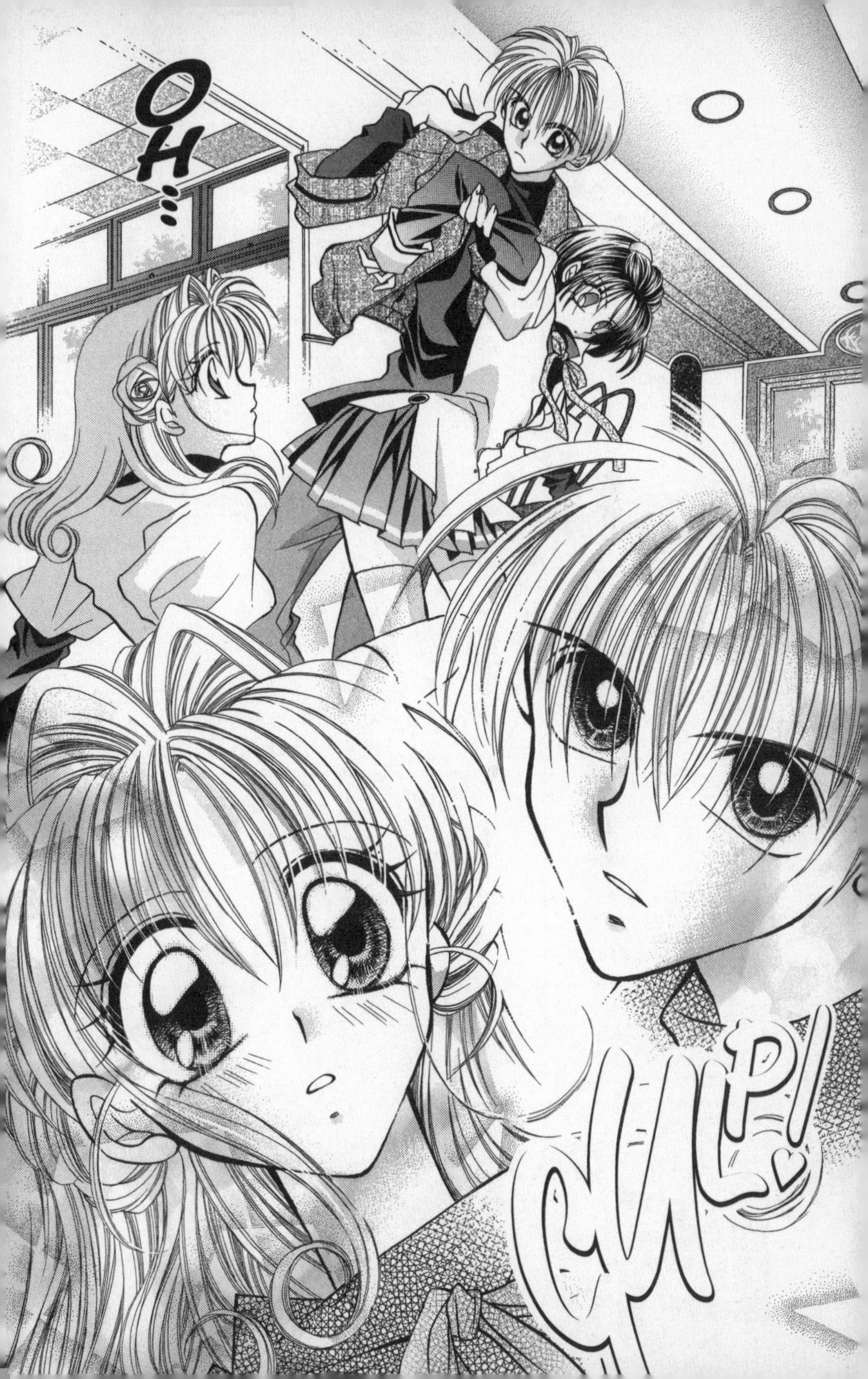
OH...
GULP!

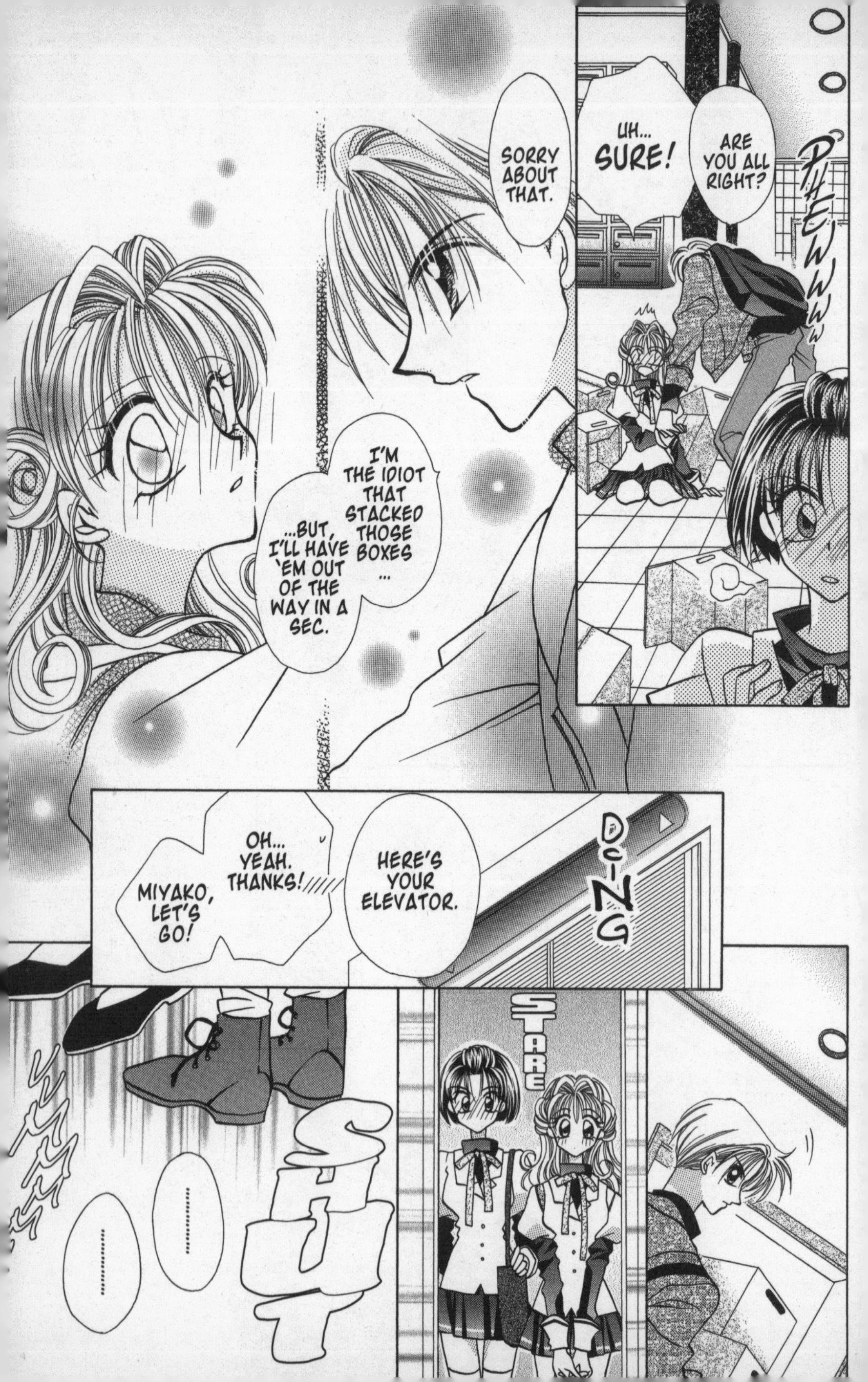
ARE YOU ALL RIGHT?
PHEWWWWW
UH... SURE!
SORRY ABOUT THAT.
I'M THE IDIOT THAT STACKED THOSE BOXES ...
...BUT, I'LL HAVE 'EM OUT OF THE WAY IN A SEC.
DING
HERE'S YOUR ELEVATOR.
OH... YEAH. THANKS!
MIYAKO, LET'S GO!
STARE
SHUT
....
....

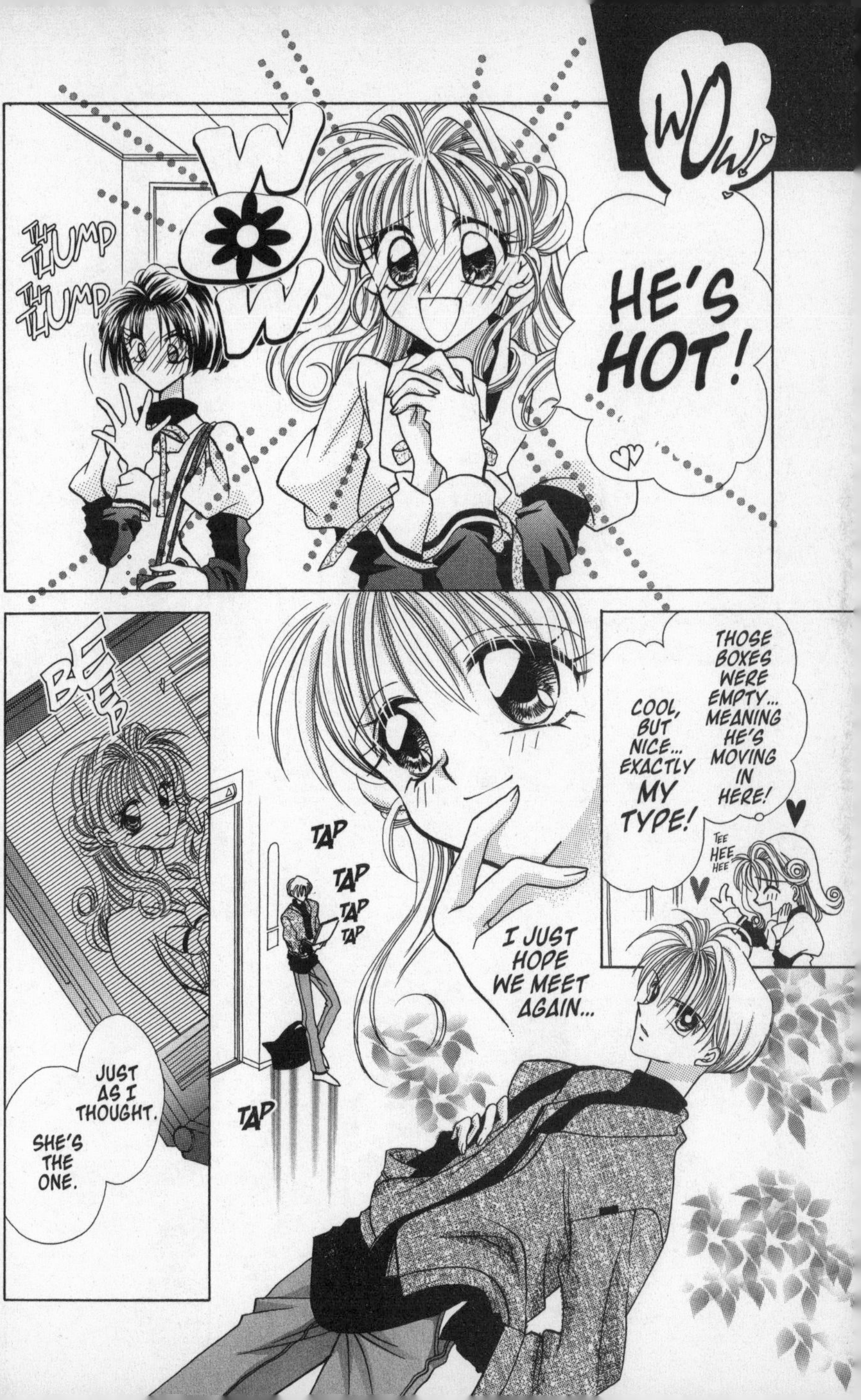
WOW!
HE'S HOT!
WOW
THUMP THUMP
THUMP THUMP
THOSE BOXES WERE EMPTY... MEANING HE'S MOVING IN HERE!
COOL, BUT NICE... EXACTLY MY TYPE!
TEE HEE HEE
I JUST HOPE WE MEET AGAIN...
TAP
TAP
TAP
TAP
TAP
BEEP
JUST AS I THOUGHT.
SHE'S THE ONE.

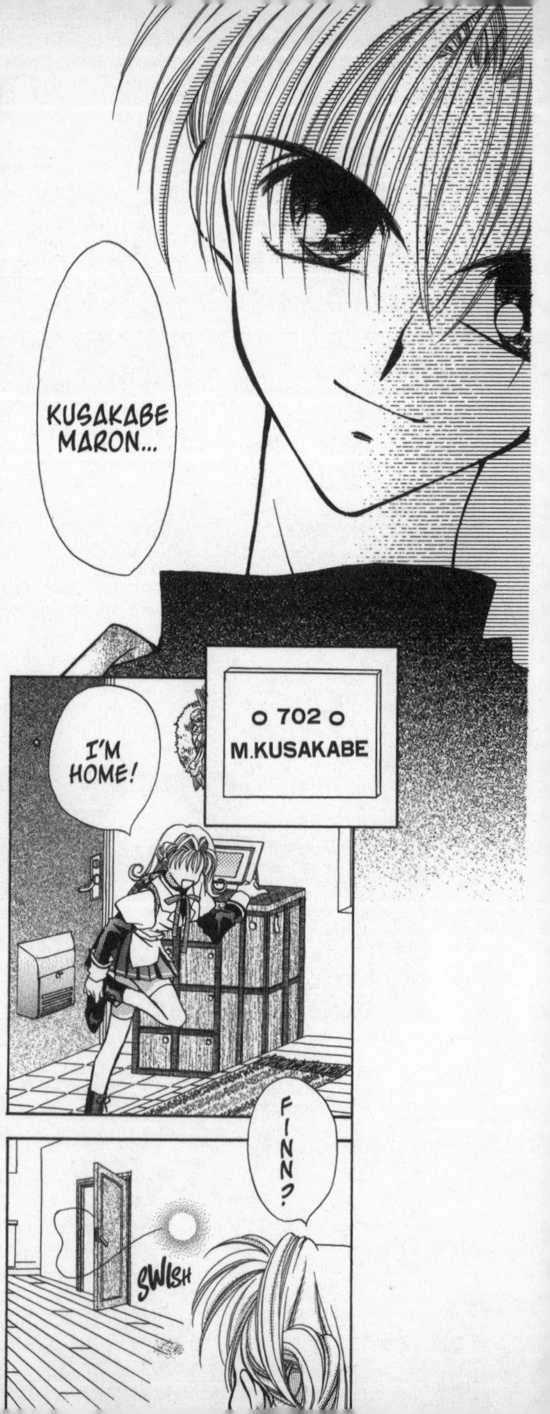
KUSAKABE MARON...
○ 702 ○
M.KUSAKABE
I'M HOME!
FINN?
SWISH

GREETINGS

Hello to all my new readers and all my not-so-new readers! I'm Arina Tanemura. Finally, it's out! The first volume of "Kamikaze Kaito Jeanne!" I'm so happy! YAYYY! This is one of the stories I've wanted to tell for a long time. (There are three of them.) I don't know how long I'll be able to keep the story going, but I hope you'll stick with me and read it through to the end!

ARINA TANEMURA PROFILE

I got a haircut!

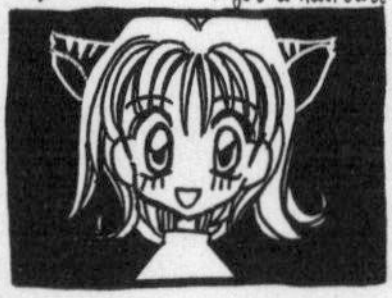

Date of birth: March 12, 1978
Blood type: A
Star sign: Pisces

Y'know, since becoming a comic artist, I've gained 22 pounds(!), so finally, I got a membership at a sports club...but I've been so busy that I haven't had a chance to go at all! So, that's two months' worth of membership wasted!

SNIFFLE

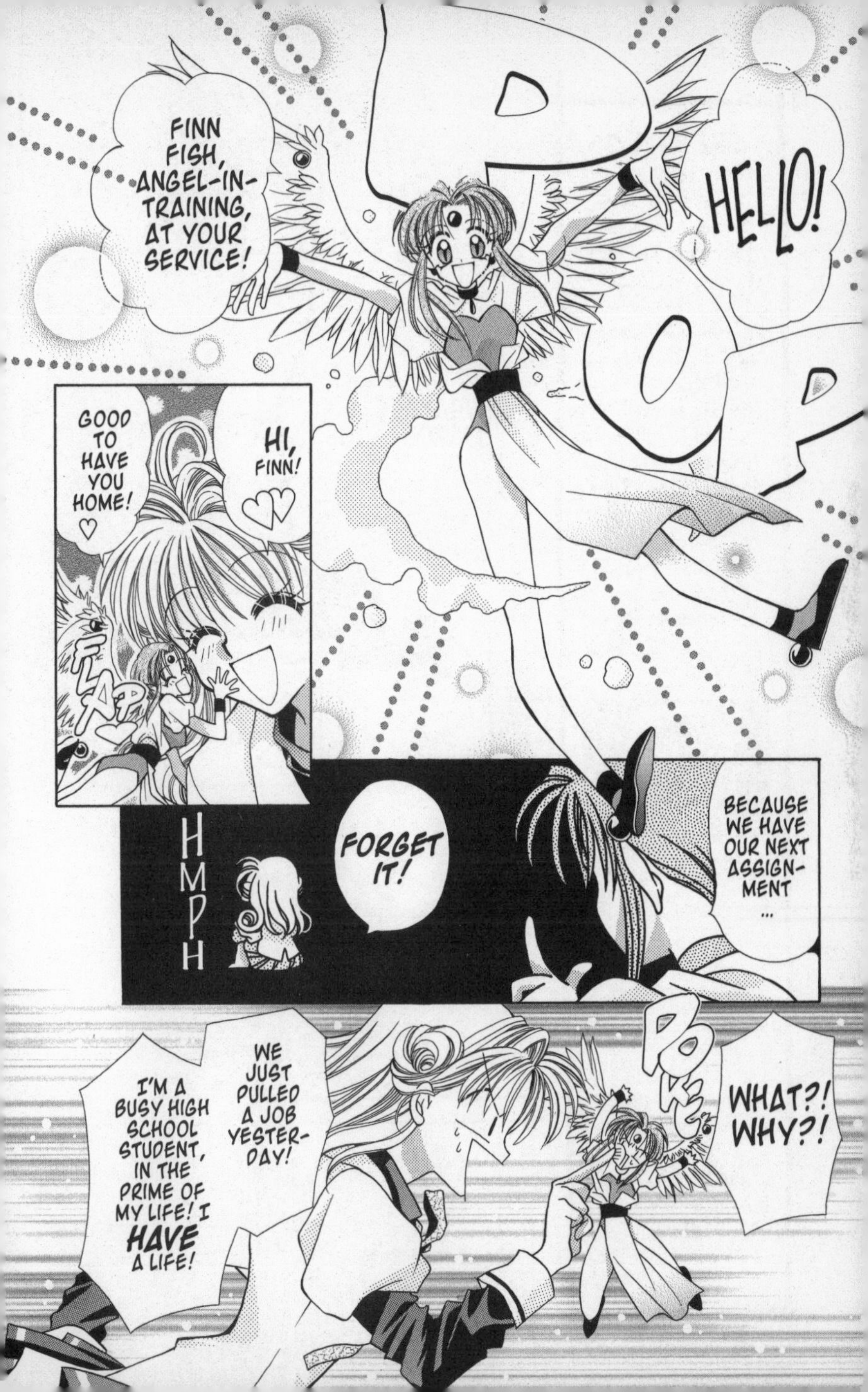
POP
HELLO!
FINN FISH, ANGEL-IN-TRAINING, AT YOUR SERVICE!
HI, FINN! ♡♡
GOOD TO HAVE YOU HOME! ♡
FLAP
BECAUSE WE HAVE OUR NEXT ASSIGNMENT...
FORGET IT!
HMPH
WHAT?! WHY?!
POKE
WE JUST PULLED A JOB YESTERDAY!
I'M A BUSY HIGH SCHOOL STUDENT, IN THE PRIME OF MY LIFE! I **HAVE** A LIFE!

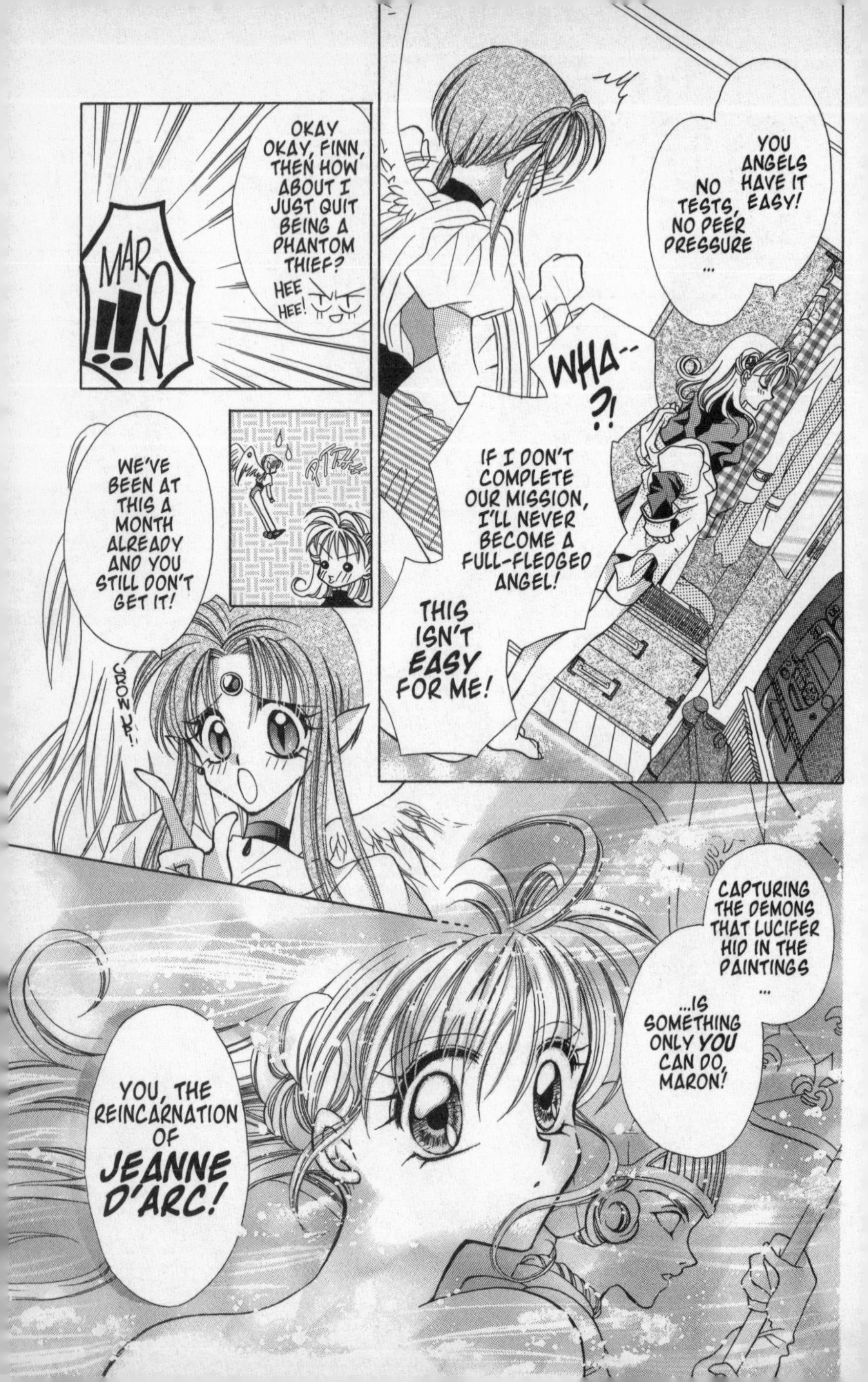
YOU ANGELS HAVE IT EASY!
NO TESTS, NO PEER PRESSURE ...
WHA--?!
IF I DON'T COMPLETE OUR MISSION, I'LL NEVER BECOME A FULL-FLEDGED ANGEL!
THIS ISN'T EASY FOR ME!
OKAY OKAY, FINN, THEN HOW ABOUT I JUST QUIT BEING A PHANTOM THIEF?
HEE HEE!
MARON!!
WE'VE BEEN AT THIS A MONTH ALREADY AND YOU STILL DON'T GET IT!
GROW UP!
CAPTURING THE DEMONS THAT LUCIFER HID IN THE PAINTINGS ...
...IS SOMETHING ONLY YOU CAN DO, MARON!
YOU, THE REINCARNATION OF JEANNE D'ARC!

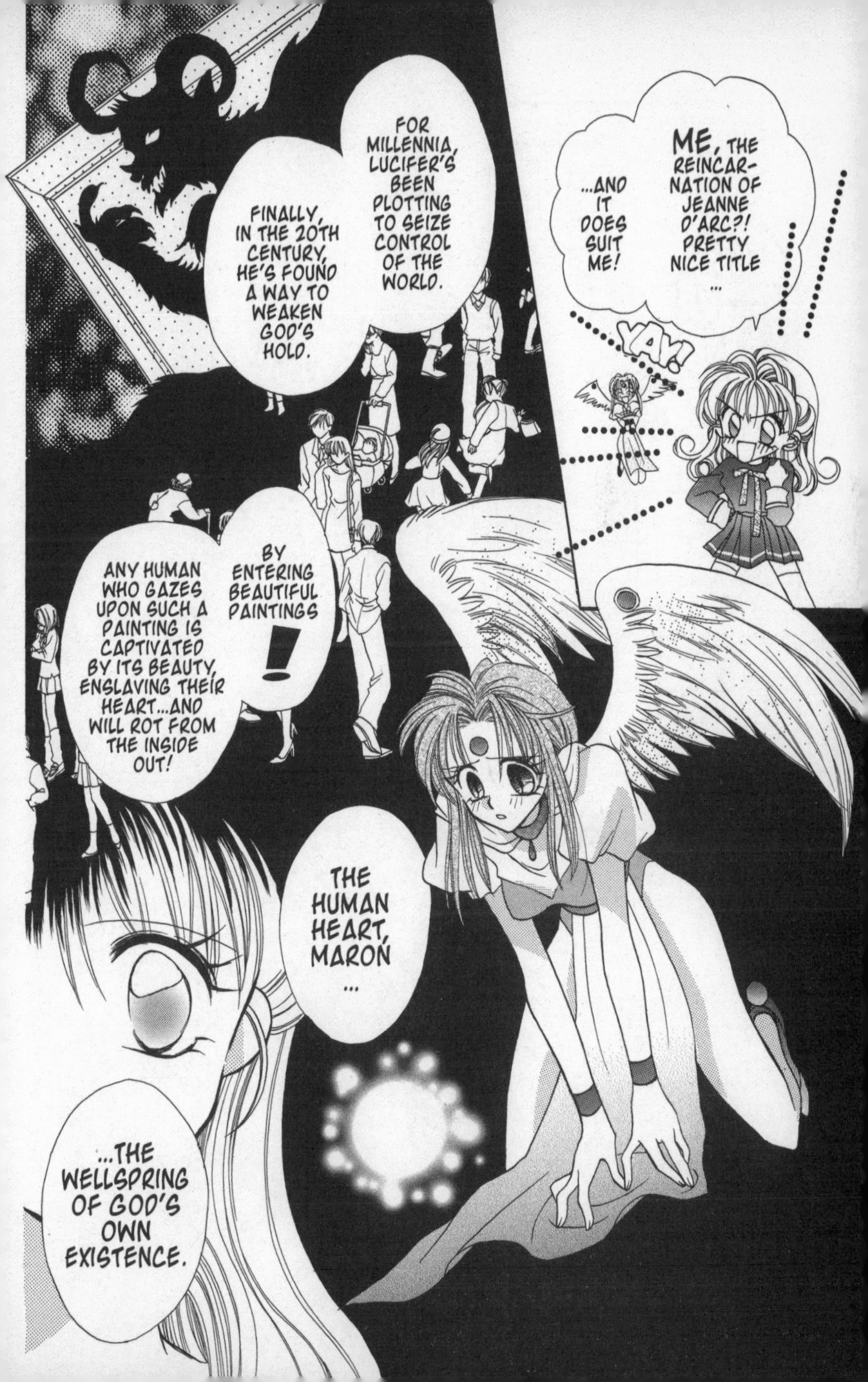
ME, THE REINCARNATION OF JEANNE D'ARC?! PRETTY NICE TITLE ...
...AND IT DOES SUIT ME!
YAY!
FOR MILLENNIA, LUCIFER'S BEEN PLOTTING TO SEIZE CONTROL OF THE WORLD.
FINALLY, IN THE 20TH CENTURY, HE'S FOUND A WAY TO WEAKEN GOD'S HOLD.
BY ENTERING BEAUTIFUL PAINTINGS !
ANY HUMAN WHO GAZES UPON SUCH A PAINTING IS CAPTIVATED BY ITS BEAUTY, ENSLAVING THEIR HEART...AND WILL ROT FROM THE INSIDE OUT!
THE HUMAN HEART, MARON ...
...THE WELLSPRING OF GOD'S OWN EXISTENCE.

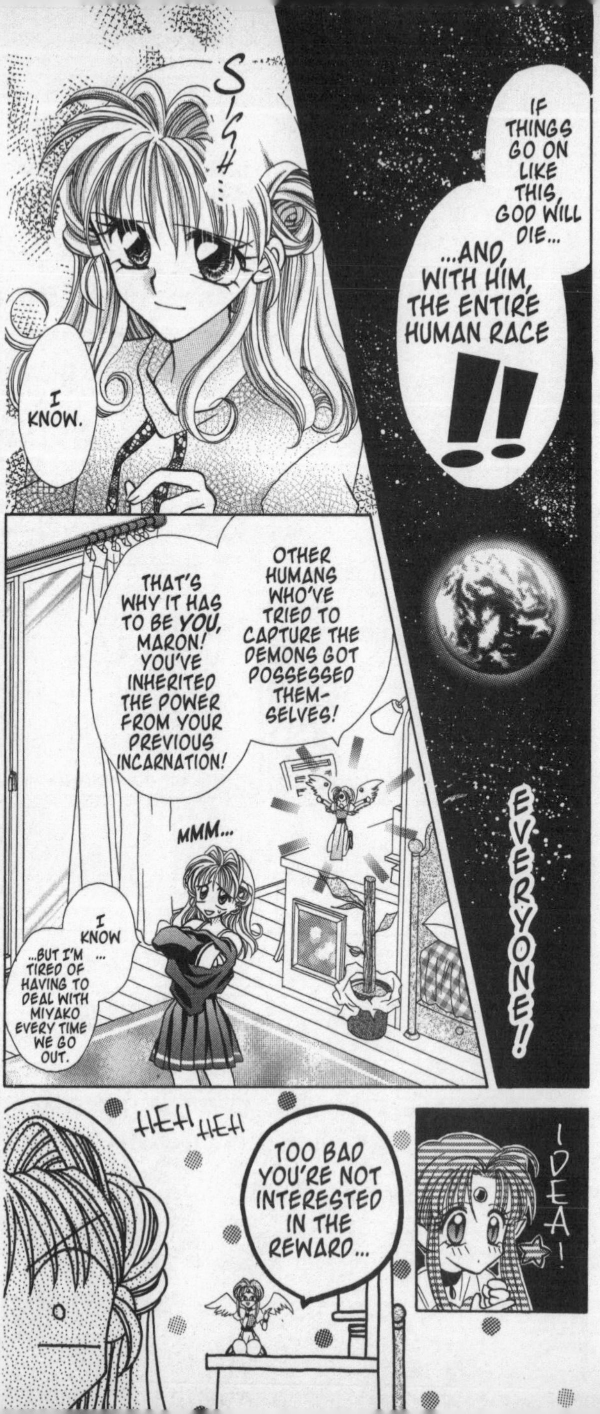
IF THINGS GO ON LIKE THIS, GOD WILL DIE...
...AND, WITH HIM, THE ENTIRE HUMAN RACE!!
EVERYONE!
SISH...
I KNOW.
OTHER HUMANS WHO'VE TRIED TO CAPTURE THE DEMONS GOT POSSESSED THEMSELVES!
THAT'S WHY IT HAS TO BE YOU, MARON! YOU'VE INHERITED THE POWER FROM YOUR PREVIOUS INCARNATION!
MMM...
I KNOW ...BUT I'M TIRED OF HAVING TO DEAL WITH MIYAKO EVERY TIME WE GO OUT.
IDEA!
HEH HEH
TOO BAD YOU'RE NOT INTERESTED IN THE REWARD...

THE PRIVATE LIFE OF ARINA TANEMURA, PART 5

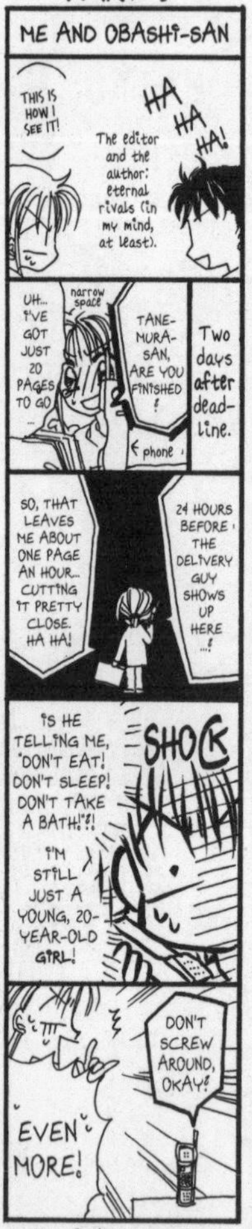
ME AND OBASHI-SAN
HA HA HA!
The editor and the author: eternal rivals (in my mind, at least).
THIS IS HOW I SEE IT!
Two days after deadline.
TANE-MURA-SAN, ARE YOU FINISHED?
narrow space
UH... I'VE GOT JUST 20 PAGES TO GO...
← phone
24 HOURS BEFORE THE DELIVERY GUY SHOWS UP HERE...!
SO, THAT LEAVES ME ABOUT ONE PAGE AN HOUR... CUTTING IT PRETTY CLOSE. HA HA!
SHOCK
IS HE TELLING ME, "DON'T EAT! DON'T SLEEP! DON'T TAKE A BATH!"?!
I'M STILL JUST A YOUNG, 20-YEAR-OLD GIRL!
DON'T SCREW AROUND, OKAY?
EVEN MORE!

Well, I drew the above (HA HA), but really, I appreciate my editor... and I should apologize for recently taking Sundays off!

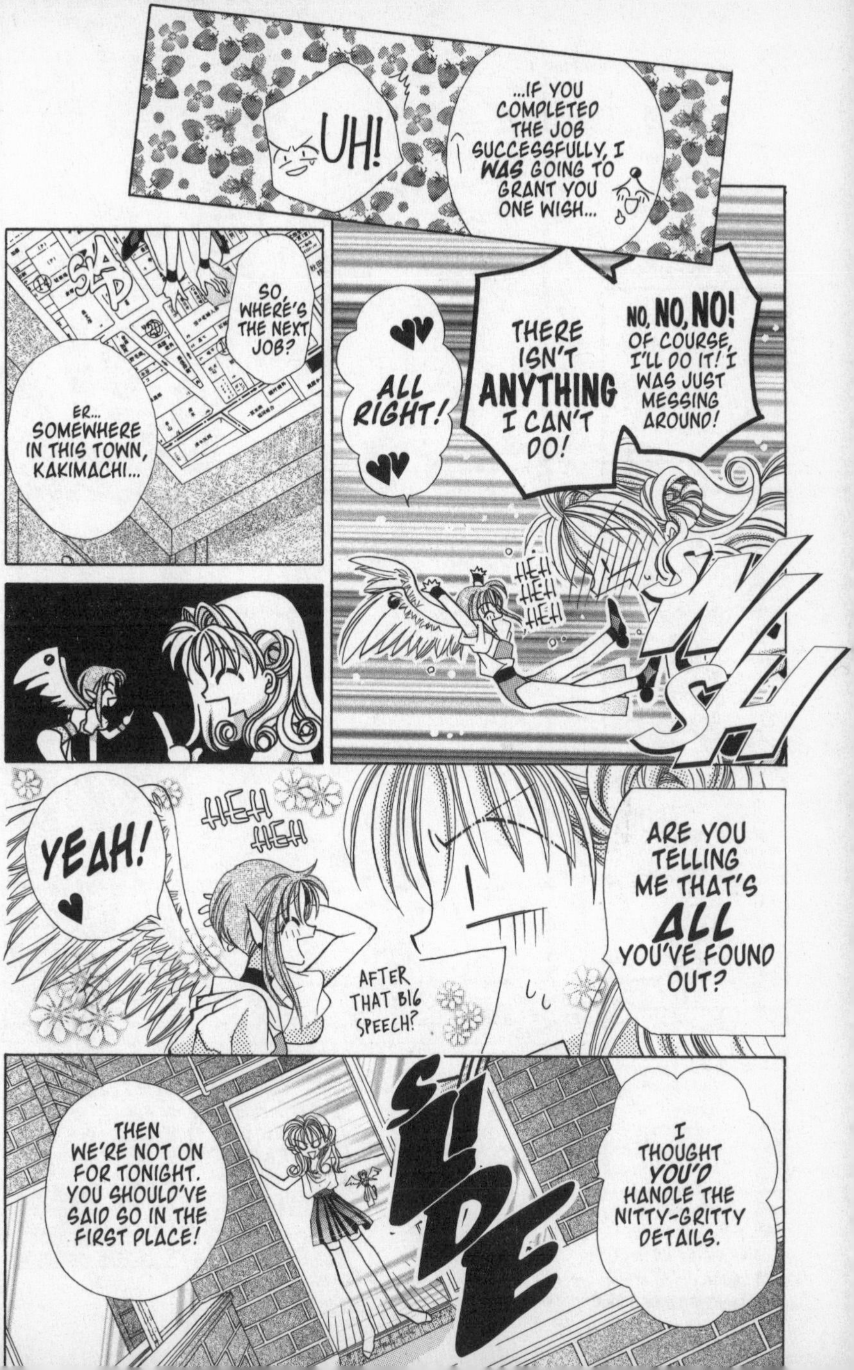
...IF YOU COMPLETED THE JOB SUCCESSFULLY, I WAS GOING TO GRANT YOU ONE WISH...
UH!
NO, NO, NO! OF COURSE, I'LL DO IT! I WAS JUST MESSING AROUND!
THERE ISN'T ANYTHING I CAN'T DO!
ALL RIGHT!
HEH HEH HEH
SWISH
SO, WHERE'S THE NEXT JOB?
ER... SOMEWHERE IN THIS TOWN, KAKIMACHI...
ARE YOU TELLING ME THAT'S ALL YOU'VE FOUND OUT?
AFTER THAT BIG SPEECH?
HEH HEH
YEAH!
I THOUGHT YOU'D HANDLE THE NITTY-GRITTY DETAILS.
SLIDE
THEN WE'RE NOT ON FOR TONIGHT. YOU SHOULD'VE SAID SO IN THE FIRST PLACE!

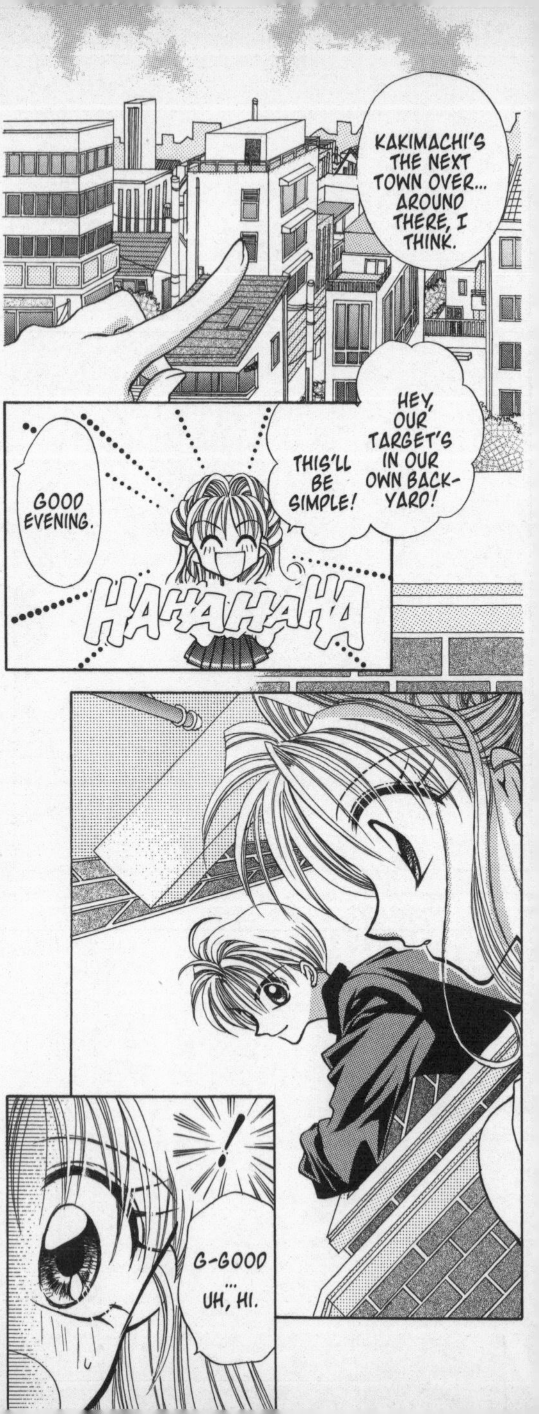
KAKIMACHI'S THE NEXT TOWN OVER... AROUND THERE, I THINK.
HEY, OUR TARGET'S IN OUR OWN BACK-YARD!
THIS'LL BE SIMPLE!
GOOD EVENING.
HAHAHAHA
!
G-GOOD ... UH, HI.

AT A SIGNING

①

The other day (July 25th), I went to Ribon's All-Japan Summer Caravan, and the signing that they sponsored. The event was held at eight places all over Japan, and I participated in two of them, in Tokyo and Nagoya.
In the morning, my editor and I left the hotel together (after meeting in the lobby) and walked towards the venue. On the way, we passed by some girls already heading back from the convention, which made me slightly nervous given that it was still morning! That day's signing was in Shinjuku, Tokyo, and was supposed to start at 11am.

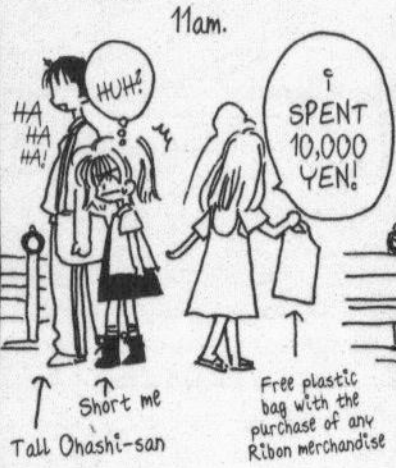
HA HA HA!
HUH?
I SPENT 10,000 YEN!
Short me
Tall Ohashi-san
Free plastic bag with the purchase of any Ribon merchandise

According to my editor, so many people had lined up by 10am that people had to be let in. Even then, it was so crowded, a lot of fans had to wait outside for, like, three hours. (Though the fans who could get autographs at the signing were chosen by lottery, the Caravan event itself was free--so anybody could come...and they did.)

→ CONTINUED IN PART #2>>>

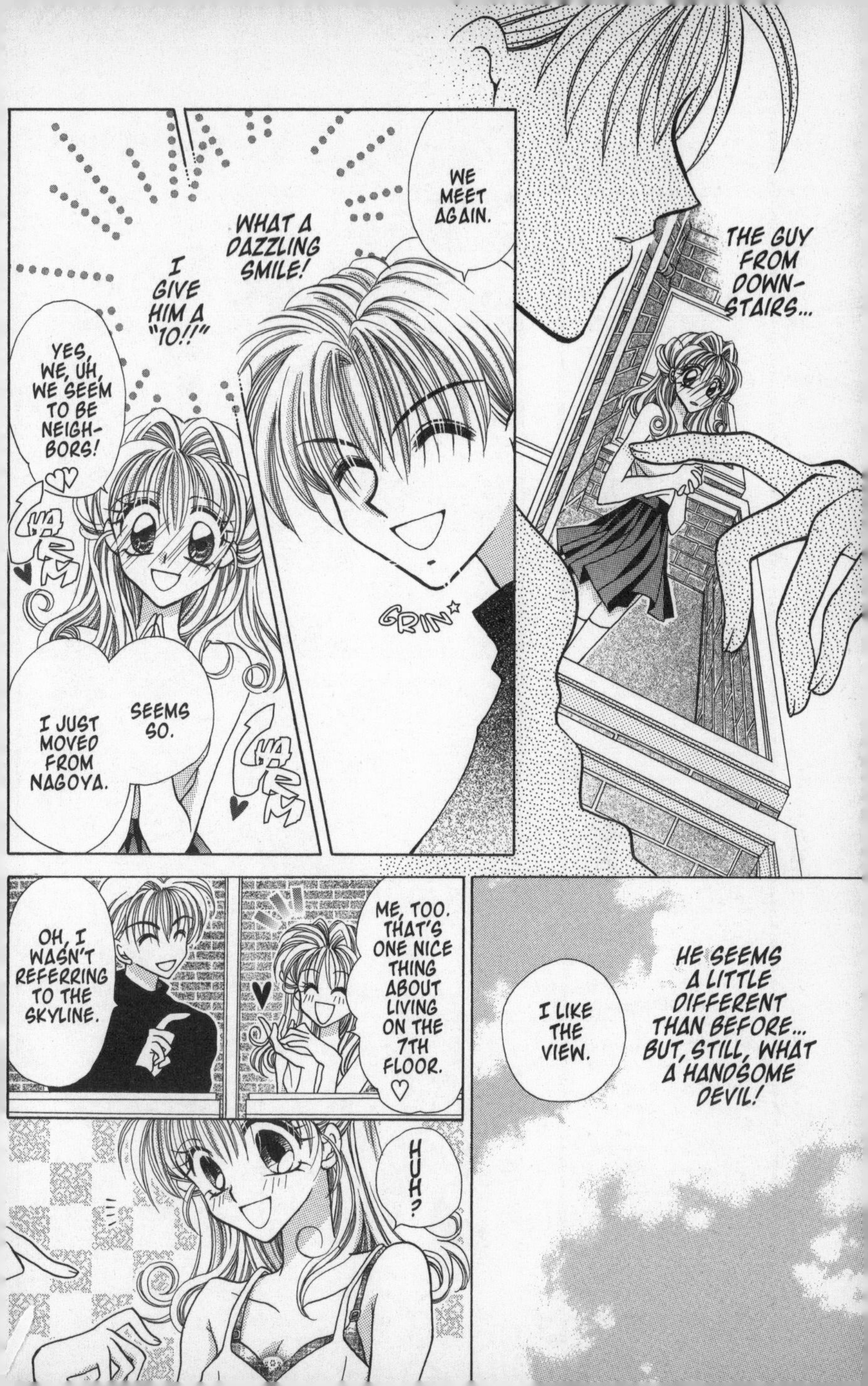
THE GUY FROM DOWN-STAIRS...
WE MEET AGAIN.
WHAT A DAZZLING SMILE!
I GIVE HIM A "10!!"
GRIN☆
YES, WE, UH, WE SEEM TO BE NEIGH-BORS! ♡
CHARM
SEEMS SO.
I JUST MOVED FROM NAGOYA.
CHARM
HE SEEMS A LITTLE DIFFERENT THAN BEFORE... BUT, STILL, WHAT A HANDSOME DEVIL!
I LIKE THE VIEW.
ME, TOO. THAT'S ONE NICE THING ABOUT LIVING ON THE 7TH FLOOR. ♡
OH, I WASN'T REFERRING TO THE SKYLINE.
HUH?

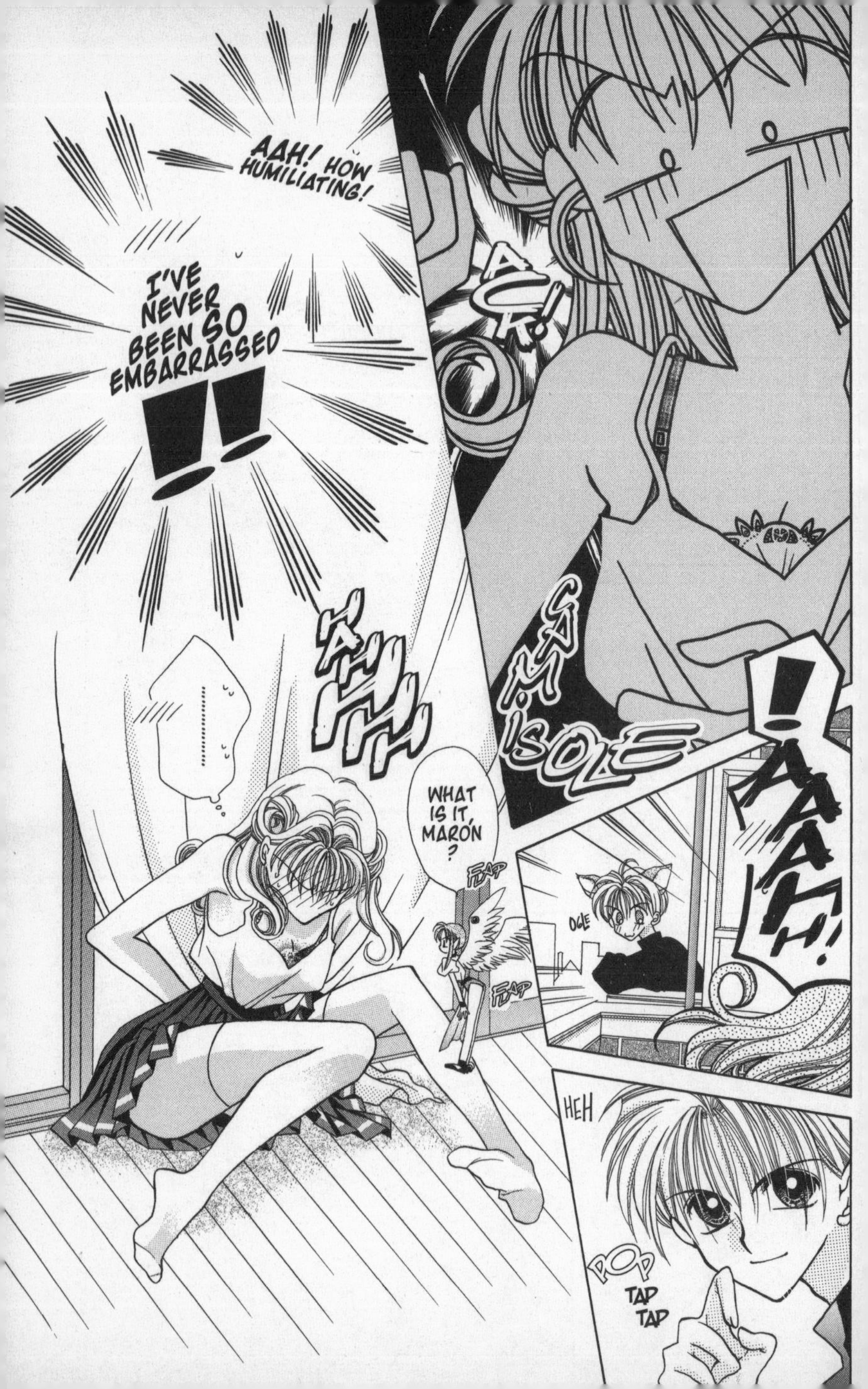
ACK!
CAMISOLE
!
AAAH!
OGLE
HEH
POP
TAP TAP
AAH! HOW HUMILIATING!
I'VE NEVER BEEN SO EMBARRASSED!!
AAHHH
......
WHAT IS IT, MARON?
FLAP
FLAP

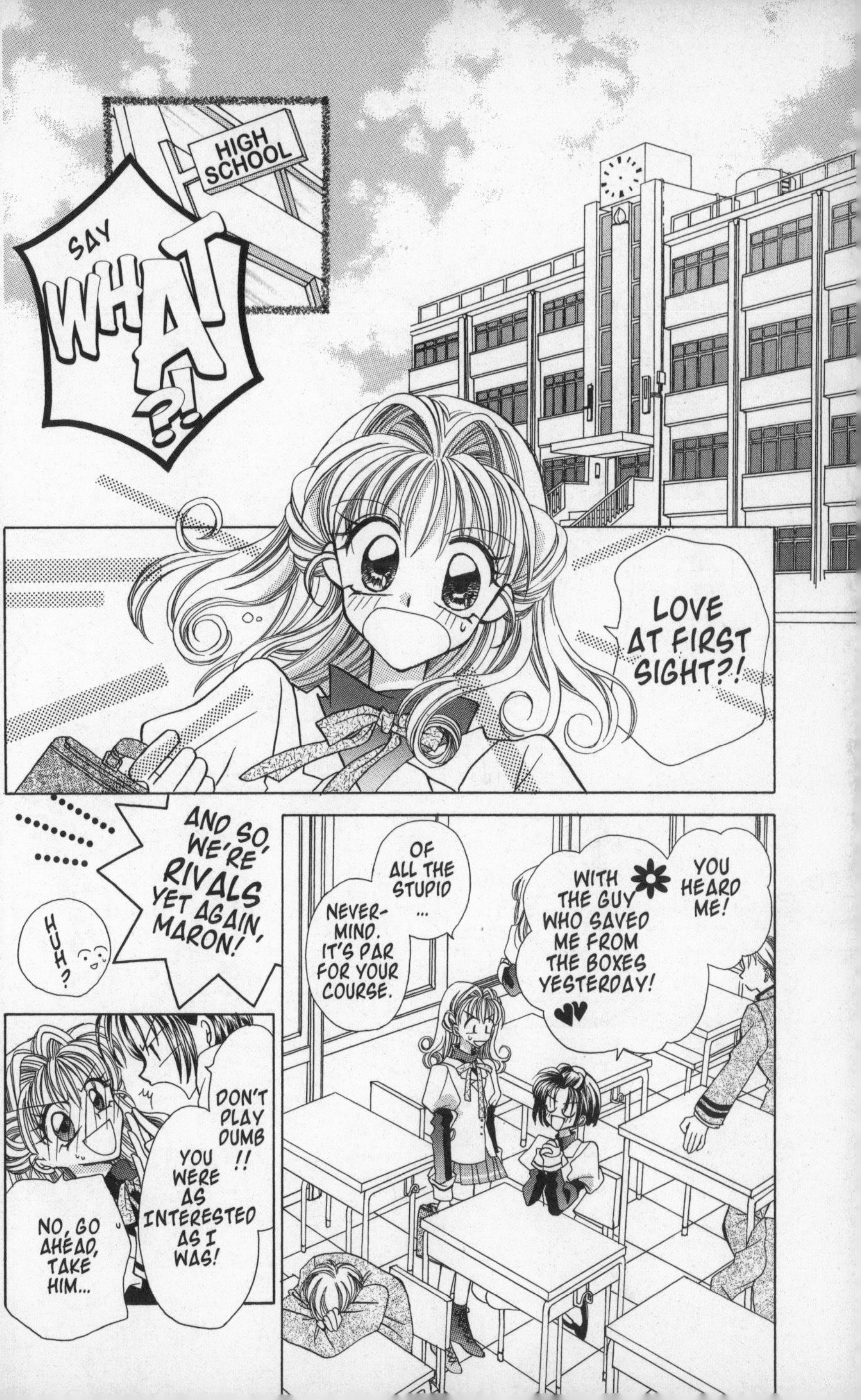

HIGH SCHOOL
SAY WHAT?!
LOVE AT FIRST SIGHT?!
YOU HEARD ME!
WITH THE GUY WHO SAVED ME FROM THE BOXES YESTERDAY!
OF ALL THE STUPID ...
NEVER-MIND. IT'S PAR FOR YOUR COURSE.
AND SO, WE'RE RIVALS YET AGAIN, MARON!
......
HUH?
DON'T PLAY DUMB!!
YOU WERE AS INTERESTED AS I WAS!
NO, GO AHEAD, TAKE HIM...

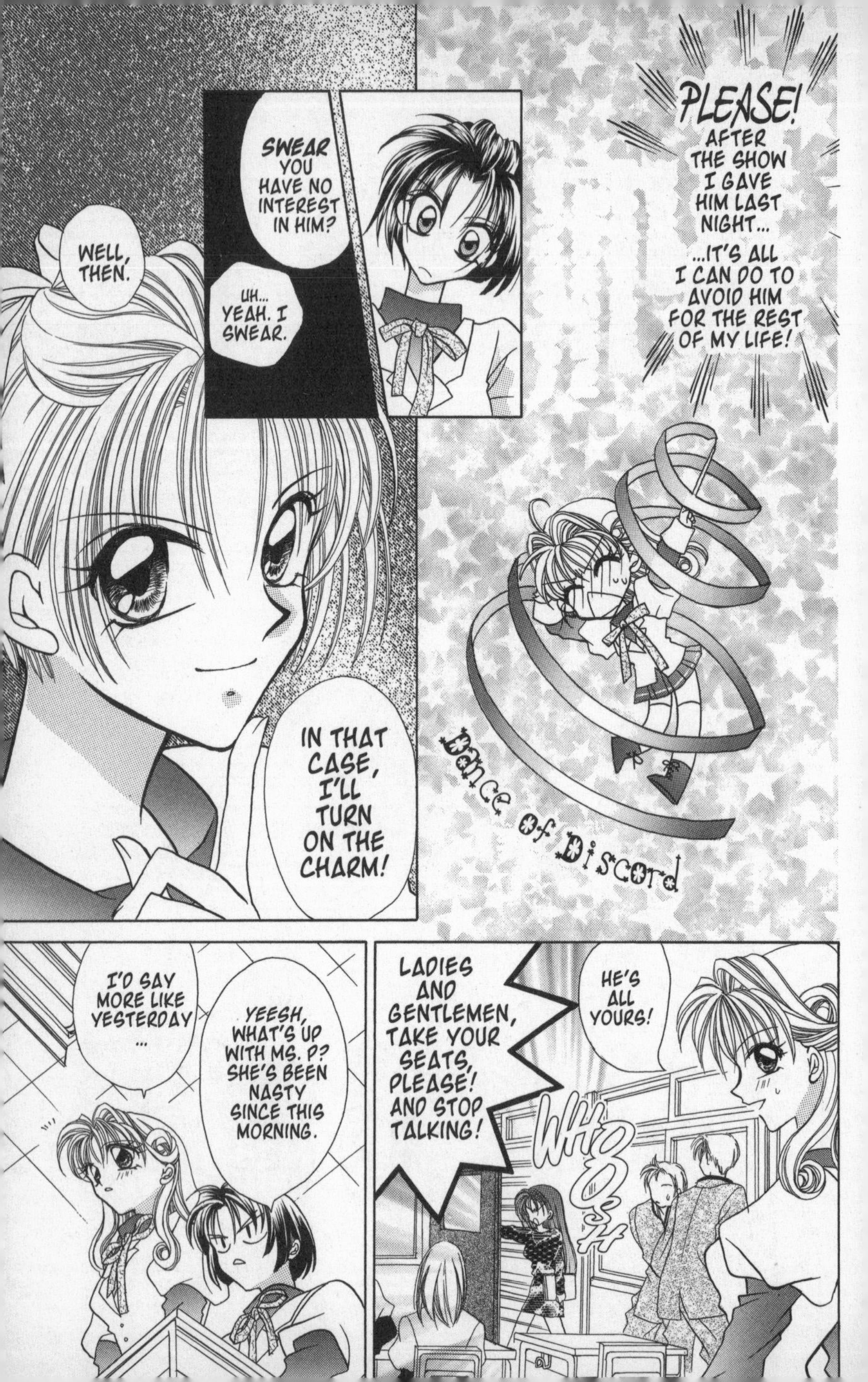
PLEASE! AFTER THE SHOW I GAVE HIM LAST NIGHT... ...IT'S ALL I CAN DO TO AVOID HIM FOR THE REST OF MY LIFE!
Dance of Discord
SWEAR YOU HAVE NO INTEREST IN HIM?
UH... YEAH. I SWEAR.
WELL, THEN.
IN THAT CASE, I'LL TURN ON THE CHARM!
HE'S ALL YOURS!
LADIES AND GENTLEMEN, TAKE YOUR SEATS, PLEASE! AND STOP TALKING!
WHOOSH
YEESH, WHAT'S UP WITH MS. P? SHE'S BEEN NASTY SINCE THIS MORNING.
I'D SAY MORE LIKE YESTERDAY ...

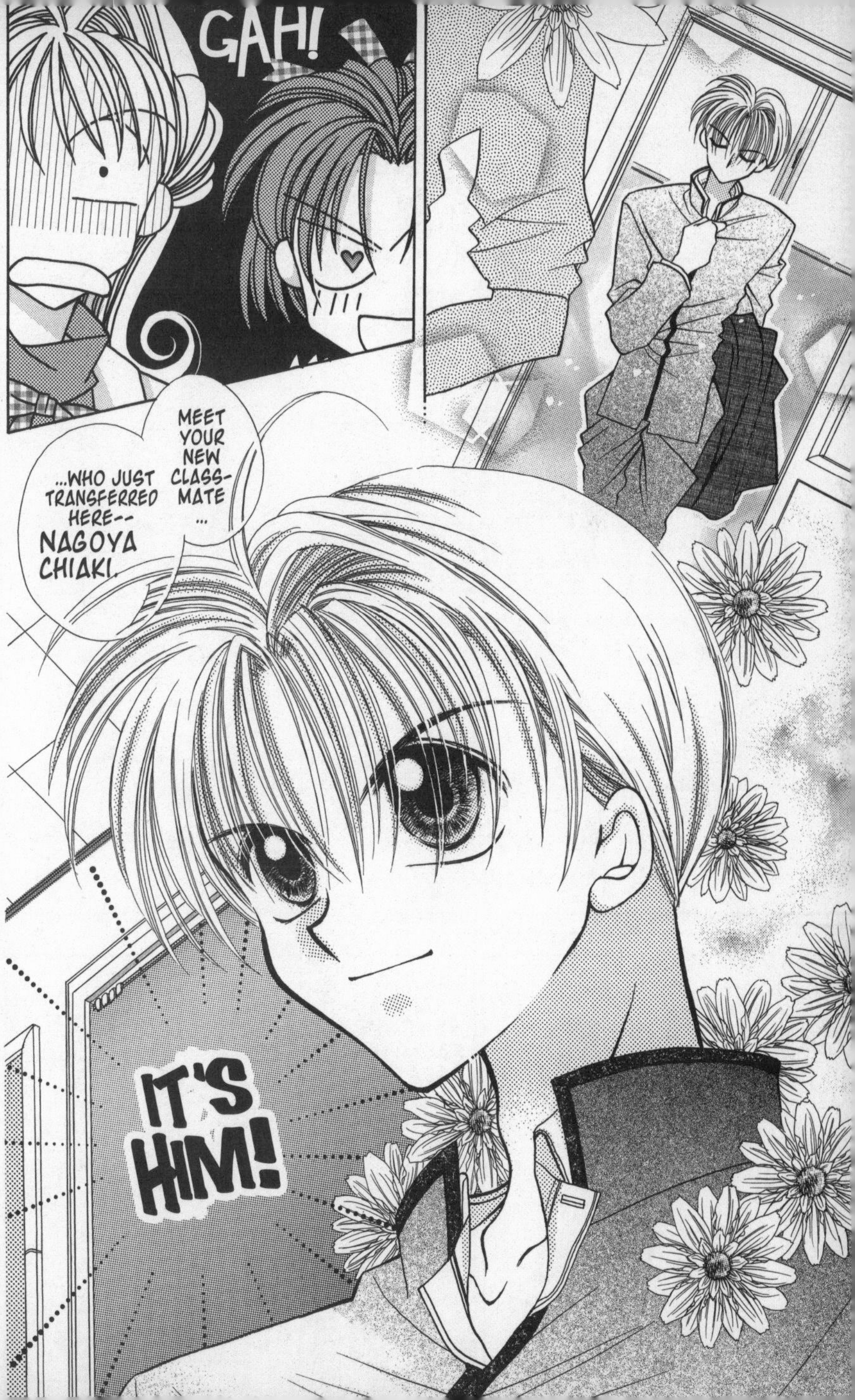
GAH!
MEET YOUR NEW CLASS-MATE ...
...WHO JUST TRANSFERRED HERE-- NAGOYA CHIAKI.
IT'S HIM!

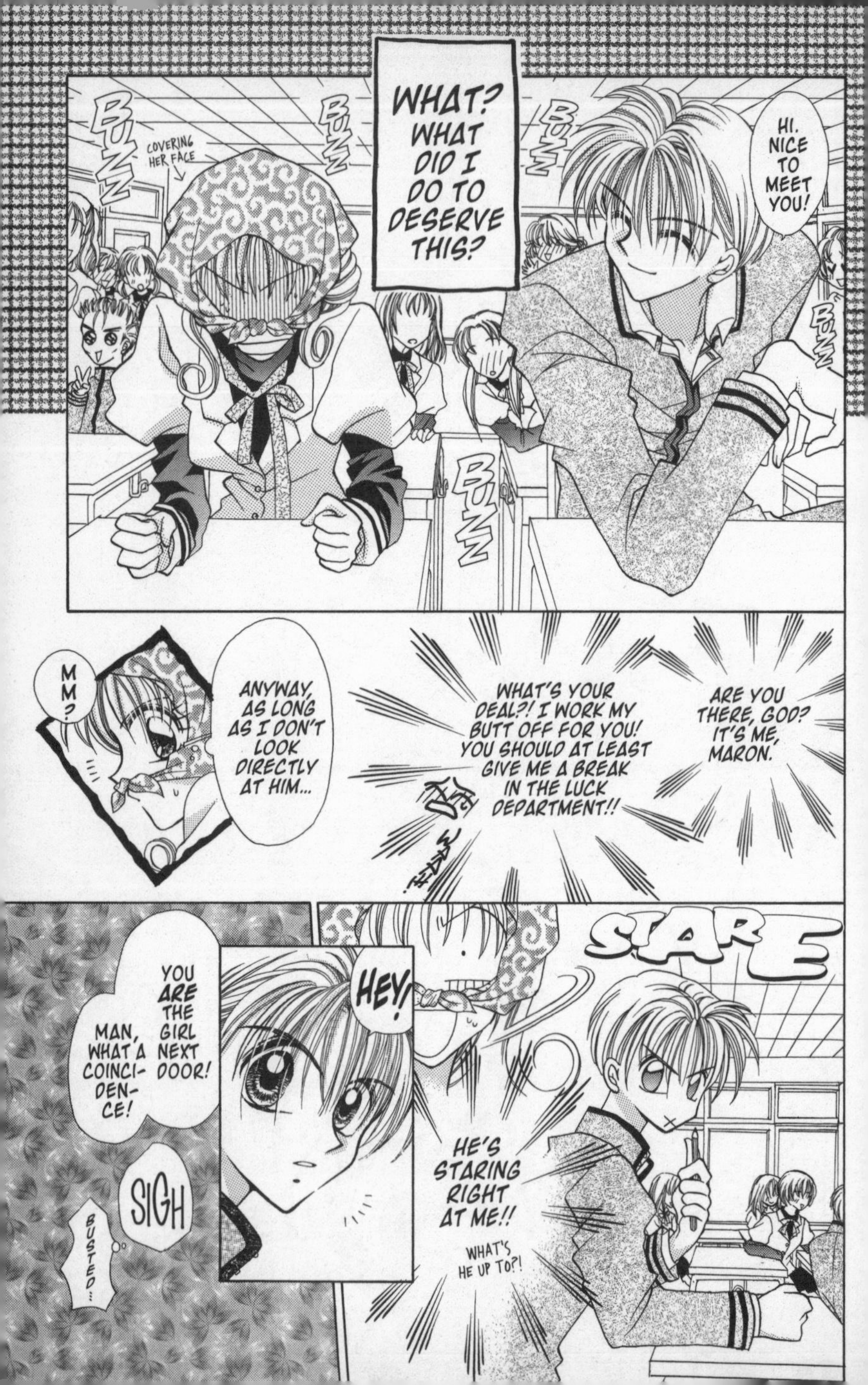
HI. NICE TO MEET YOU!
BUZZ
BUZZ
WHAT? WHAT DID I DO TO DESERVE THIS?
BUZZ
COVERING HER FACE
BUZZ
BUZZ
ARE YOU THERE, GOD? IT'S ME, MARON.
WHAT'S YOUR DEAL?! I WORK MY BUTT OFF FOR YOU! YOU SHOULD AT LEAST GIVE ME A BREAK IN THE LUCK DEPARTMENT!!
ANYWAY, AS LONG AS I DON'T LOOK DIRECTLY AT HIM...
MM?
STARE
HE'S STARING RIGHT AT ME!!
WHAT'S HE UP TO?!
HEY!
YOU ARE THE GIRL NEXT DOOR!
MAN, WHAT A COINCI-DEN-CE!
SIGH
BUSTED...

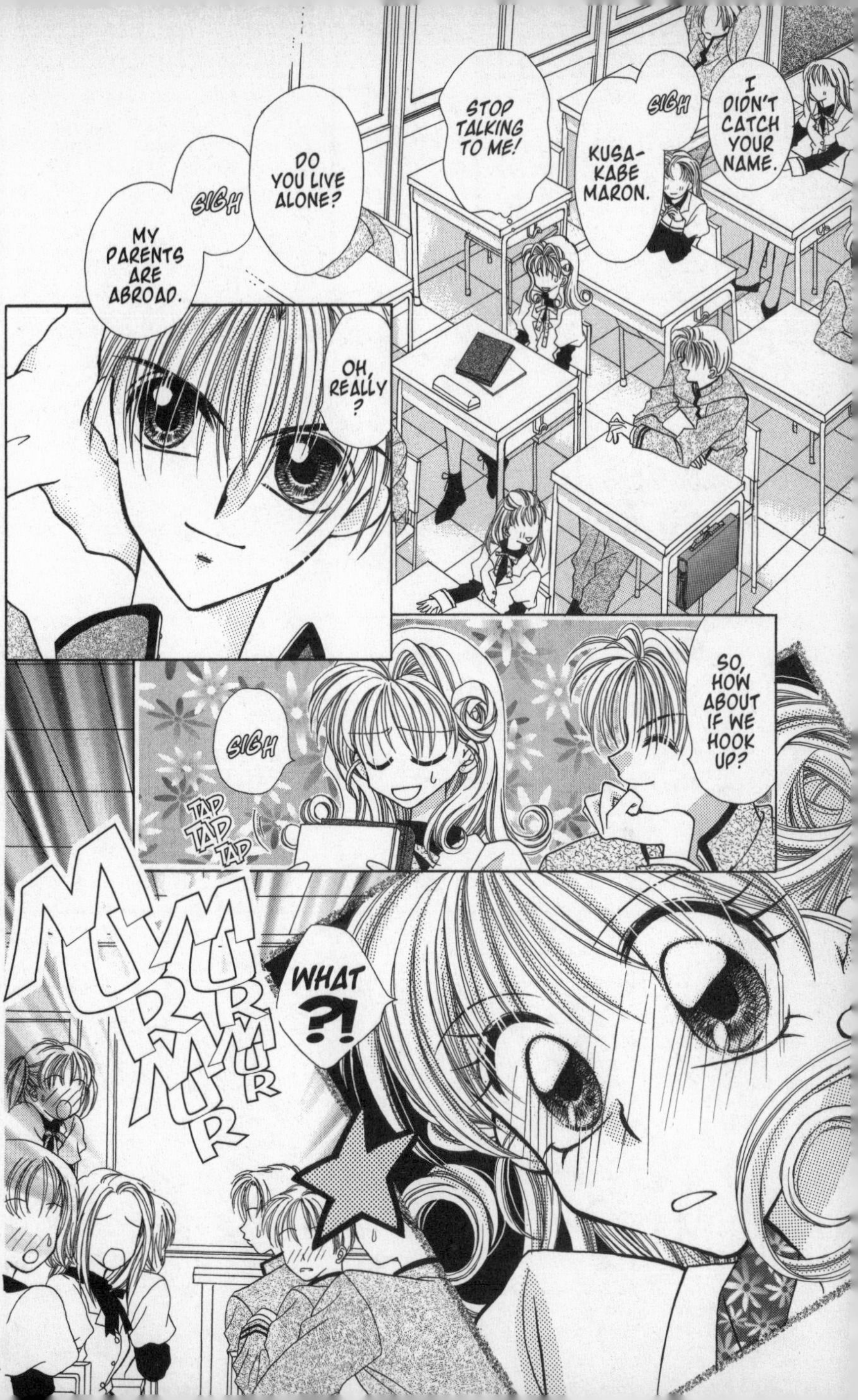

I DIDN'T CATCH YOUR NAME.
SIGH
KUSA-KABE MARON.
STOP TALKING TO ME!
DO YOU LIVE ALONE?
SIGH
MY PARENTS ARE ABROAD.
OH, REALLY?
SO, HOW ABOUT IF WE HOOK UP?
SIGH
TAP TAP TAP
WHAT?!
MURMUR
MURMUR

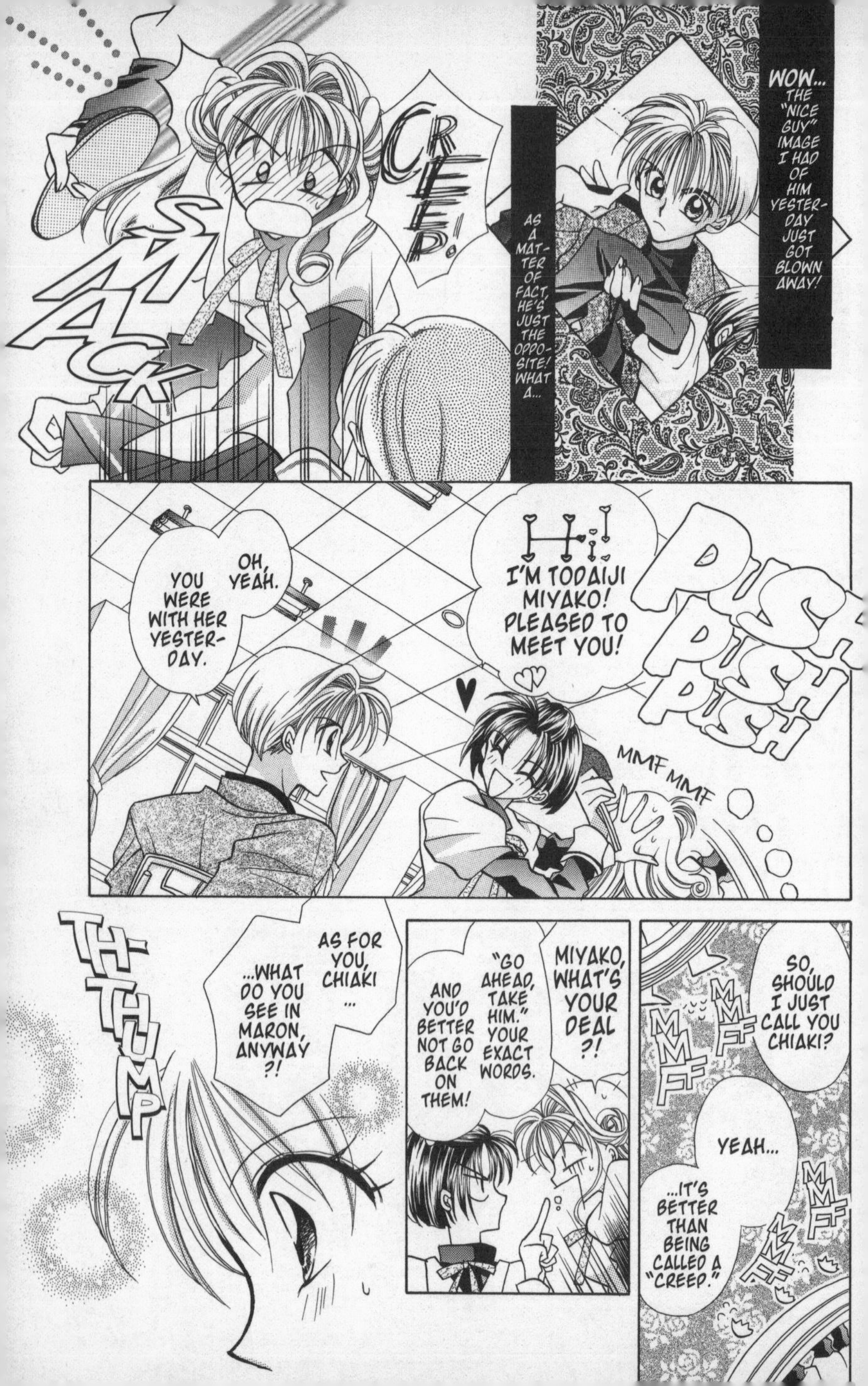
WOW... THE "NICE GUY" IMAGE I HAD OF HIM YESTERDAY JUST GOT BLOWN AWAY!
AS A MATTER OF FACT, HE'S JUST THE OPPOSITE! WHAT A...
CREEP!
SMACK
PISH PISH PISH
Hi! I'M TODAIJI MIYAKO! PLEASED TO MEET YOU!
OH, YEAH. YOU WERE WITH HER YESTERDAY.
MMF MMF
SO, SHOULD I JUST CALL YOU CHIAKI?
MMMF MMMF
YEAH...
...IT'S BETTER THAN BEING CALLED A "CREEP."
MMMF MMMF
MIYAKO, WHAT'S YOUR DEAL?!
"GO AHEAD, TAKE HIM." YOUR EXACT WORDS.
AND YOU'D BETTER NOT GO BACK ON THEM!
AS FOR YOU, CHIAKI...
...WHAT DO YOU SEE IN MARON, ANYWAY?!
TH-THUMP

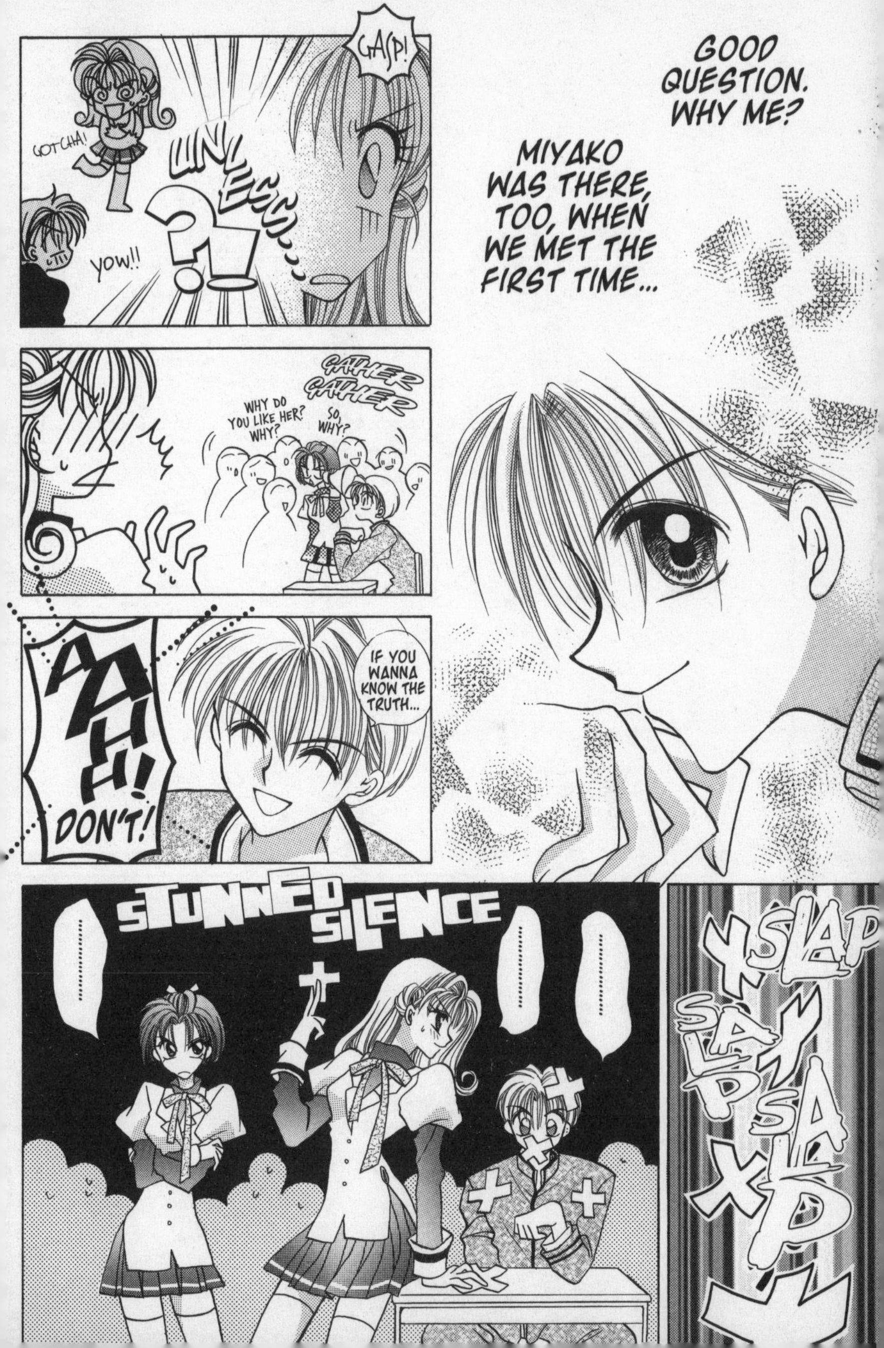
GOOD QUESTION. WHY ME?
MIYAKO WAS THERE, TOO, WHEN WE MET THE FIRST TIME...
GASP!
UNLESS...?
GOTCHA!
YOW!!
GATHER GATHER
SO, WHY?
WHY DO YOU LIKE HER? WHY?
IF YOU WANNA KNOW THE TRUTH...
AAHH! DON'T!
SLAP SLAP SLAP SLAP
STUNNED SILENCE
....
....
....

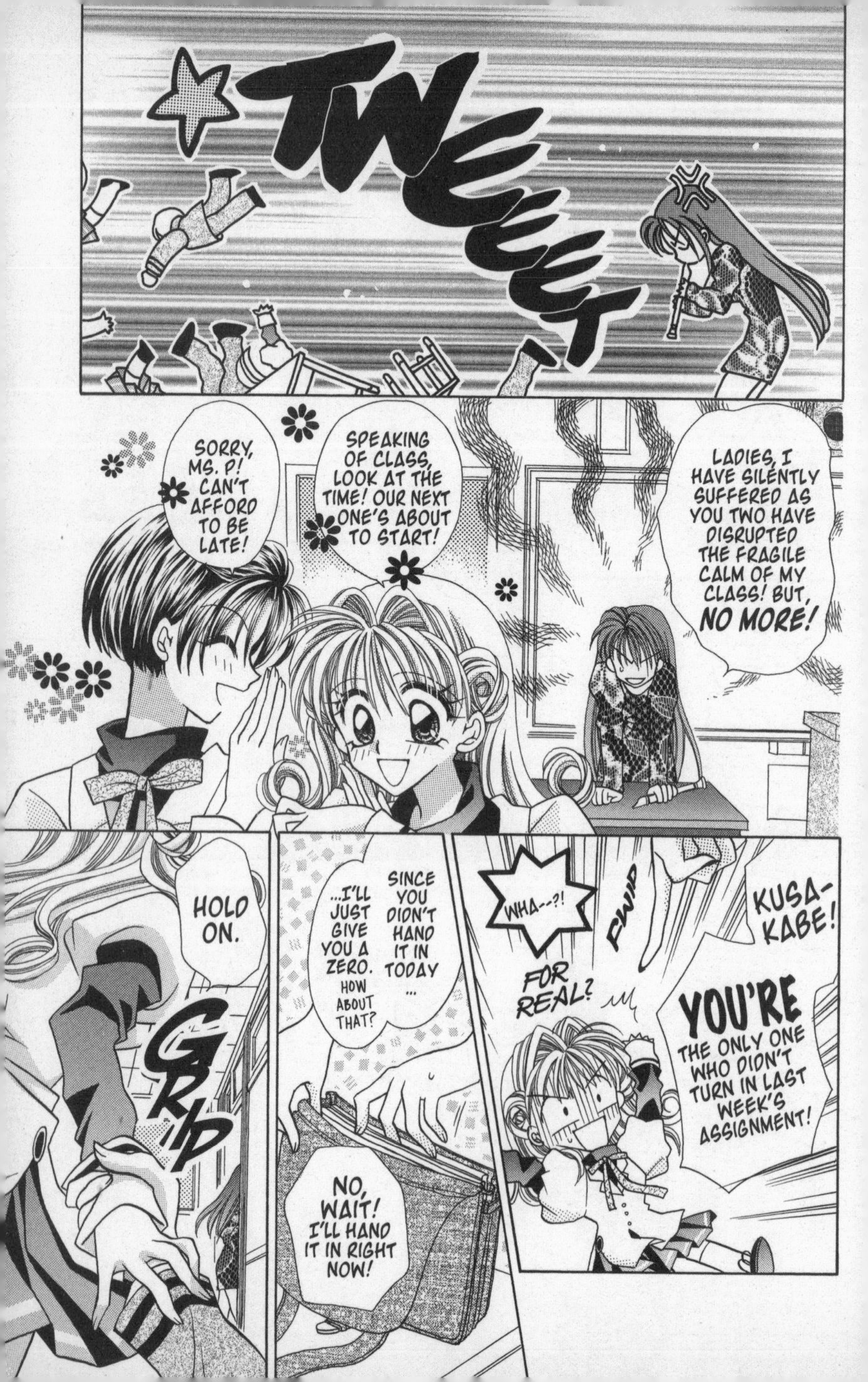
TWEEEET
LADIES, I HAVE SILENTLY SUFFERED AS YOU TWO HAVE DISRUPTED THE FRAGILE CALM OF MY CLASS! BUT, NO MORE!
SPEAKING OF CLASS, LOOK AT THE TIME! OUR NEXT ONE'S ABOUT TO START!
SORRY, MS. P! CAN'T AFFORD TO BE LATE!
KUSA-KABE!
YOU'RE THE ONLY ONE WHO DIDN'T TURN IN LAST WEEK'S ASSIGNMENT!
FWIP
WHA--?!
FOR REAL?
SINCE YOU DIDN'T HAND IT IN TODAY...
...I'LL JUST GIVE YOU A ZERO. HOW ABOUT THAT?
NO, WAIT! I'LL HAND IT IN RIGHT NOW!
HOLD ON.
GRIP

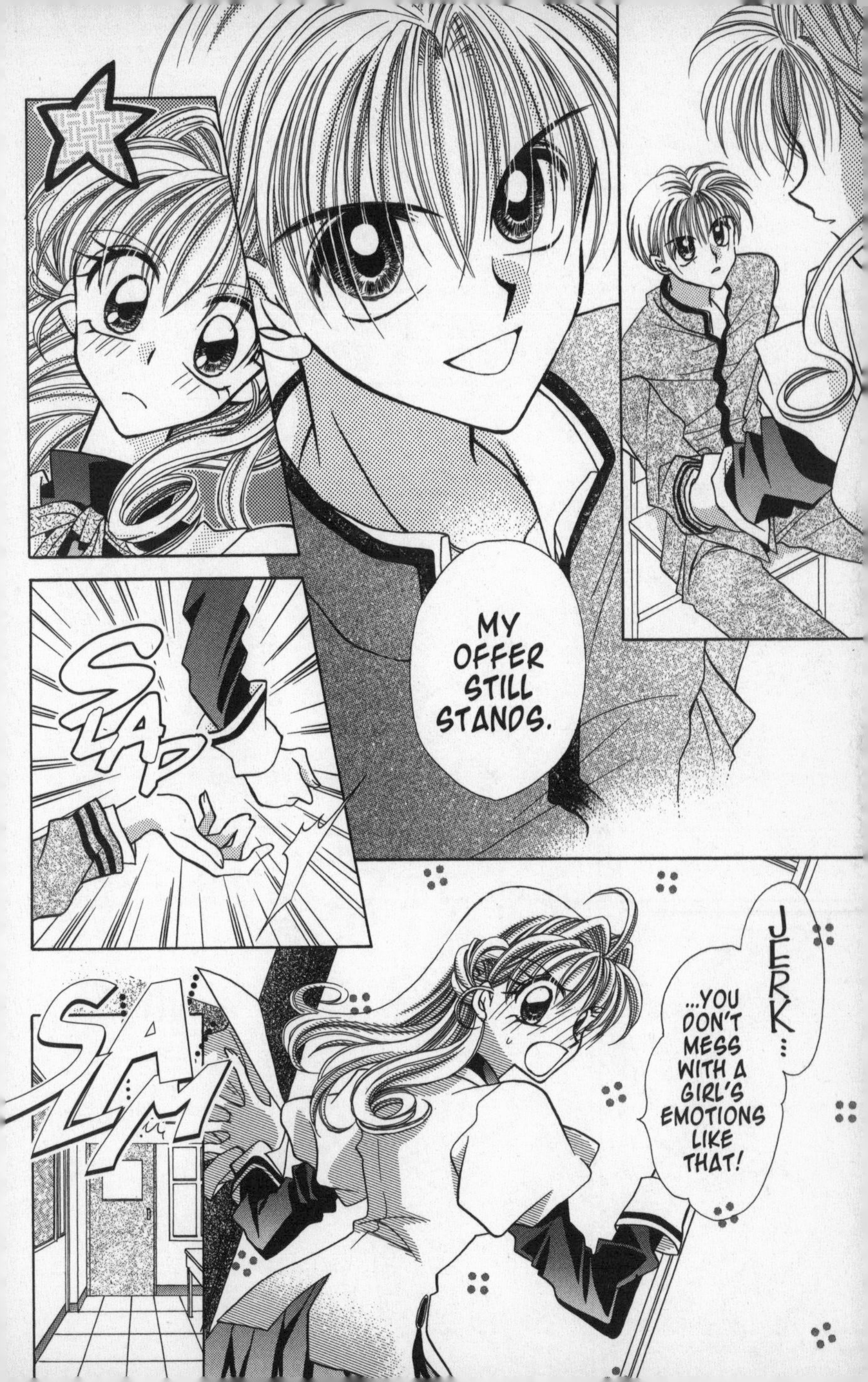
MY OFFER STILL STANDS.
SLAP
JERK...
...YOU DON'T MESS WITH A GIRL'S EMOTIONS LIKE THAT!
SLAM

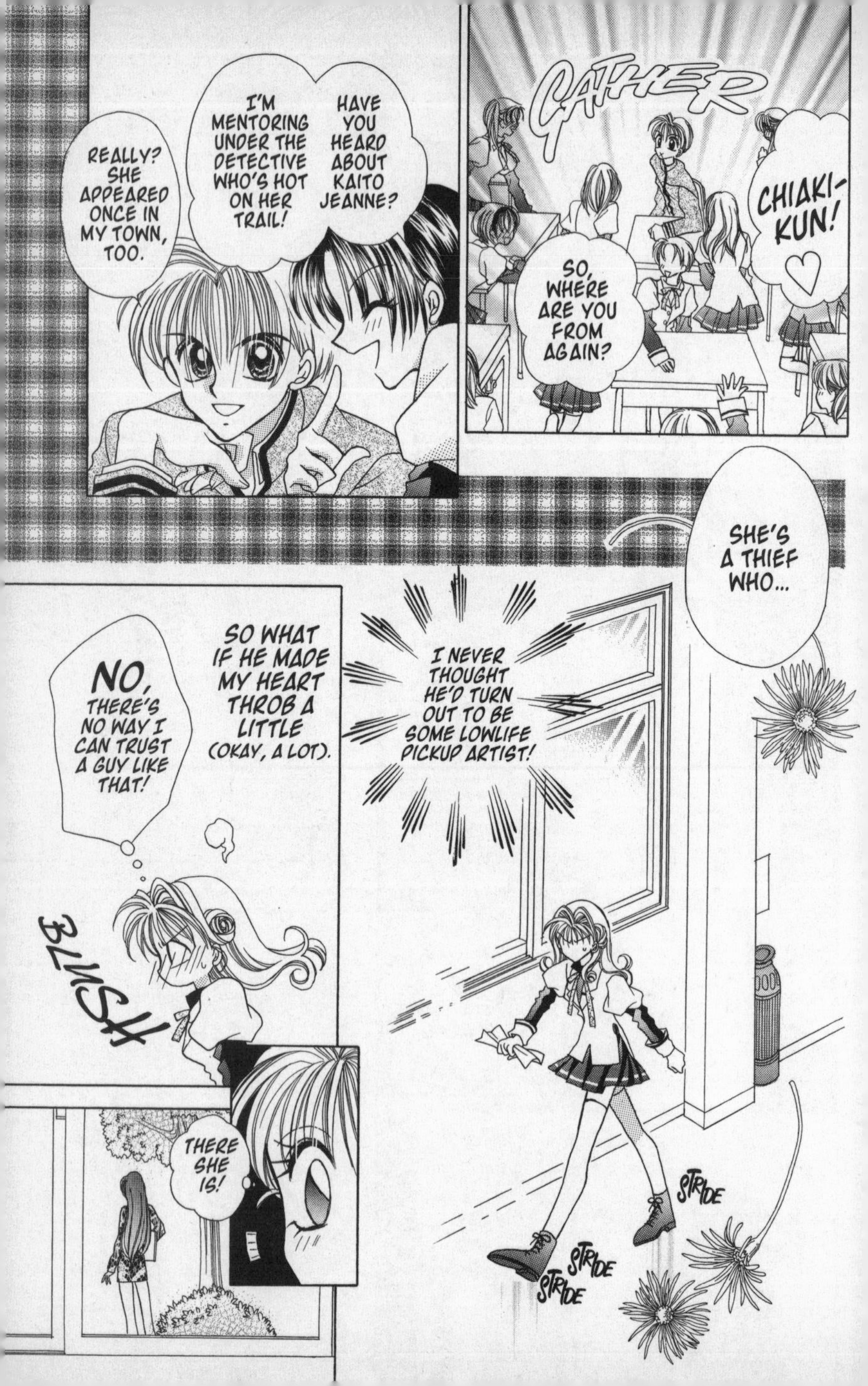
GATHER
CHIAKI-KUN!
SO, WHERE ARE YOU FROM AGAIN?
HAVE YOU HEARD ABOUT KAITO JEANNE?
I'M MENTORING UNDER THE DETECTIVE WHO'S HOT ON HER TRAIL!
REALLY? SHE APPEARED ONCE IN MY TOWN, TOO.
SHE'S A THIEF WHO...
I NEVER THOUGHT HE'D TURN OUT TO BE SOME LOWLIFE PICKUP ARTIST!
STRIDE
STRIDE
STRIDE
SO WHAT IF HE MADE MY HEART THROB A LITTLE (OKAY, A LOT).
NO, THERE'S NO WAY I CAN TRUST A GUY LIKE THAT!
BLUSH
THERE SHE IS!

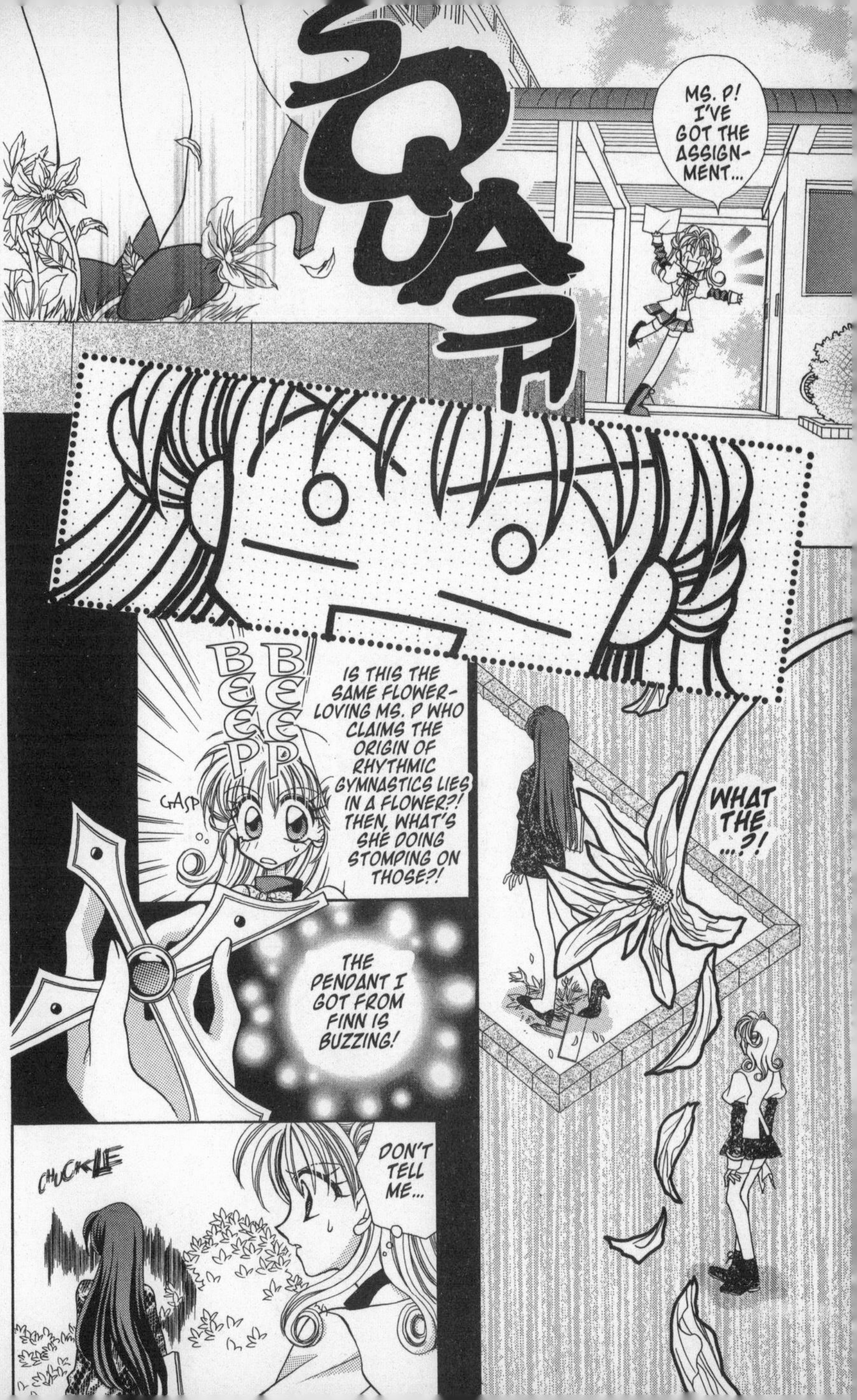
MS. P! I'VE GOT THE ASSIGNMENT...
SQUASH
WHAT THE ...?!
IS THIS THE SAME FLOWER-LOVING MS. P WHO CLAIMS THE ORIGIN OF RHYTHMIC GYMNASTICS LIES IN A FLOWER?! THEN, WHAT'S SHE DOING STOMPING ON THOSE?!
BEEP BEEP
GASP
THE PENDANT I GOT FROM FINN IS BUZZING!
DON'T TELL ME...
CHUCKLE

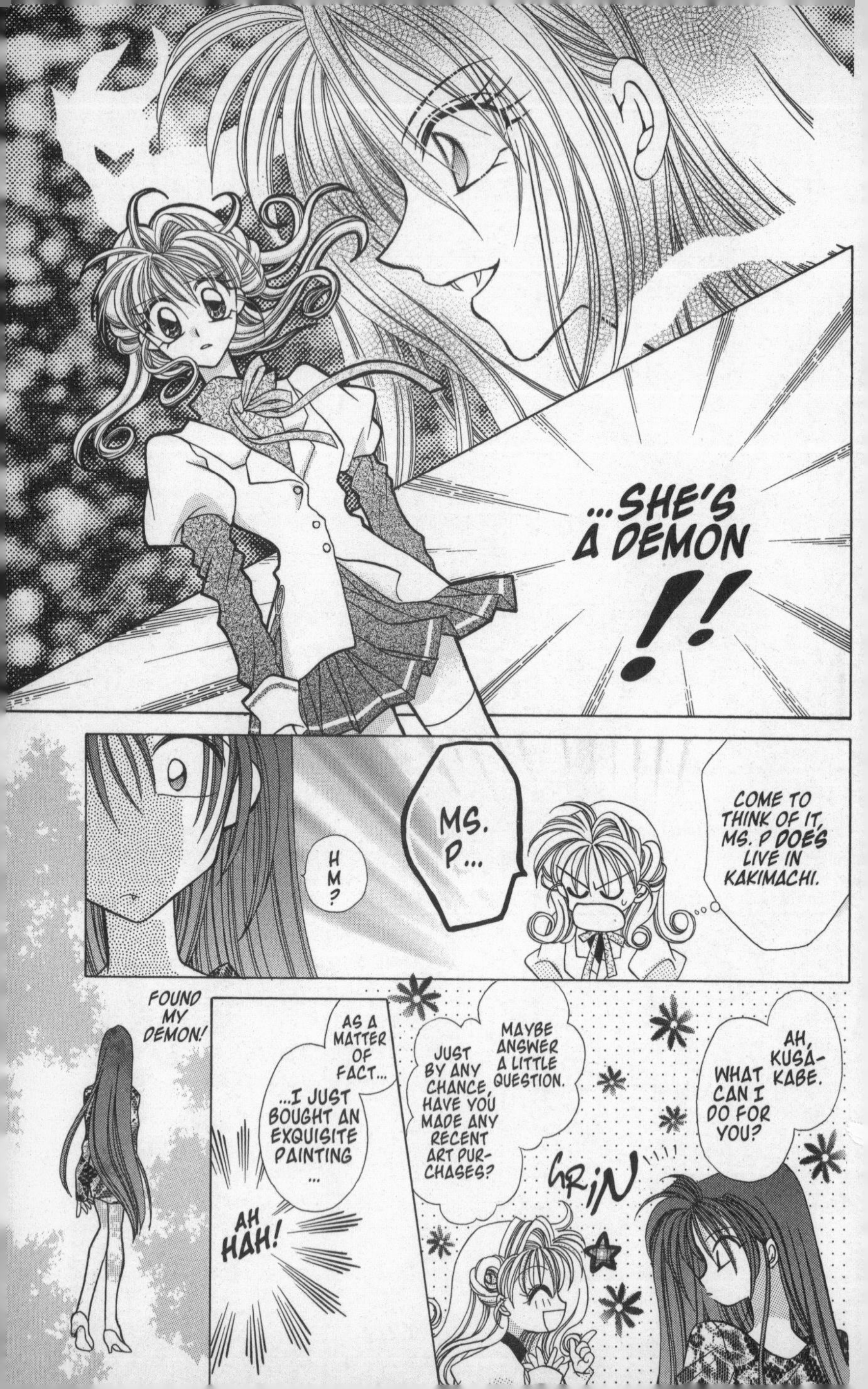
...SHE'S A DEMON !!
COME TO THINK OF IT, MS. P DOES LIVE IN KAKIMACHI.
MS. P...
HM?
AH, KUSAKABE. WHAT CAN I DO FOR YOU?
GRIN
MAYBE ANSWER A LITTLE QUESTION.
JUST BY ANY CHANCE, HAVE YOU MADE ANY RECENT ART PURCHASES?
AS A MATTER OF FACT...
...I JUST BOUGHT AN EXQUISITE PAINTING ...
AH HAH!
FOUND MY DEMON!

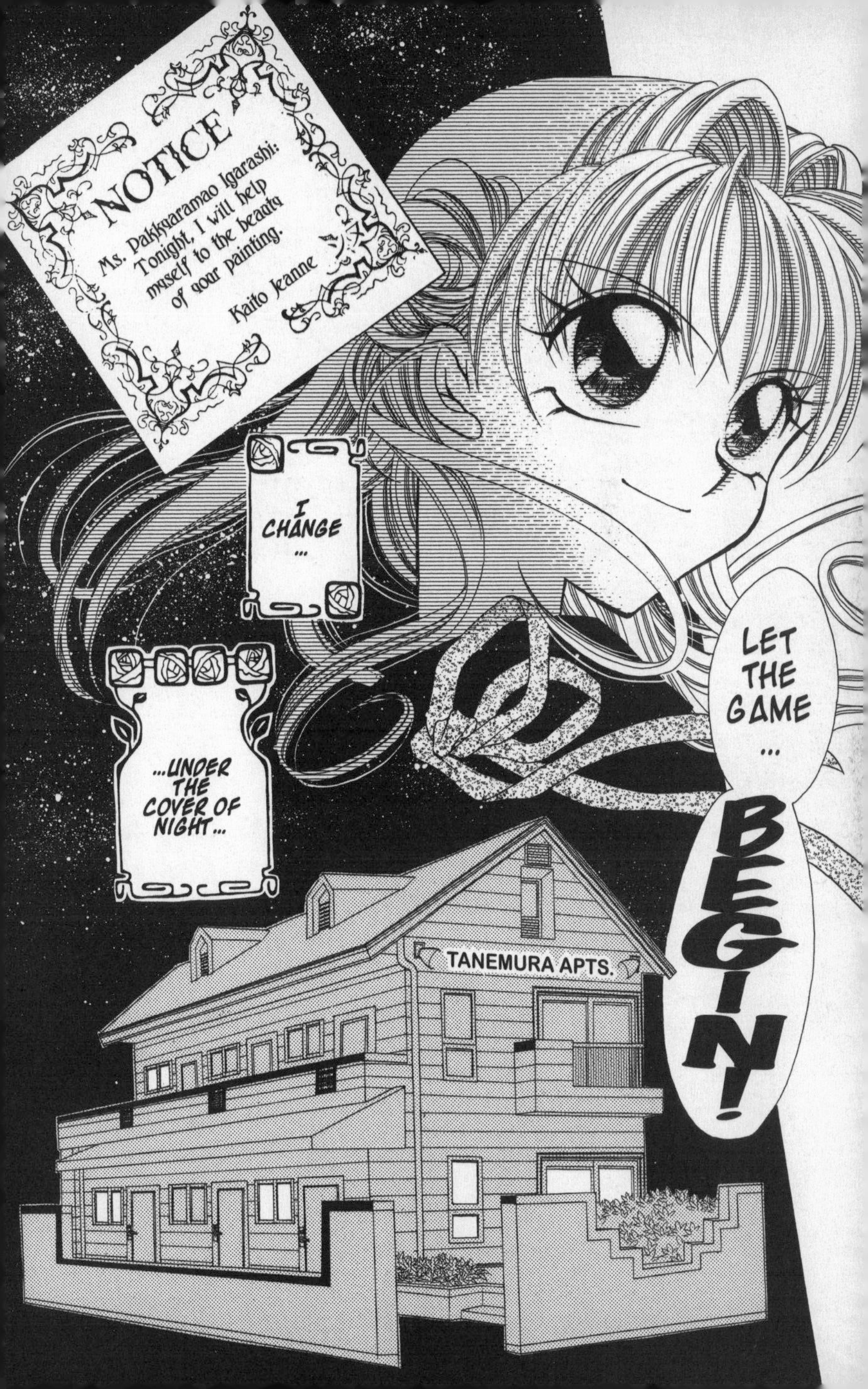
NOTICE
Ms. Pakkgaramao Igarashi:
Tonight, I will help myself to the beauty of your painting.
Kaito Jeanne
LET THE GAME ... BEGIN!
I CHANGE ...
...UNDER THE COVER OF NIGHT...
TANEMURA APTS.

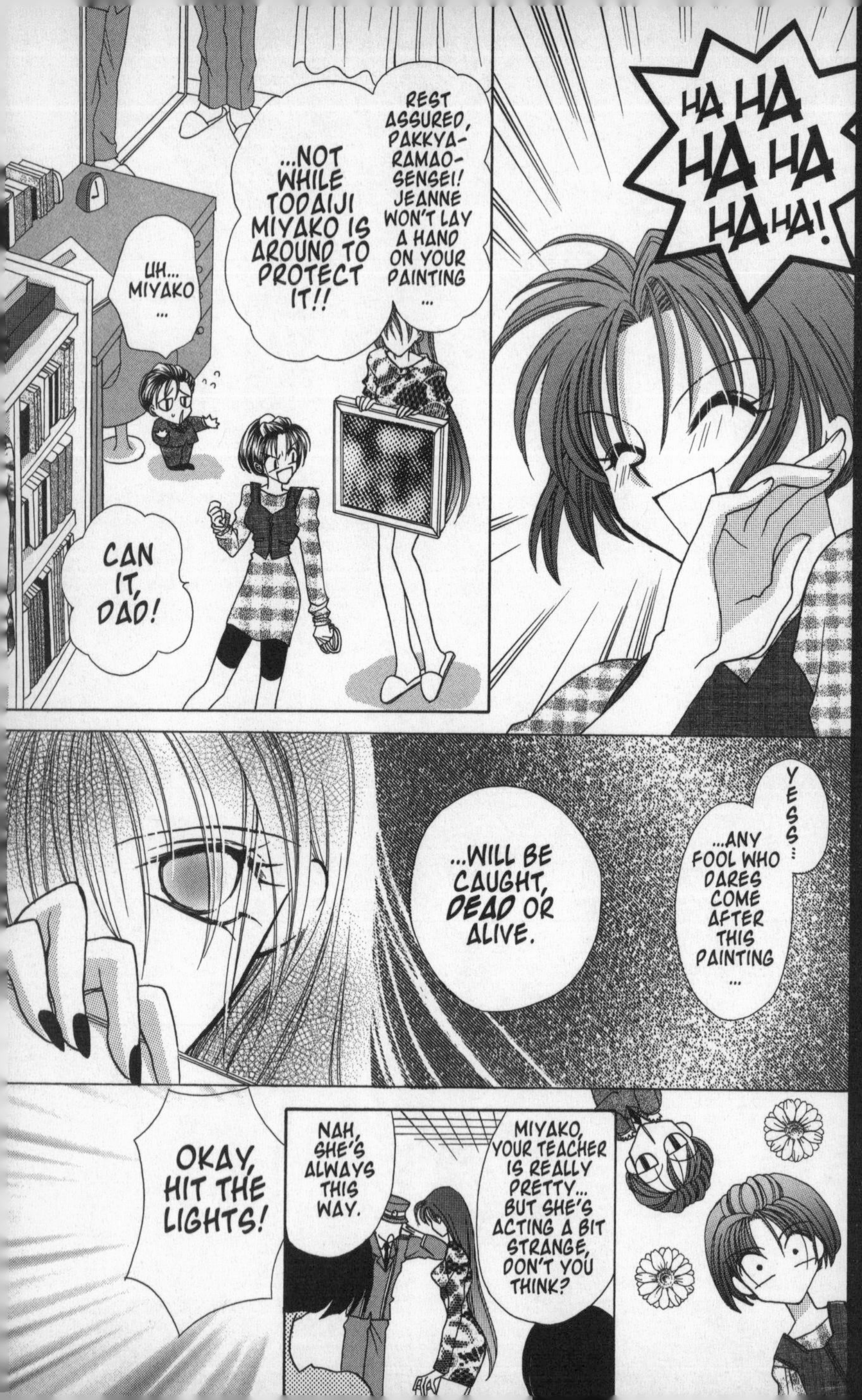
HA HA HA HA HA HA!
REST ASSURED, PAKKYA-RAMAO-SENSEI! JEANNE WON'T LAY A HAND ON YOUR PAINTING ...
...NOT WHILE TODAIJI MIYAKO IS AROUND TO PROTECT IT!!
UH... MIYAKO ...
CAN IT, DAD!
YESS...
...ANY FOOL WHO DARES COME AFTER THIS PAINTING ...
...WILL BE CAUGHT, DEAD OR ALIVE.
MIYAKO, YOUR TEACHER IS REALLY PRETTY... BUT SHE'S ACTING A BIT STRANGE, DON'T YOU THINK?
NAH, SHE'S ALWAYS THIS WAY.
OKAY, HIT THE LIGHTS!

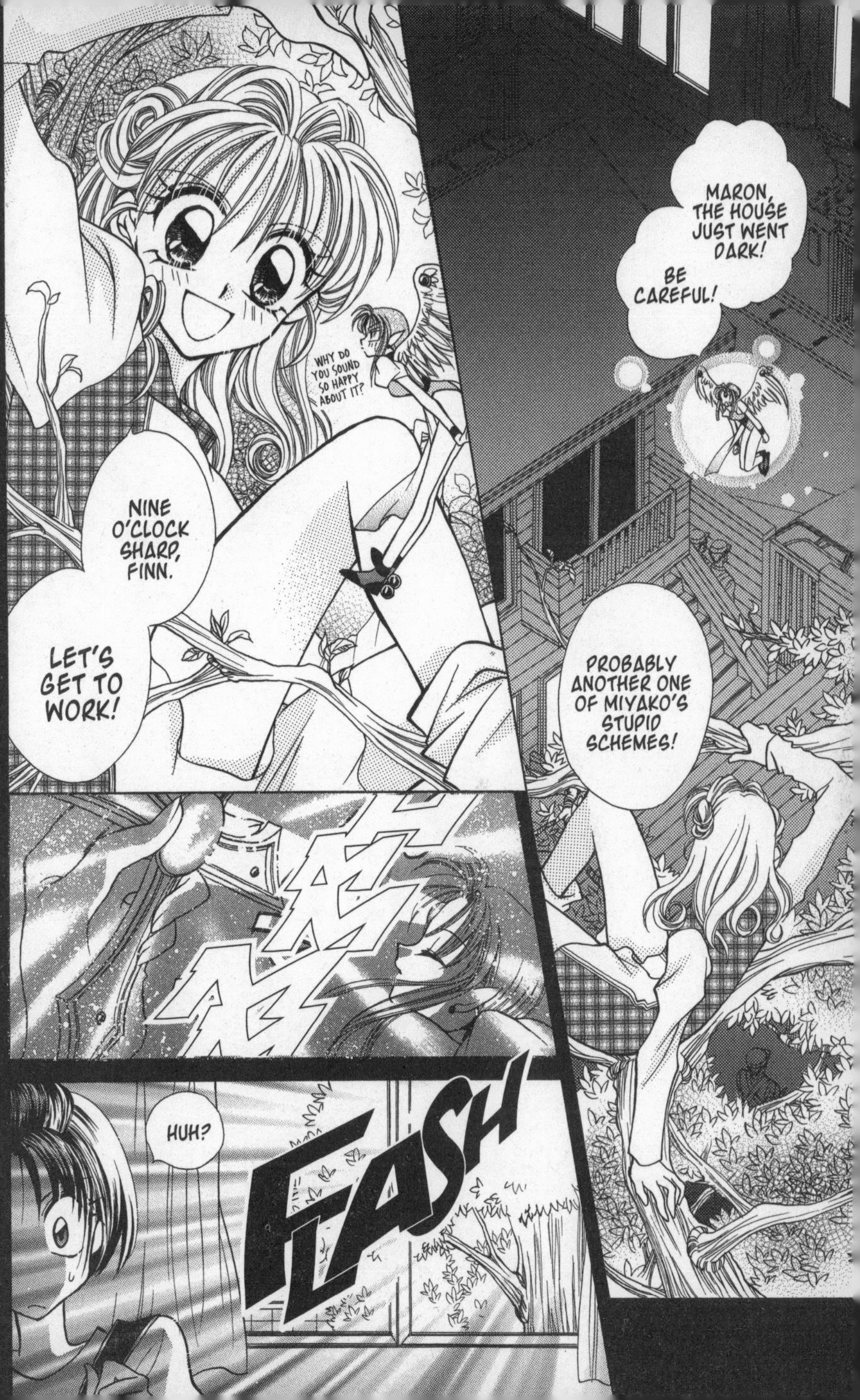
MARON, THE HOUSE JUST WENT DARK!
BE CAREFUL!
PROBABLY ANOTHER ONE OF MIYAKO'S STUPID SCHEMES!
NINE O'CLOCK SHARP, FINN.
WHY DO YOU SOUND SO HAPPY ABOUT IT?
LET'S GET TO WORK!
FLASH
HUH?

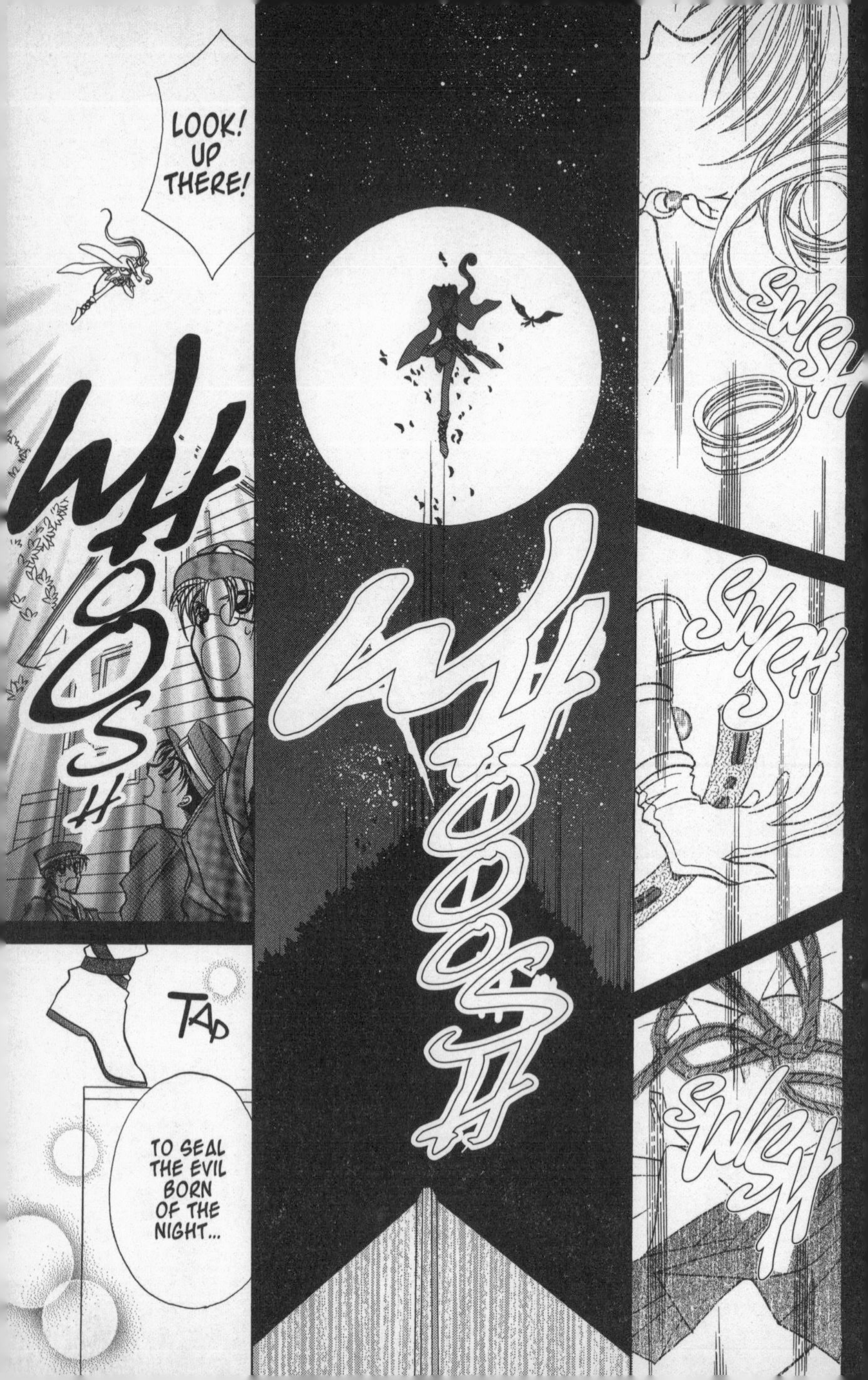
SWISH
SWISH
SWISH
WHOOSH
LOOK! UP THERE!
WHOOSH
TAP
TO SEAL THE EVIL BORN OF THE NIGHT...

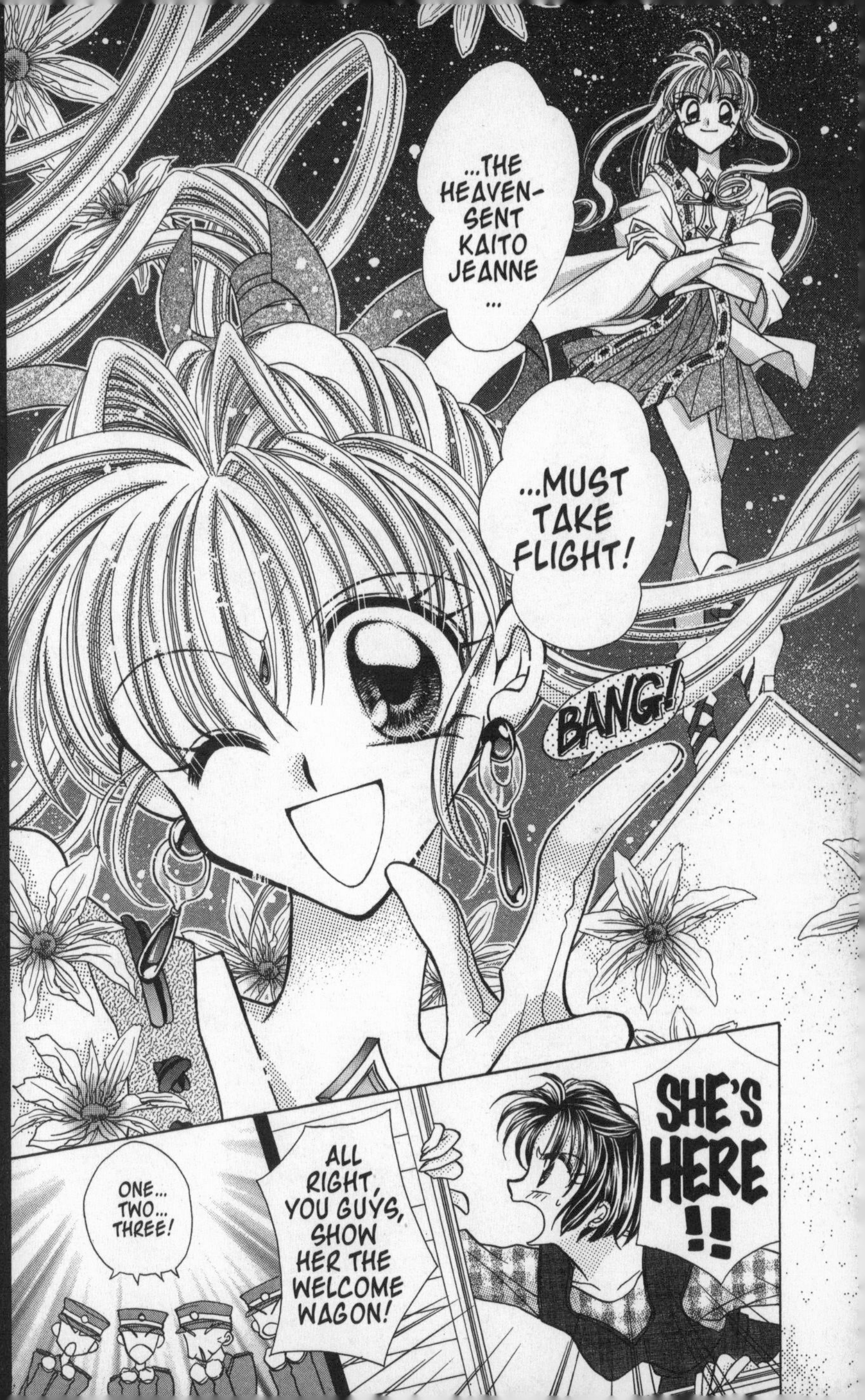
...THE HEAVEN-SENT KAITO JEANNE ...
...MUST TAKE FLIGHT!
BANG!
SHE'S HERE!!
ALL RIGHT, YOU GUYS, SHOW HER THE WELCOME WAGON!
ONE... TWO... THREE!

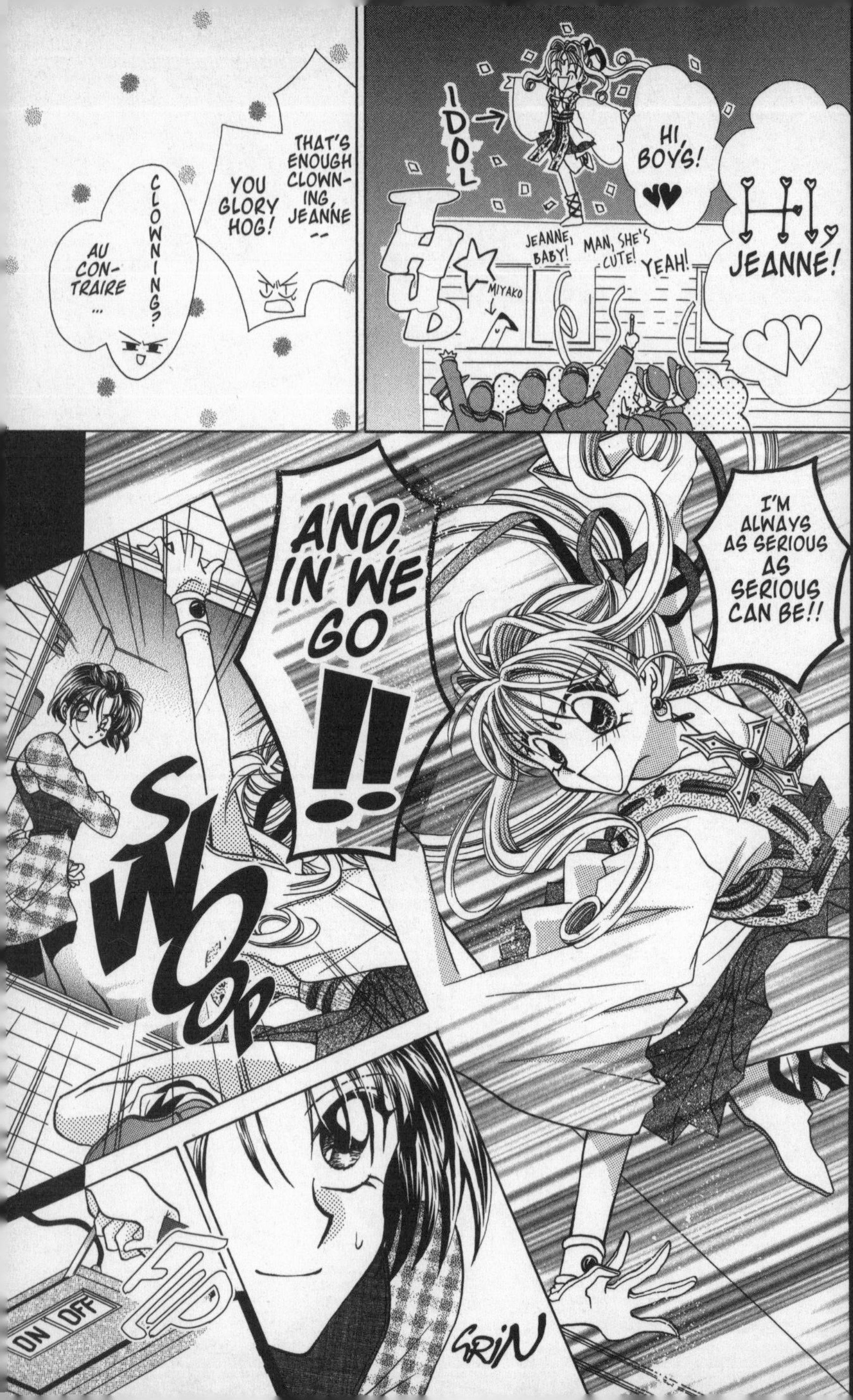
HI, BOYS! ♥♥
HI JEANNE!
IDOL →
THUD
JEANNE, BABY!
MAN, SHE'S CUTE!
YEAH!
MIYAKO
THAT'S ENOUGH CLOWNING, JEANNE --
YOU GLORY HOG!
CLOWNING?
AU CONTRAIRE ...
I'M ALWAYS AS SERIOUS AS SERIOUS CAN BE!!
AND IN WE GO !!
SWOOP
ON OFF
GRIN

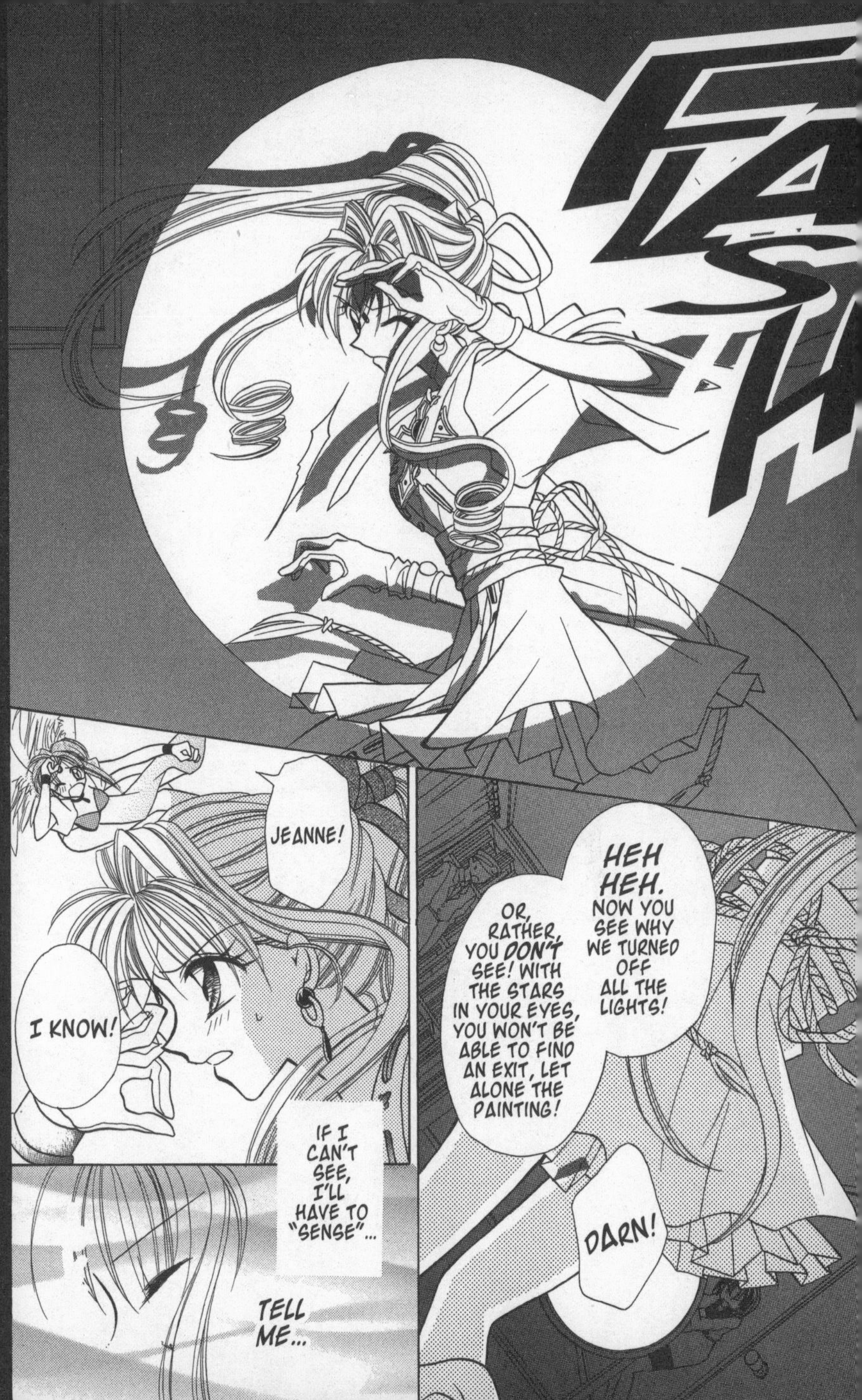
HEH HEH. NOW YOU SEE WHY WE TURNED OFF ALL THE LIGHTS!
OR, RATHER, YOU DON'T SEE! WITH THE STARS IN YOUR EYES, YOU WON'T BE ABLE TO FIND AN EXIT, LET ALONE THE PAINTING!
DARN!
JEANNE!
I KNOW!
IF I CAN'T SEE, I'LL HAVE TO "SENSE"...
TELL ME...

JEANNE D'ARC... THE ORIGINAL, SLEEPING INSIDE OF ME... PLEASE, JEANNE, WAKE UP AND TELL ME WHERE...

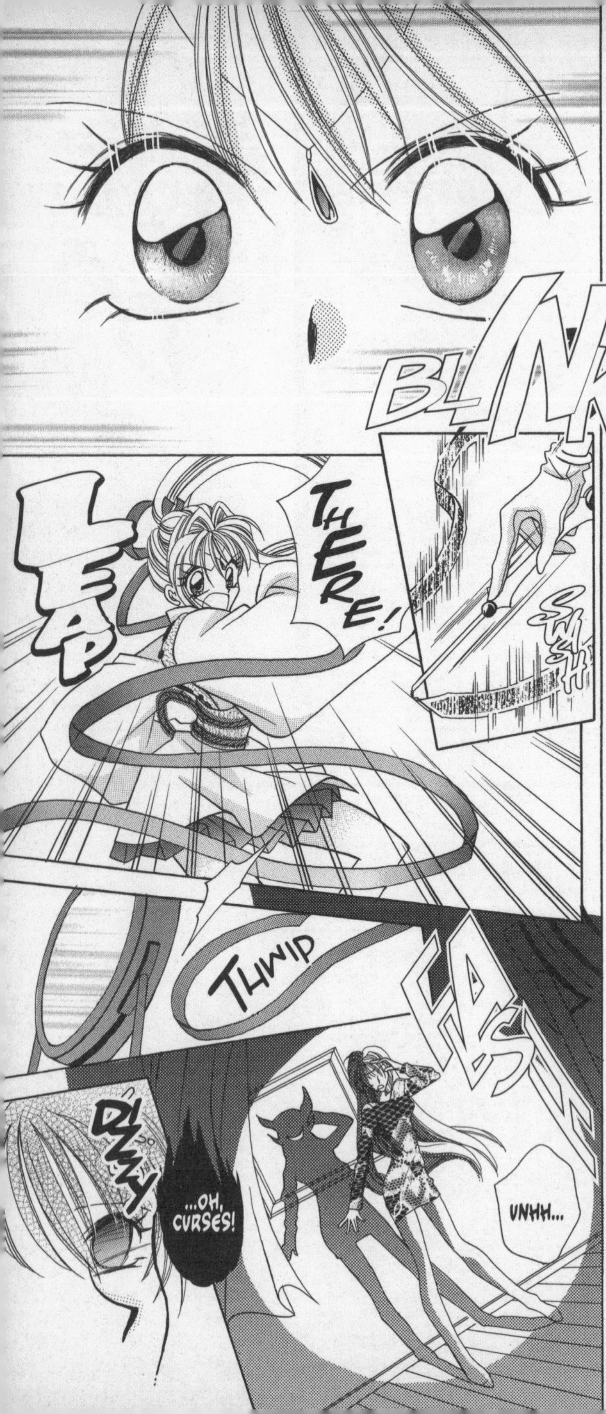
BLINK
SWISH
THERE!
LEAP
FLASH
THWIP
UNHH...
...OH, CURSES!
DIZZY

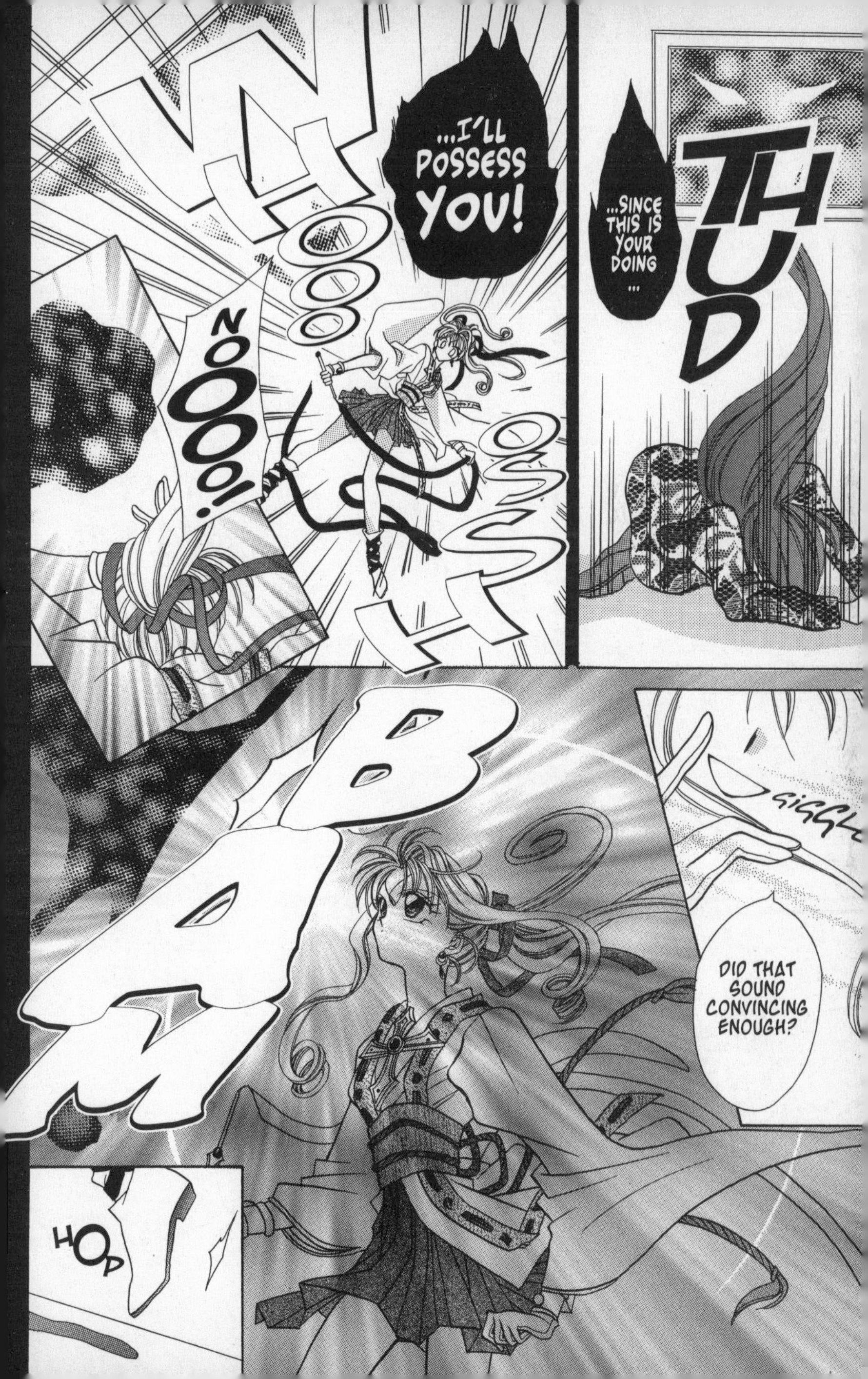
THUD
...SINCE THIS IS YOUR DOING ...
...I'LL POSSESS YOU!
WHOOOOOSH
NOOOOO!
GIGGL
DID THAT SOUND CONVINCING ENOUGH?
BAM
HOP

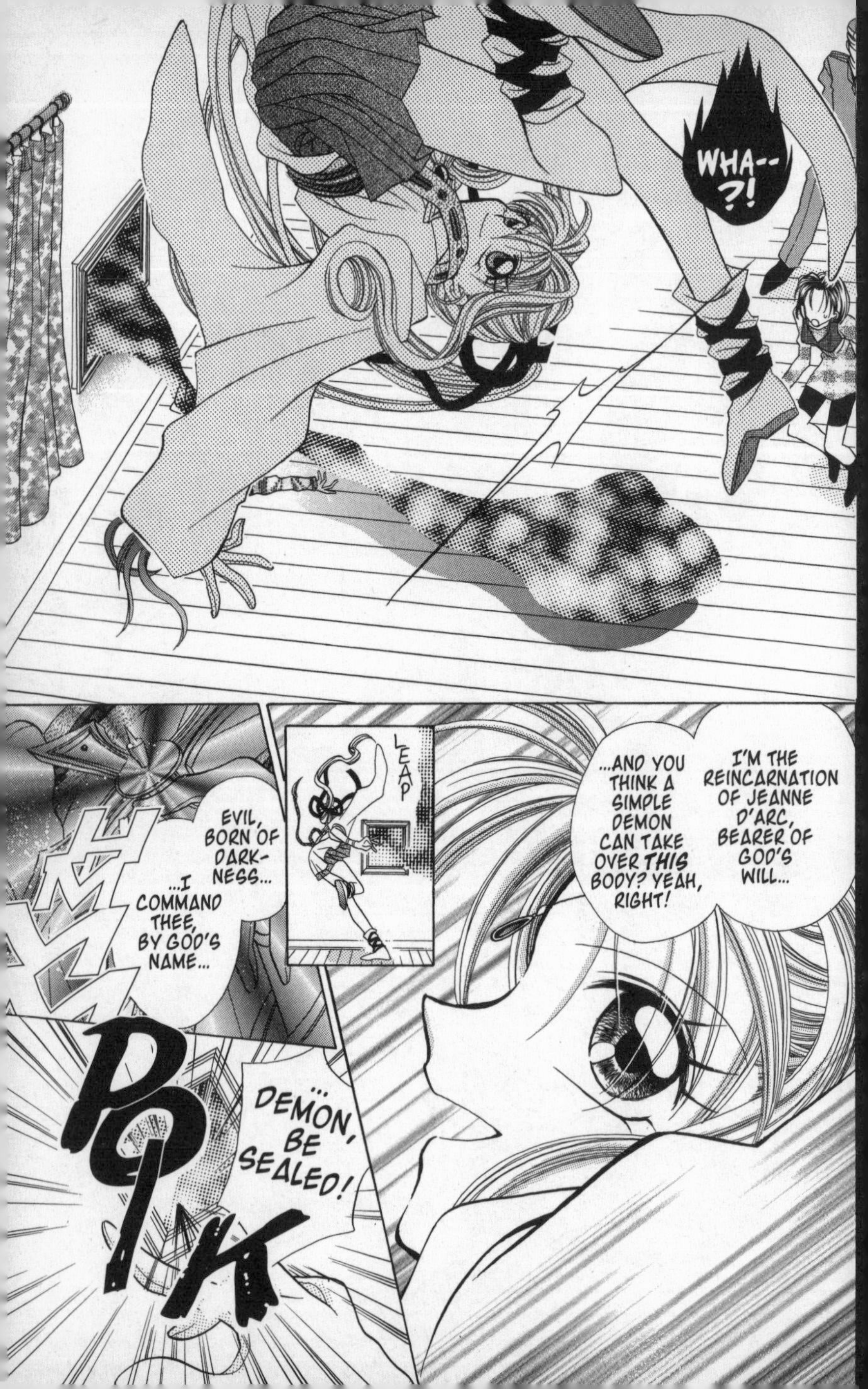
WHA--?!
I'M THE REINCARNATION OF JEANNE D'ARC, BEARER OF GOD'S WILL...
...AND YOU THINK A SIMPLE DEMON CAN TAKE OVER THIS BODY? YEAH, RIGHT!
LEAP
EVIL, BORN OF DARKNESS...
...I COMMAND THEE, BY GOD'S NAME...
...DEMON, BE SEALED!

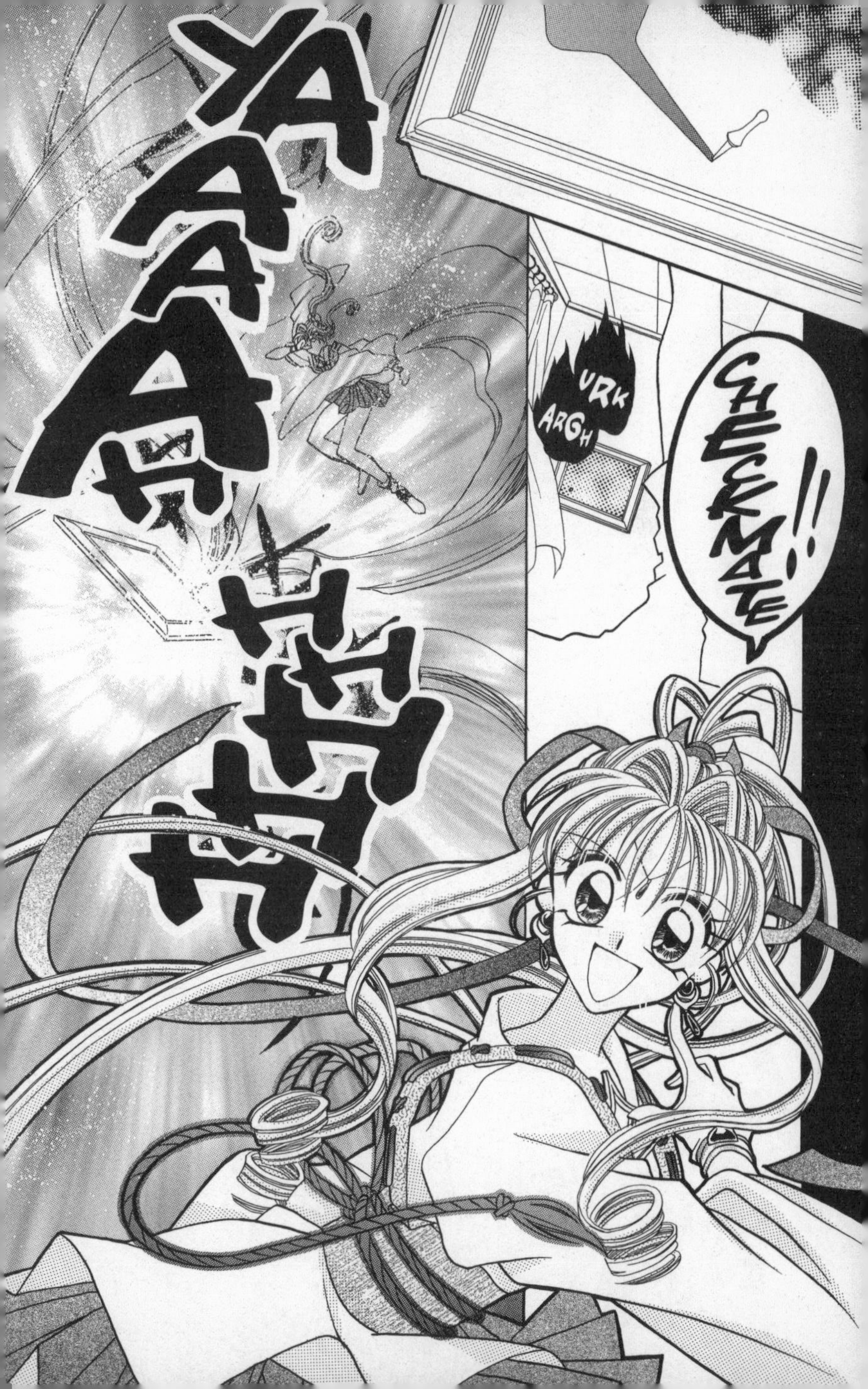
CHECKMATE!!
URK
ARGH

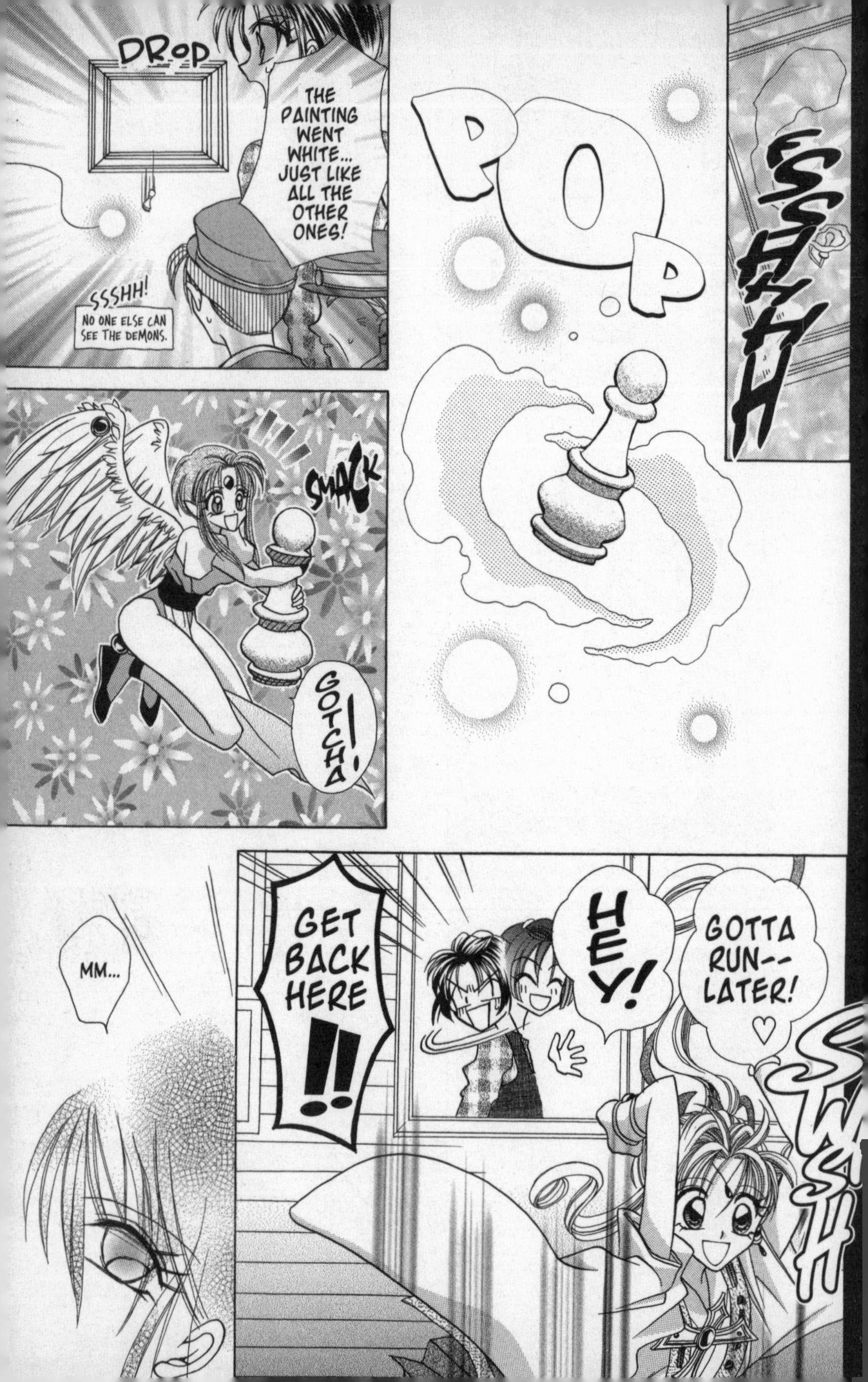
ESHHHH
POP
DROP
THE PAINTING WENT WHITE... JUST LIKE ALL THE OTHER ONES!
SSSHH!
NO ONE ELSE CAN SEE THE DEMONS.
SMACK
GOTCHA!
GOTTA RUN-- LATER! ♡
SWISH
HEY!
GET BACK HERE!!
MM...

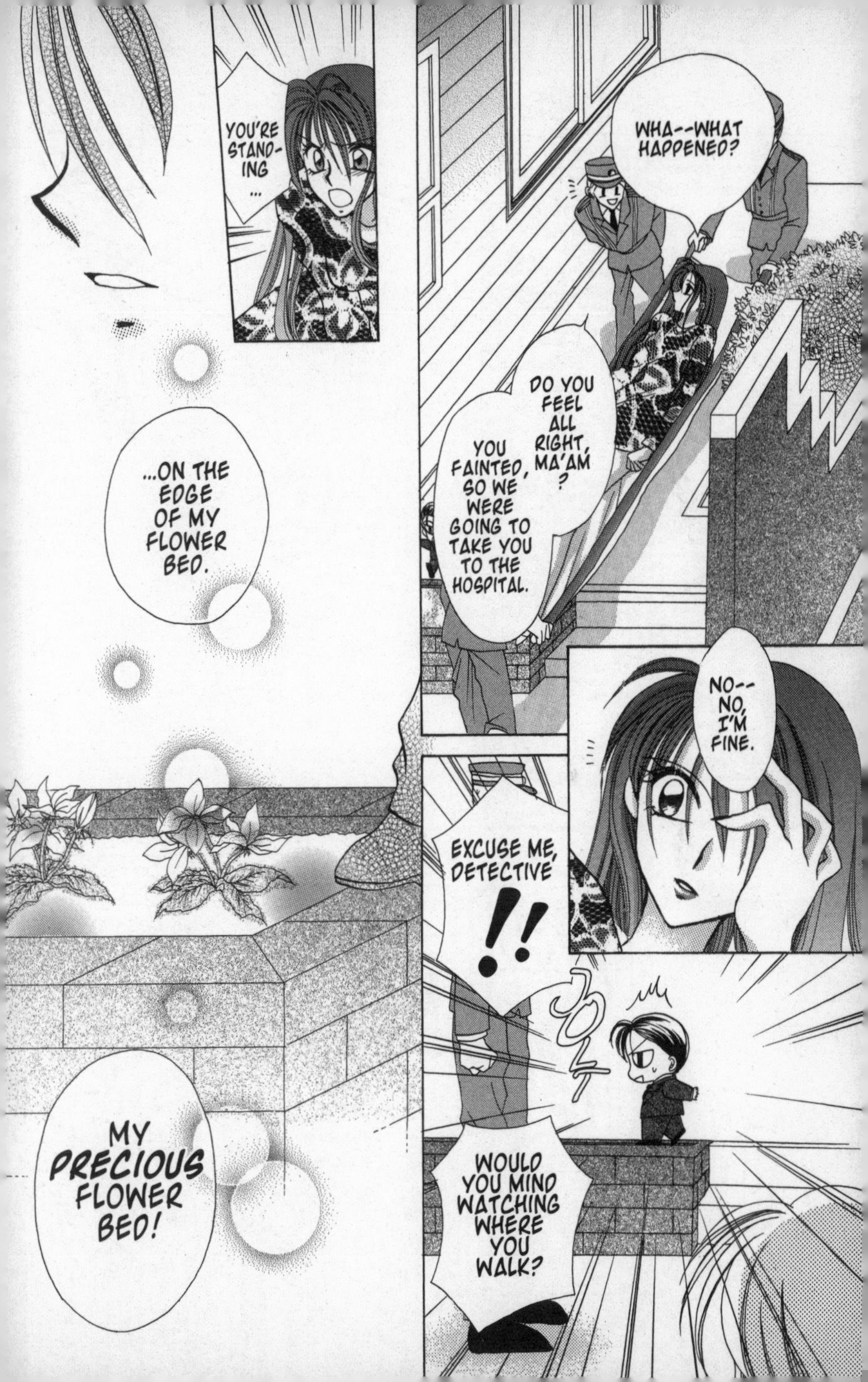
WHA--WHAT HAPPENED?
DO YOU FEEL ALL RIGHT, MA'AM?
YOU FAINTED, SO WE WERE GOING TO TAKE YOU TO THE HOSPITAL.
NO--NO, I'M FINE.
EXCUSE ME, DETECTIVE
!!
WOULD YOU MIND WATCHING WHERE YOU WALK?
YOU'RE STANDING ...
...ON THE EDGE OF MY FLOWER BED.
MY PRECIOUS FLOWER BED!

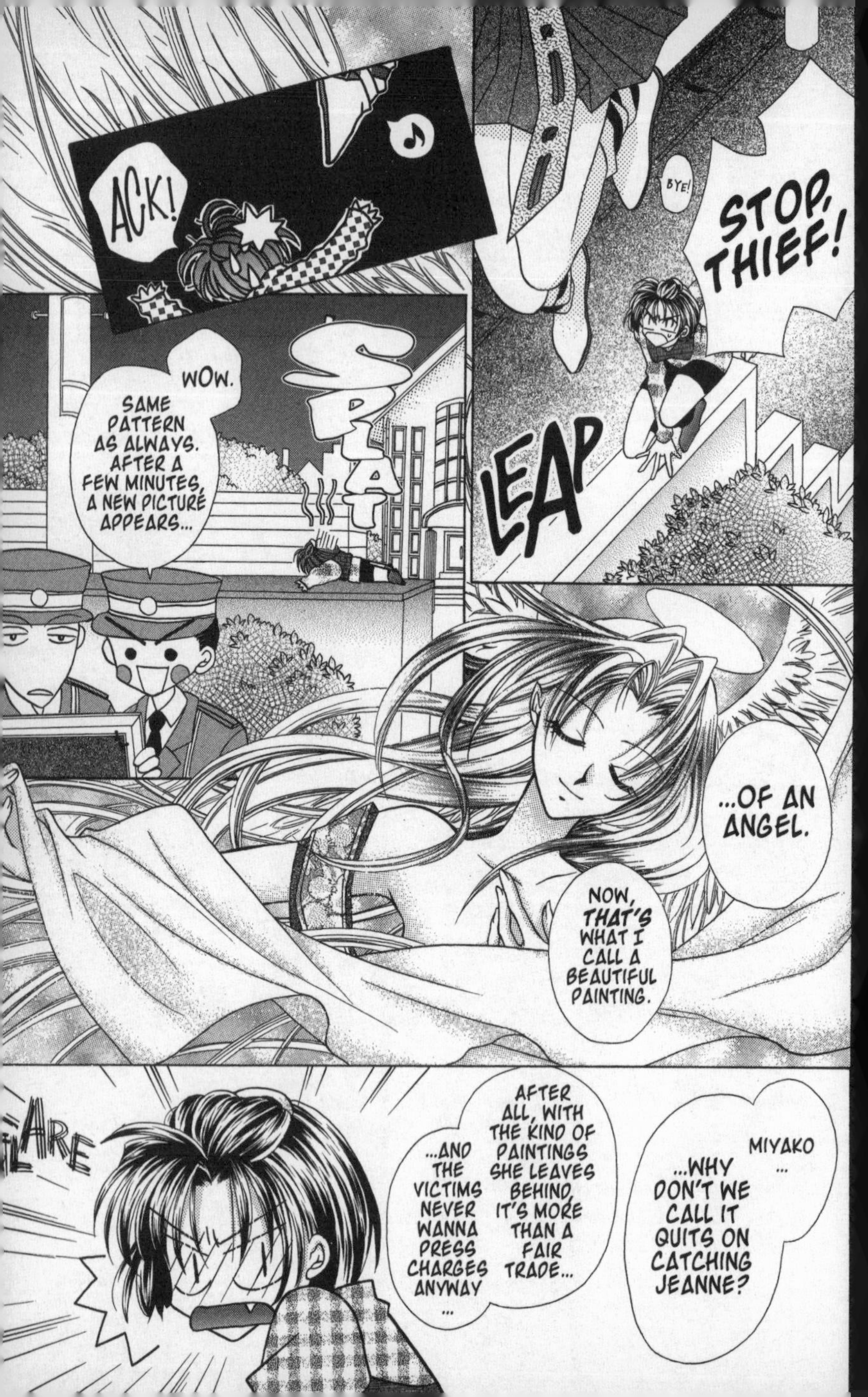
BYE!
STOP, THIEF!
LEAP
ACK!
WOW.
SAME PATTERN AS ALWAYS. AFTER A FEW MINUTES, A NEW PICTURE APPEARS...
SPLAT
...OF AN ANGEL.
NOW, THAT'S WHAT I CALL A BEAUTIFUL PAINTING.
MIYAKO ...
...WHY DON'T WE CALL IT QUITS ON CATCHING JEANNE?
AFTER ALL, WITH THE KIND OF PAINTINGS SHE LEAVES BEHIND, IT'S MORE THAN A FAIR TRADE...
...AND THE VICTIMS NEVER WANNA PRESS CHARGES ANYWAY ...

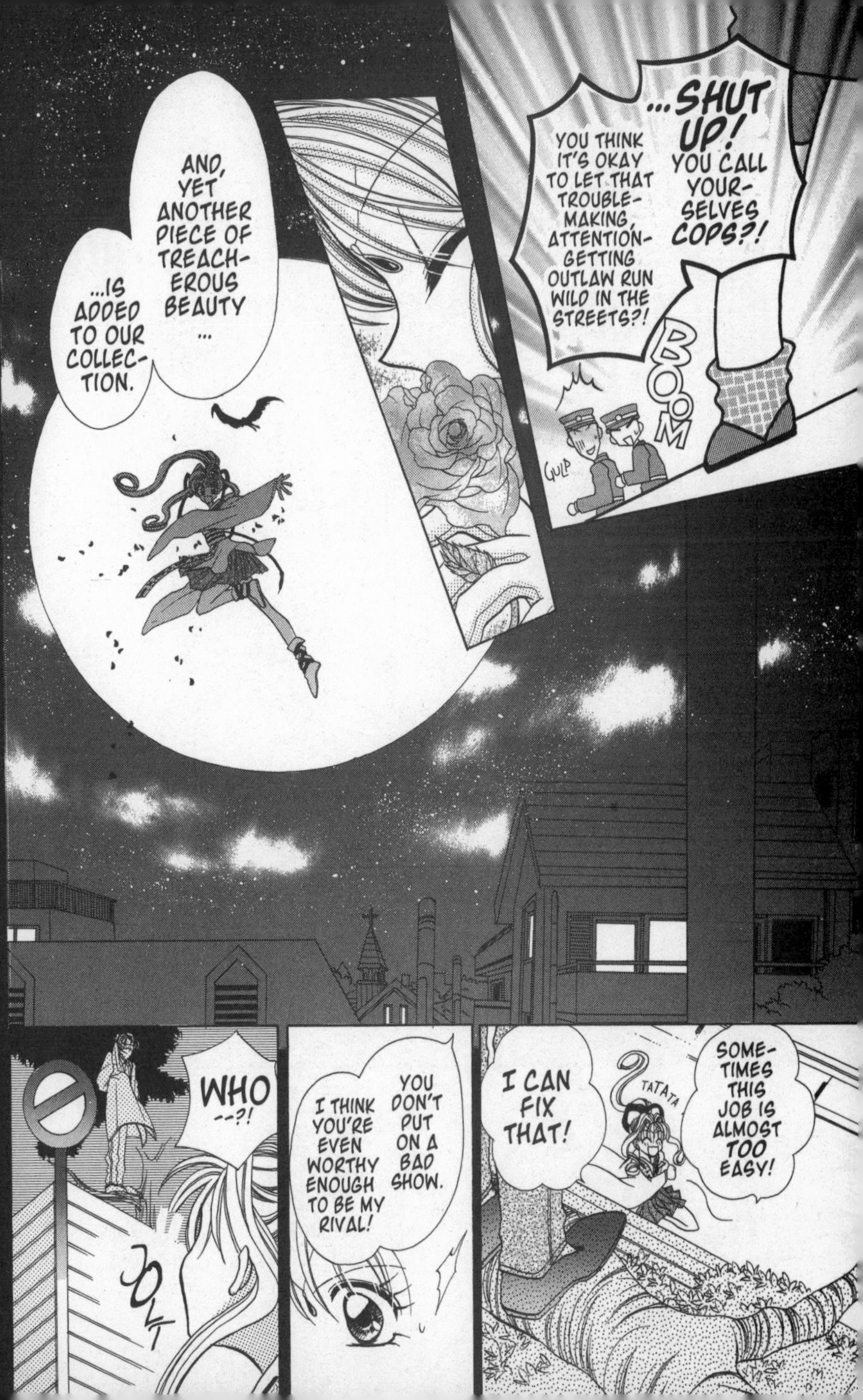
...SHUT UP! YOU CALL YOURSELVES COPS?!
YOU THINK IT'S OKAY TO LET THAT TROUBLE-MAKING, ATTENTION-GETTING OUTLAW RUN WILD IN THE STREETS?!
BOOM
GULP
AND, YET ANOTHER PIECE OF TREACHEROUS BEAUTY...
...IS ADDED TO OUR COLLECTION.
SOMETIMES THIS JOB IS ALMOST TOO EASY!
TATATA
I CAN FIX THAT!
YOU DON'T PUT ON A BAD SHOW.
I THINK YOU'RE EVEN WORTHY ENOUGH TO BE MY RIVAL!
WHO--?!
JOLT

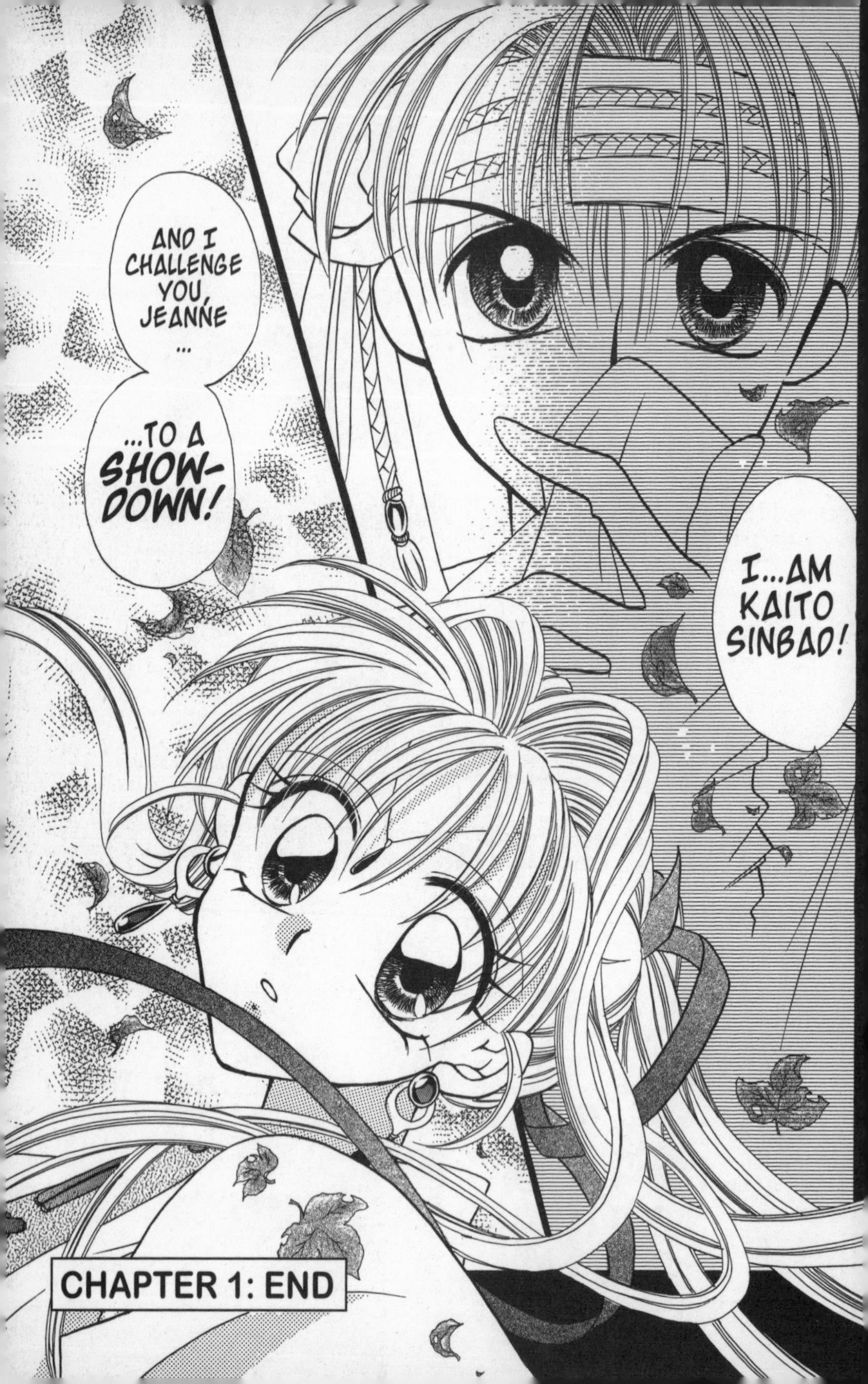
I...AM KAITO SINBAD!
AND I CHALLENGE YOU, JEANNE ...
...TO A SHOW-DOWN!
CHAPTER 1: END

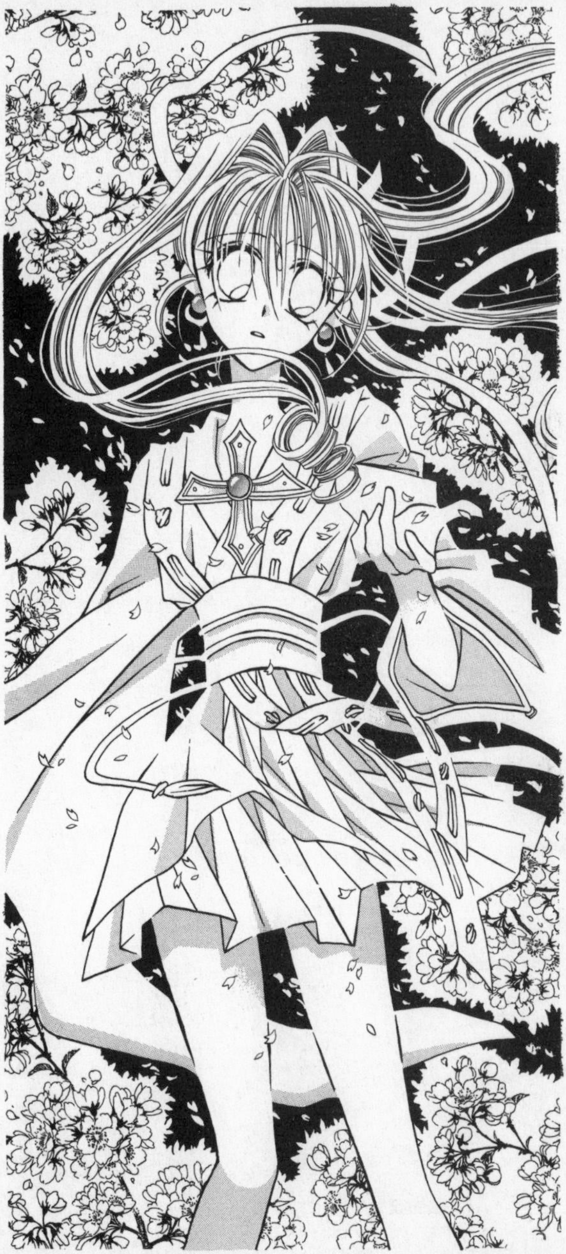

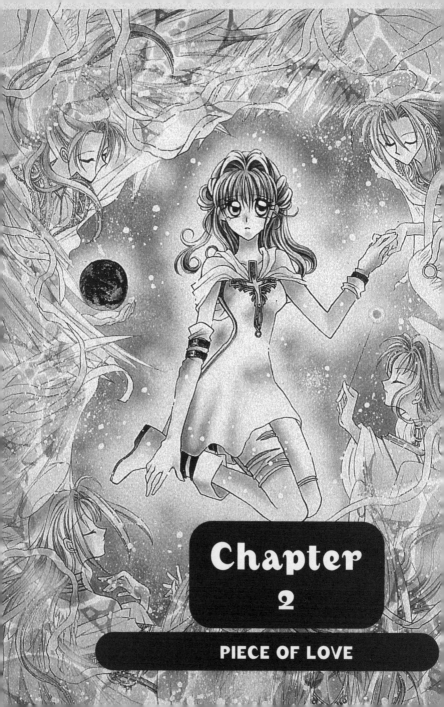

Chapter
2

PIECE OF LOVE

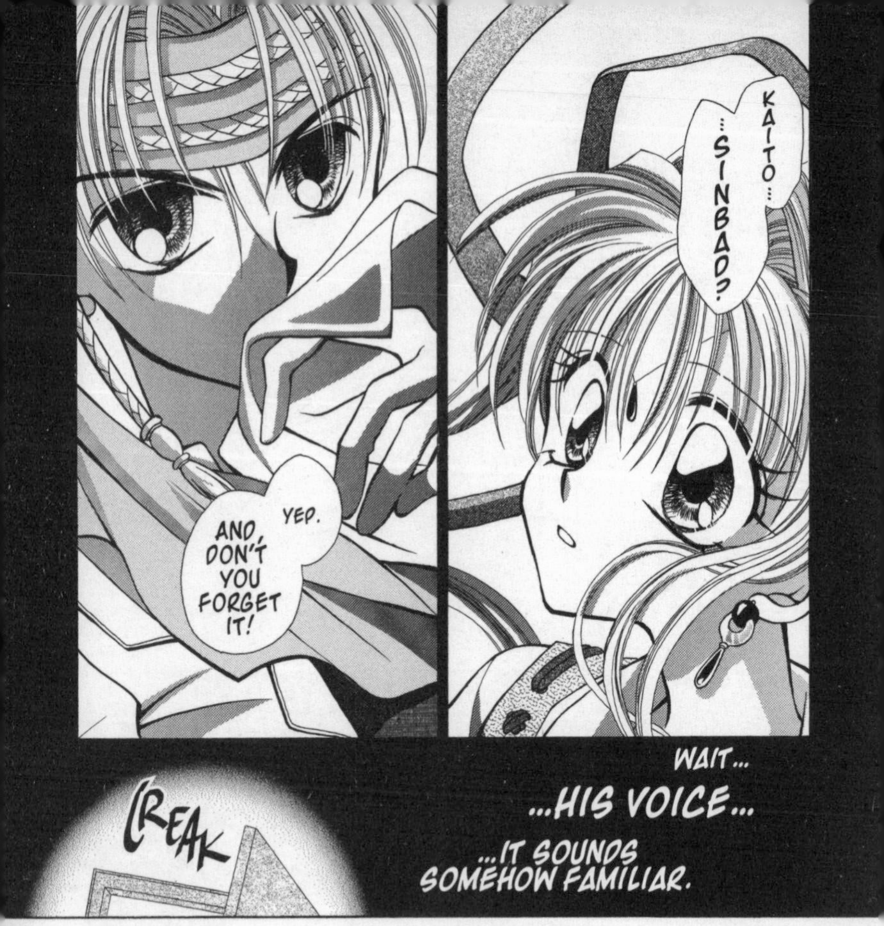
KAITO...
...SINBAD?
YEP.
AND, DON'T YOU FORGET IT!
WAIT...
...HIS VOICE...
...IT SOUNDS SOMEHOW FAMILIAR.
CREAK

TITLE DRAWING AND STORY COMMENTS 2

CONTINUED>>>

And if I accept that as being the case, I decided that I would try to make one unhappy girl living in my world happy. That became the basis for this story. By the way, my prototype story from way back was just frantic action. Not that it's gone to waste; I've fit it in here, making it the model for episode four.

CHAPTER 2: PIECE OF LOVE

"With a sacred heart, the world will be saved."

I love the title page of this episode! Okay, specifically, the shadings, Maron's expression, the position of her body, the globe that the angel is holding, etc. I think this one page turned out really well! I loooove being able to draw my favorite things into the "Jeanne" title page artwork. (For example, I'm into drawing angels and mermaids and so on. Basically, I love drawing anything mythological, whether the characters look serious or are laughing uproariously.) About the story itself, all I can remember is rushing to get it done...mmm...I'll try to think of better memories for the next story.

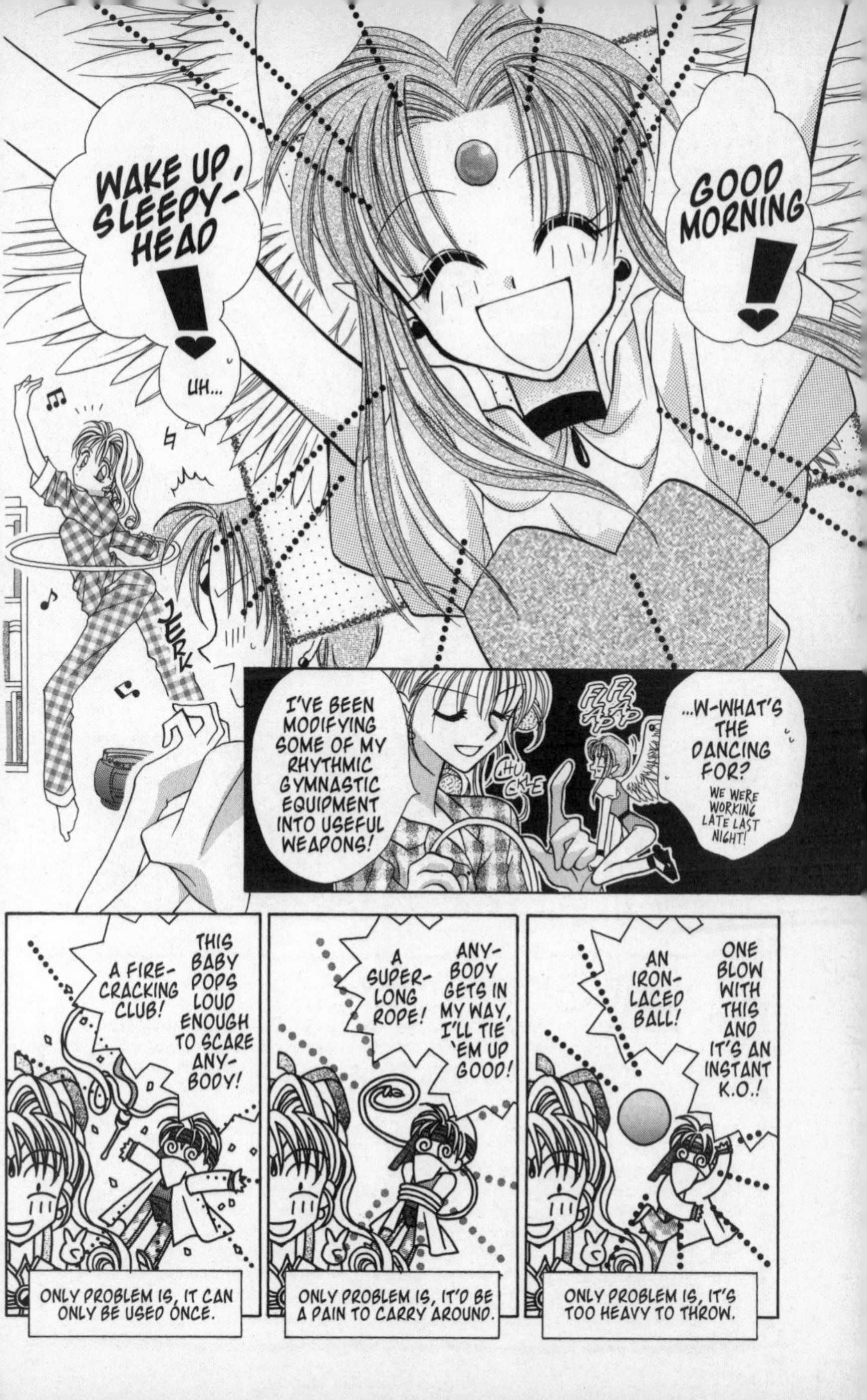
GOOD MORNING!
WAKE UP, SLEEPY-HEAD!
UH...
JERK
...W-WHAT'S THE DANCING FOR?
WE WERE WORKING LATE LAST NIGHT!
FLAP FLAP
CHUCKLE
I'VE BEEN MODIFYING SOME OF MY RHYTHMIC GYMNASTIC EQUIPMENT INTO USEFUL WEAPONS!
ONE BLOW WITH THIS AND IT'S AN INSTANT K.O.!
AN IRON-LACED BALL!
ONLY PROBLEM IS, IT'S TOO HEAVY TO THROW.
ANY-BODY GETS IN MY WAY, I'LL TIE 'EM UP GOOD!
A SUPER-LONG ROPE!
ONLY PROBLEM IS, IT'D BE A PAIN TO CARRY AROUND.
THIS BABY POPS LOUD ENOUGH TO SCARE ANY-BODY!
A FIRE-CRACKING CLUB!
ONLY PROBLEM IS, IT CAN ONLY BE USED ONCE.

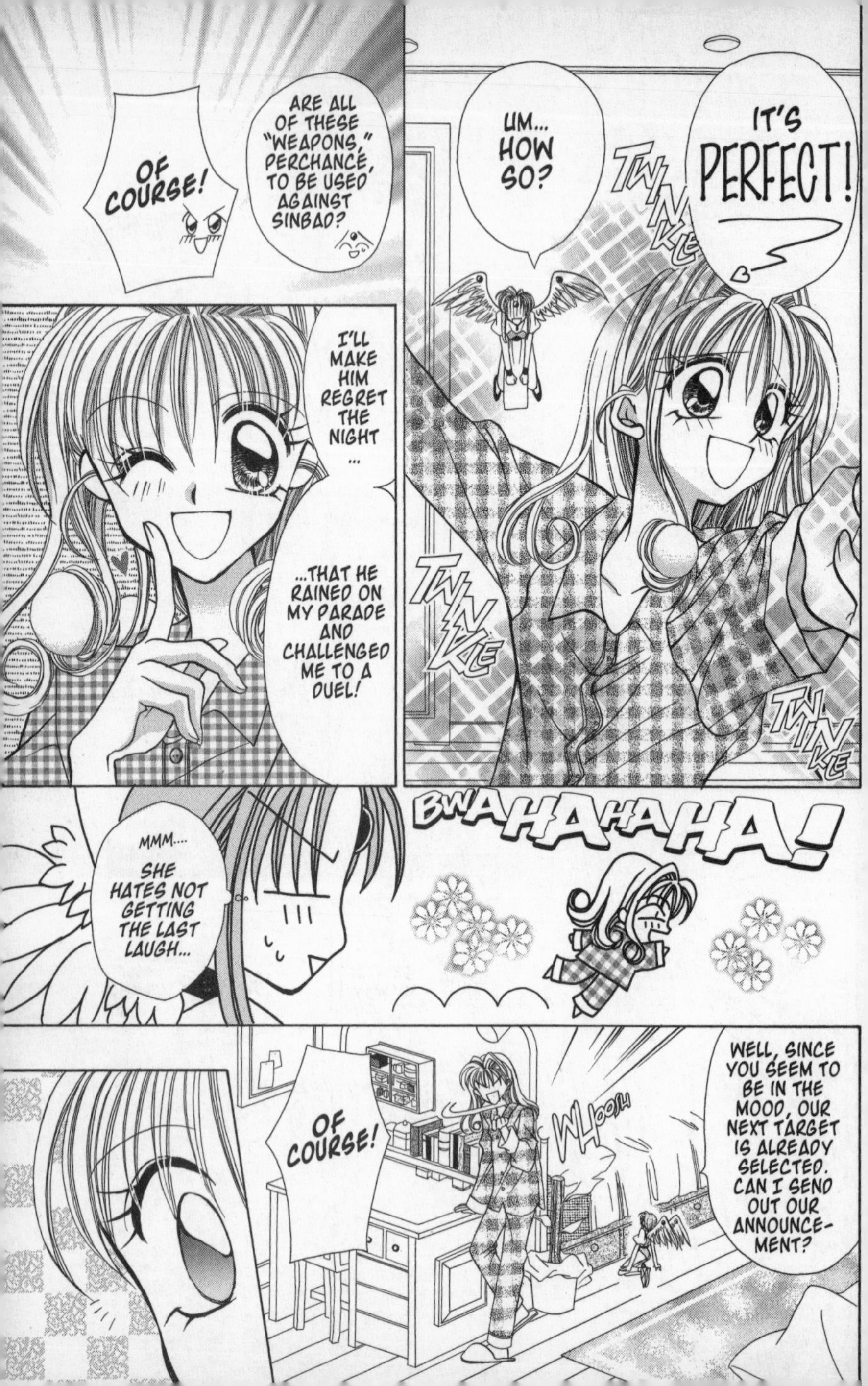
IT'S PERFECT!
TWINKLE
TWINKLE
TWINKLE
UM... HOW SO?
ARE ALL OF THESE "WEAPONS," PERCHANCE, TO BE USED AGAINST SINBAD?
OF COURSE!
I'LL MAKE HIM REGRET THE NIGHT...
...THAT HE RAINED ON MY PARADE AND CHALLENGED ME TO A DUEL!
BWAHAHAHAHA!
MMM.... SHE HATES NOT GETTING THE LAST LAUGH...
WELL, SINCE YOU SEEM TO BE IN THE MOOD, OUR NEXT TARGET IS ALREADY SELECTED. CAN I SEND OUT OUR ANNOUNCEMENT?
WHOOSH
OF COURSE!

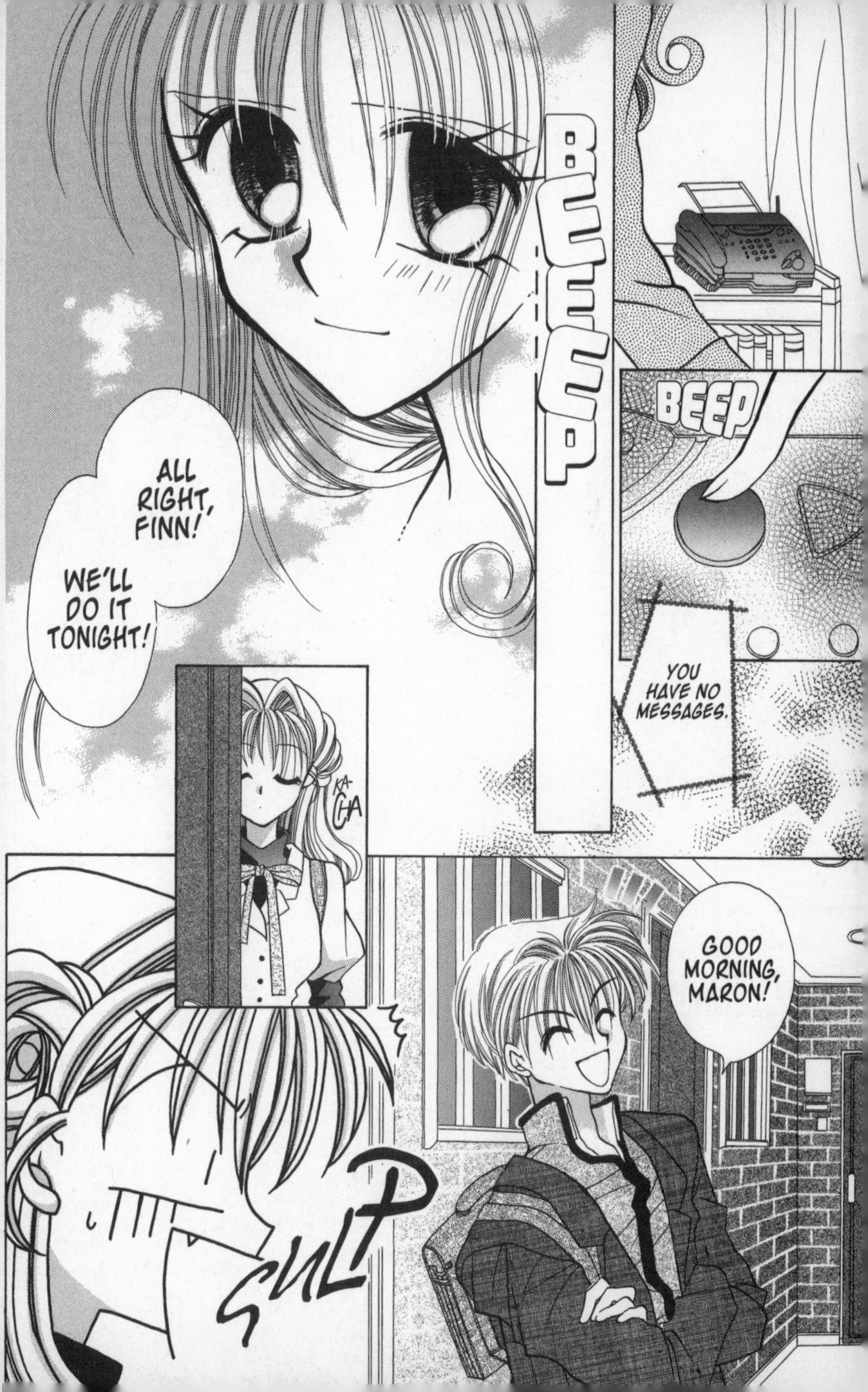
BEEEEP
BEEP
YOU HAVE NO MESSAGES.
ALL RIGHT, FINN!
WE'LL DO IT TONIGHT!
KA-CHA
GOOD MORNING, MARON!
GULP

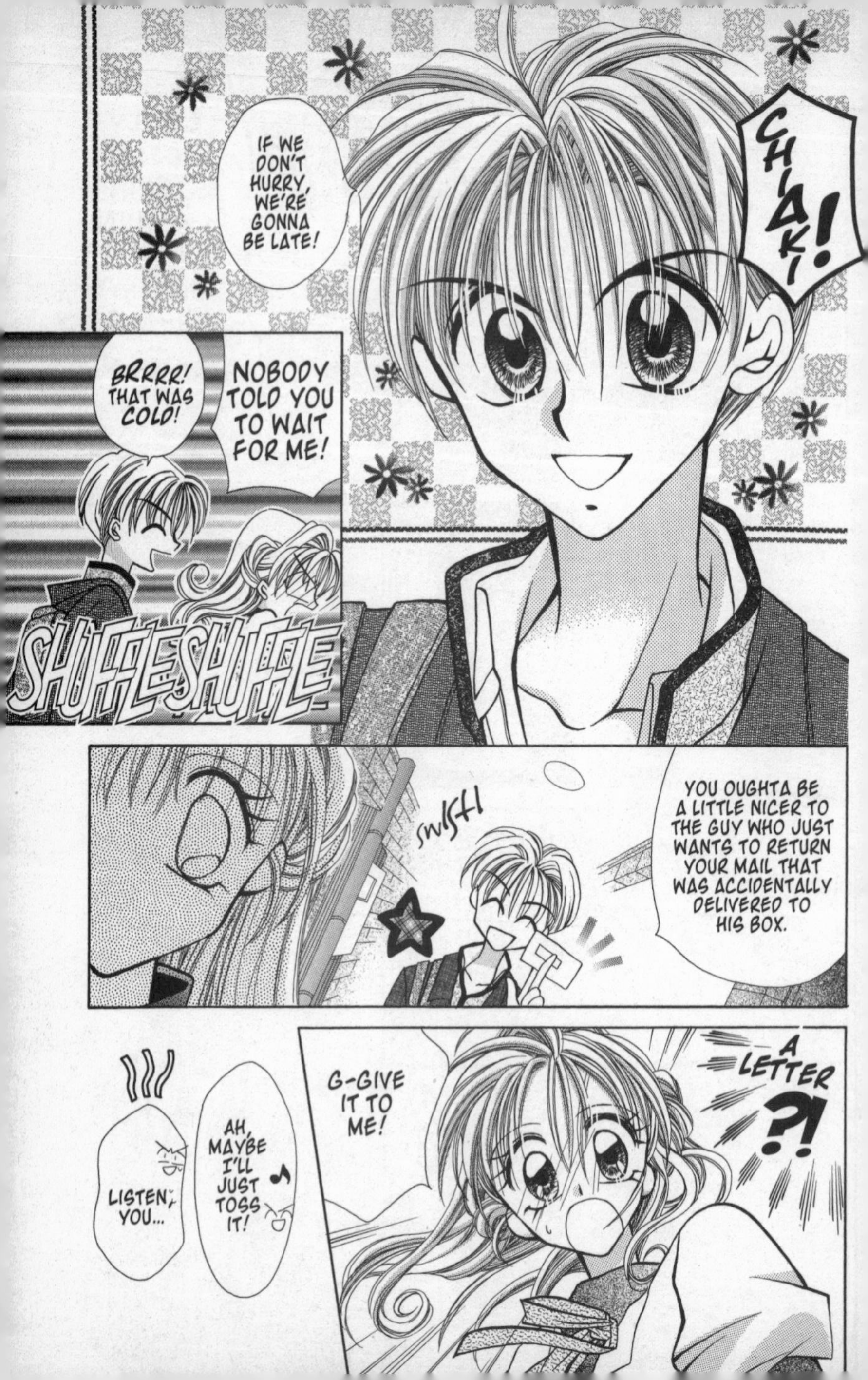
CHIAKI!
IF WE DON'T HURRY, WE'RE GONNA BE LATE!
NOBODY TOLD YOU TO WAIT FOR ME!
BRRRR! THAT WAS COLD!
SHUFFLESHUFFLE
YOU OUGHTA BE A LITTLE NICER TO THE GUY WHO JUST WANTS TO RETURN YOUR MAIL THAT WAS ACCIDENTALLY DELIVERED TO HIS BOX.
SWISH!
A LETTER?!
G-GIVE IT TO ME!
AH, MAYBE I'LL JUST TOSS IT!
LISTEN, YOU...

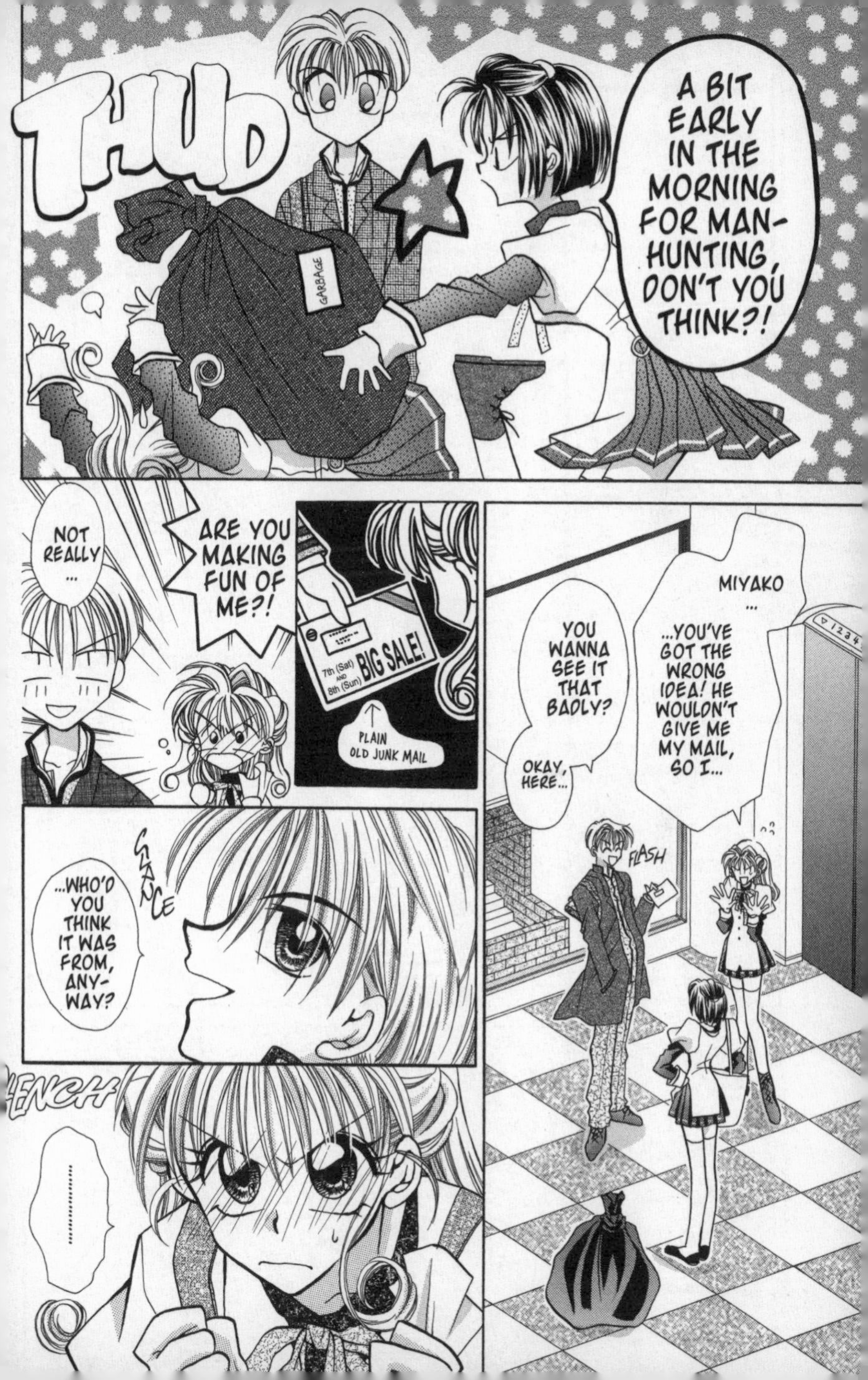
THUD
A BIT EARLY IN THE MORNING FOR MAN-HUNTING, DON'T YOU THINK?!
GARBAGE
MIYAKO ...
...YOU'VE GOT THE WRONG IDEA! HE WOULDN'T GIVE ME MY MAIL, SO I...
YOU WANNA SEE IT THAT BADLY?
OKAY, HERE...
FLASH
7th (Sat) AND 8th (Sun) BIG SALE!
PLAIN OLD JUNK MAIL
ARE YOU MAKING FUN OF ME?!
NOT REALLY ...
GLANCE
...WHO'D YOU THINK IT WAS FROM, ANYWAY?
CLENCH
....

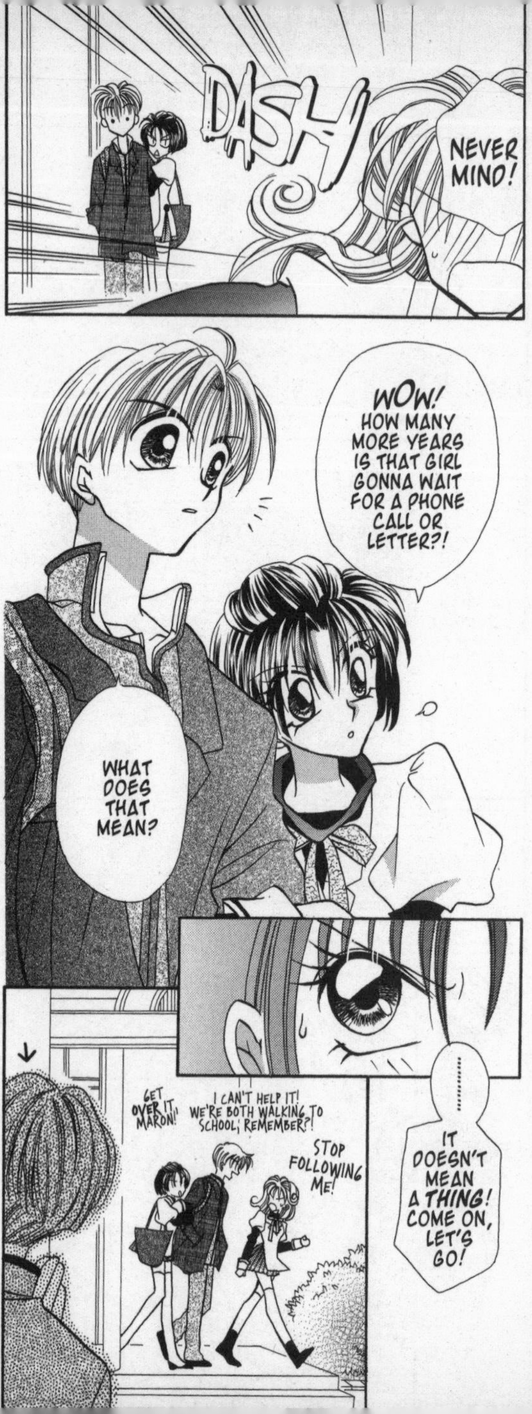
DASH
NEVER MIND!
WOW! HOW MANY MORE YEARS IS THAT GIRL GONNA WAIT FOR A PHONE CALL OR LETTER?!
WHAT DOES THAT MEAN?
......
IT DOESN'T MEAN A THING! COME ON, LET'S GO!
STOP FOLLOWING ME!
I CAN'T HELP IT! WE'RE BOTH WALKING TO SCHOOL, REMEMBER?!
GET OVER IT MARON!

AT A SIGNING 2

When I arrived at the venue, I was met with the sight of a line of people...that started from up several flights of stairs inside the building and extended all the way outside.

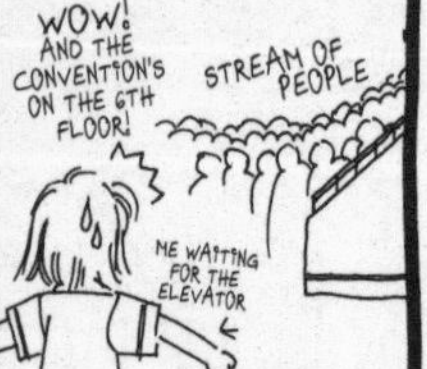
WOW! AND THE CONVENTION'S ON THE 6TH FLOOR!
STREAM OF PEOPLE
ME WAITING FOR THE ELEVATOR

The causes of this situation seem to have been both a location that was slightly too small for the event and a blunder on the part of the convention organizers, who greatly underestimated the number of people who would show up. I'm sorry about the fans who reportedly waited in line for a long time but finally gave up and went home, daunted. Actually, I wanted to see the original art exhibition, have a picture taken with my Jeanne-chan at a photo booth and so on, but it was just so crowded, I couldn't even get in to the convention hall, let alone buy a single product. (The convention and signing were held in the same building, but on different floors.)

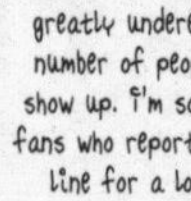

Afterwards, I heard that people had to wait five hours to get in if they arrived at one o'clock and later. One woman told me to "Hold the next one at Tokyo Big Site or some other place with more space."

→ CONTINUED IN PART #3>>

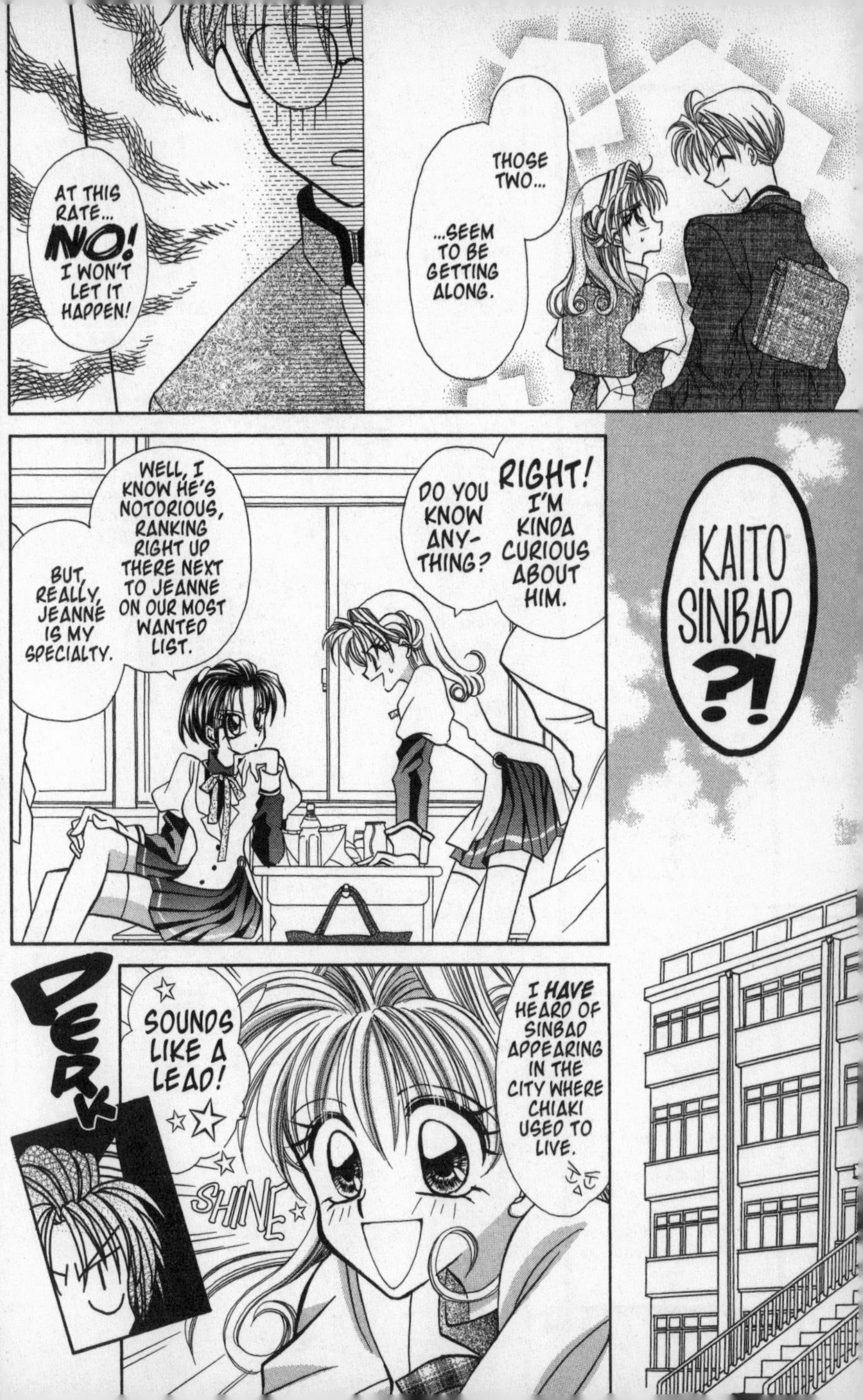
THOSE TWO...
...SEEM TO BE GETTING ALONG.
AT THIS RATE... NO! I WON'T LET IT HAPPEN!
KAITO SINBAD ?!
RIGHT! I'M KINDA CURIOUS ABOUT HIM.
DO YOU KNOW ANYTHING?
WELL, I KNOW HE'S NOTORIOUS, RANKING RIGHT UP THERE NEXT TO JEANNE ON OUR MOST WANTED LIST.
BUT, REALLY, JEANNE IS MY SPECIALTY.
I HAVE HEARD OF SINBAD APPEARING IN THE CITY WHERE CHIAKI USED TO LIVE.
SOUNDS LIKE A LEAD!
SHINE
PERK

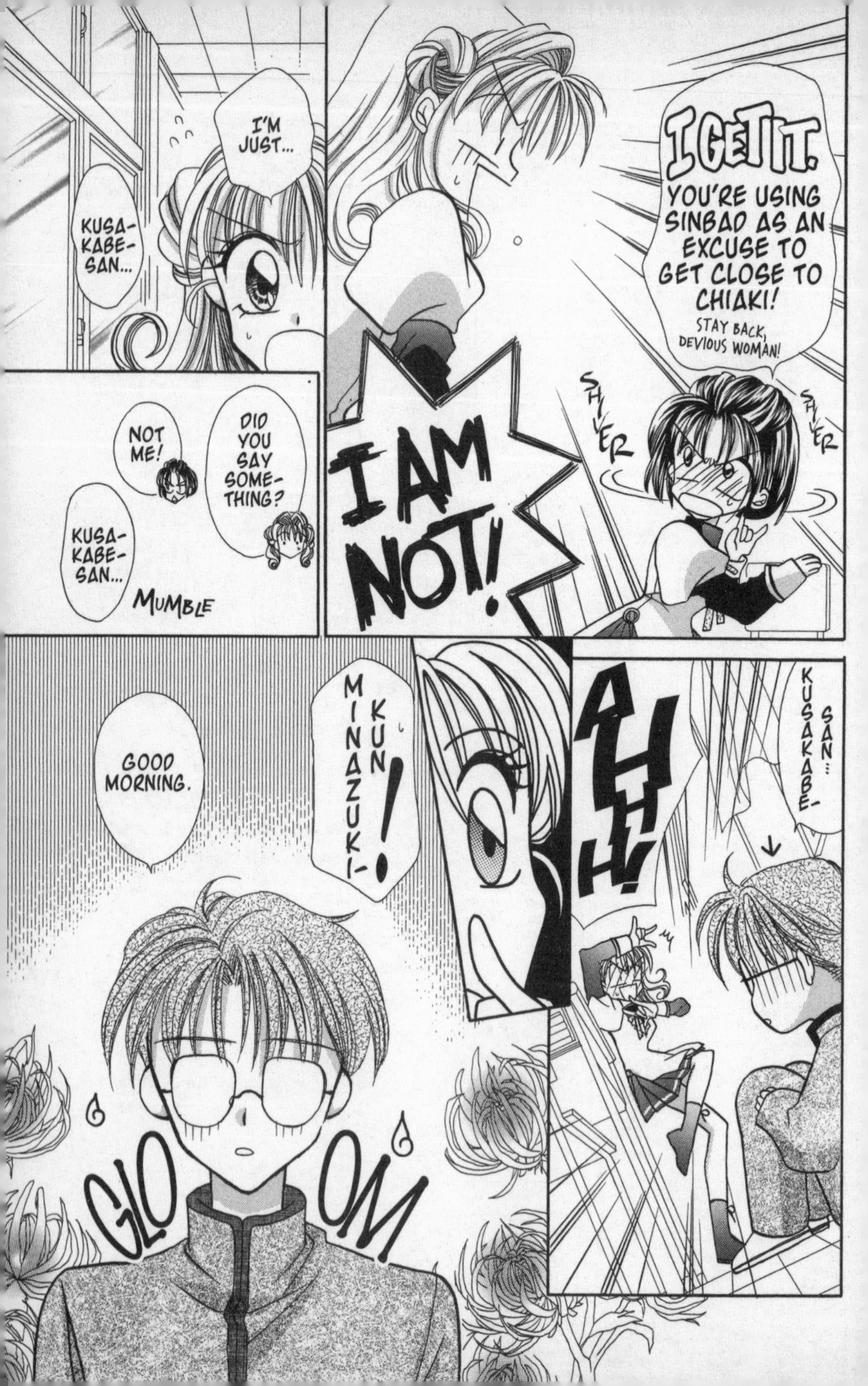
I GET IT.
YOU'RE USING SINBAD AS AN EXCUSE TO GET CLOSE TO CHIAKI!
STAY BACK, DEVIOUS WOMAN!
SHIVER
SHIVER
I AM NOT!
I'M JUST...
KUSA-KABE-SAN...
DID YOU SAY SOME-THING?
NOT ME!
KUSA-KABE-SAN...
MUMBLE
KUSAKABE-SAN...
AHH!
MINAZUKI-KUN!
GOOD MORNING.
GLOOM

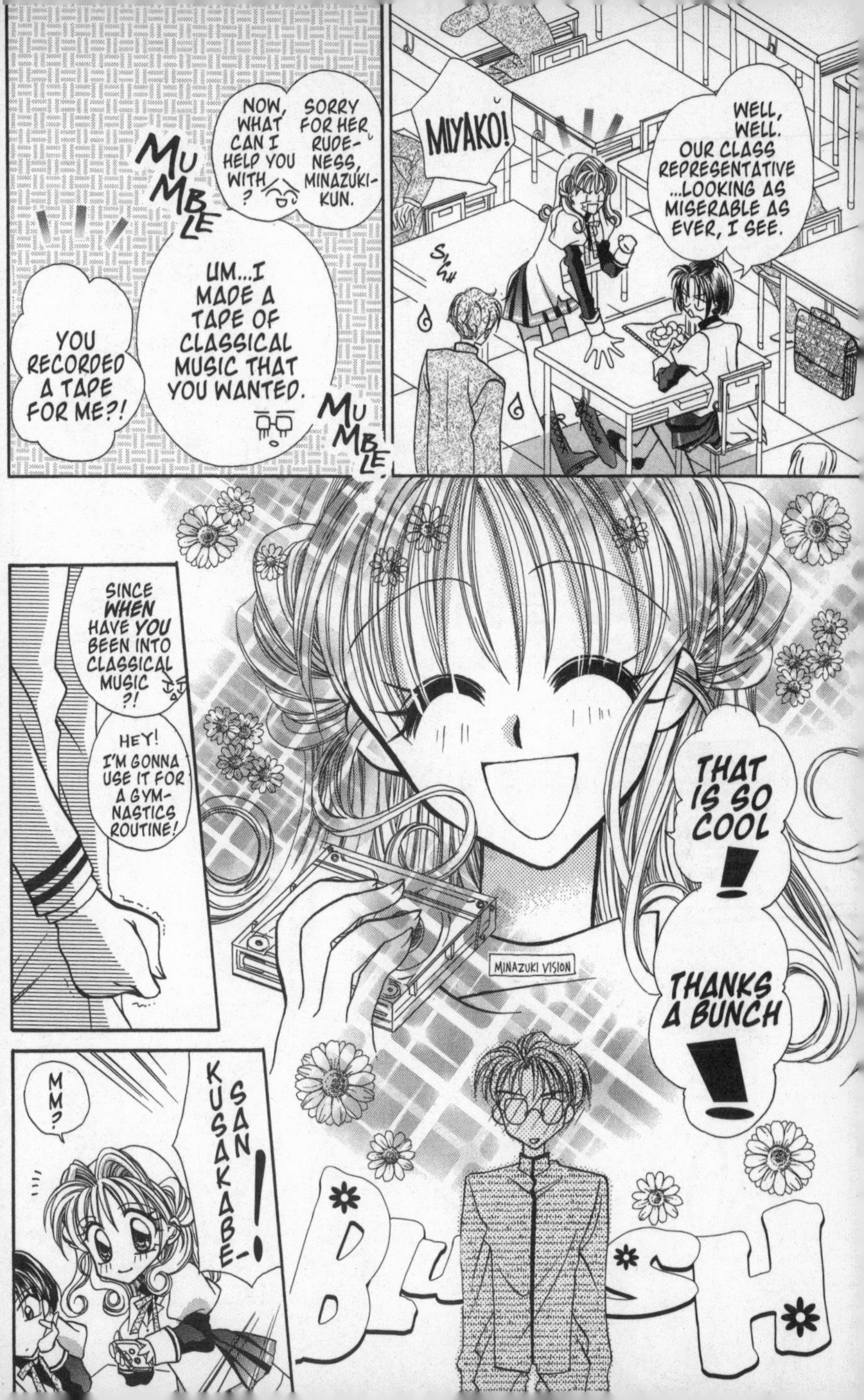
WELL, WELL. OUR CLASS REPRESENTATIVE ...LOOKING AS MISERABLE AS EVER, I SEE.
MIYAKO!
SORRY FOR HER RUDENESS, MINAZUKI-KUN.
NOW, WHAT CAN I HELP YOU WITH?
MUMBLE
UM...I MADE A TAPE OF CLASSICAL MUSIC THAT YOU WANTED.
MUMBLE
YOU RECORDED A TAPE FOR ME?!
THAT IS SO COOL!
THANKS A BUNCH!
MINAZUKI VISION
SINCE WHEN HAVE YOU BEEN INTO CLASSICAL MUSIC?!
HEY! I'M GONNA USE IT FOR A GYMNASTICS ROUTINE!
KUSAKABE-SAN!
MM?

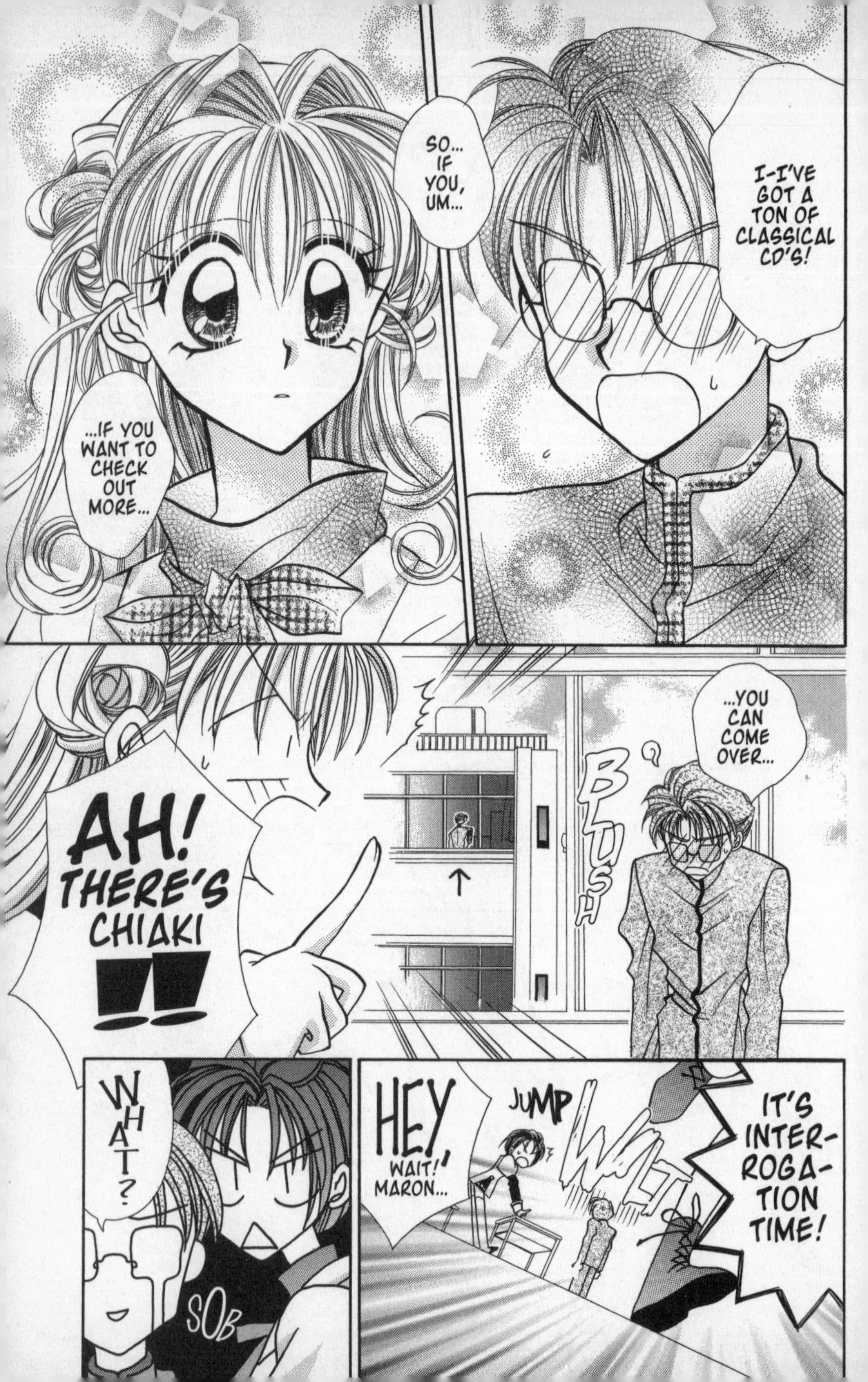
I-I'VE GOT A TON OF CLASSICAL CD'S!
SO... IF YOU, UM...
...IF YOU WANT TO CHECK OUT MORE...
...YOU CAN COME OVER...
BLUSH
AH! THERE'S CHIAKI!!
IT'S INTER-ROGA-TION TIME!
WAIT
JUMP
HEY, WAIT! MARON...
WHAT?
SOB

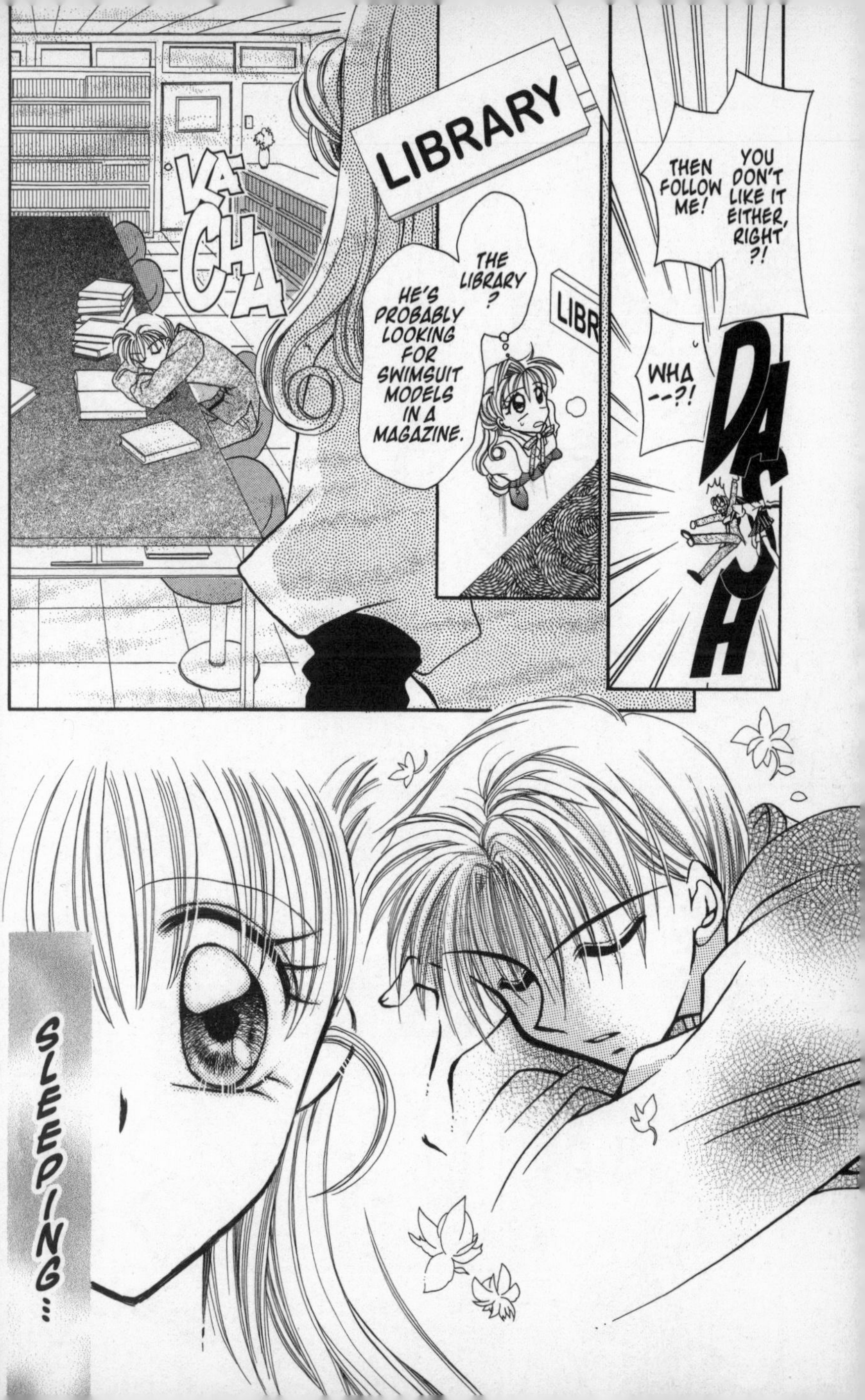
YOU DON'T LIKE IT EITHER, RIGHT?!
THEN FOLLOW ME!
WHA--?!
DASH
LIBRARY
THE LIBRARY?
HE'S PROBABLY LOOKING FOR SWIMSUIT MODELS IN A MAGAZINE.
LIBR
KA-CHA
SLEEPING...

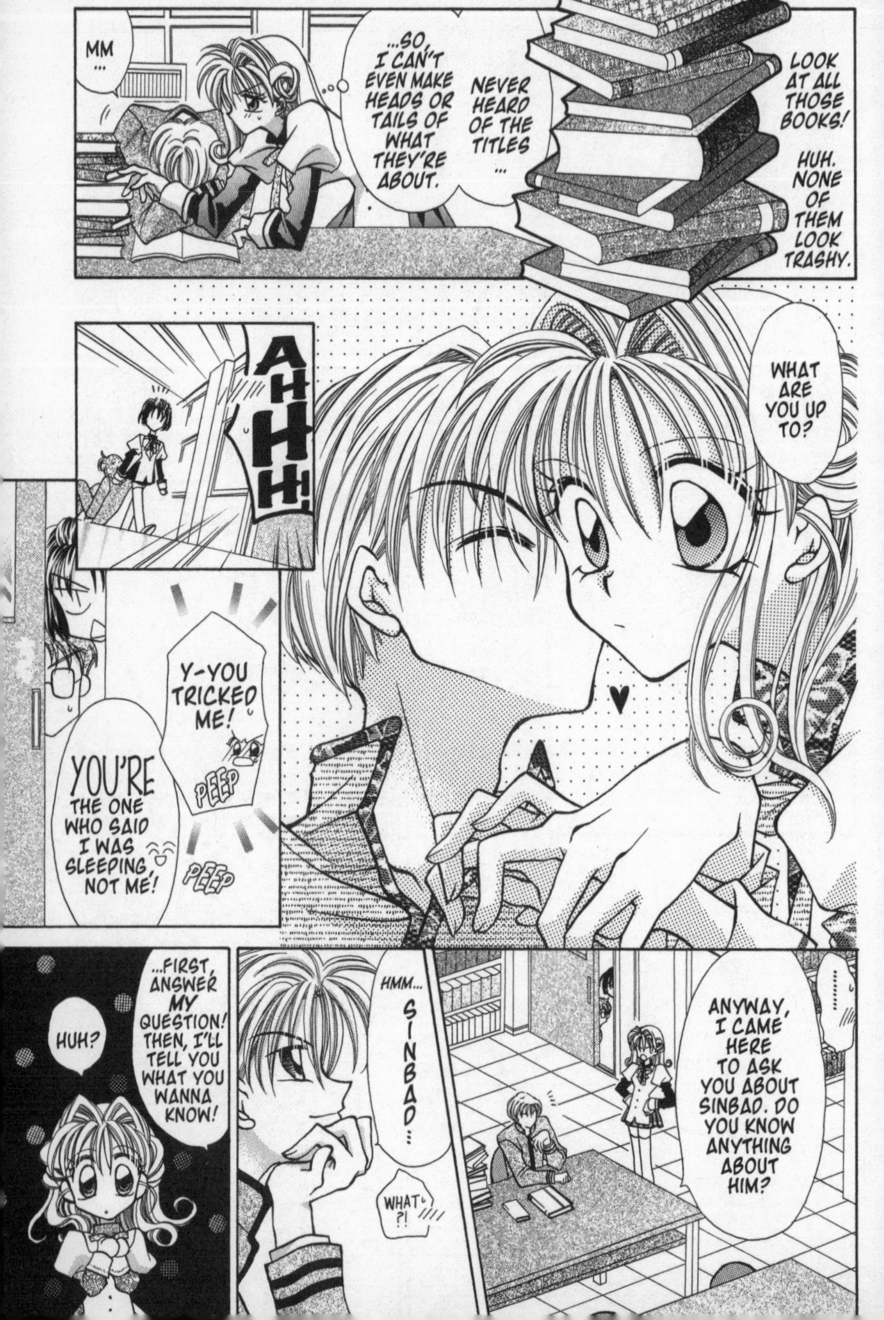
LOOK AT ALL THOSE BOOKS!
HUH. NONE OF THEM LOOK TRASHY.
NEVER HEARD OF THE TITLES ...
...SO, I CAN'T EVEN MAKE HEADS OR TAILS OF WHAT THEY'RE ABOUT.
MM ...
WHAT ARE YOU UP TO?
AHHH!
Y-YOU TRICKED ME!
PEEP
YOU'RE THE ONE WHO SAID I WAS SLEEPING, NOT ME!
PEEP
......
ANYWAY, I CAME HERE TO ASK YOU ABOUT SINBAD. DO YOU KNOW ANYTHING ABOUT HIM?
WHAT?!
HMM... SINBAD...
...FIRST, ANSWER MY QUESTION! THEN, I'LL TELL YOU WHAT YOU WANNA KNOW!
HUH?

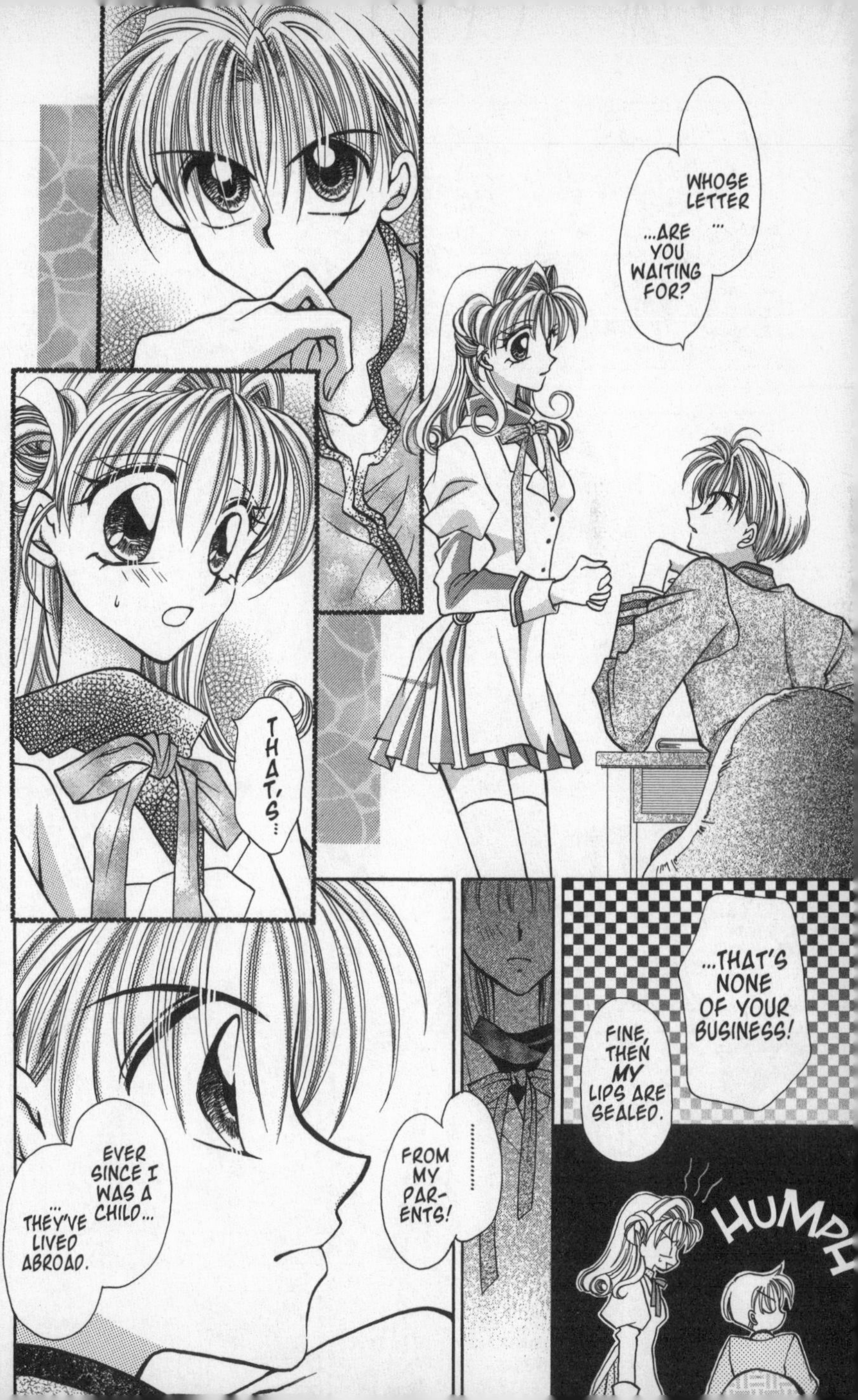
WHOSE LETTER ...
...ARE YOU WAITING FOR?
THAT'S...
...THAT'S NONE OF YOUR BUSINESS!
FINE, THEN MY LIPS ARE SEALED.
HUMPH
......
FROM MY PAR-ENTS!
EVER SINCE I WAS A CHILD...
...THEY'VE LIVED ABROAD.

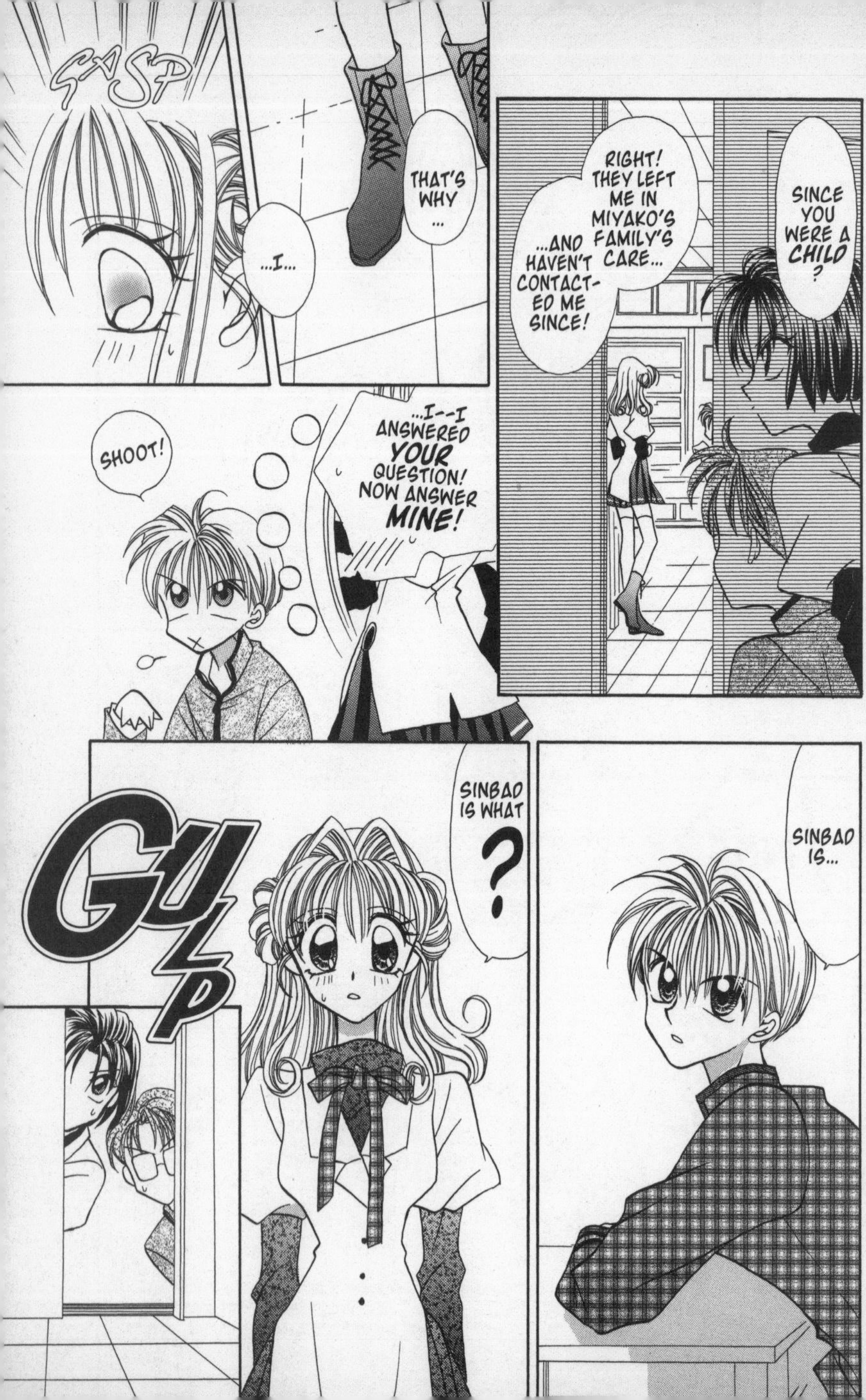
SINCE YOU WERE A CHILD?
RIGHT! THEY LEFT ME IN MIYAKO'S FAMILY'S CARE...
...AND HAVEN'T CONTACT-ED ME SINCE!
THAT'S WHY ...
...I...
GASP
...I--I ANSWERED YOUR QUESTION! NOW ANSWER MINE!
SHOOT!
SINBAD IS...
SINBAD IS WHAT ?
GULP

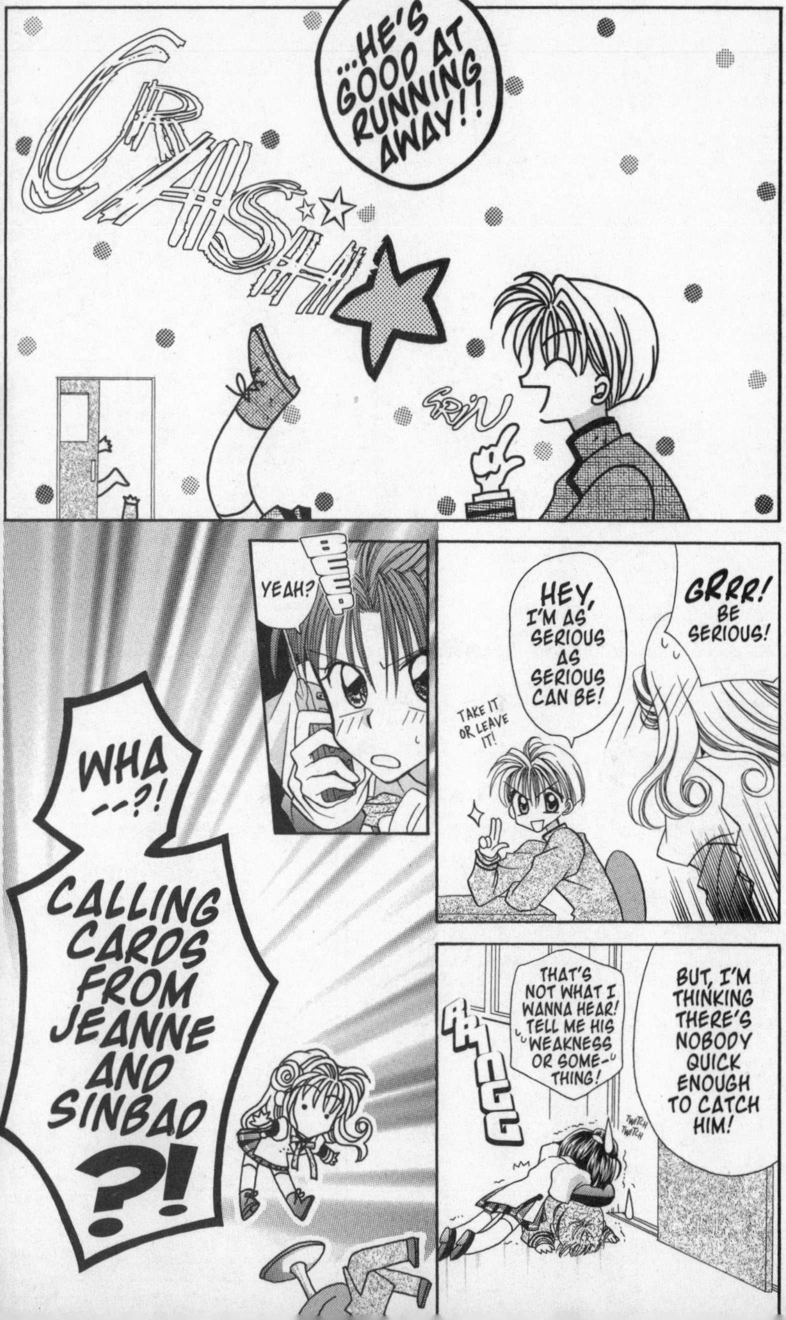
...HE'S GOOD AT RUNNING AWAY!!
CRASH
GRIN
GRRR! BE SERIOUS!
HEY, I'M AS SERIOUS AS SERIOUS CAN BE!
TAKE IT OR LEAVE IT!
BUT, I'M THINKING THERE'S NOBODY QUICK ENOUGH TO CATCH HIM!
THAT'S NOT WHAT I WANNA HEAR! TELL ME HIS WEAKNESS OR SOME-THING!
RRINGG
TWITCH TWITCH
BEEP
YEAH?
WHA--?!
CALLING CARDS FROM JEANNE AND SINBAD ?!

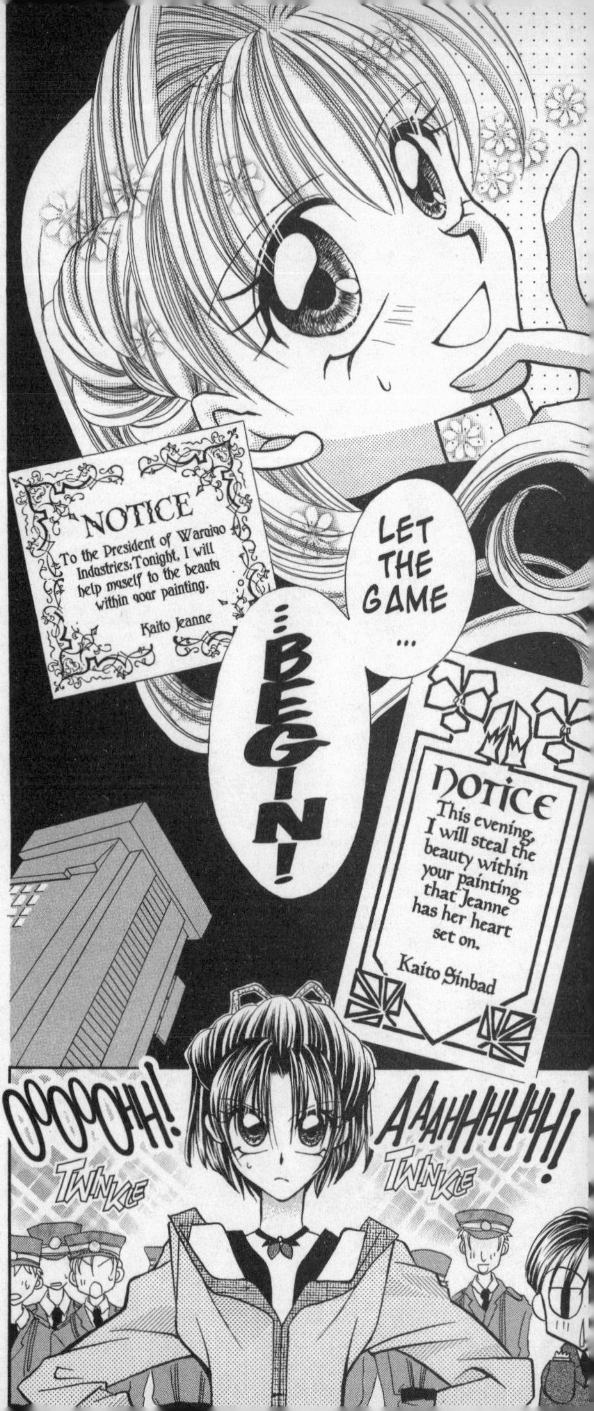
LET THE GAME...
BEGIN!
NOTICE
To the President of Waraigo Industries: Tonight, I will help myself to the beauty within your painting.
Kaito Jeanne
NOTICE
This evening, I will steal the beauty within your painting that Jeanne has her heart set on.
Kaito Sinbad
AAAHHHHHH!
TWINKLE
OOOOOHH!
TWINKLE

THE PRIVATE LIFE OF ARINA TANEMURA, PART 6

What kinda title is this, anyway?!

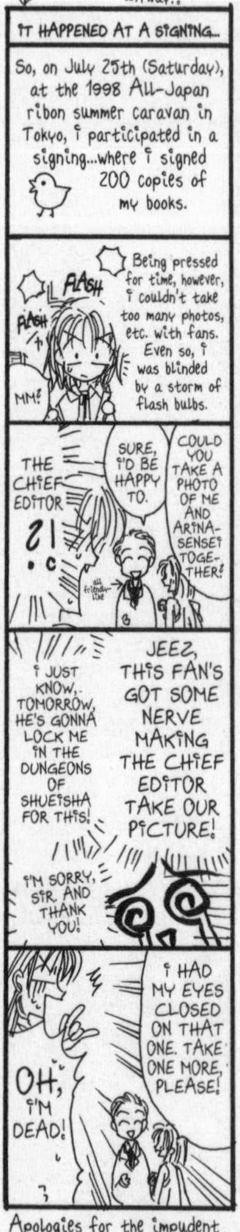
IT HAPPENED AT A SIGNING...
So, on July 25th (Saturday), at the 1998 All-Japan ribon summer caravan in Tokyo, I participated in a signing...where I signed 200 copies of my books.
Being pressed for time, however, I couldn't take too many photos, etc. with fans. Even so, I was blinded by a storm of flash bulbs.
FLASH
FLASH
MM!
COULD YOU TAKE A PHOTO OF ME AND ARINA-SENSEI TOGETHER?
SURE, I'D BE HAPPY TO.
THE CHIEF EDITOR?!
all friendly-like
JEEZ, THIS FAN'S GOT SOME NERVE MAKING THE CHIEF EDITOR TAKE OUR PICTURE!
I JUST KNOW, TOMORROW, HE'S GONNA LOCK ME IN THE DUNGEONS OF SHUEISHA FOR THIS!
I'M SORRY, SIR. AND THANK YOU!
I HAD MY EYES CLOSED ON THAT ONE. TAKE ONE MORE, PLEASE!
OH, I'M DEAD!

Apologies for the impudent fan, chief! Otherwise, I had a great time and hope I can go again! ♡

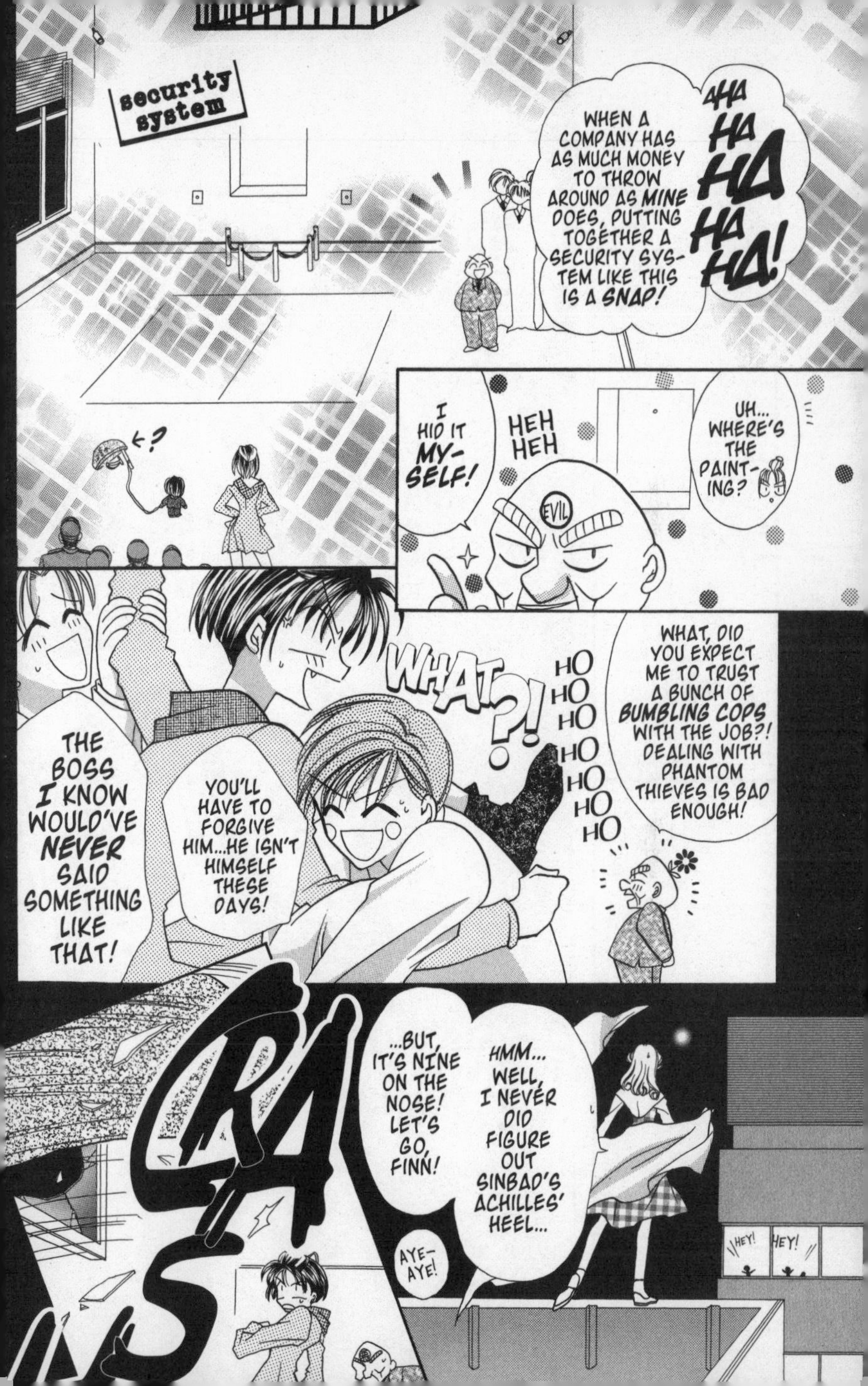
security system
AHA HA HA HA HA!
WHEN A COMPANY HAS AS MUCH MONEY TO THROW AROUND AS MINE DOES, PUTTING TOGETHER A SECURITY SYSTEM LIKE THIS IS A SNAP!
UH... WHERE'S THE PAINTING?
HEH HEH
I HID IT MYSELF!
WHAT, DID YOU EXPECT ME TO TRUST A BUNCH OF BUMBLING COPS WITH THE JOB?! DEALING WITH PHANTOM THIEVES IS BAD ENOUGH!
HO HO HO HO HO HO HO
WHAT?!
YOU'LL HAVE TO FORGIVE HIM...HE ISN'T HIMSELF THESE DAYS!
THE BOSS I KNOW WOULD'VE NEVER SAID SOMETHING LIKE THAT!
HEY!
HEY!
HMM... WELL, I NEVER DID FIGURE OUT SINBAD'S ACHILLES' HEEL...
...BUT, IT'S NINE ON THE NOSE! LET'S GO, FINN!
AYE-AYE!
CRASH

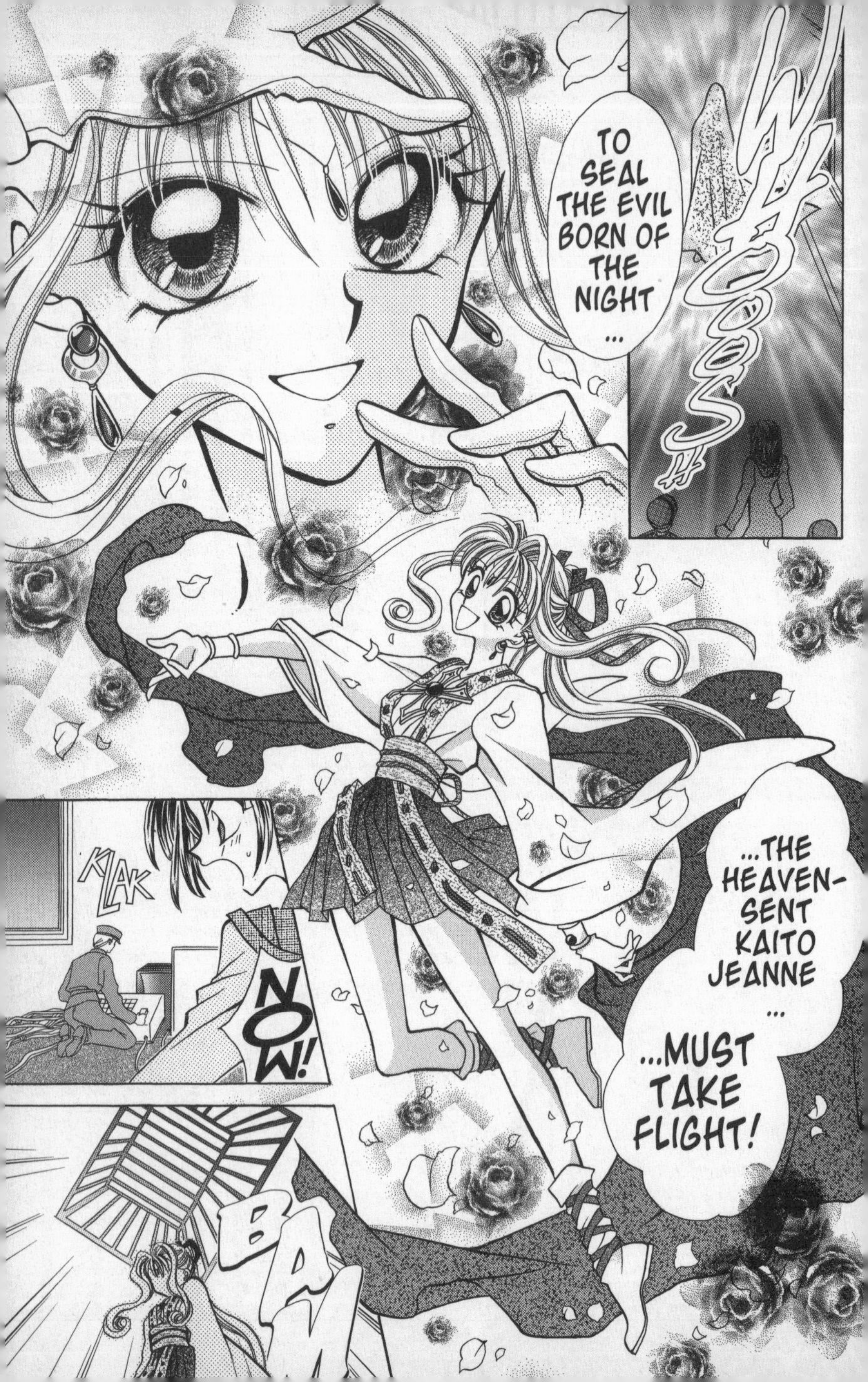
WHOOSH
TO SEAL THE EVIL BORN OF THE NIGHT ...
...THE HEAVEN-SENT KAITO JEANNE ...
KLAK
NOW!
...MUST TAKE FLIGHT!
BA

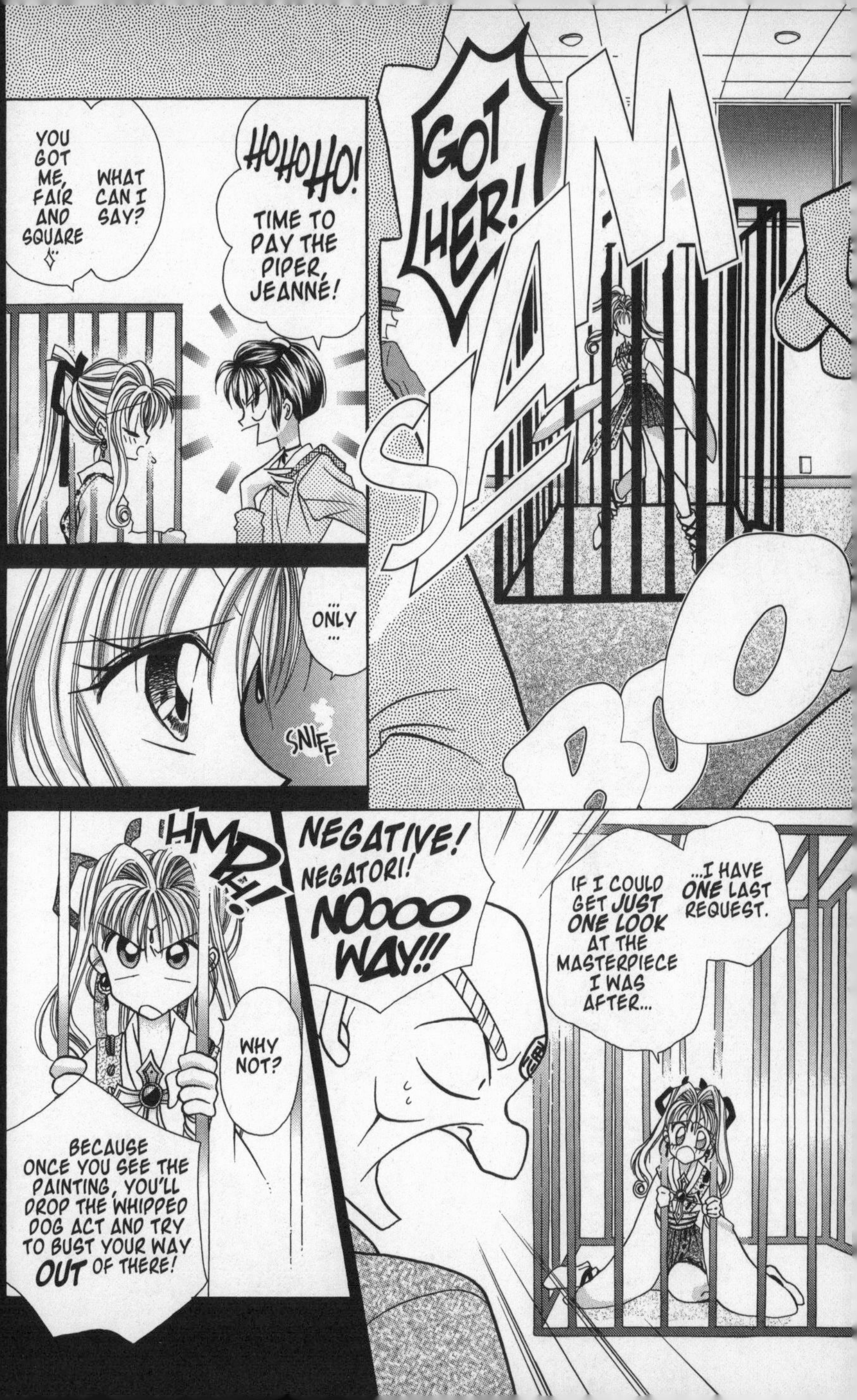
GOT HER!
SLAM
BOOM
HO HO HO!
TIME TO PAY THE PIPER, JEANNÉ!
YOU GOT ME, FAIR AND SQUARE
WHAT CAN I SAY?
... ONLY ...
SNIFF
...I HAVE ONE LAST REQUEST.
IF I COULD GET JUST ONE LOOK AT THE MASTERPIECE I WAS AFTER...
NEGATIVE! NEGATORI! NOOOO WAY!!
HMPH!
WHY NOT?
BECAUSE ONCE YOU SEE THE PAINTING, YOU'LL DROP THE WHIPPED DOG ACT AND TRY TO BUST YOUR WAY OUT OF THERE!

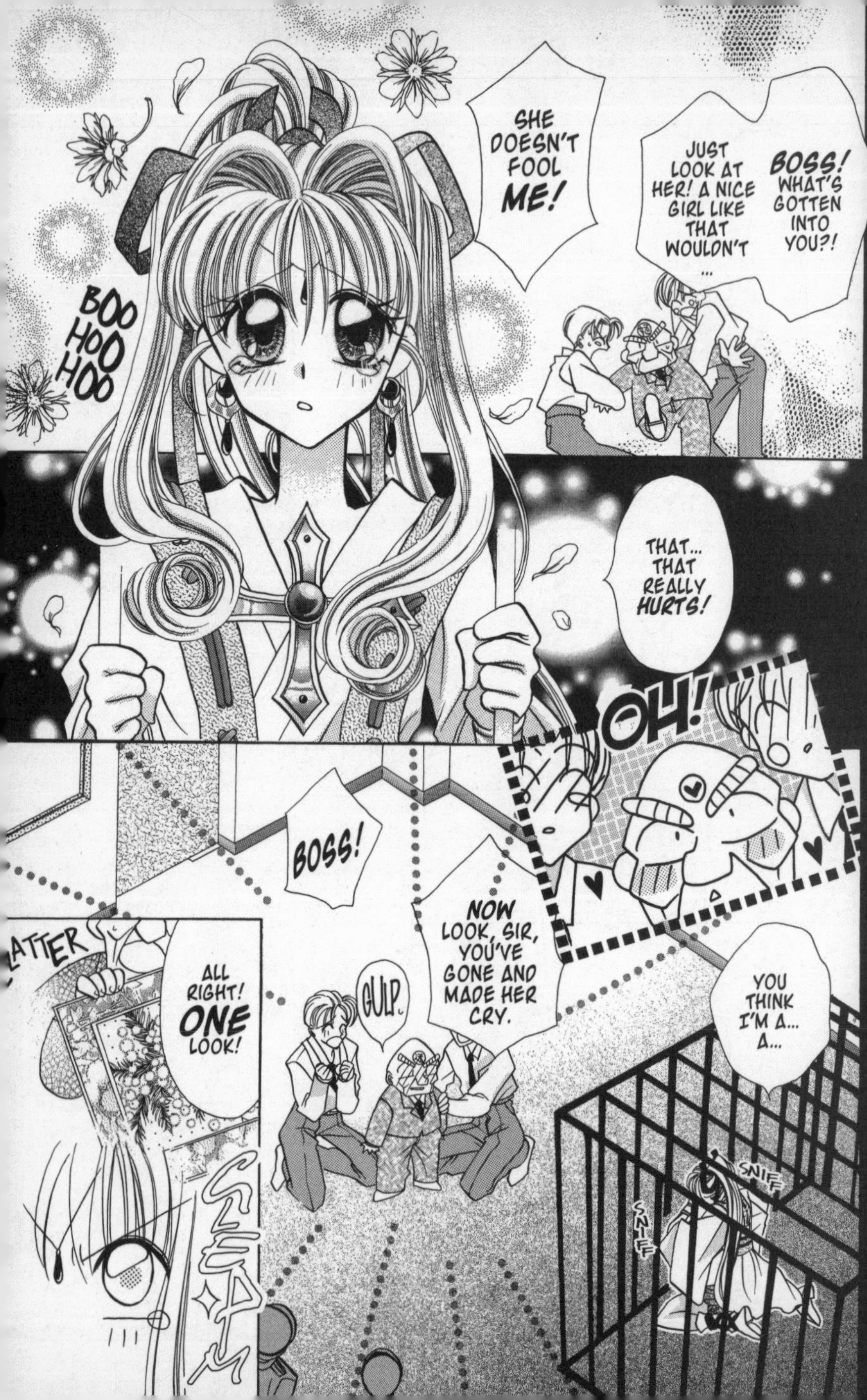
BOSS! WHAT'S GOTTEN INTO YOU?!
JUST LOOK AT HER! A NICE GIRL LIKE THAT WOULDN'T ...
SHE DOESN'T FOOL ME!
BOO HOO HOO
THAT... THAT REALLY HURTS!
OH!
BOSS!
YOU THINK I'M A... A...
SNIFF
SNIFF
NOW LOOK, SIR, YOU'VE GONE AND MADE HER CRY.
GULP
ALL RIGHT! ONE LOOK!
GLEAM

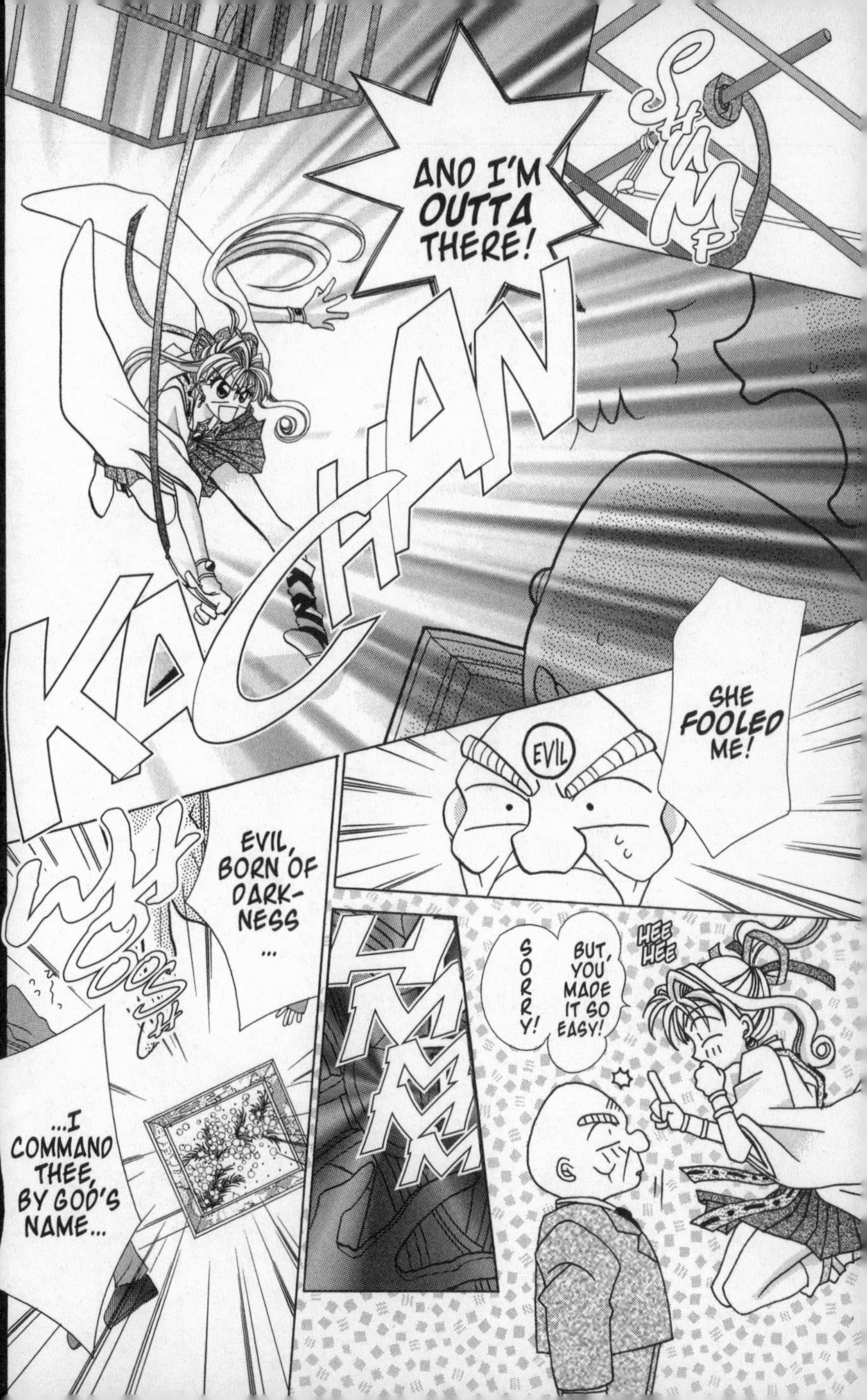
SHUMP
AND I'M OUTTA THERE!
KACHAN
SHE FOOLED ME!
EVIL
EVIL, BORN OF DARKNESS ...
WHOOSH
HEE HEE
BUT, YOU MADE IT SO EASY!
SORRY!
HMMM
...I COMMAND THEE, BY GOD'S NAME...

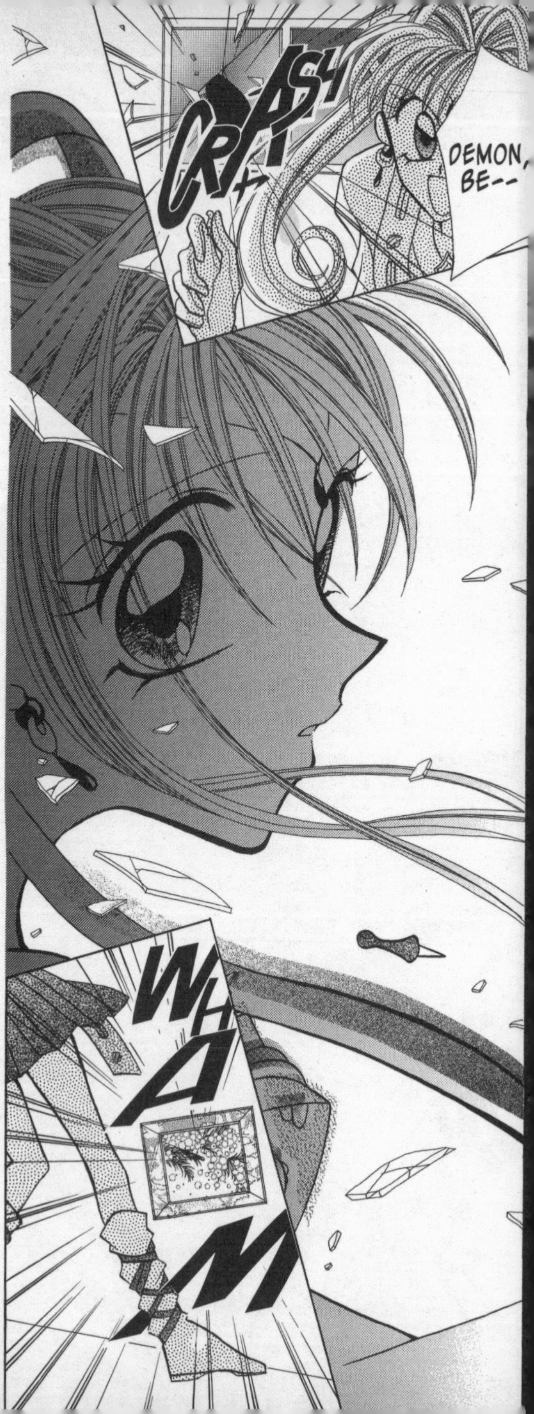
CRASH
DEMON, BE--
WHAM

AT A SIGNING: 3

The signing was from 1 to about 1:30. After that, on the same floor (7th), I had lunch in a private room...

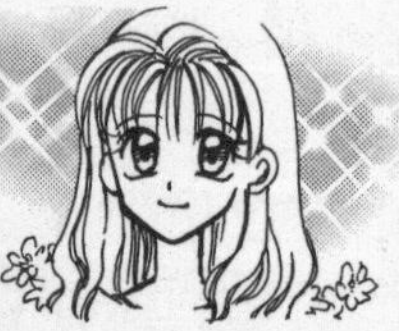

when OBANA-SENSEI showed up!

WOW, SHE IS SOOOO BEAUTIFUL!

AND SLIM! AND CHARMING!

I mean, compared to me. we're night and day...apples and oranges...salt and pepper...
Anyway, I was thrilled (but nervous) and she talked to me so kindly and even gave me her autograph! So, thank you very much, Obana-sensei!

To digress, just outside the private lunchroom was a restaurant with glass walls. From where I was sitting, I could see one of the seats perfectly; a girl sat there having spaghetti while reading "I.O.N." (one of my comics!), which made me so happy! I wondered whether she'd bought it at the event. It looked like she had read all of "I.O.N." and "Kandama," another of mine, really quickly...

CONTINUED IN #4>>

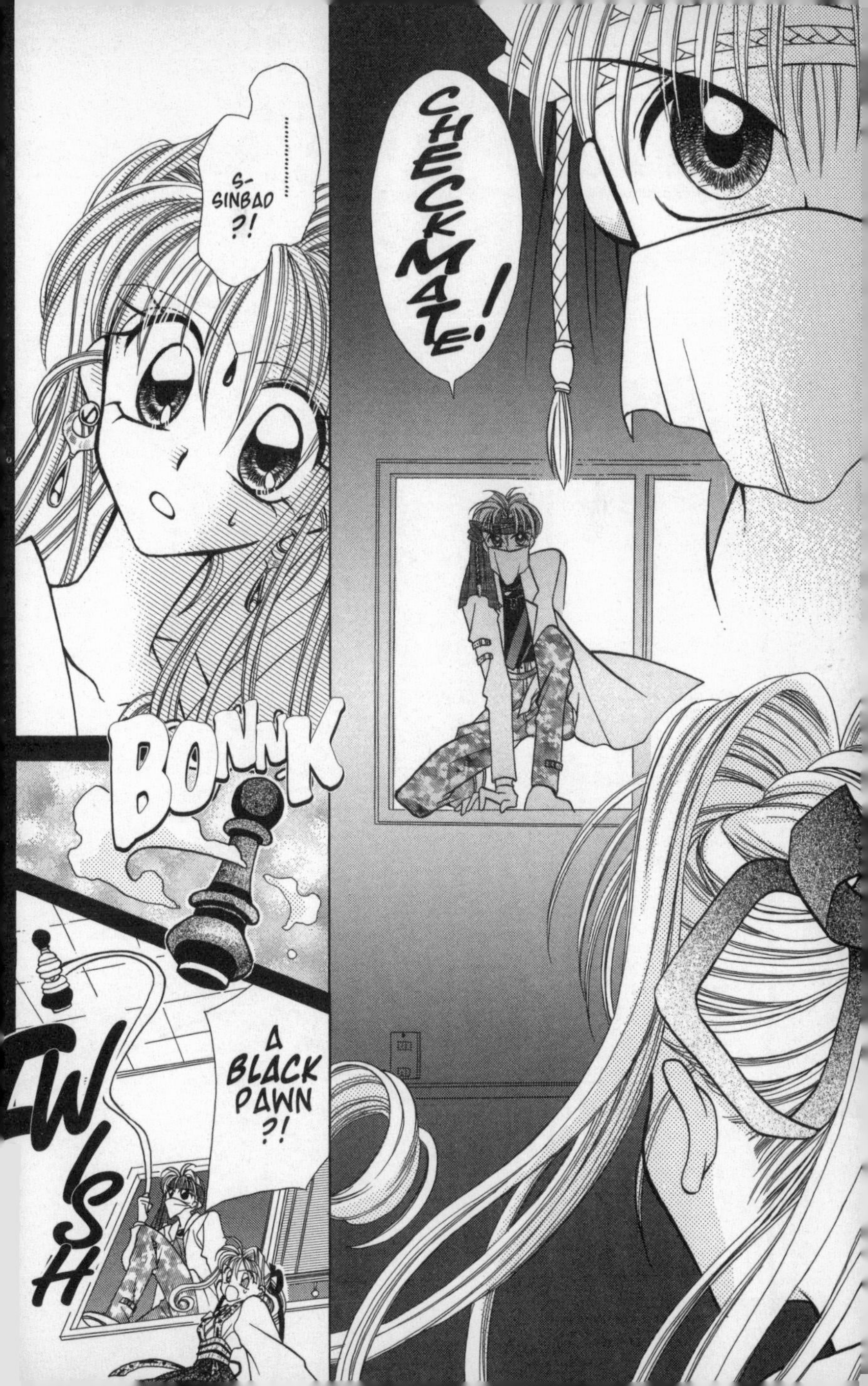
CHECKMATE!
......
S-SINBAD?!
BONNK
A BLACK PAWN?!
WISH

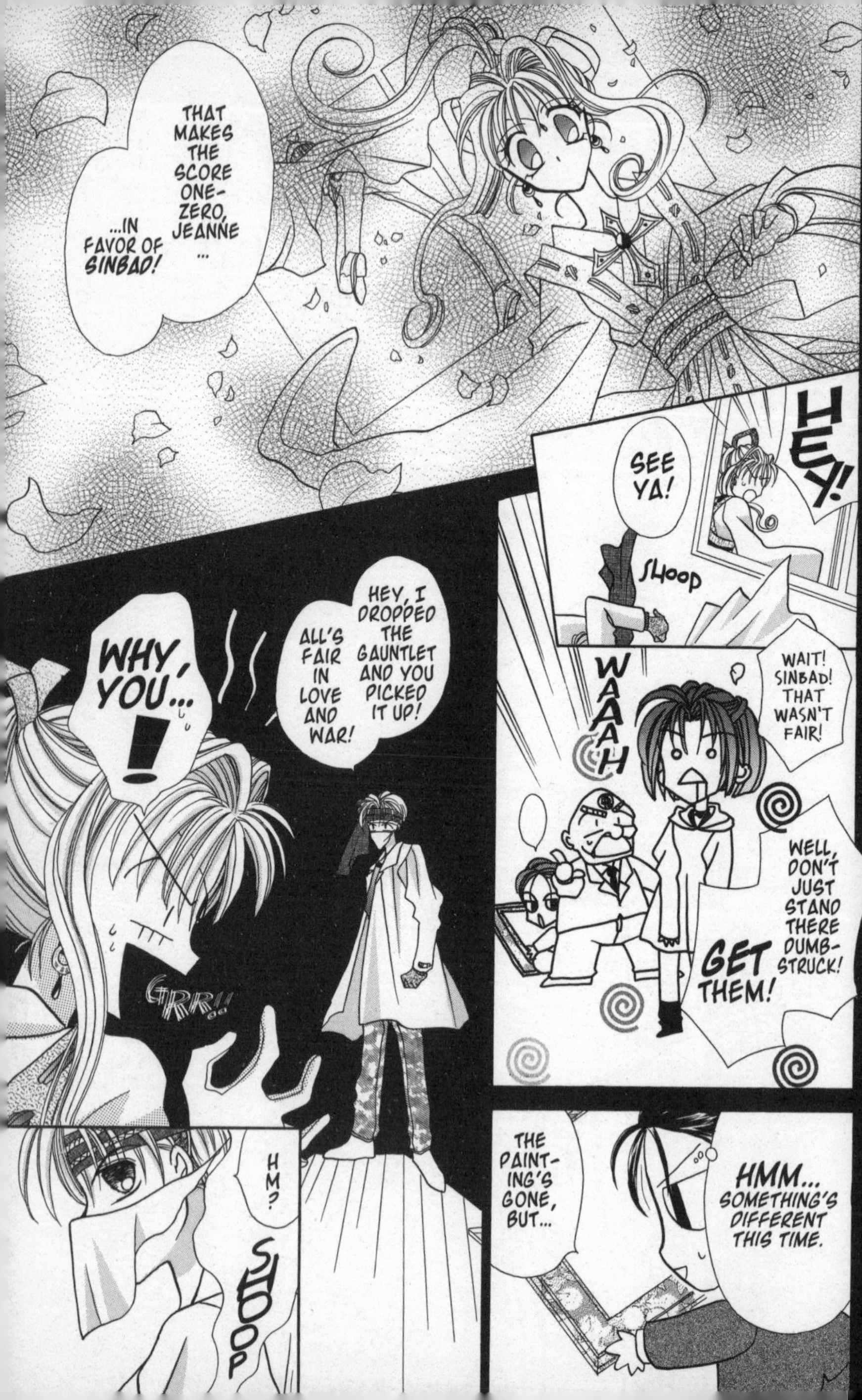
THAT MAKES THE SCORE ONE-ZERO, JEANNE ...
...IN FAVOR OF SINBAD!
HEY!
SEE YA!
SHOOP
WAAAH
WAIT! SINBAD! THAT WASN'T FAIR!
WELL, DON'T JUST STAND THERE DUMBSTRUCK!
GET THEM!
HEY, I DROPPED THE GAUNTLET AND YOU PICKED IT UP!
ALL'S FAIR IN LOVE AND WAR!
WHY, YOU...!
GRR!!
THE PAINTING'S GONE, BUT...
HMM... SOMETHING'S DIFFERENT THIS TIME.
HM?
SHOOP

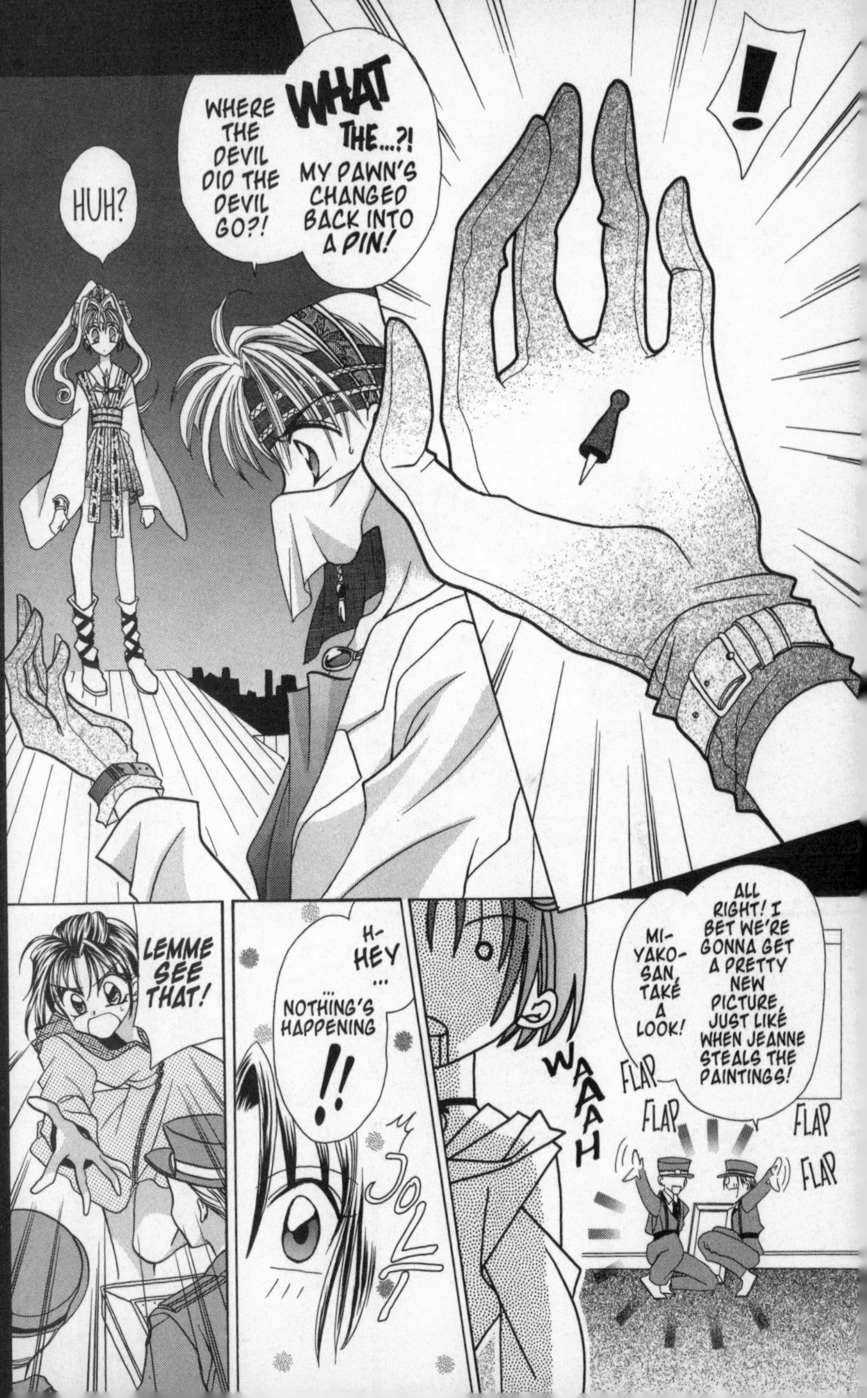
!
WHAT THE...?! MY PAWN'S CHANGED BACK INTO A PIN!
WHERE THE DEVIL DID THE DEVIL GO?!
HUH?
ALL RIGHT! I BET WE'RE GONNA GET A PRETTY NEW PICTURE, JUST LIKE WHEN JEANNE STEALS THE PAINTINGS!
MI-YAKO-SAN, TAKE A LOOK!
FLAP
FLAP
FLAP
FLAP
WAAAH
H-HEY ... NOTHING'S HAPPENING
!!
JOLT
LEMME SEE THAT!

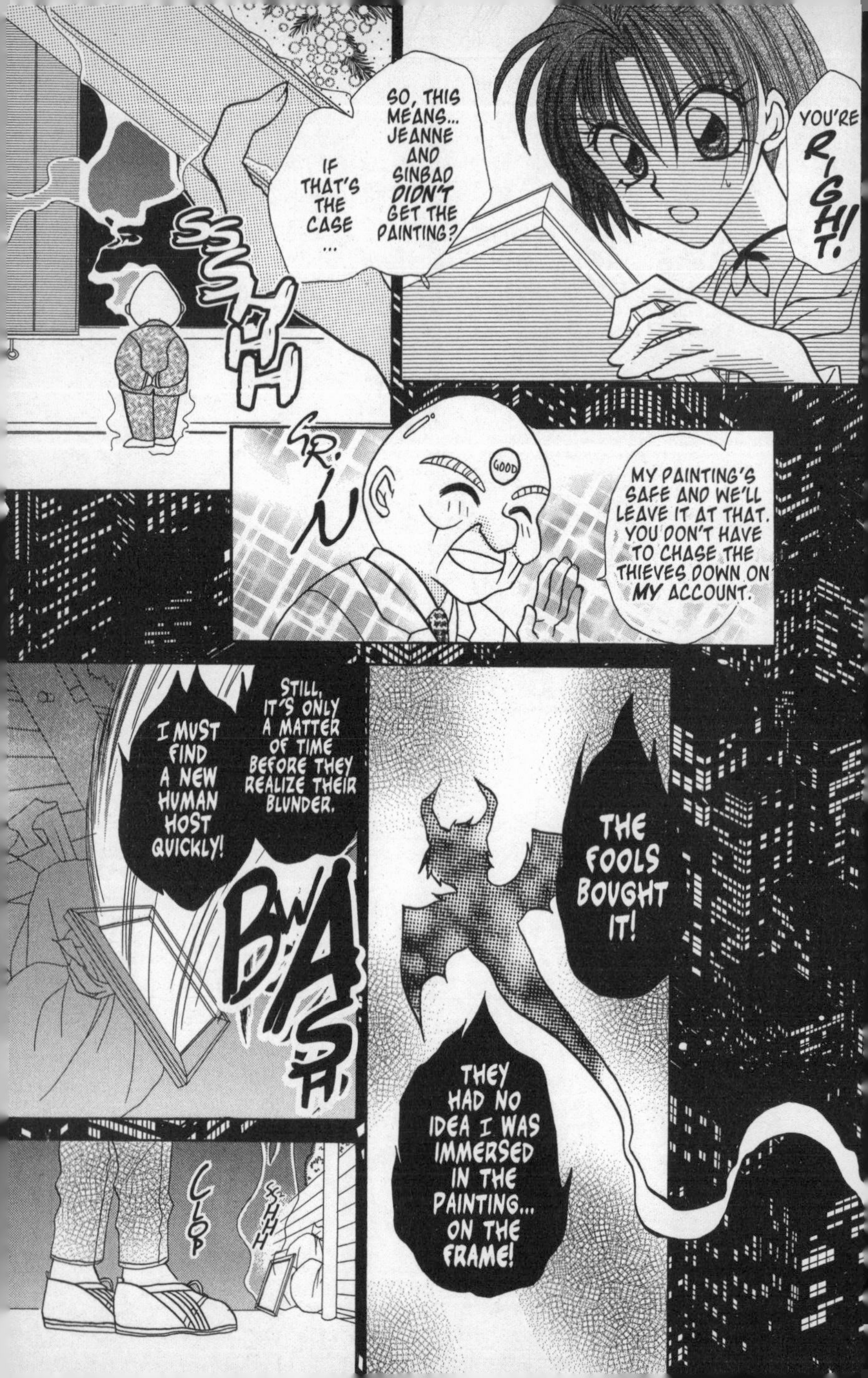
YOU'RE RIGHT!
SO, THIS MEANS... JEANNE AND SINBAD DIDN'T GET THE PAINTING?
IF THAT'S THE CASE...
SSSHH
GRIN
MY PAINTING'S SAFE AND WE'LL LEAVE IT AT THAT. YOU DON'T HAVE TO CHASE THE THIEVES DOWN ON MY ACCOUNT.
GOOD
THE FOOLS BOUGHT IT!
THEY HAD NO IDEA I WAS IMMERSED IN THE PAINTING... ON THE FRAME!
STILL, IT'S ONLY A MATTER OF TIME BEFORE THEY REALIZE THEIR BLUNDER.
I MUST FIND A NEW HUMAN HOST QUICKLY!
BWASH
CLOP
SHHH

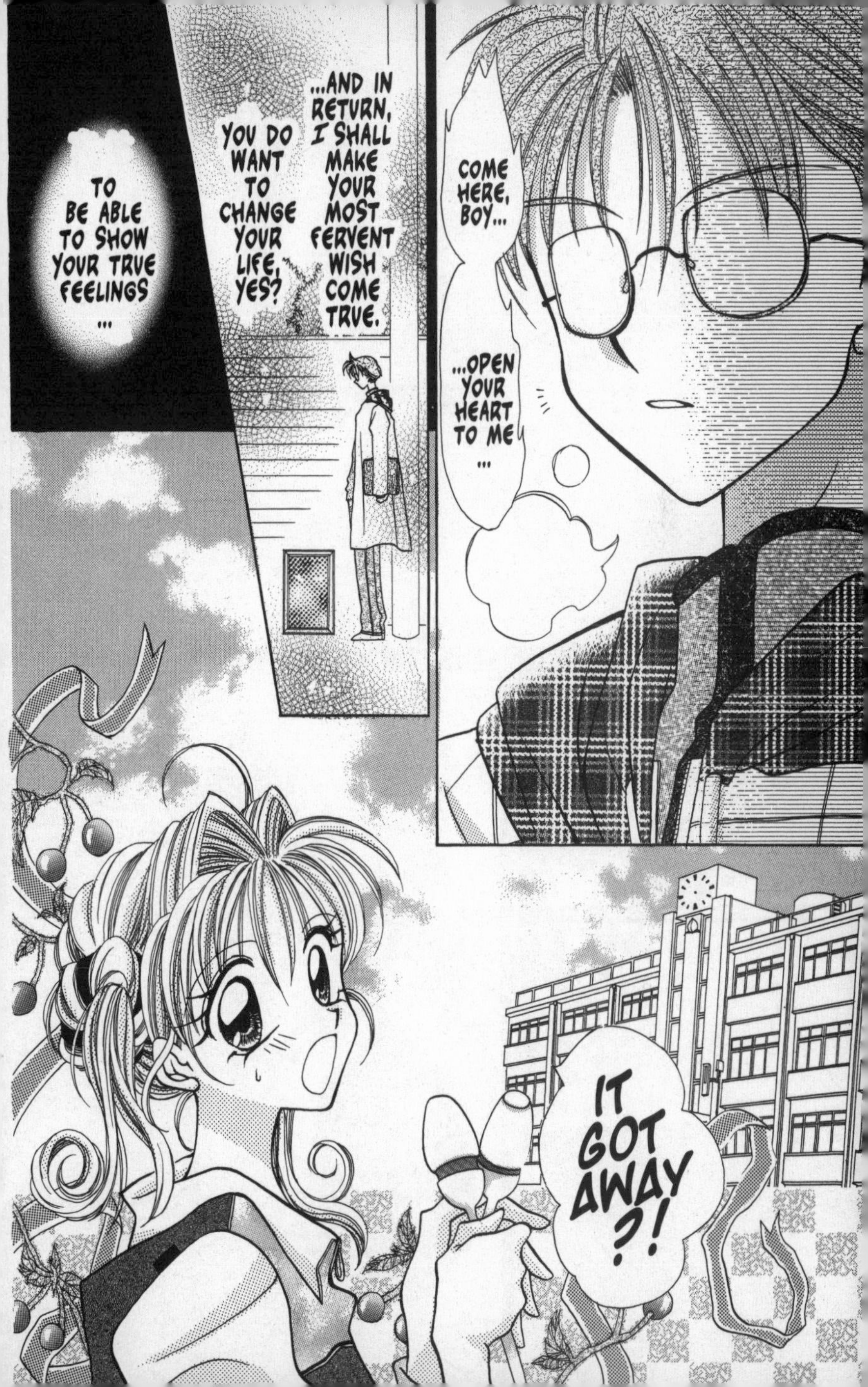
COME HERE, BOY...
...OPEN YOUR HEART TO ME ...
...AND IN RETURN, I SHALL MAKE YOUR MOST FERVENT WISH COME TRUE.
YOU DO WANT TO CHANGE YOUR LIFE, YES?
TO BE ABLE TO SHOW YOUR TRUE FEELINGS ...
IT GOT AWAY?!

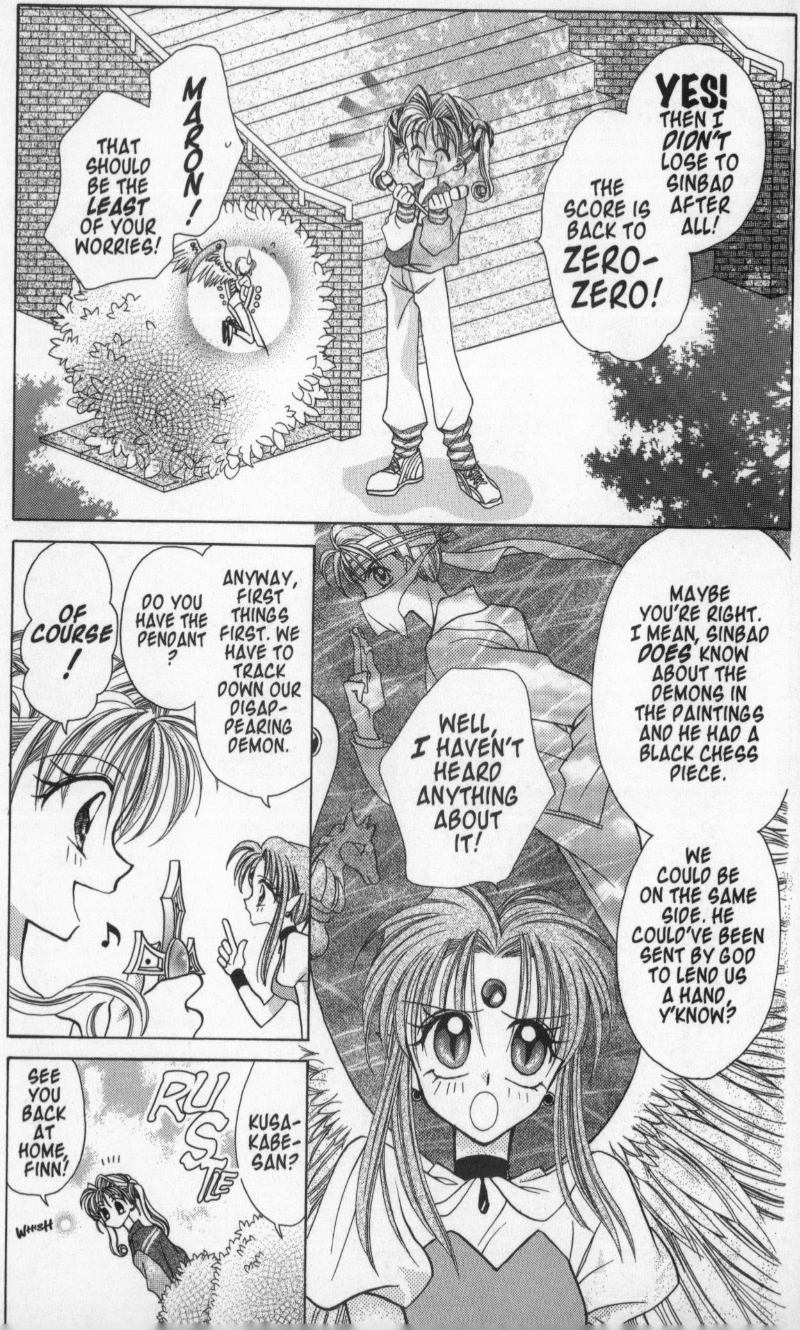
YES! THEN I DIDN'T LOSE TO SINBAD AFTER ALL!
THE SCORE IS BACK TO ZERO-ZERO!
MARON!
THAT SHOULD BE THE LEAST OF YOUR WORRIES!
MAYBE YOU'RE RIGHT. I MEAN, SINBAD DOES KNOW ABOUT THE DEMONS IN THE PAINTINGS AND HE HAD A BLACK CHESS PIECE.
WE COULD BE ON THE SAME SIDE. HE COULD'VE BEEN SENT BY GOD TO LEND US A HAND, Y'KNOW?
WELL, I HAVEN'T HEARD ANYTHING ABOUT IT!
ANYWAY, FIRST THINGS FIRST. WE HAVE TO TRACK DOWN OUR DISAPPEARING DEMON.
DO YOU HAVE THE PENDANT?
OF COURSE!
KUSA-KABE-SAN?
RUSTLE
SEE YOU BACK AT HOME, FINN!
WHISH

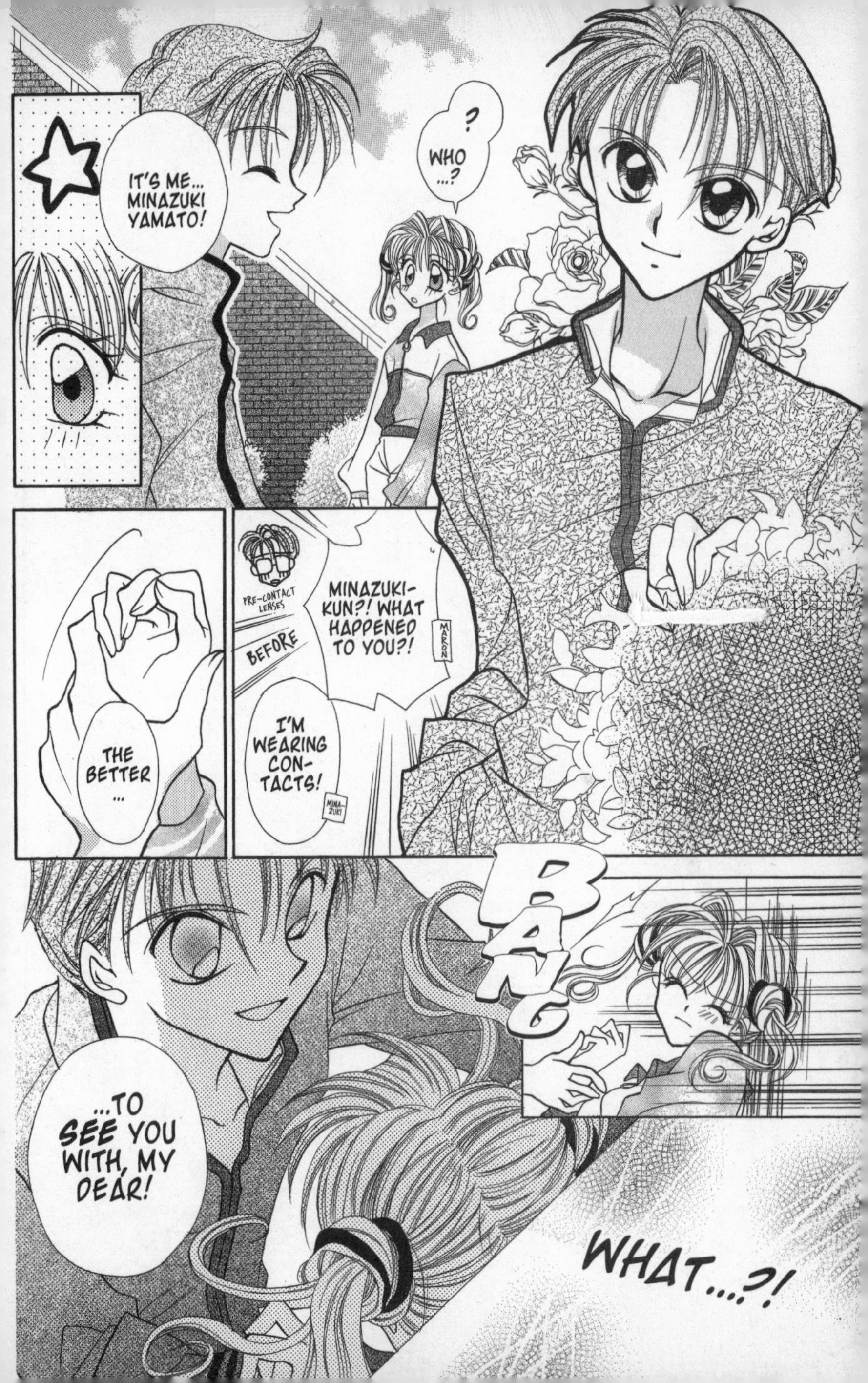
?
WHO ...?
IT'S ME... MINAZUKI YAMATO!
MINAZUKI-KUN?! WHAT HAPPENED TO YOU?!
MARON
I'M WEARING CONTACTS!
MINA-ZUKI
BEFORE
PRE-CONTACT LENSES
THE BETTER ...
BANG
...TO SEE YOU WITH, MY DEAR!
WHAT...?!

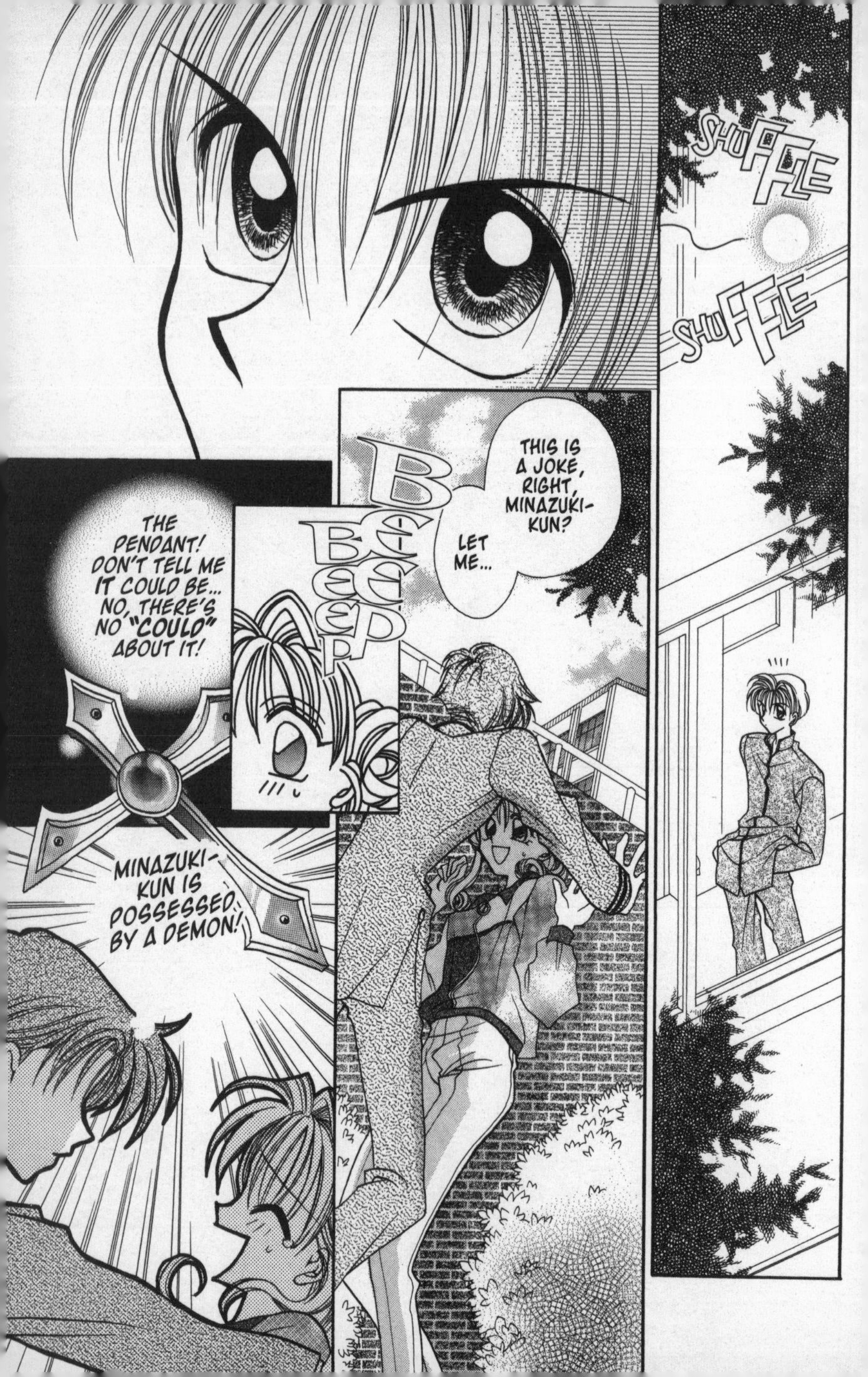
SHUFFLE
SHUFFLE
THIS IS A JOKE, RIGHT, MINAZUKI-KUN?
LET ME...
BEEEP
THE PENDANT! DON'T TELL ME IT COULD BE... NO, THERE'S NO "COULD" ABOUT IT!
MINAZUKI-KUN IS POSSESSED BY A DEMON!

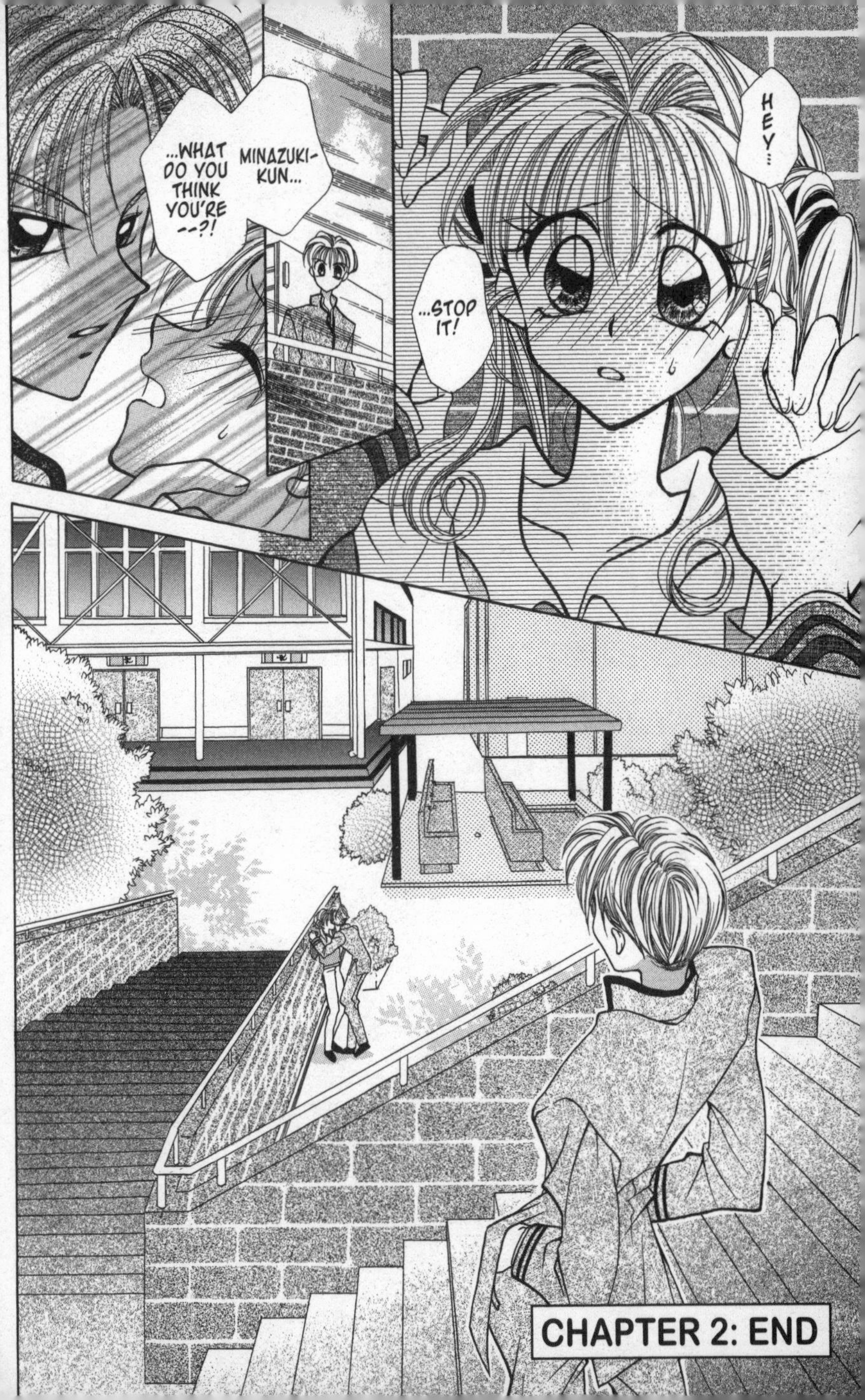
HEY...
...STOP IT!
MINAZUKI-KUN...
...WHAT DO YOU THINK YOU'RE --?!
CHAPTER 2: END

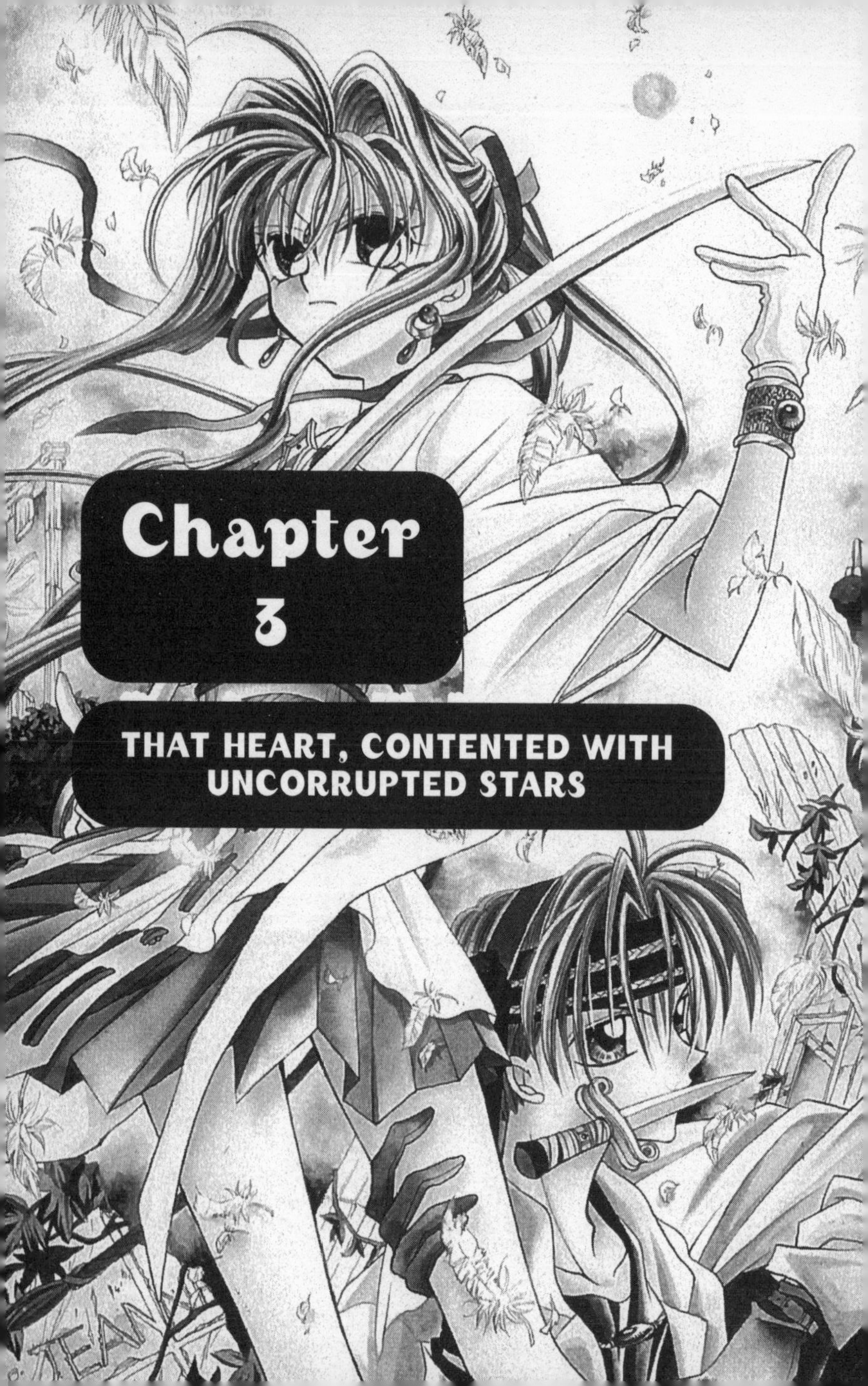
Chapter
3
THAT HEART, CONTENTED WITH UNCORRUPTED STARS

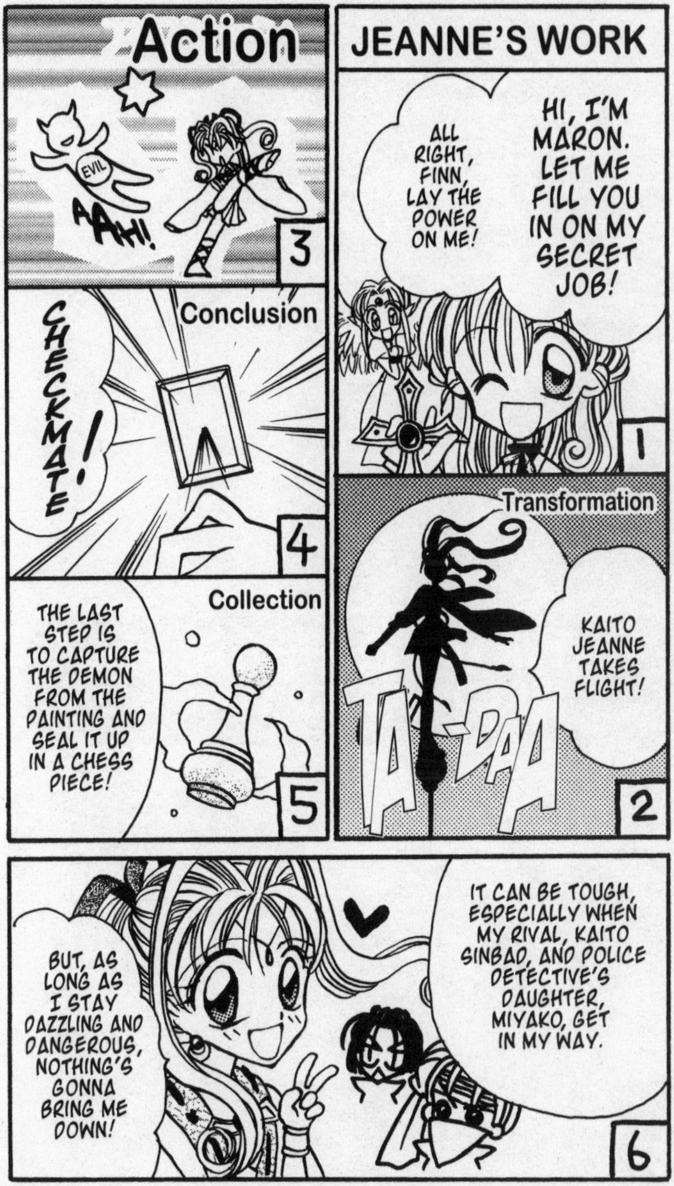
JEANNE'S WORK
HI, I'M MARON. LET ME FILL YOU IN ON MY SECRET JOB!
ALL RIGHT, FINN, LAY THE POWER ON ME!
1
Transformation
KAITO JEANNE TAKES FLIGHT!
TA-DAA
2
Action
EVIL
AAHH!
3
Conclusion
CHECKMATE!
4
Collection
THE LAST STEP IS TO CAPTURE THE DEMON FROM THE PAINTING AND SEAL IT UP IN A CHESS PIECE!
5
IT CAN BE TOUGH, ESPECIALLY WHEN MY RIVAL, KAITO SINBAD, AND POLICE DETECTIVE'S DAUGHTER, MIYAKO, GET IN MY WAY.
BUT, AS LONG AS I STAY DAZZLING AND DANGEROUS, NOTHING'S GONNA BRING ME DOWN!
6

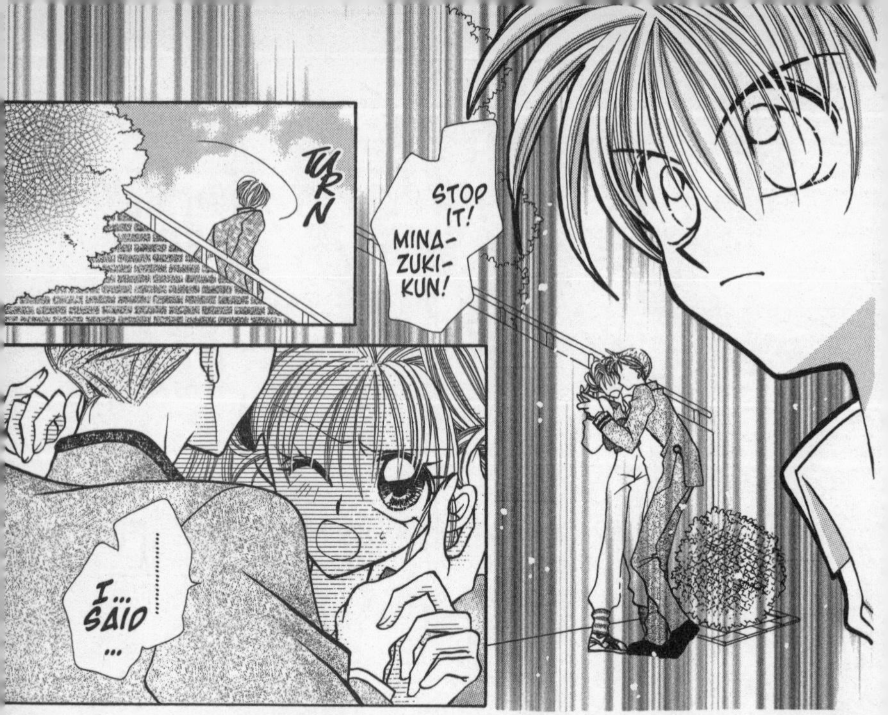
STOP IT! MINA-ZUKI-KUN!
TURN
......
I... SAID ...

CHAPTER 3: THAT HEART, CONTENTED WITH UNCORRUPTED STARS

"It is my destiny to battle in this form!"

I love the heck out of the title page art for this episode, too (although I think the black and white shading is crummy)! Check out how Sinbad-sama is groping Jeanne's thigh! Sexy! HEH HEH HEH! Even though a lot of my friends told me that page has punch, my editor called it "grim," so obviously it's not one of his faves. Regarding the story, it's one I had in mind since conceiving of the series and added extra pages to it as a bonus. Also, I was so psyched when I thought of the title for this tale! In it, we start to see different sides of Maron and her relationship with Chiaki progressing. In fact, the whole linchpin of the series might be right here. MMM...yeah, I like this one.

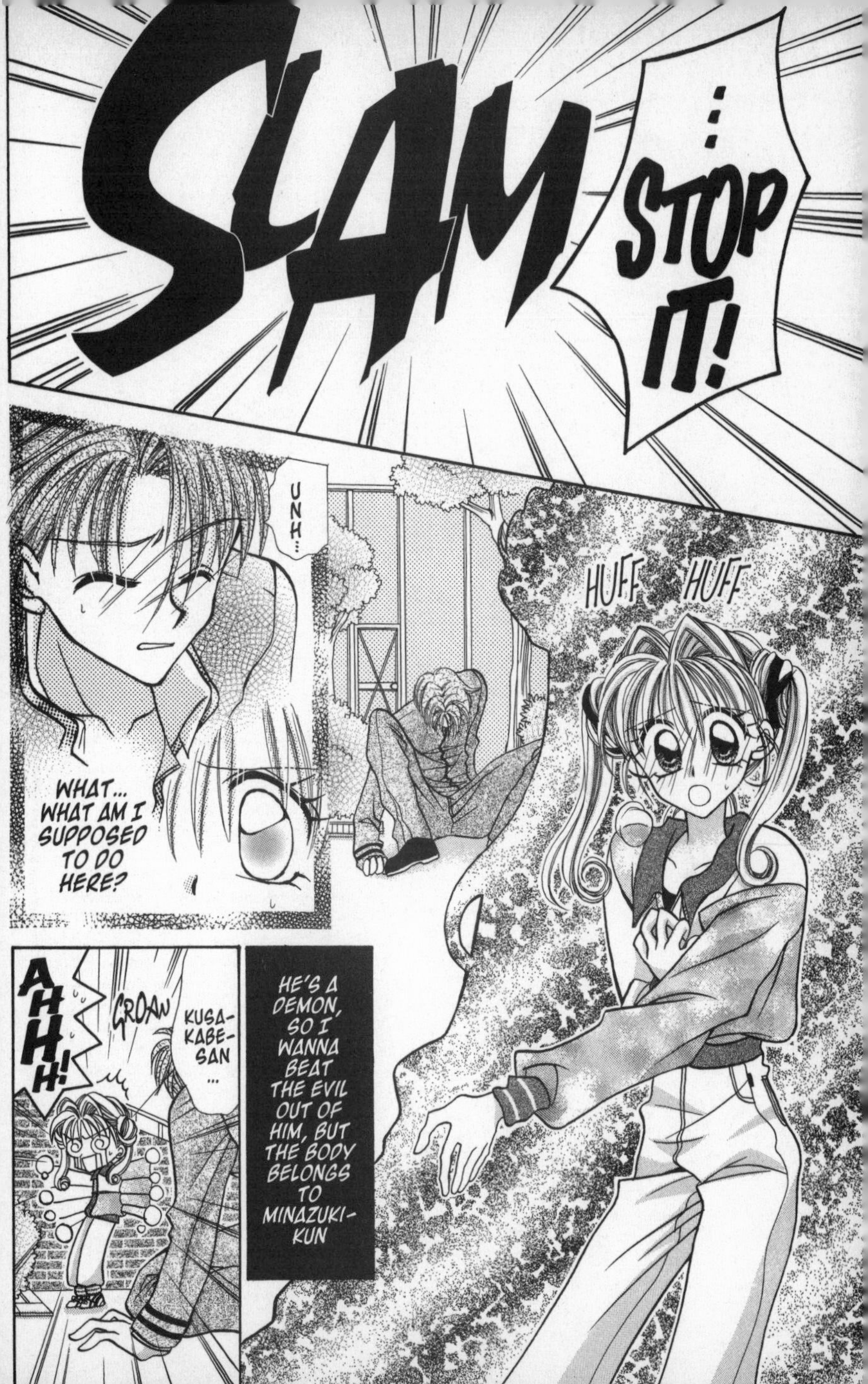
SLAM
...STOP IT!
UNH...
HUFF HUFF
WHAT... WHAT AM I SUPPOSED TO DO HERE?
HE'S A DEMON, SO I WANNA BEAT THE EVIL OUT OF HIM, BUT THE BODY BELONGS TO MINAZUKI-KUN
KUSA-KABE-SAN ...
GROAN
AHHHH!

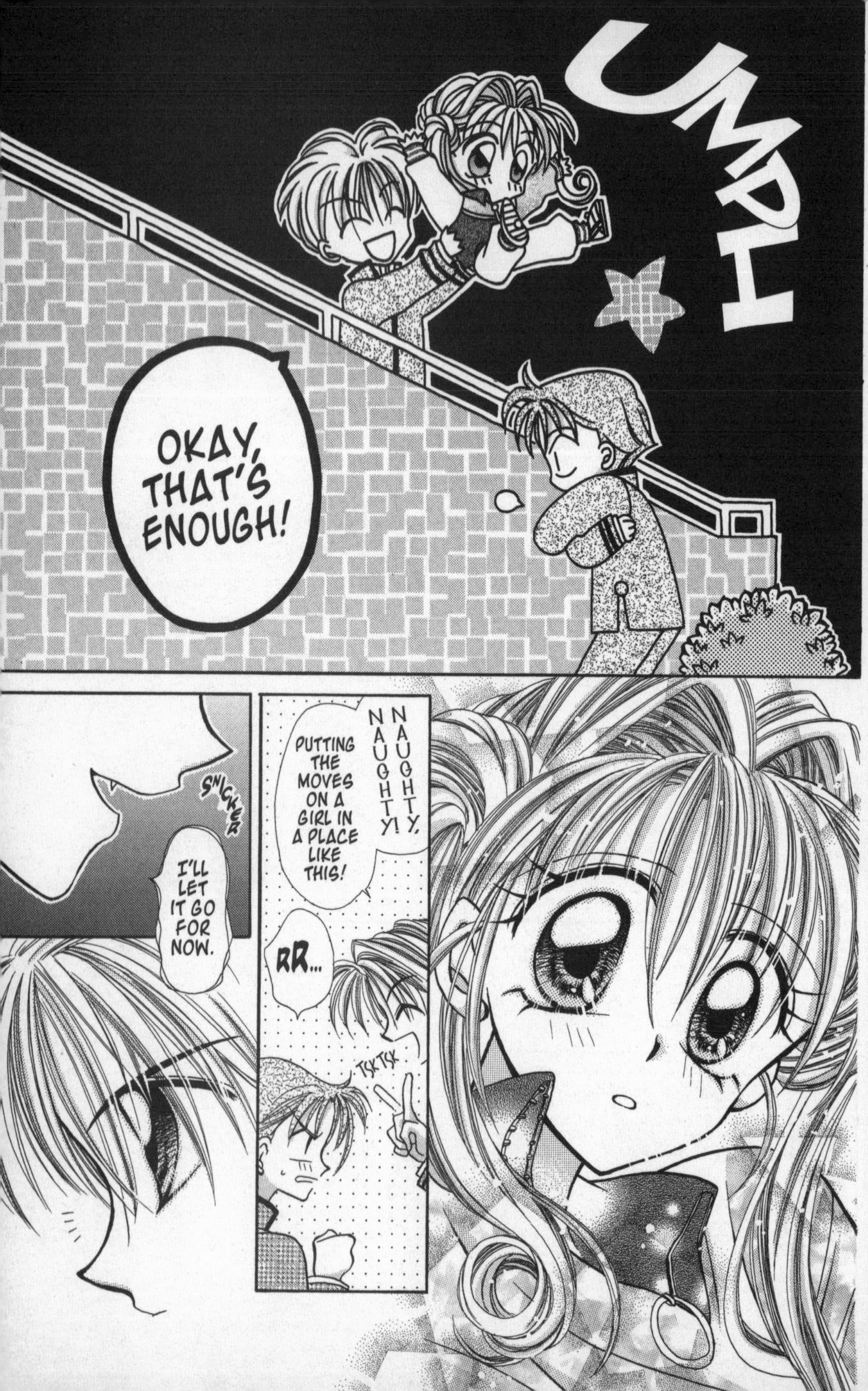
UMPH
OKAY, THAT'S ENOUGH!
NAUGHTY, NAUGHTY!
PUTTING THE MOVES ON A GIRL IN A PLACE LIKE THIS!
RR...
TSK TSK
SNICKER
I'LL LET IT GO FOR NOW.

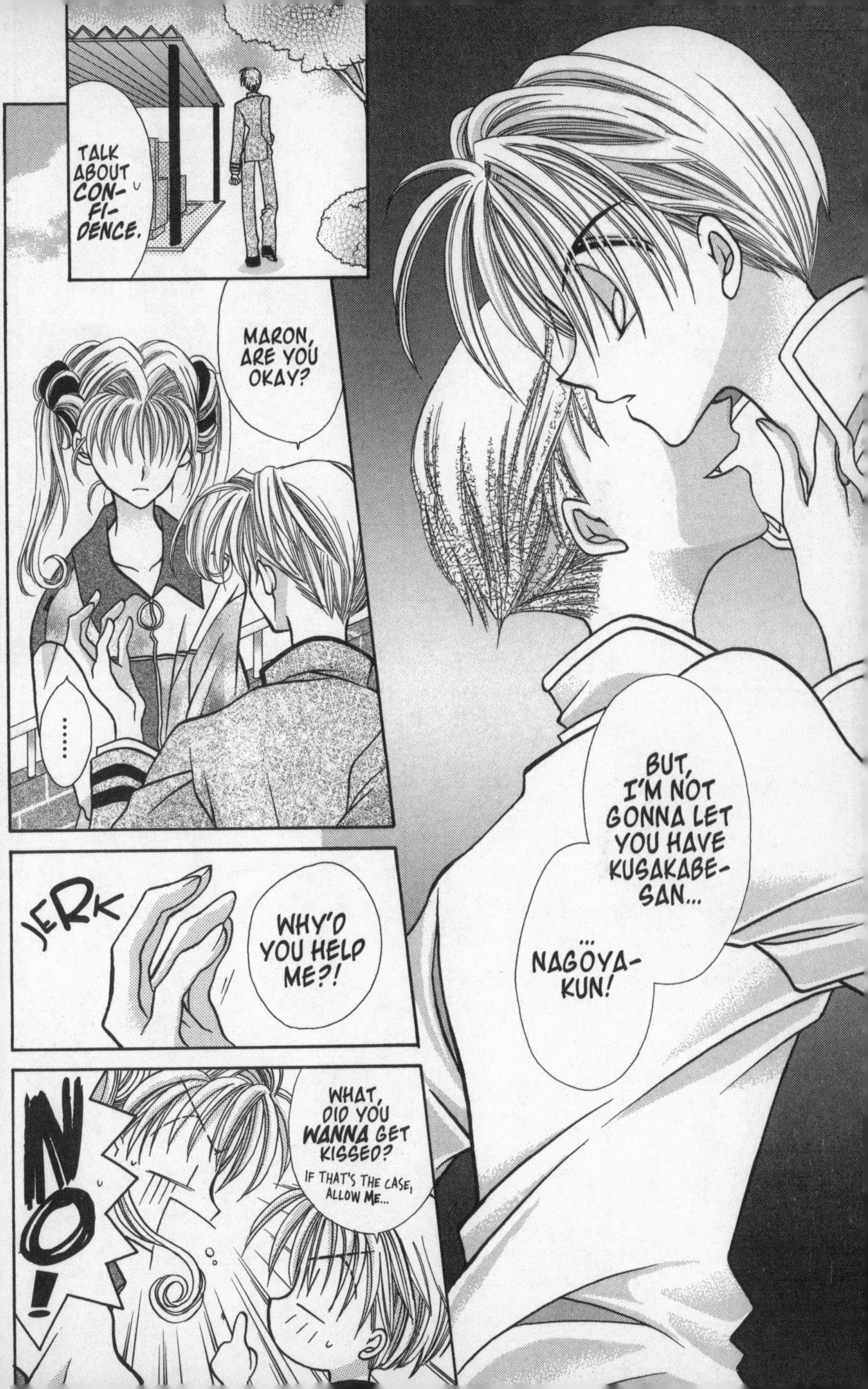
BUT, I'M NOT GONNA LET YOU HAVE KUSAKABE-SAN...
... NAGOYA-KUN!
TALK ABOUT CON-FI-DENCE.
MARON, ARE YOU OKAY?
......
JERK
WHY'D YOU HELP ME?!
WHAT, DID YOU WANNA GET KISSED?
IF THAT'S THE CASE, ALLOW ME...
NO!

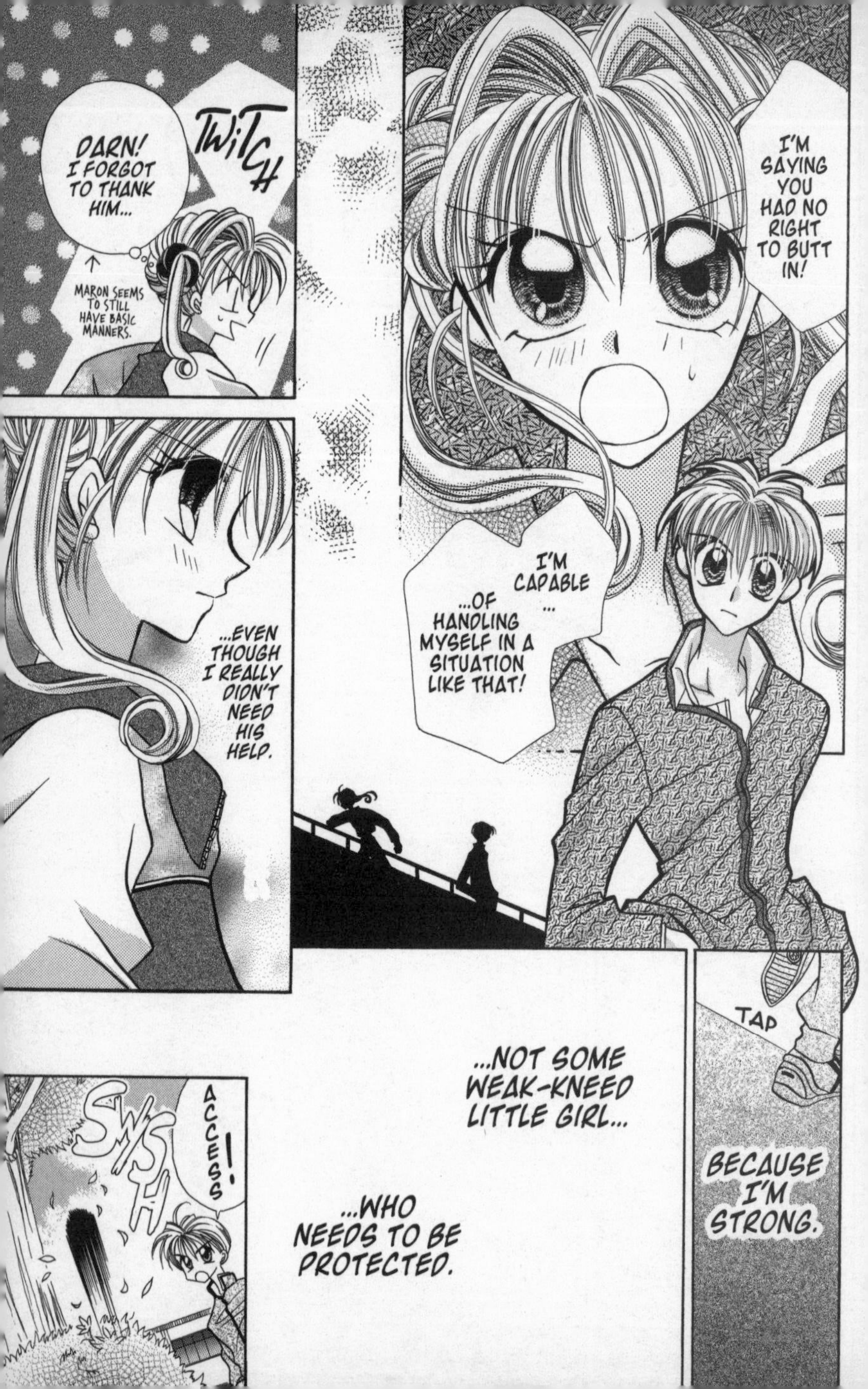
I'M SAYING YOU HAD NO RIGHT TO BUTT IN!
I'M CAPABLE ...
...OF HANDLING MYSELF IN A SITUATION LIKE THAT!
TWITCH
DARN! I FORGOT TO THANK HIM...
MARON SEEMS TO STILL HAVE BASIC MANNERS.
...EVEN THOUGH I REALLY DIDN'T NEED HIS HELP.
TAP
BECAUSE I'M STRONG.
...NOT SOME WEAK-KNEED LITTLE GIRL...
...WHO NEEDS TO BE PROTECTED.
ACCESS!
SWISH

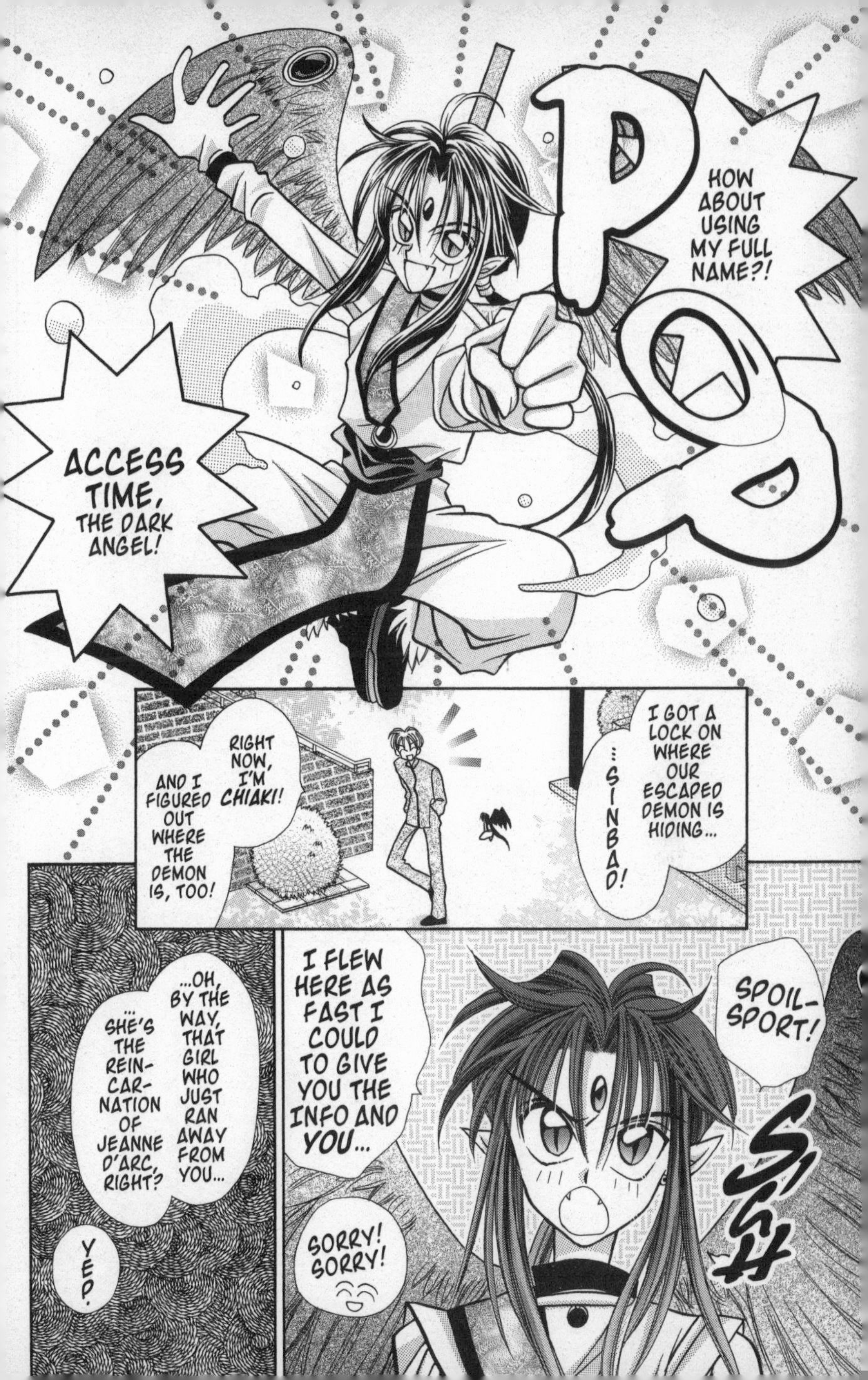
POP
HOW ABOUT USING MY FULL NAME?!
ACCESS TIME, THE DARK ANGEL!
I GOT A LOCK ON WHERE OUR ESCAPED DEMON IS HIDING...
...SINBAD!
RIGHT NOW, I'M CHIAKI!
AND I FIGURED OUT WHERE THE DEMON IS, TOO!
SPOIL-SPORT!
I FLEW HERE AS FAST I COULD TO GIVE YOU THE INFO AND YOU...
SIGH
SORRY! SORRY!
...OH, BY THE WAY, THAT GIRL WHO JUST RAN AWAY FROM YOU...
...SHE'S THE REIN-CAR-NATION OF JEANNE D'ARC, RIGHT?
YEP.

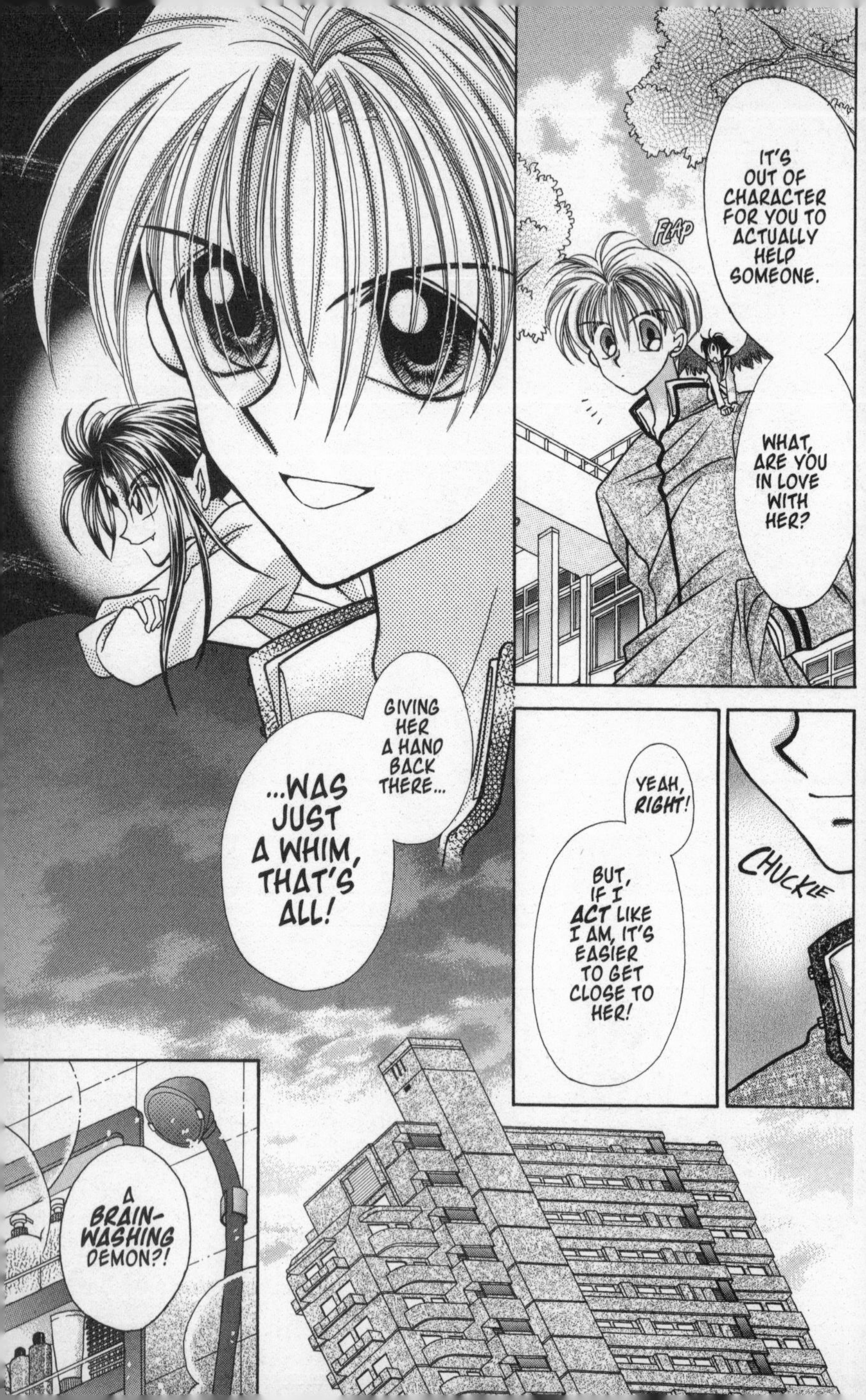
IT'S OUT OF CHARACTER FOR YOU TO ACTUALLY HELP SOMEONE.
FLAP
WHAT, ARE YOU IN LOVE WITH HER?
CHUCKLE
YEAH, RIGHT!
BUT, IF I ACT LIKE I AM, IT'S EASIER TO GET CLOSE TO HER!
GIVING HER A HAND BACK THERE...
...WAS JUST A WHIM, THAT'S ALL!
A BRAIN-WASHING DEMON?!

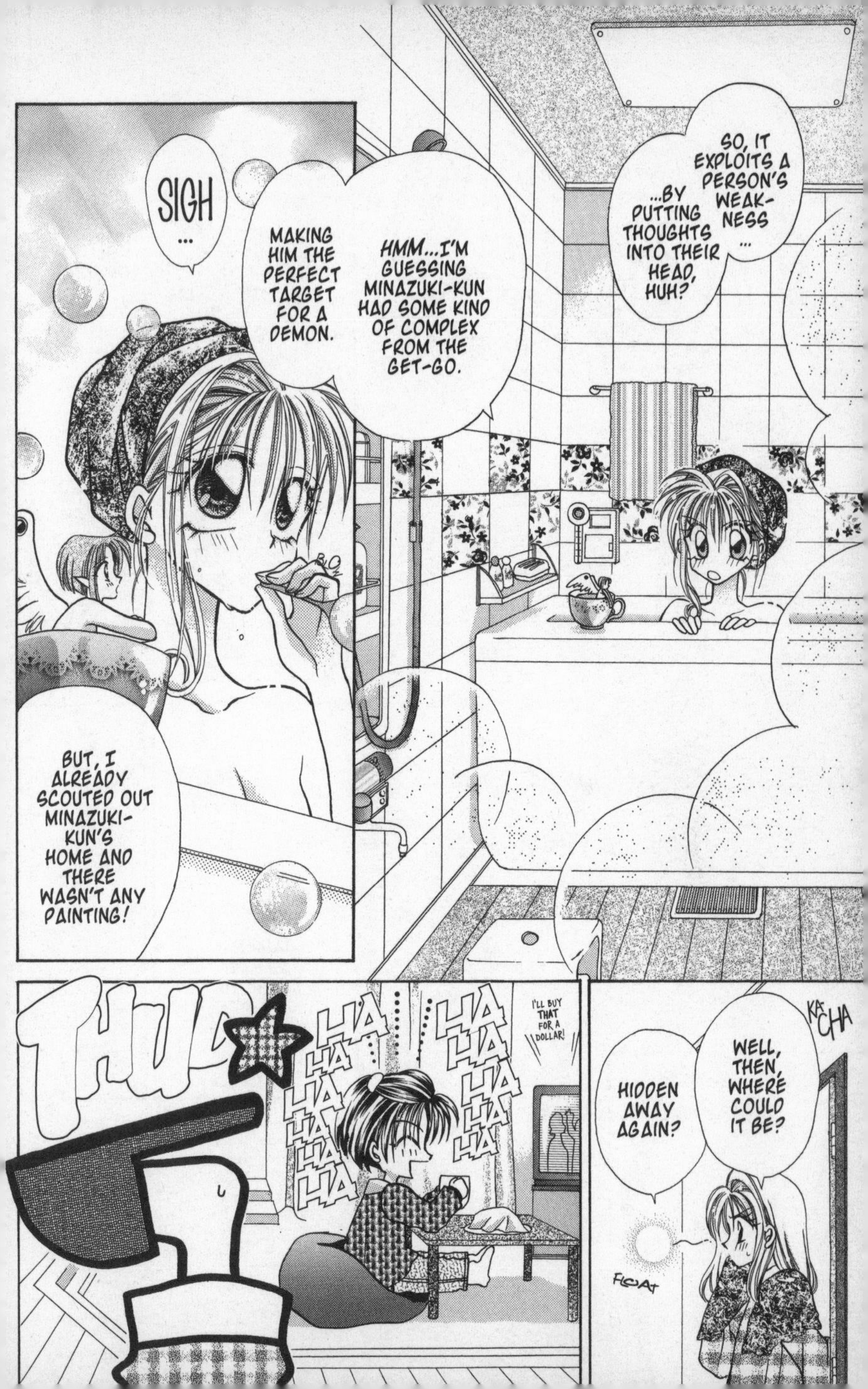
SO, IT EXPLOITS A PERSON'S WEAKNESS...
...BY PUTTING THOUGHTS INTO THEIR HEAD, HUH?
HMM...I'M GUESSING MINAZUKI-KUN HAD SOME KIND OF COMPLEX FROM THE GET-GO.
MAKING HIM THE PERFECT TARGET FOR A DEMON.
SIGH...
BUT, I ALREADY SCOUTED OUT MINAZUKI-KUN'S HOME AND THERE WASN'T ANY PAINTING!
KACHA
WELL, THEN, WHERE COULD IT BE?
HIDDEN AWAY AGAIN?
FLOAT
HA HA HA HA HA HA
HA HA HA HA HA HA HA
I'LL BUY THAT FOR A DOLLAR!
THUD

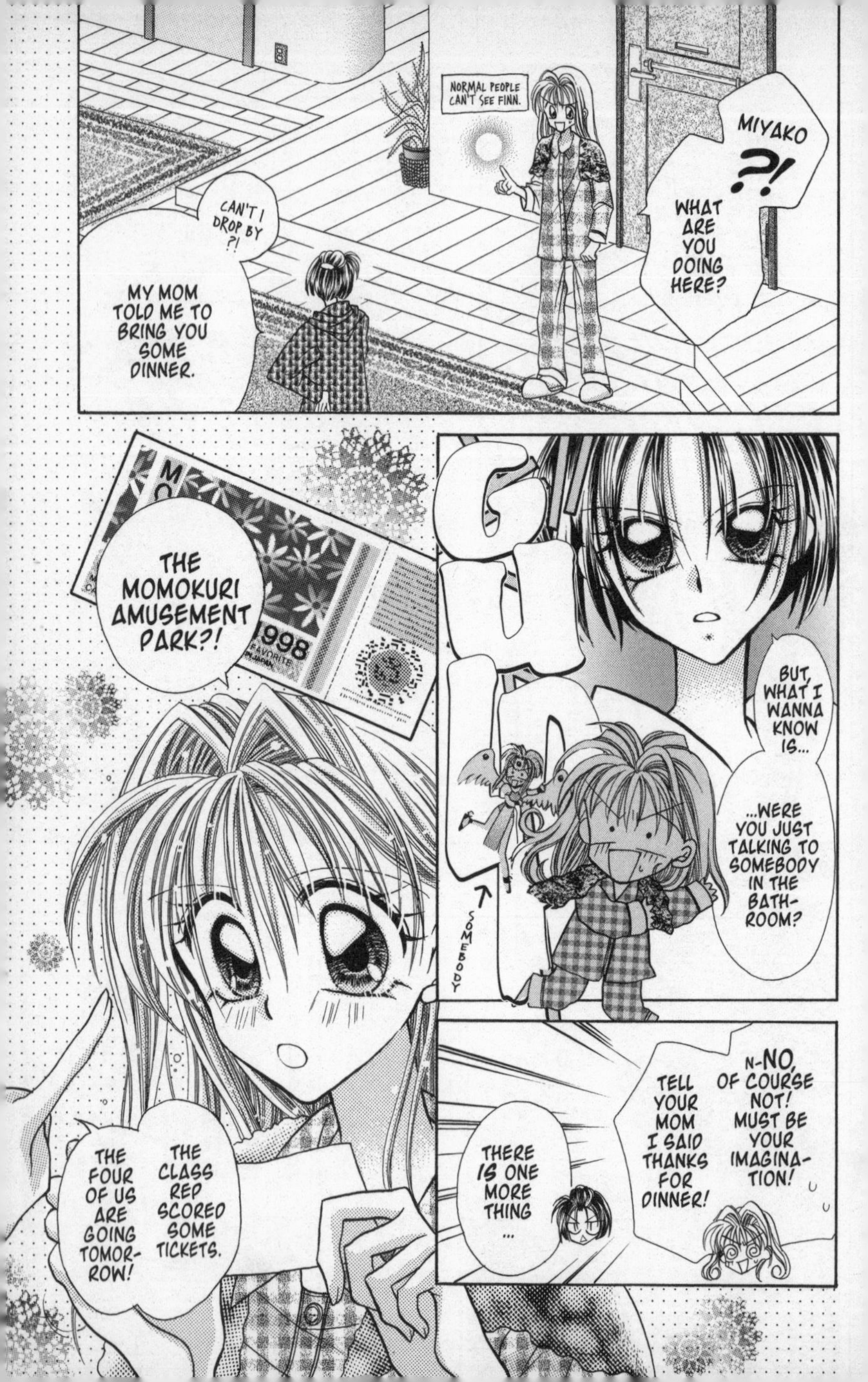
MIYAKO ?!
WHAT ARE YOU DOING HERE?
NORMAL PEOPLE CAN'T SEE FINN.
CAN'T I DROP BY ?!
MY MOM TOLD ME TO BRING YOU SOME DINNER.
BUT, WHAT I WANNA KNOW IS...
...WERE YOU JUST TALKING TO SOMEBODY IN THE BATH-ROOM?
SOMEBODY
N-NO, OF COURSE NOT! MUST BE YOUR IMAGINATION!
TELL YOUR MOM I SAID THANKS FOR DINNER!
THERE *IS* ONE MORE THING ...
THE MOMOKURI AMUSEMENT PARK?!
THE CLASS REP SCORED SOME TICKETS.
THE FOUR OF US ARE GOING TOMORROW!

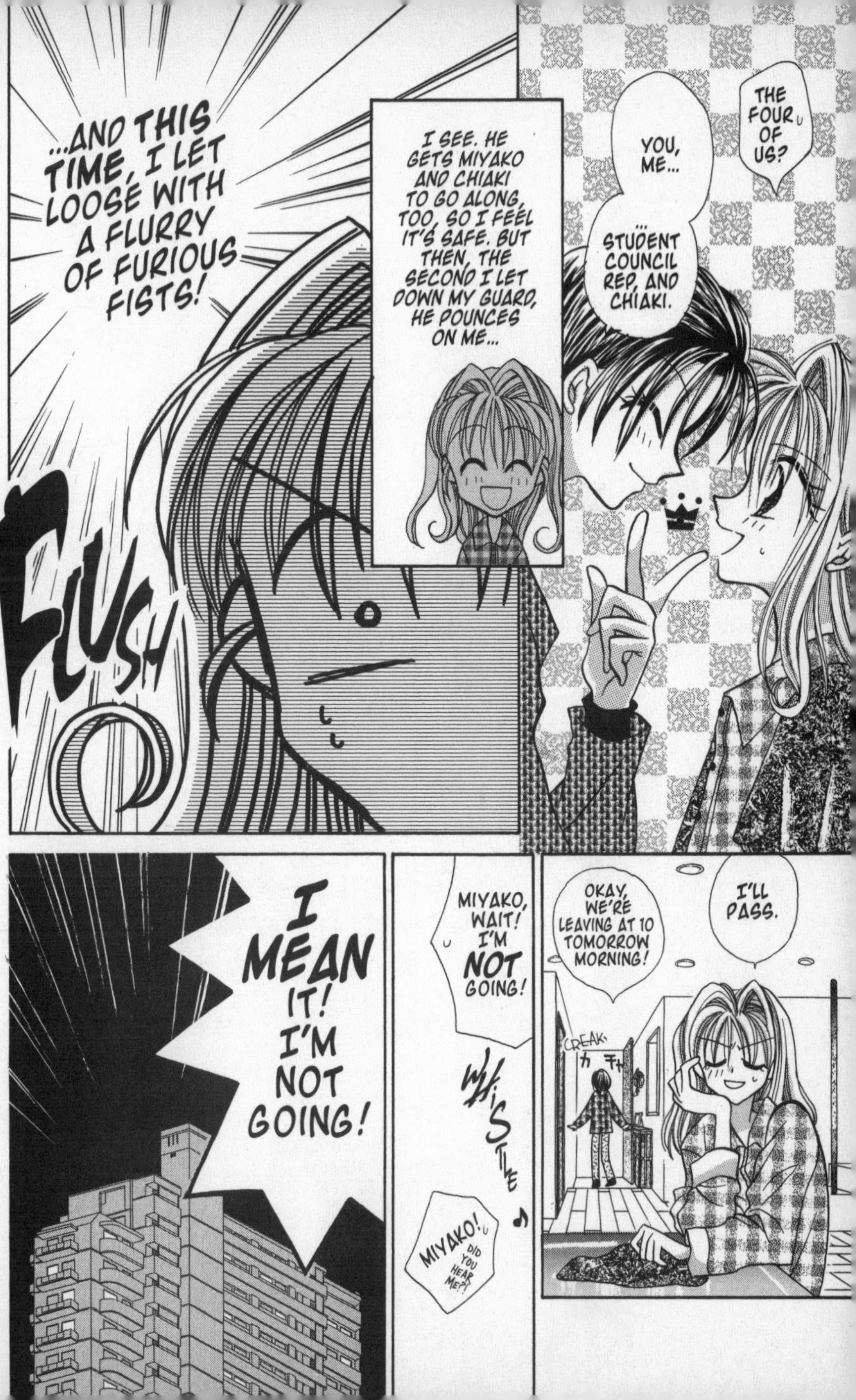
THE FOUR OF US?
YOU, ME... ...STUDENT COUNCIL REP, AND CHIAKI.
I SEE. HE GETS MIYAKO AND CHIAKI TO GO ALONG, TOO, SO I FEEL IT'S SAFE. BUT THEN, THE SECOND I LET DOWN MY GUARD, HE POUNCES ON ME...
...AND THIS TIME, I LET LOOSE WITH A FLURRY OF FURIOUS FISTS!
FLUSH
I'LL PASS.
OKAY, WE'RE LEAVING AT 10 TOMORROW MORNING!
CREAK
MIYAKO, WAIT! I'M NOT GOING!
WHISTLE
MIYAKO! DID YOU HEAR ME?!
I MEAN IT! I'M NOT GOING!

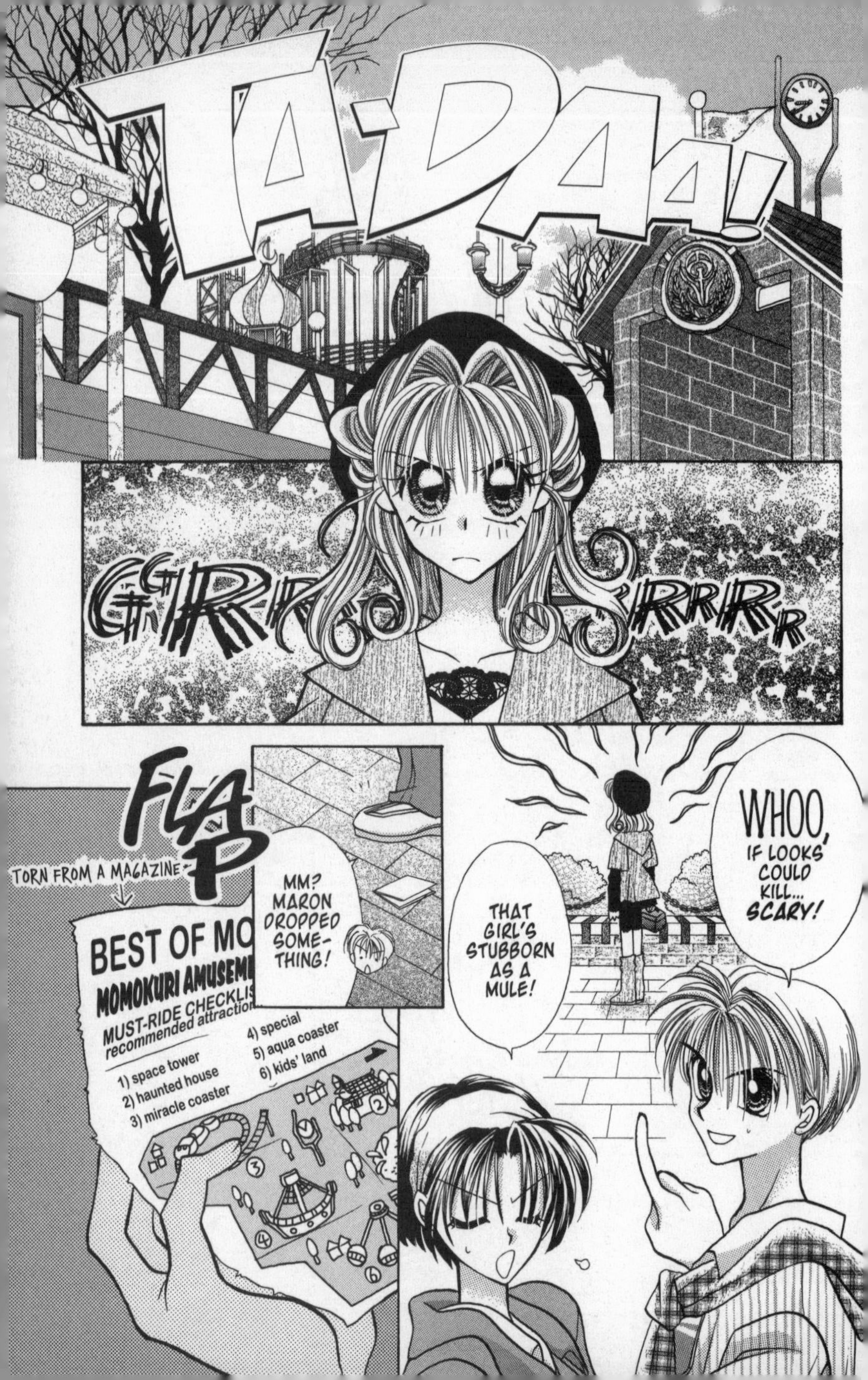
TA-DAA!
GRRR
RRRRR
WHOO, IF LOOKS COULD KILL... SCARY!
THAT GIRL'S STUBBORN AS A MULE!
MM? MARON DROPPED SOME-THING!
FLAP
TORN FROM A MAGAZINE
BEST OF MO
MOMOKURI AMUSEME
MUST-RIDE CHECKLIS
recommended attraction
1) space tower
2) haunted house
3) miracle coaster
4) special
5) aqua coaster
6) kids' land

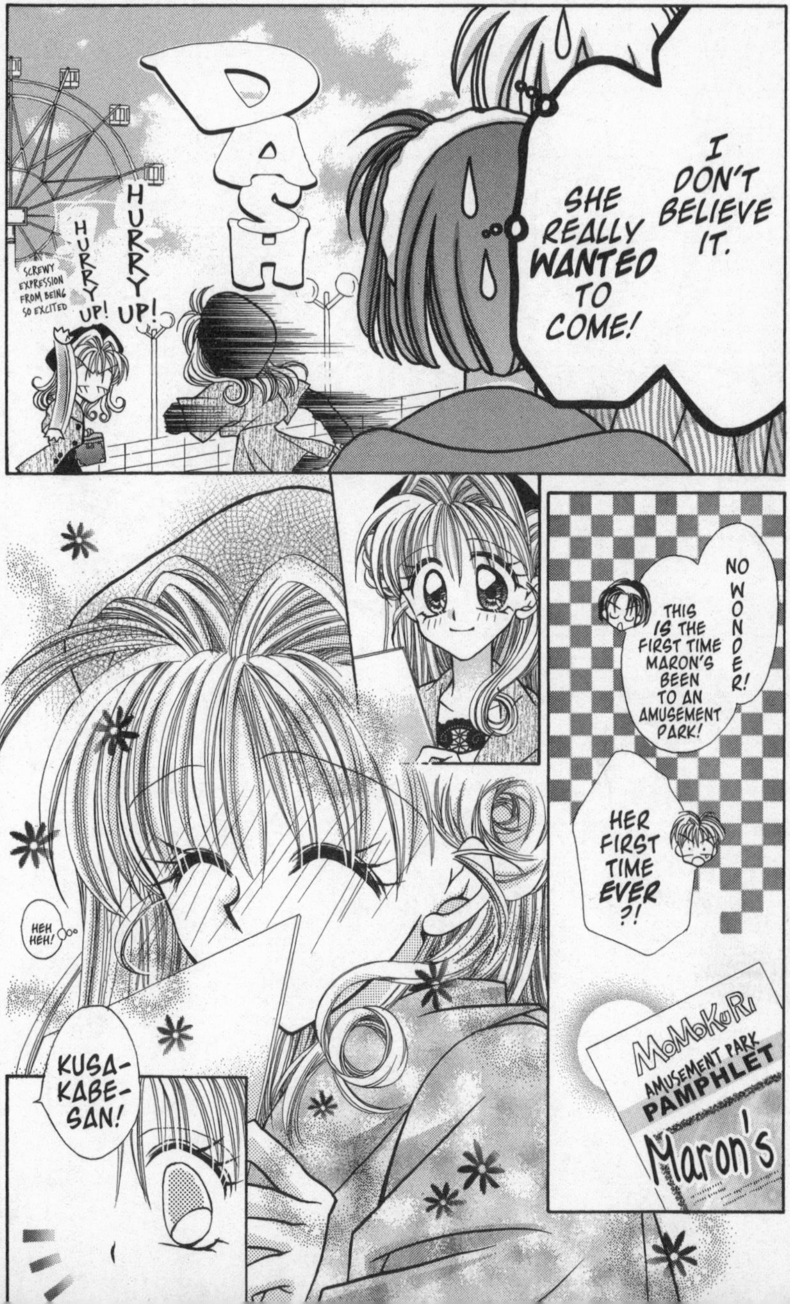
I DON'T BELIEVE IT.
SHE REALLY WANTED TO COME!
DASH
HURRY UP!
HURRY UP!
SCREWY EXPRESSION FROM BEING SO EXCITED
NO WONDER!
THIS IS THE FIRST TIME MARON'S BEEN TO AN AMUSEMENT PARK!
HER FIRST TIME EVER?!
HEH HEH!
MOMOKURI AMUSEMENT PARK PAMPHLET
Maron's
KUSA-KABE-SAN!

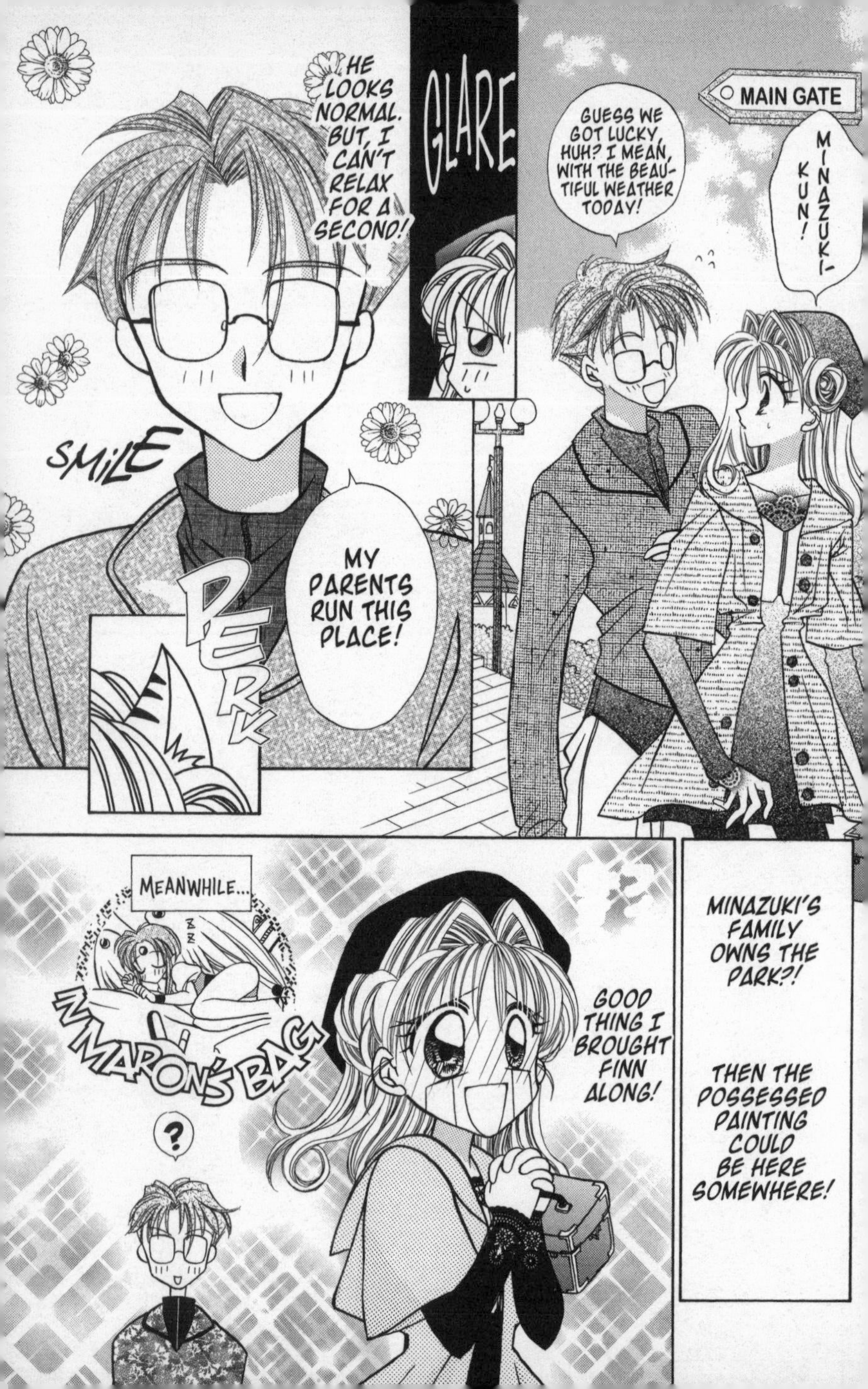
MAIN GATE
MINAZUKI-KUN!
GUESS WE GOT LUCKY HUH? I MEAN, WITH THE BEAUTIFUL WEATHER TODAY!
GLARE
HE LOOKS NORMAL. BUT, I CAN'T RELAX FOR A SECOND!
MY PARENTS RUN THIS PLACE!
SMILE
PERK
MINAZUKI'S FAMILY OWNS THE PARK?!
THEN THE POSSESSED PAINTING COULD BE HERE SOMEWHERE!
GOOD THING I BROUGHT FINN ALONG!
MEANWHILE...
IN MARON'S BAG
?

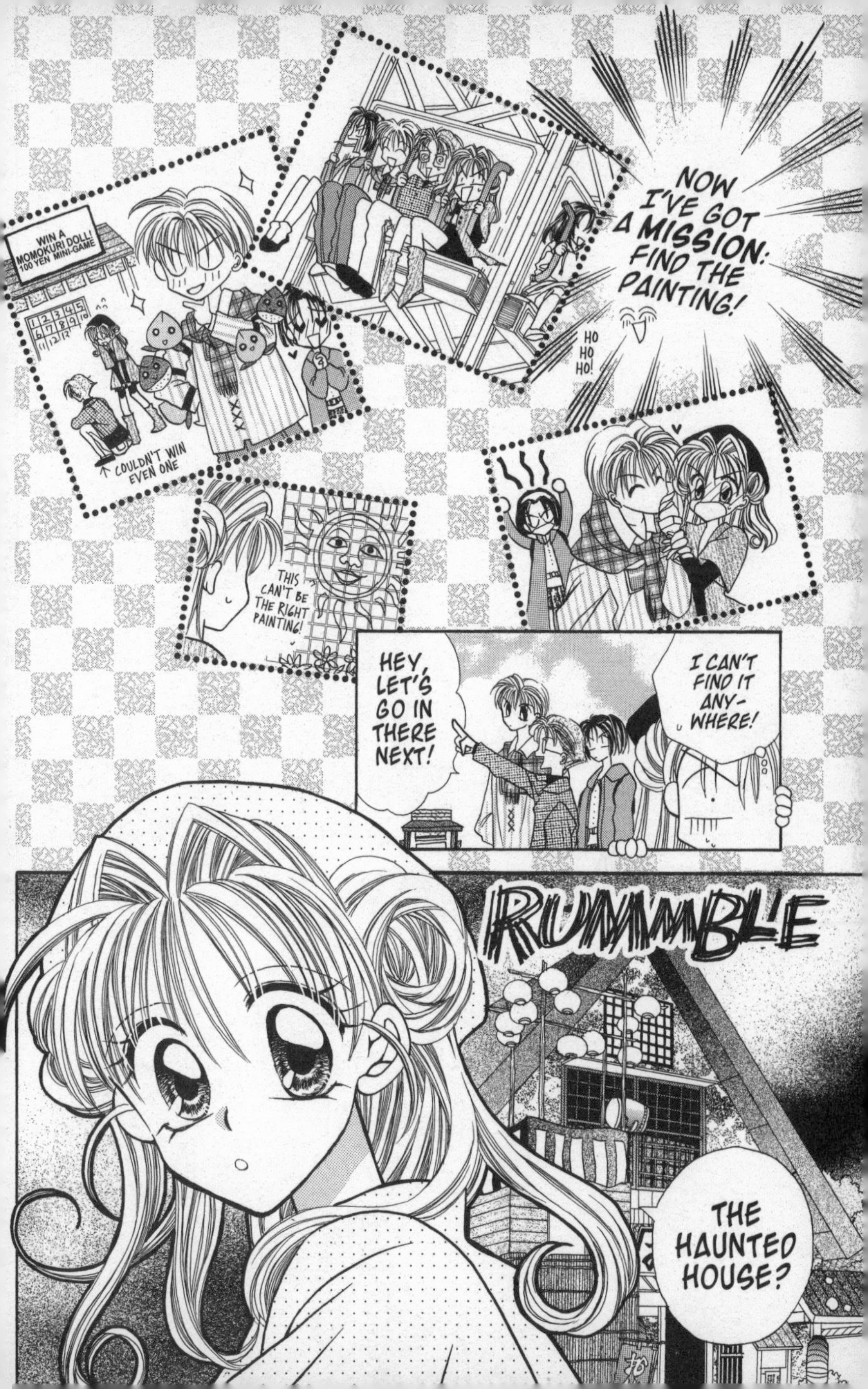
NOW I'VE GOT A MISSION: FIND THE PAINTING!
HO HO HO!
WIN A MOMOKURI DOLL! 100 YEN MINI-GAME
COULDN'T WIN EVEN ONE
THIS CAN'T BE THE RIGHT PAINTING!
I CAN'T FIND IT ANY-WHERE!
HEY, LET'S GO IN THERE NEXT!
RUMMBLE
THE HAUNTED HOUSE?

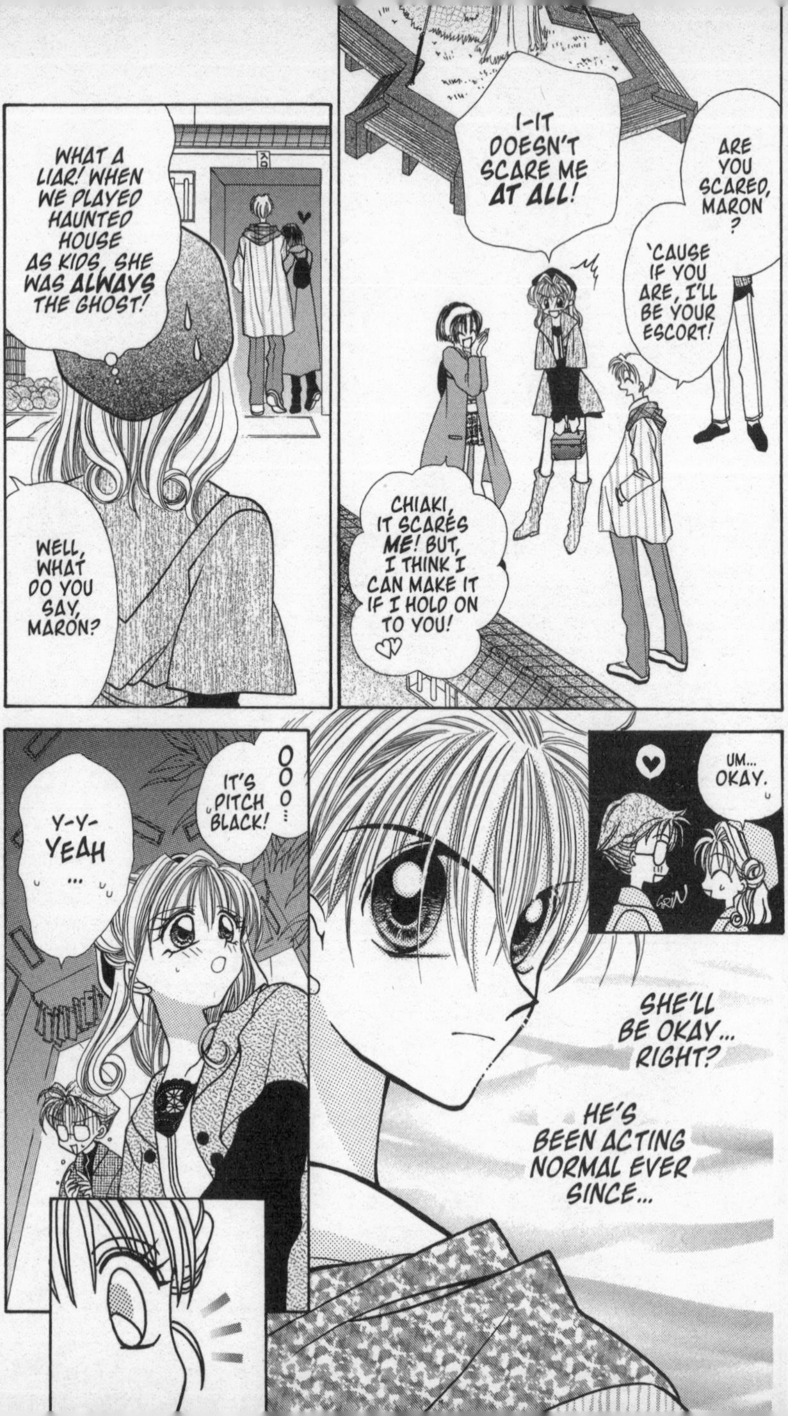
ARE YOU SCARED, MARON?
'CAUSE IF YOU ARE, I'LL BE YOUR ESCORT!
I-IT DOESN'T SCARE ME AT ALL!
CHIAKI, IT SCARES ME! BUT, I THINK I CAN MAKE IT IF I HOLD ON TO YOU!
WHAT A LIAR! WHEN WE PLAYED HAUNTED HOUSE AS KIDS, SHE WAS ALWAYS THE GHOST!
WELL, WHAT DO YOU SAY, MARON?
UM... OKAY.
GRIN
SHE'LL BE OKAY... RIGHT?
HE'S BEEN ACTING NORMAL EVER SINCE...
OOO...
IT'S PITCH BLACK!
Y-Y-YEAH ...

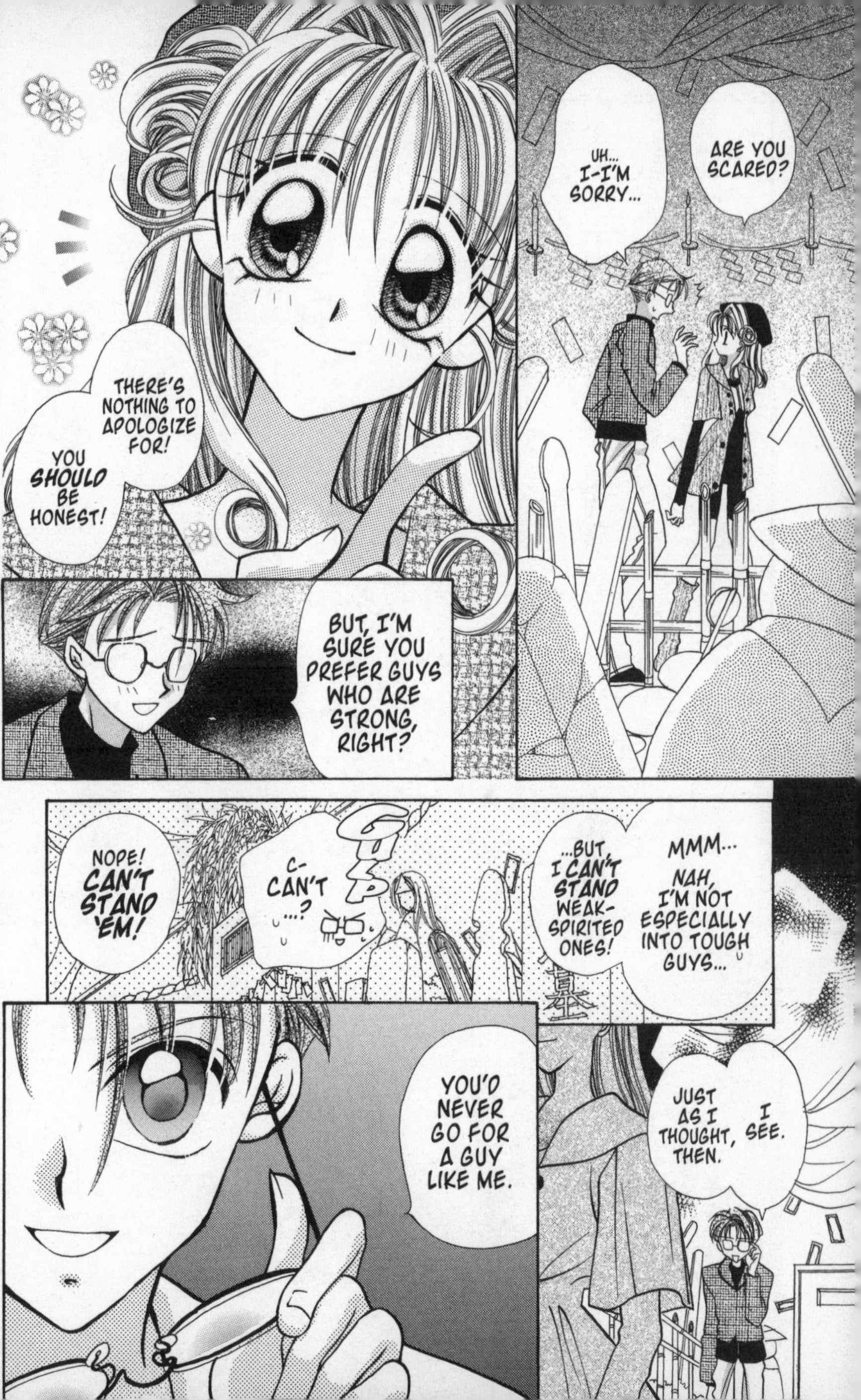
ARE YOU SCARED?
UH... I-I'M SORRY...
THERE'S NOTHING TO APOLOGIZE FOR!
YOU SHOULD BE HONEST!
BUT, I'M SURE YOU PREFER GUYS WHO ARE STRONG, RIGHT?
MMM... NAH, I'M NOT ESPECIALLY INTO TOUGH GUYS...
...BUT, I CAN'T STAND WEAK-SPIRITED ONES!
GULP
C- CAN'T ...?
NOPE! CAN'T STAND 'EM!
I SEE.
JUST AS I THOUGHT, THEN.
YOU'D NEVER GO FOR A GUY LIKE ME.

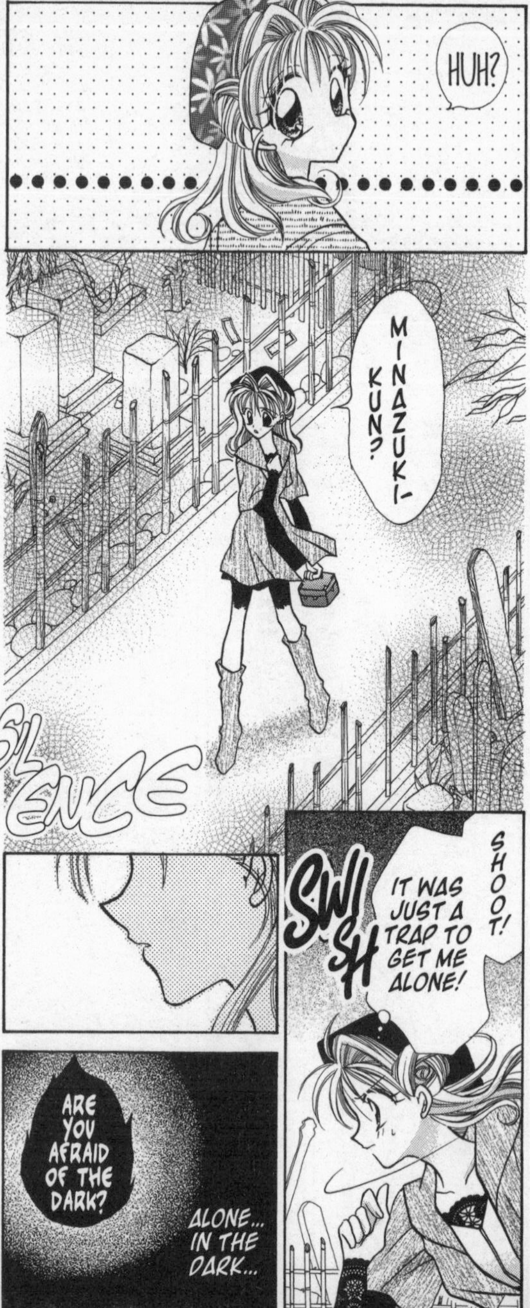
HUH?
MINAZUKI-KUN?
SILENCE
SHOOT!
IT WAS JUST A TRAP TO GET ME ALONE!
SWISH
ARE YOU AFRAID OF THE DARK?
ALONE... IN THE DARK...

AT A SIGNING: 4

So, finally, the signing began and the fans came right up to me one after another. But, because it was my first fan exposure as well as the first time I had to sign so many autographs, I got majorly stressed out, which caused me to turn into a gibbering idiot!
On the other hand, a lot of fans were junior high school girls, who were so sweet! They gave me presents, letters, etc. (completely unexpected!), which made me so happy! I especially loved the beautiful flowers that I received during the 3pm signing session! Also memorable was a present that was sent to me all the way from aichi prefecture via a delivery service, but the only thing that I personally carried all the way home was that bouquet of flowers. I really love carrying flowers around in my arms, but hardly have any opportunities to do so, which is why I appreciated them all the more!

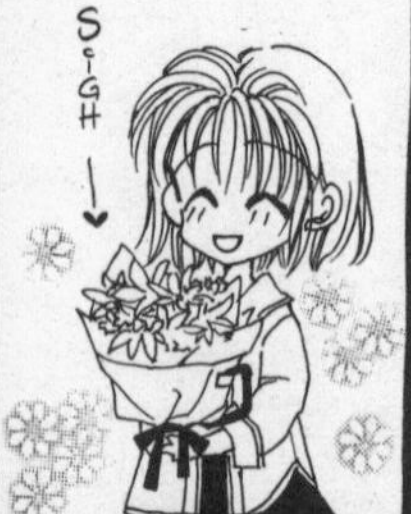
SIGH

CONTINUED IN #5>>

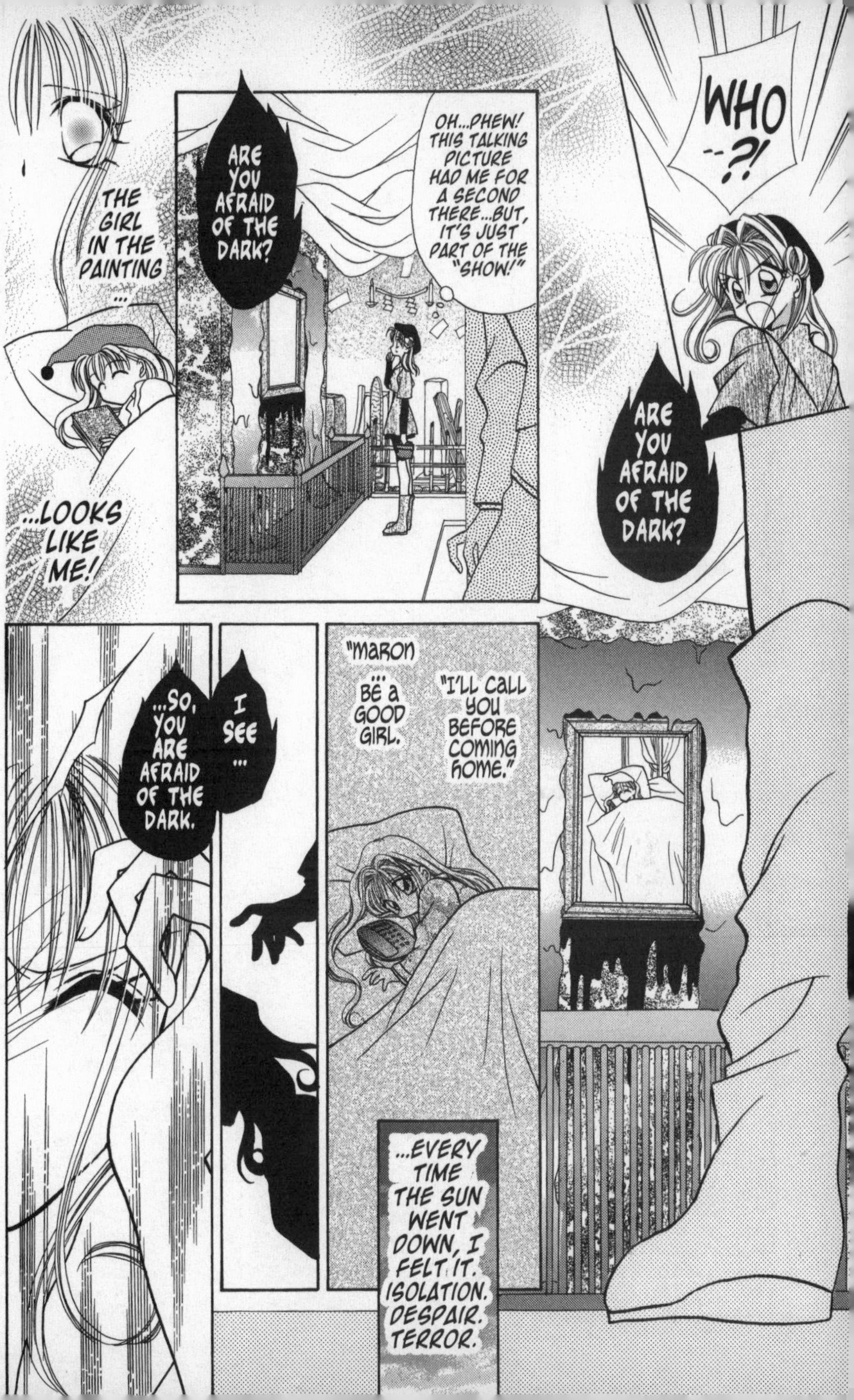
WHO --?!
ARE YOU AFRAID OF THE DARK?
OH...PHEW! THIS TALKING PICTURE HAD ME FOR A SECOND THERE...BUT, IT'S JUST PART OF THE "SHOW!"
ARE YOU AFRAID OF THE DARK?
THE GIRL IN THE PAINTING ...
...LOOKS LIKE ME!
"MARON ... BE A GOOD GIRL.
"I'LL CALL YOU BEFORE COMING HOME."
...EVERY TIME THE SUN WENT DOWN, I FELT IT. ISOLATION. DESPAIR. TERROR.
I SEE ...
...SO, YOU ARE AFRAID OF THE DARK.

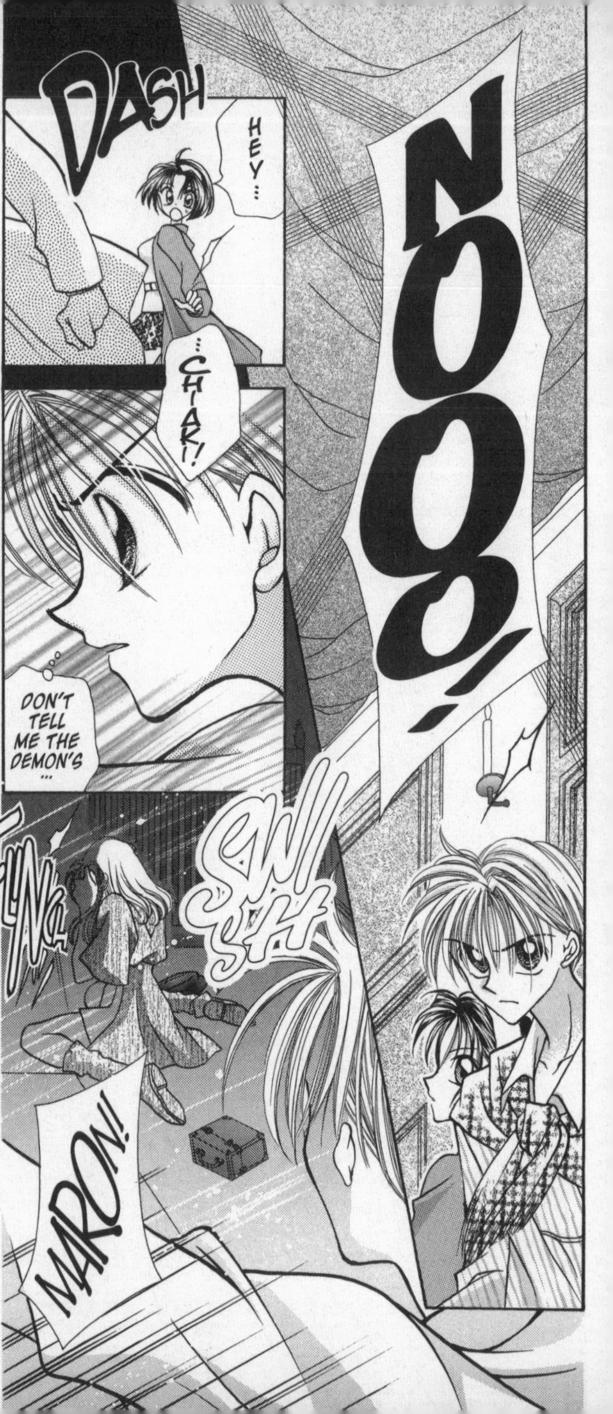
NOOO!
DASH
HEY...
...CHIAKI!
DON'T TELL ME THE DEMON'S...
SWISH
FLING
MARON!

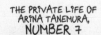

THE PRIVATE LIFE OF ARINA TANEMURA, NUMBER 7

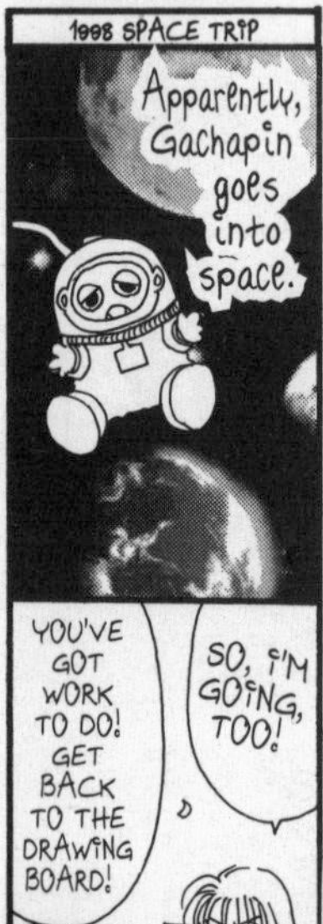
1998 SPACE TRIP
Apparently, Gachapin goes into space.
SO, I'M GOING, TOO!
YOU'VE GOT WORK TO DO! GET BACK TO THE DRAWING BOARD!
SSSS
QUIT TRYIN' TO ESCAPE!

I wonder if he'll still be in space by the time this sees print. Gachapin has been my favorite kids' TV show mascot ever since I was a little girl.
This has nothing to do with the above, but one of my assistants looks just like Gachapin. I'm talking the spitting image!

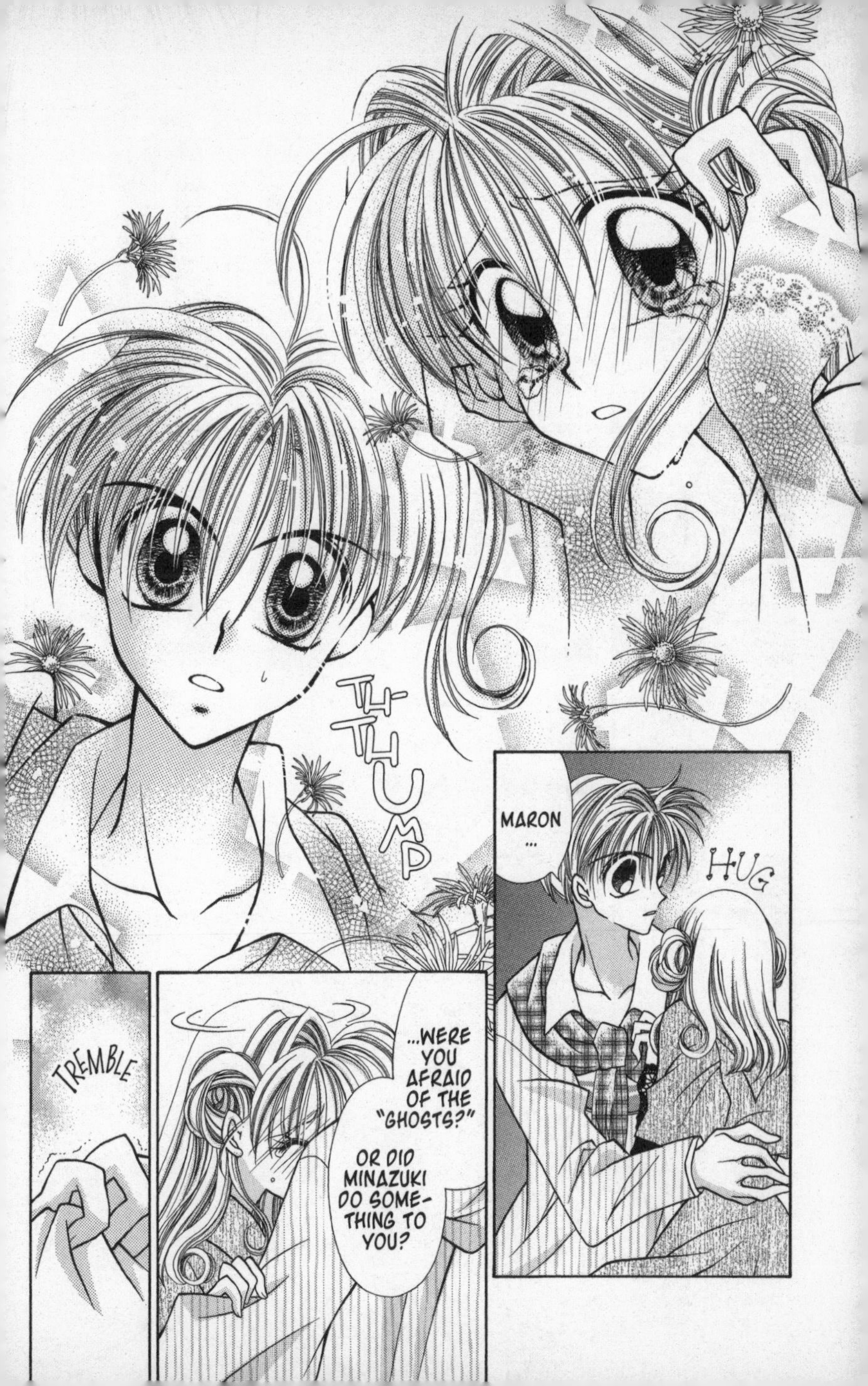
TH-THUMP
MARON ...
HUG
...WERE YOU AFRAID OF THE "GHOSTS?"
OR DID MINAZUKI DO SOME-THING TO YOU?
TREMBLE

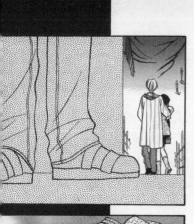

IT'S OKAY NOW.

MARON...

...YOU'RE OKAY.

YOU'RE SAFE.

CRUD!

HE HEARD HER SCREAM AND CAME RUNNING!

BUMP

OH!

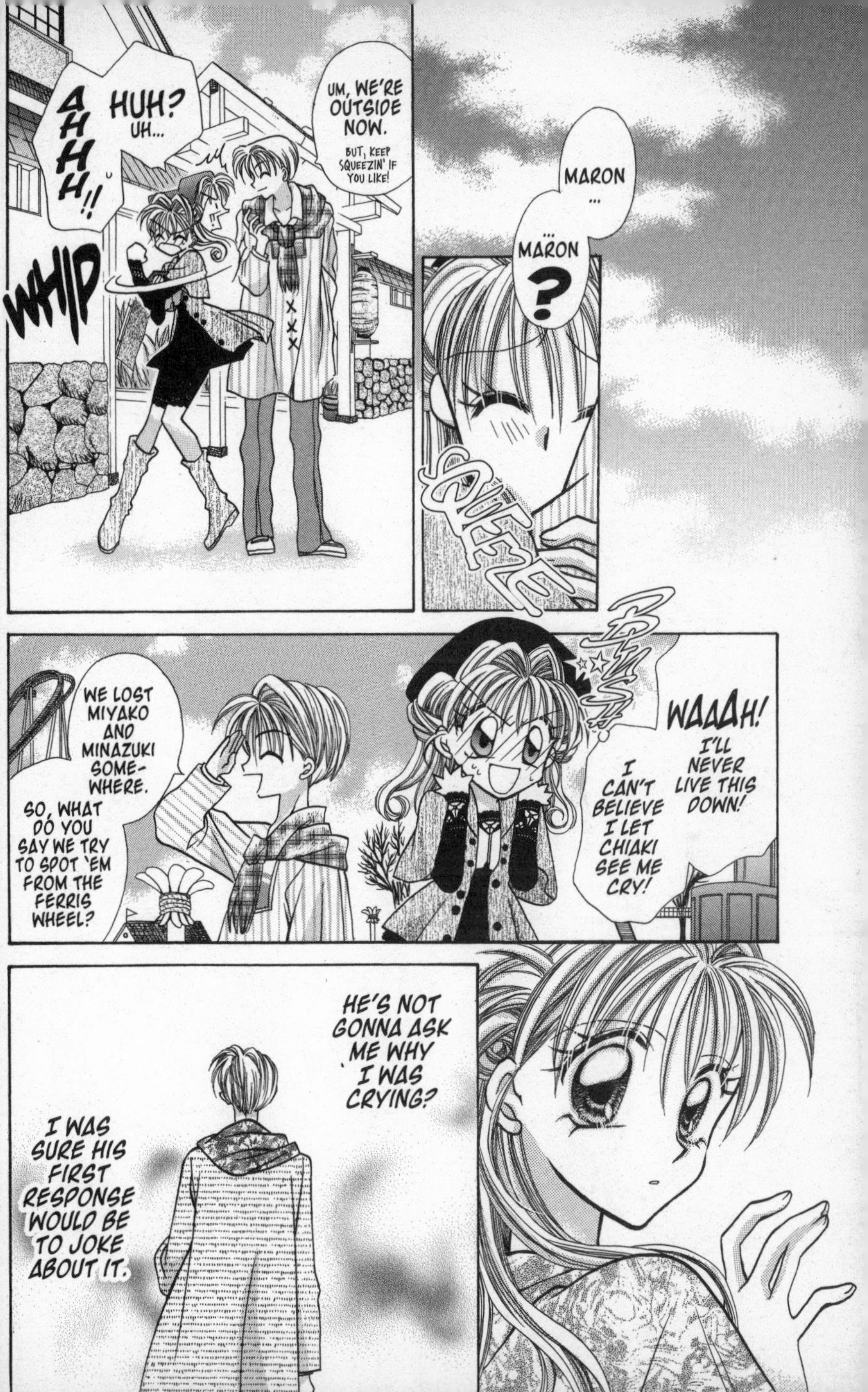
MARON ...
... MARON ?
SQUEEZE
UM, WE'RE OUTSIDE NOW.
BUT, KEEP SQUEEZIN' IF YOU LIKE!
HUH? UH...
AHHHH!!
WHIP
WAAAH!
I'LL NEVER LIVE THIS DOWN!
I CAN'T BELIEVE I LET CHIAKI SEE ME CRY!
WE LOST MIYAKO AND MINAZUKI SOME-WHERE.
SO, WHAT DO YOU SAY WE TRY TO SPOT 'EM FROM THE FERRIS WHEEL?
HE'S NOT GONNA ASK ME WHY I WAS CRYING?
I WAS SURE HIS FIRST RESPONSE WOULD BE TO JOKE ABOUT IT.

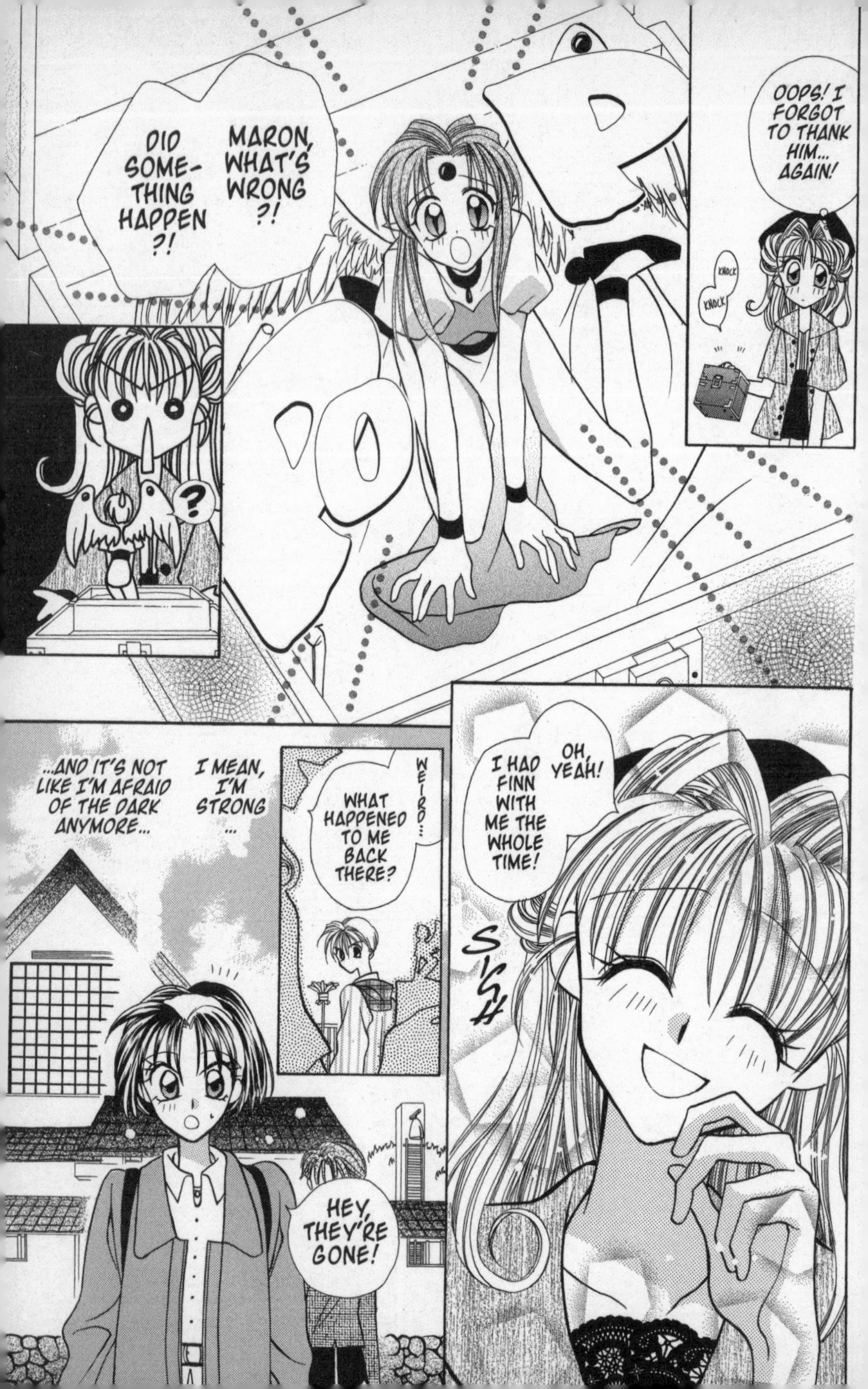
OOPS! I FORGOT TO THANK HIM... AGAIN!
KNOCK
KNOCK
MARON, WHAT'S WRONG?!
DID SOMETHING HAPPEN?!
?
OH, YEAH!
I HAD FINN WITH ME THE WHOLE TIME!
SIGH
WEIRD...
WHAT HAPPENED TO ME BACK THERE?
I MEAN, I'M STRONG...
...AND IT'S NOT LIKE I'M AFRAID OF THE DARK ANYMORE...
HEY, THEY'RE GONE!

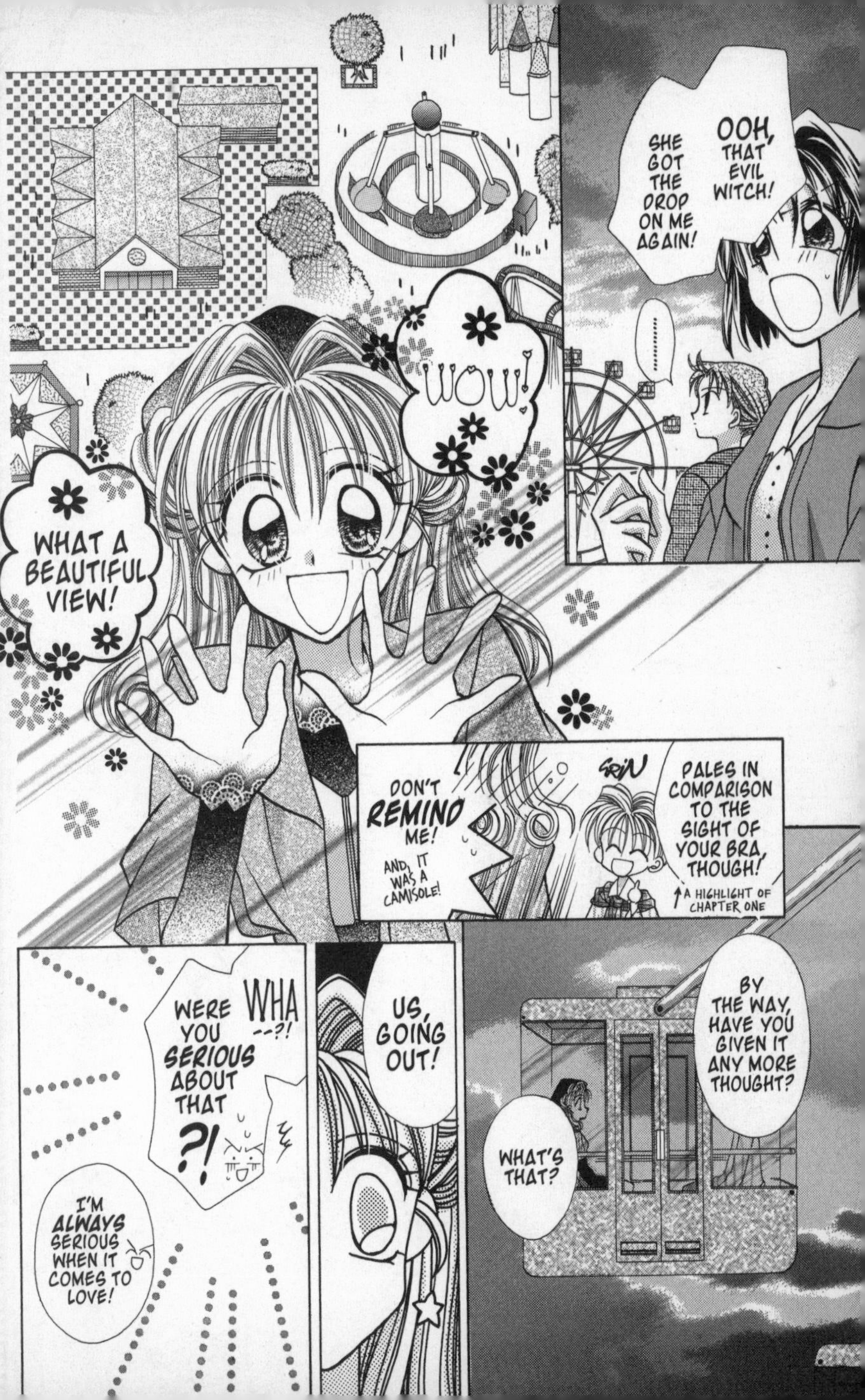

OOH, THAT EVIL WITCH!
SHE GOT THE DROP ON ME AGAIN!
......
WOW!
WHAT A BEAUTIFUL VIEW!
PALES IN COMPARISON TO THE SIGHT OF YOUR BRA, THOUGH!
GRIN
↑A HIGHLIGHT OF CHAPTER ONE
DON'T REMIND ME!
AND, IT WAS A CAMISOLE!
BY THE WAY, HAVE YOU GIVEN IT ANY MORE THOUGHT?
WHAT'S THAT?
US, GOING OUT!
WHA--?!
WERE YOU SERIOUS ABOUT THAT?!
I'M ALWAYS SERIOUS WHEN IT COMES TO LOVE!

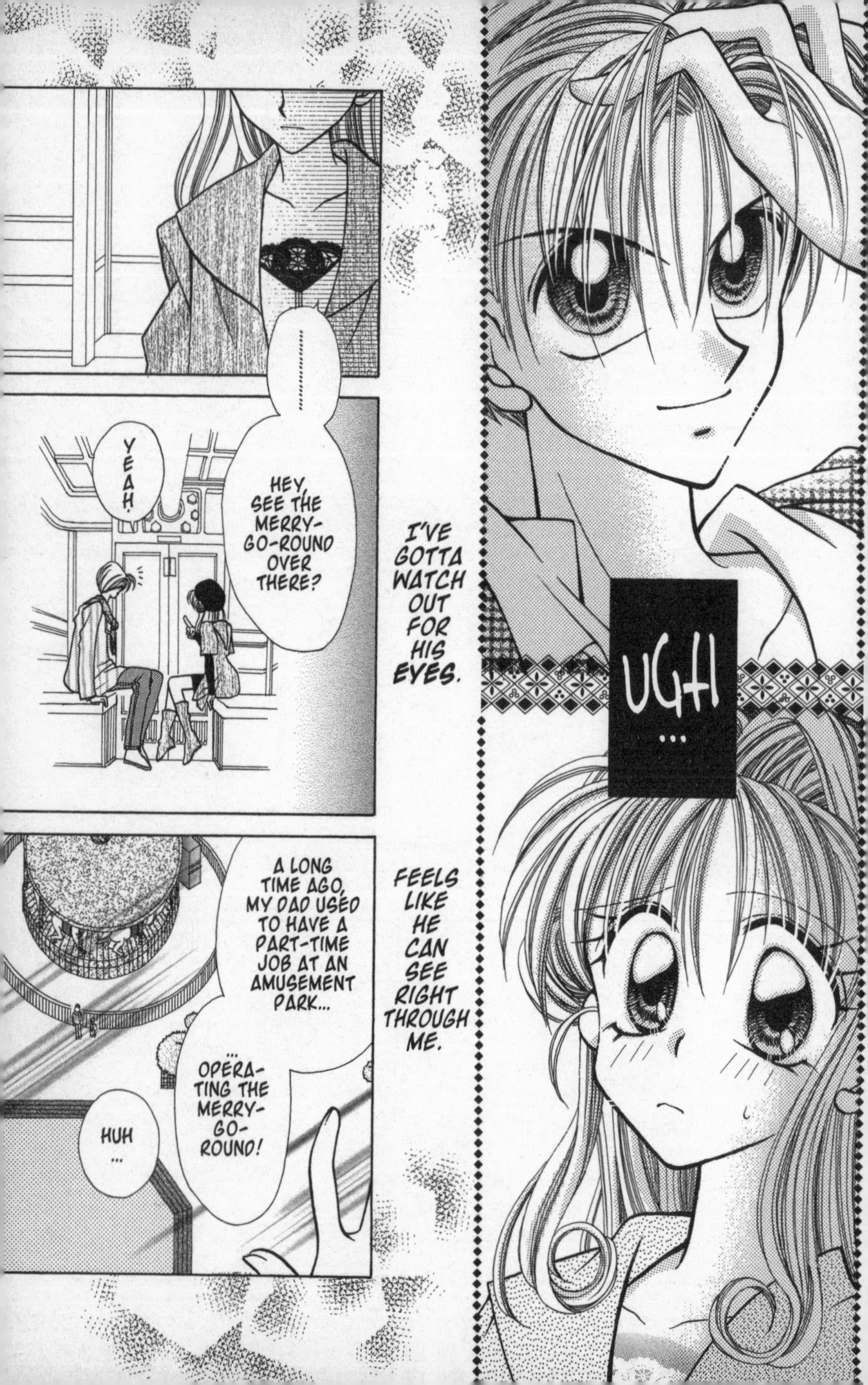
UGH...
I'VE GOTTA WATCH OUT FOR HIS EYES.
FEELS LIKE HE CAN SEE RIGHT THROUGH ME.
......
HEY, SEE THE MERRY-GO-ROUND OVER THERE?
YEAH!
A LONG TIME AGO, MY DAD USED TO HAVE A PART-TIME JOB AT AN AMUSEMENT PARK...
...OPERATING THE MERRY-GO-ROUND!
HUH...

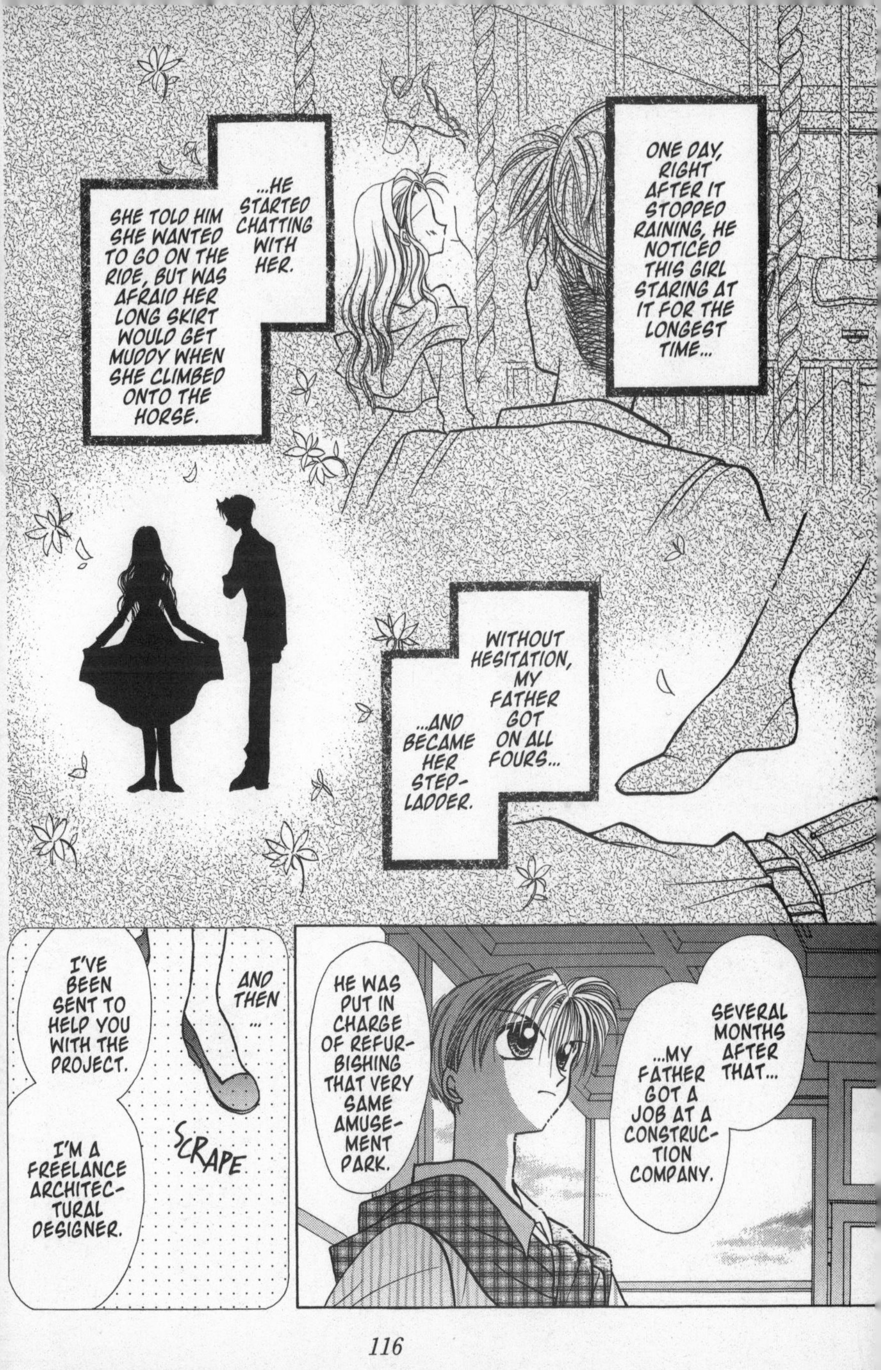
ONE DAY, RIGHT AFTER IT STOPPED RAINING, HE NOTICED THIS GIRL STARING AT IT FOR THE LONGEST TIME...
...HE STARTED CHATTING WITH HER.
SHE TOLD HIM SHE WANTED TO GO ON THE RIDE, BUT WAS AFRAID HER LONG SKIRT WOULD GET MUDDY WHEN SHE CLIMBED ONTO THE HORSE.
WITHOUT HESITATION, MY FATHER GOT ON ALL FOURS...
...AND BECAME HER STEP-LADDER.
SEVERAL MONTHS AFTER THAT...
...MY FATHER GOT A JOB AT A CONSTRUC-TION COMPANY.
HE WAS PUT IN CHARGE OF REFUR-BISHING THAT VERY SAME AMUSE-MENT PARK.
AND THEN...
I'VE BEEN SENT TO HELP YOU WITH THE PROJECT.
SCRAPE
I'M A FREELANCE ARCHITEC-TURAL DESIGNER.

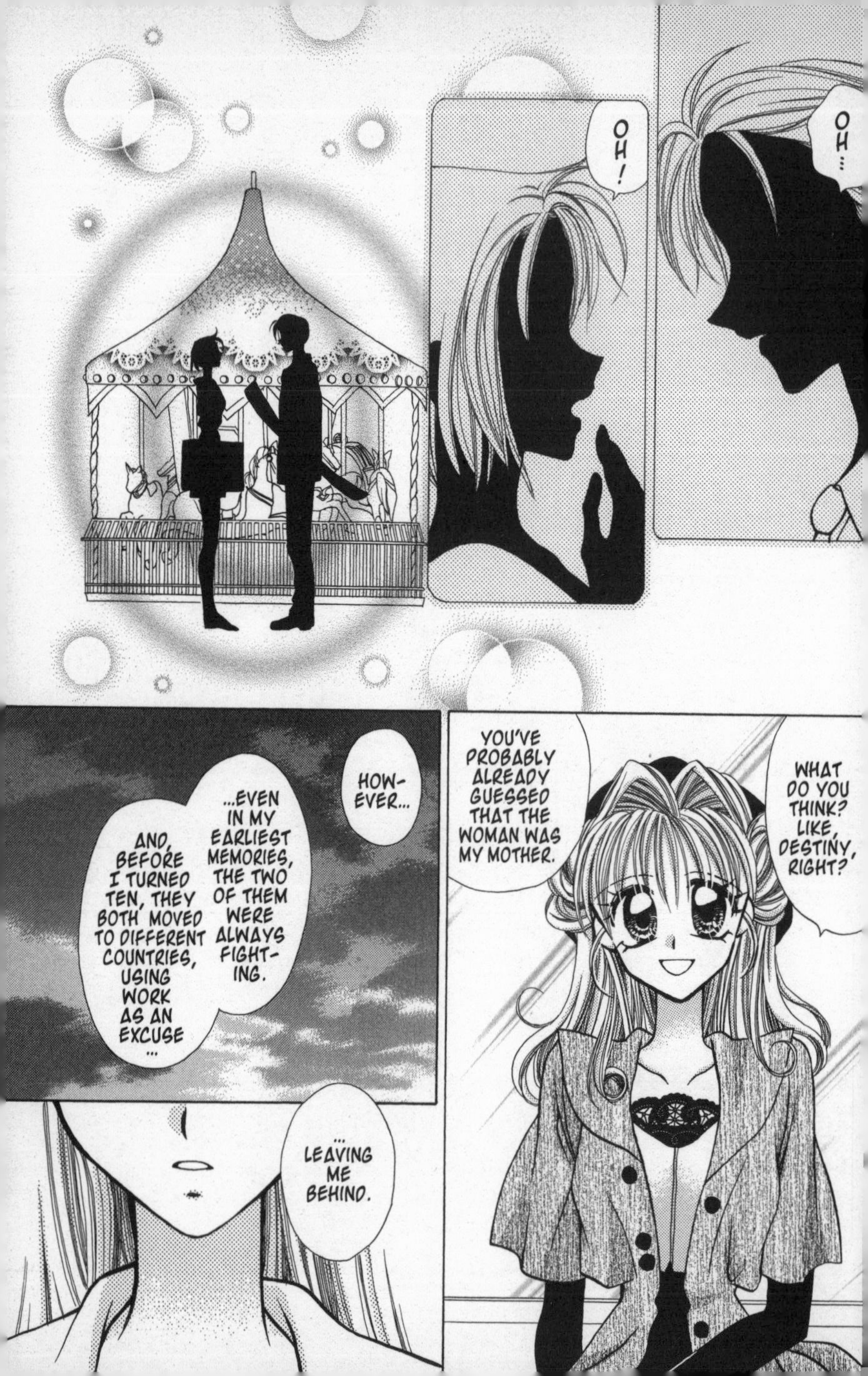
OH...
OH!
WHAT DO YOU THINK? LIKE, DESTINY, RIGHT?
YOU'VE PROBABLY ALREADY GUESSED THAT THE WOMAN WAS MY MOTHER.
HOW-EVER...
...EVEN IN MY EARLIEST MEMORIES, THE TWO OF THEM WERE ALWAYS FIGHT-ING.
AND, BEFORE I TURNED TEN, THEY BOTH MOVED TO DIFFERENT COUNTRIES, USING WORK AS AN EXCUSE ...
...LEAVING ME BEHIND.

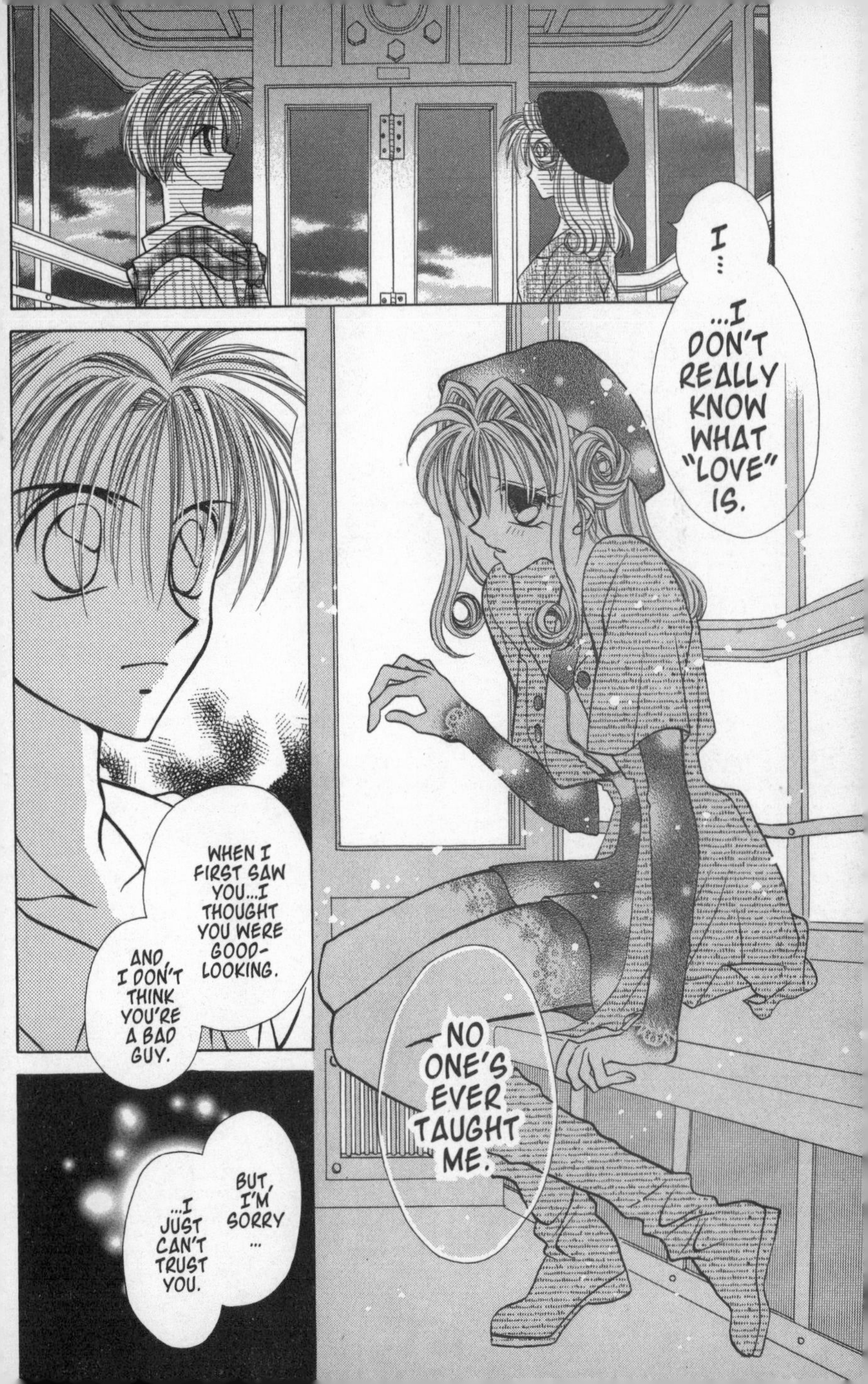
I...
...I DON'T REALLY KNOW WHAT "LOVE" IS.
NO ONE'S EVER TAUGHT ME.
WHEN I FIRST SAW YOU...I THOUGHT YOU WERE GOOD-LOOKING.
AND I DON'T THINK YOU'RE A BAD GUY.
BUT, I'M SORRY...
...I JUST CAN'T TRUST YOU.

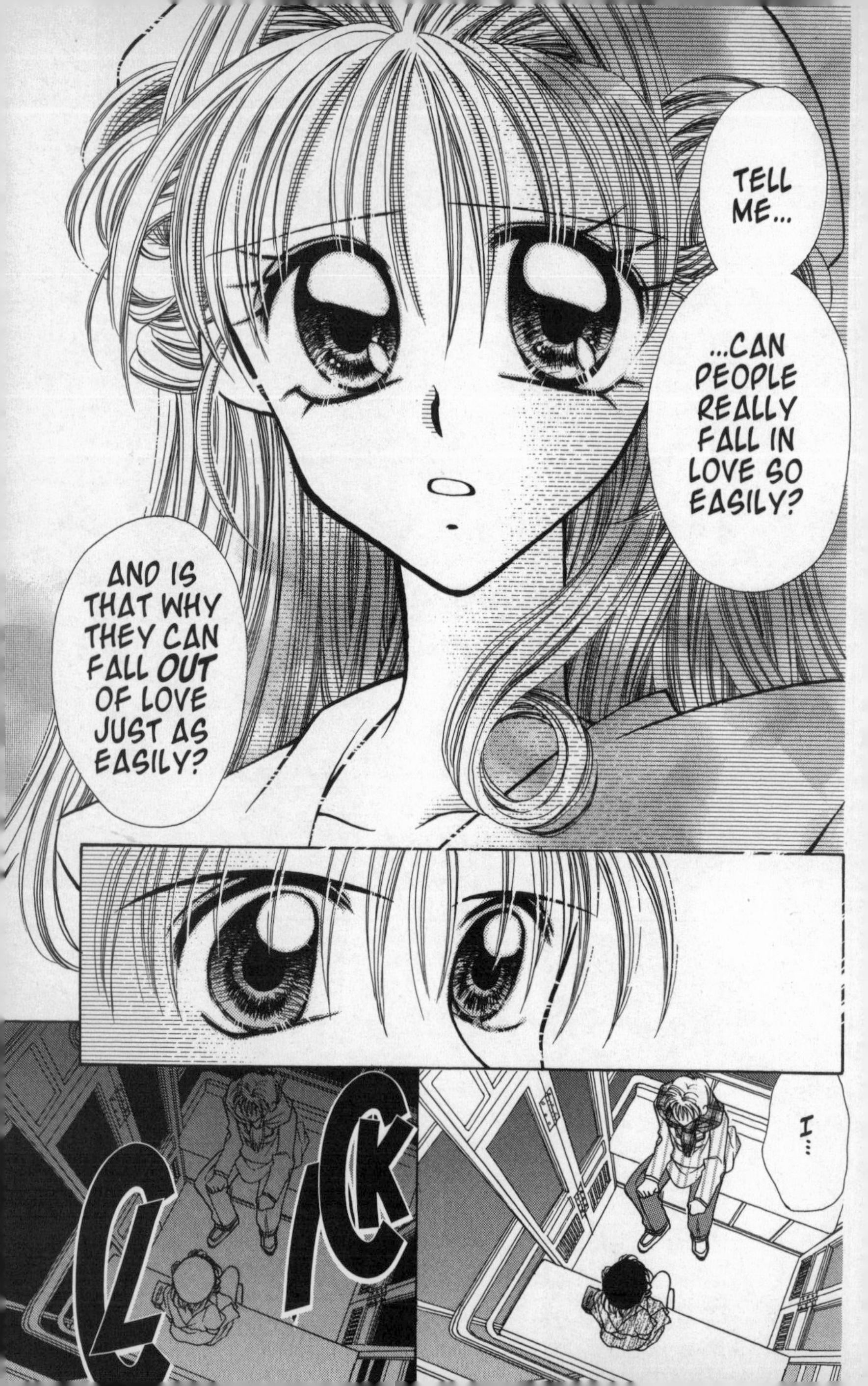
TELL ME...
...CAN PEOPLE REALLY FALL IN LOVE SO EASILY?
AND IS THAT WHY THEY CAN FALL OUT OF LOVE JUST AS EASILY?
I...
CLICK

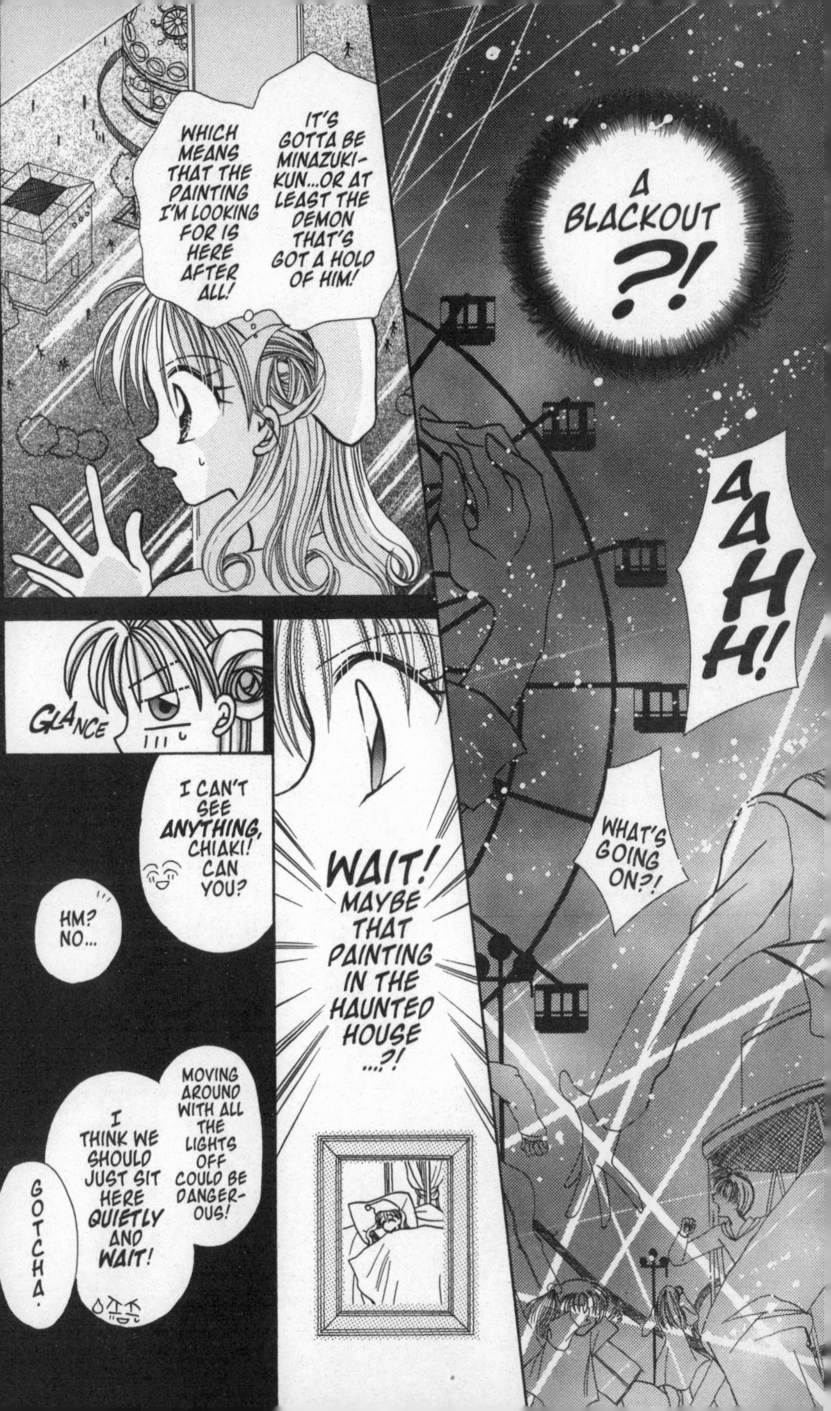
A BLACKOUT ?!
AAHH!
WHAT'S GOING ON?!
IT'S GOTTA BE MINAZUKI-KUN...OR AT LEAST THE DEMON THAT'S GOT A HOLD OF HIM!
WHICH MEANS THAT THE PAINTING I'M LOOKING FOR IS HERE AFTER ALL!
WAIT! MAYBE THAT PAINTING IN THE HAUNTED HOUSE ...?!
GLANCE
I CAN'T SEE ANYTHING, CHIAKI! CAN YOU?
HM? NO...
MOVING AROUND WITH ALL THE LIGHTS OFF COULD BE DANGEROUS!
I THINK WE SHOULD JUST SIT HERE QUIETLY AND WAIT!
GOTCHA.

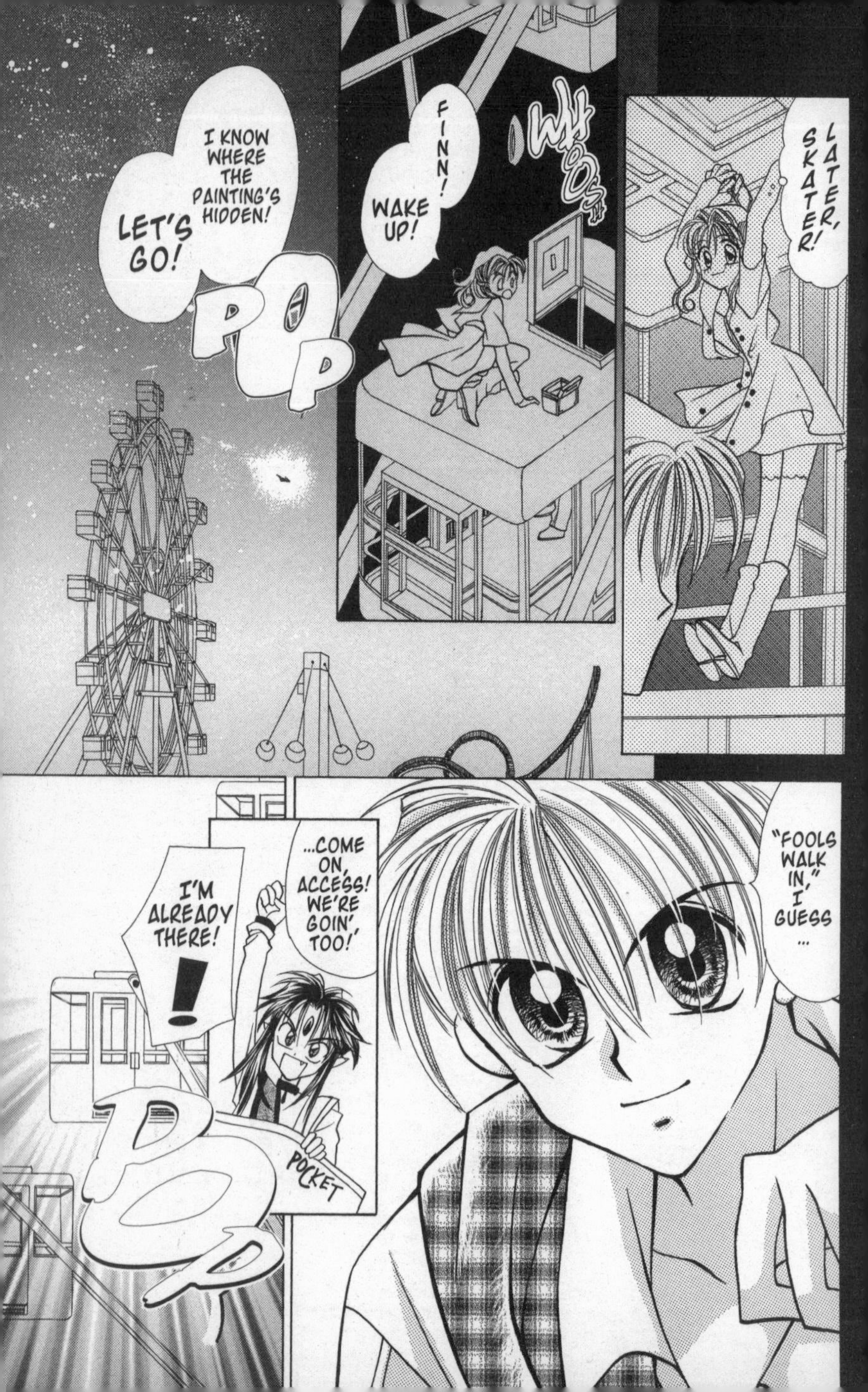
LATER, SKATER!
FINN! WAKE UP!
WHOOSH
I KNOW WHERE THE PAINTING'S HIDDEN!
LET'S GO!
POP
"FOOLS WALK IN," I GUESS ...
...COME ON, ACCESS! WE'RE GOIN' TOO!
I'M ALREADY THERE!
!
POCKET

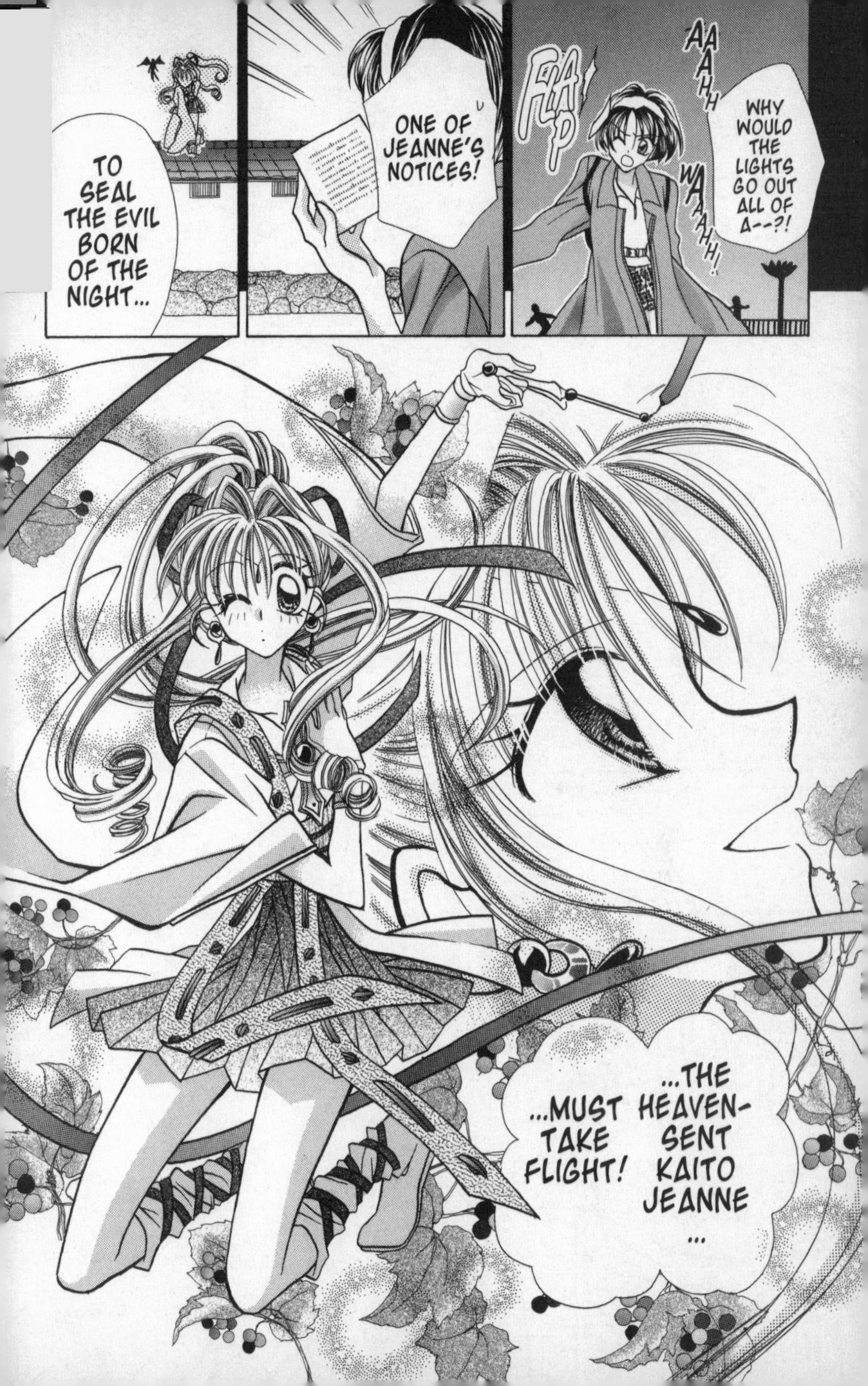
AAAAHH WAAAHH!
FLAP!
WHY WOULD THE LIGHTS GO OUT ALL OF A--?!
ONE OF JEANNE'S NOTICES!
TO SEAL THE EVIL BORN OF THE NIGHT...
...THE HEAVEN-SENT KAITO JEANNE...
...MUST TAKE FLIGHT!

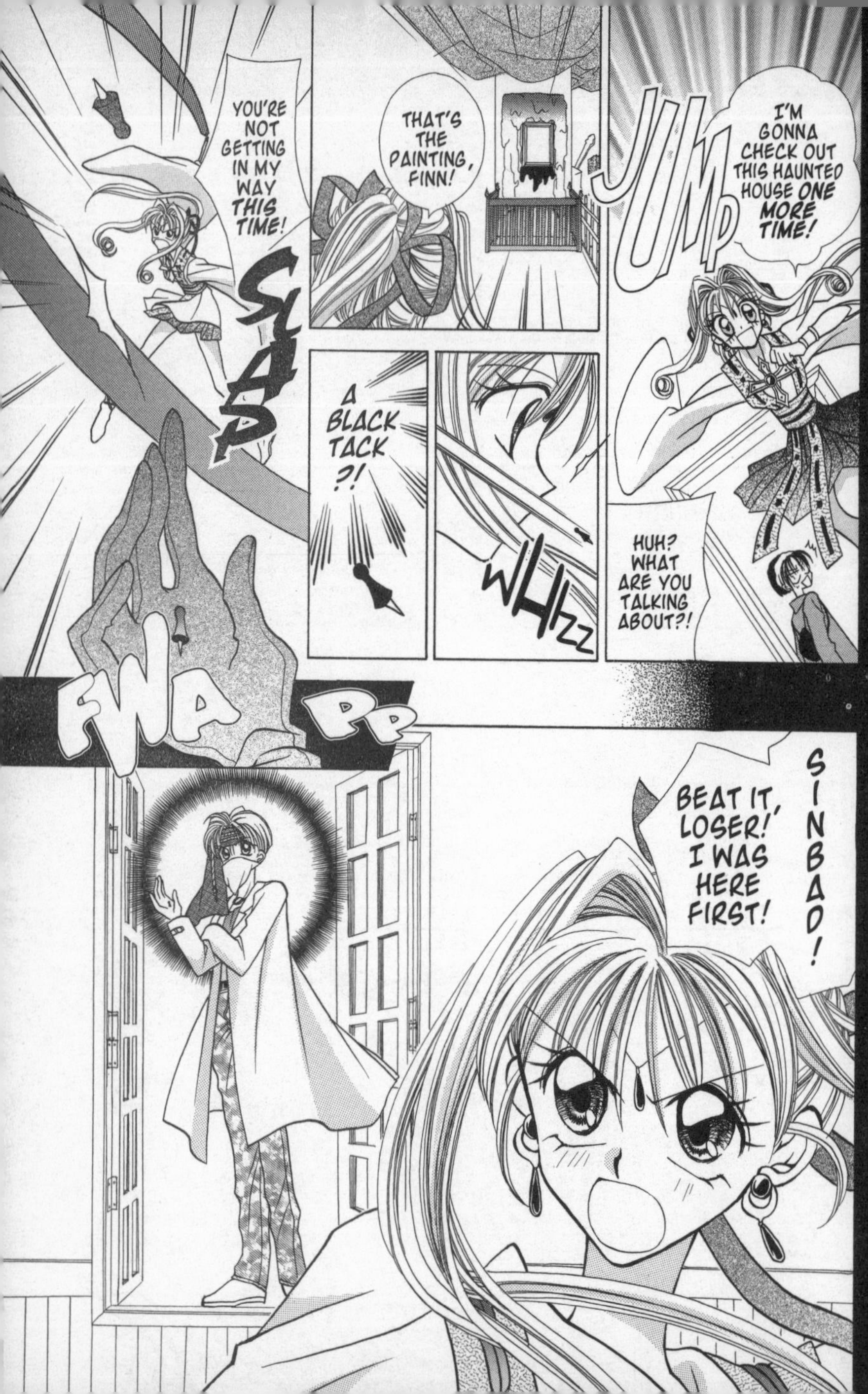

JUMP
I'M GONNA CHECK OUT THIS HAUNTED HOUSE ONE MORE TIME!
HUH? WHAT ARE YOU TALKING ABOUT?!
THAT'S THE PAINTING, FINN!
WHIZZ
A BLACK TACK ?!
YOU'RE NOT GETTING IN MY WAY THIS TIME!
SLAP
FWAPP
SINBAD!
BEAT IT, LOSER! I WAS HERE FIRST!

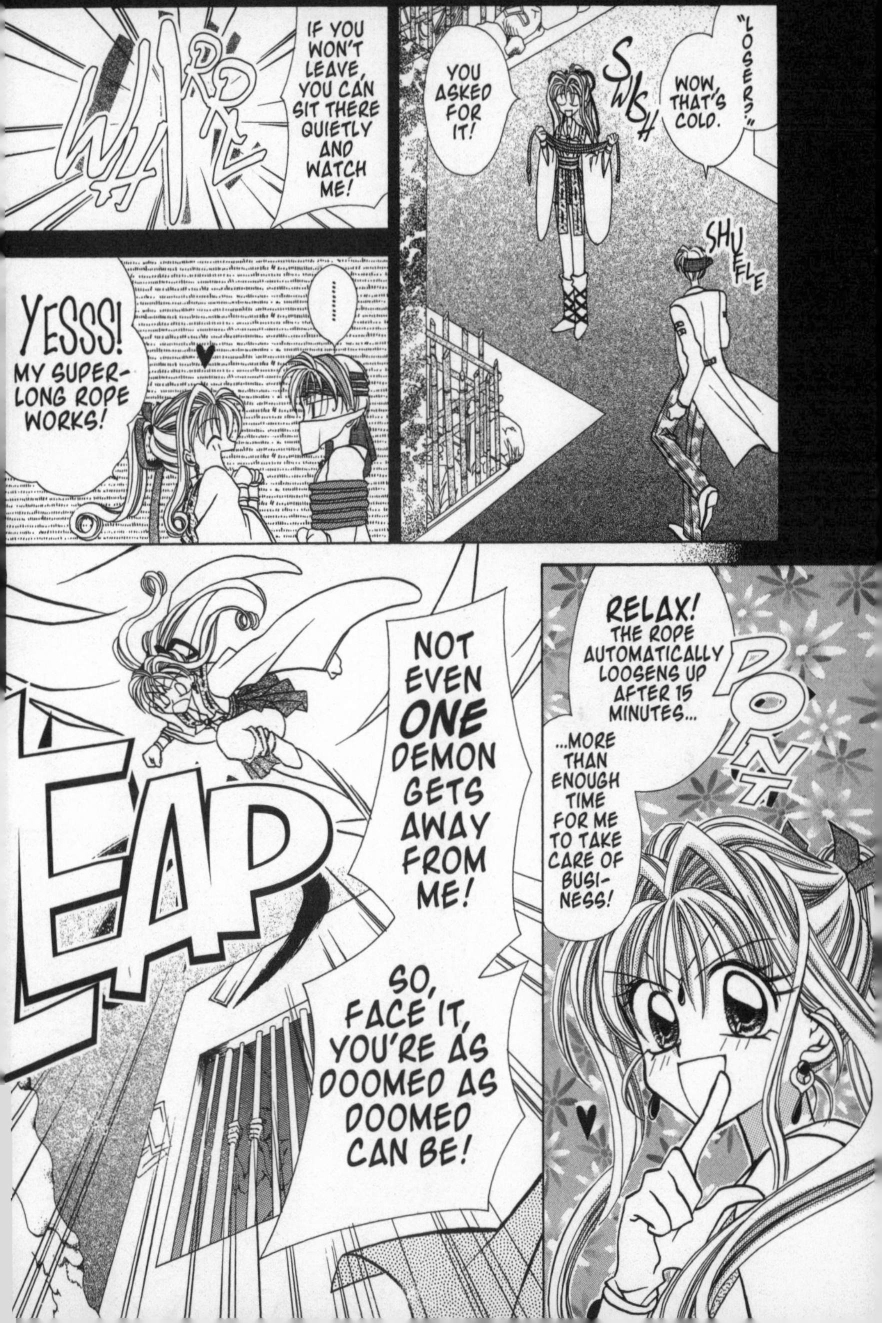
"LOSERS?"
WOW, THAT'S COLD.
SWISH
YOU ASKED FOR IT!
SHUFFLE
IF YOU WON'T LEAVE, YOU CAN SIT THERE QUIETLY AND WATCH ME!
WHIRR
......
YESSS! MY SUPER-LONG ROPE WORKS!
RELAX! THE ROPE AUTOMATICALLY LOOSENS UP AFTER 15 MINUTES...
POINT
...MORE THAN ENOUGH TIME FOR ME TO TAKE CARE OF BUSI-NESS!
NOT EVEN ONE DEMON GETS AWAY FROM ME!
SO, FACE IT, YOU'RE AS DOOMED AS DOOMED CAN BE!
LEAP

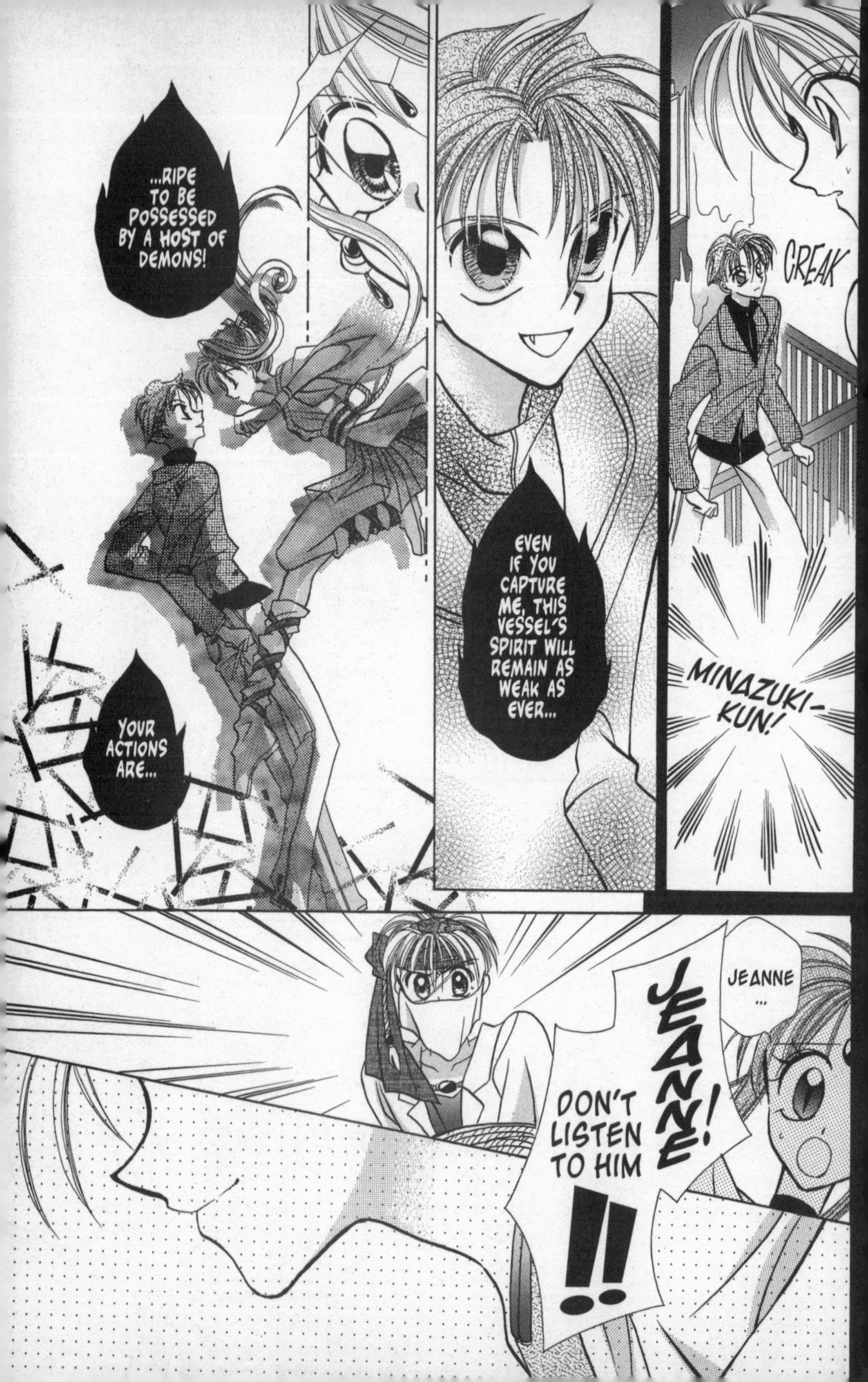
CREAK
MINAZUKI-KUN!
EVEN IF YOU CAPTURE ME, THIS VESSEL'S SPIRIT WILL REMAIN AS WEAK AS EVER...
...RIPE TO BE POSSESSED BY A HOST OF DEMONS!
YOUR ACTIONS ARE...
JEANNE ...
JEANNE!
DON'T LISTEN TO HIM!!

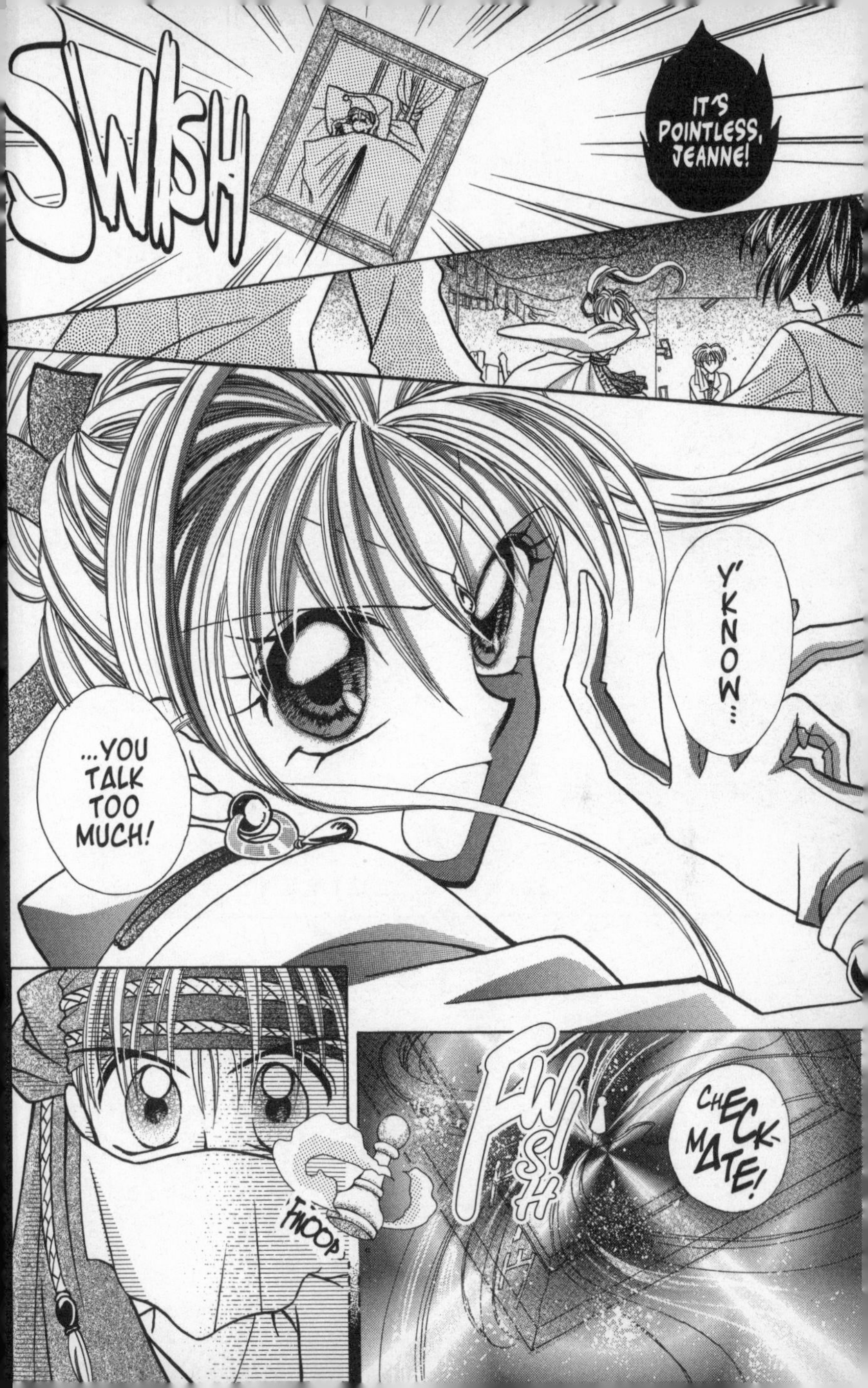
IT'S POINTLESS, JEANNE!
SWISH
Y'KNOW...
...YOU TALK TOO MUCH!
CHECK-MATE!
FWISH
FWOOP

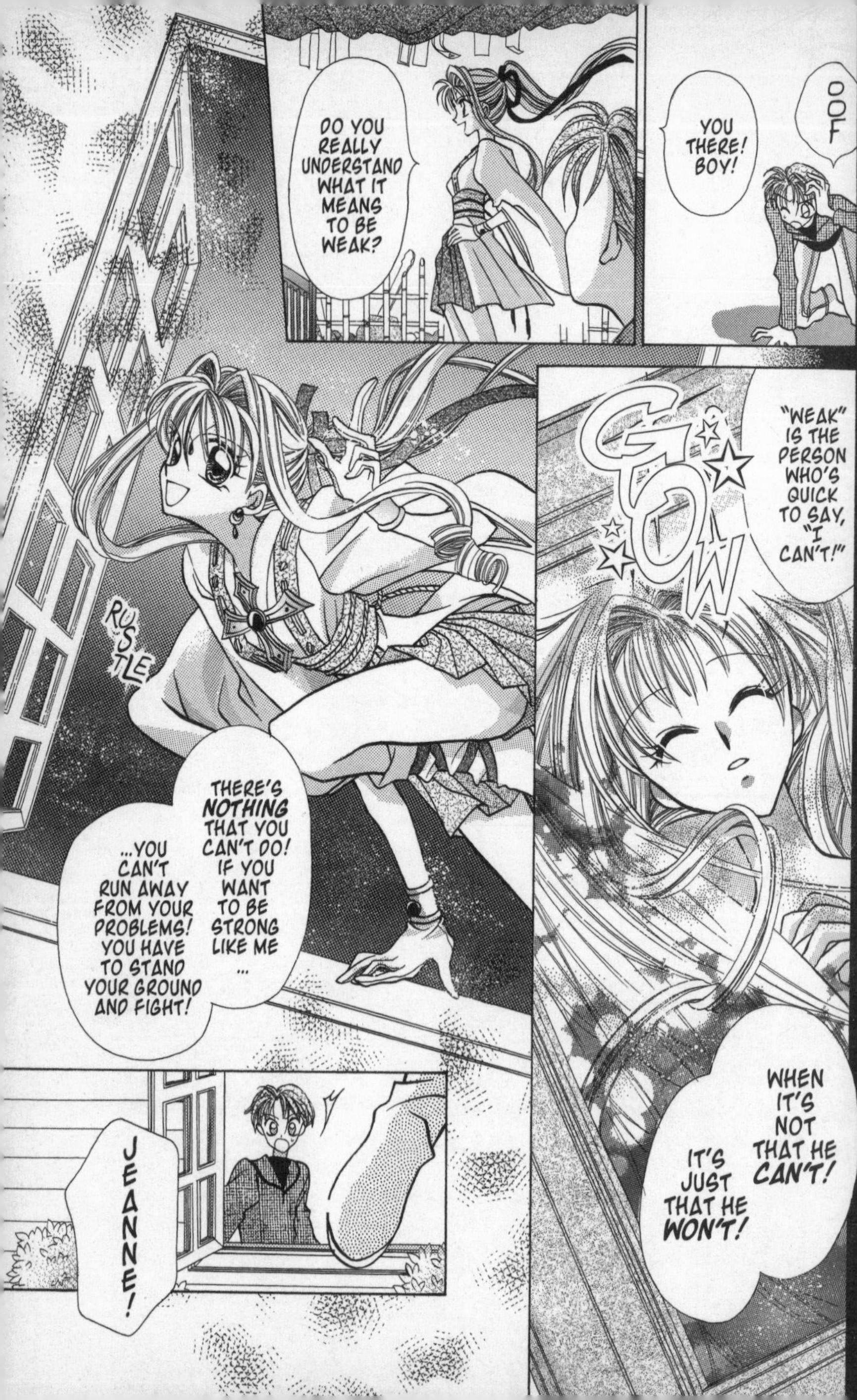
OOF
YOU THERE! BOY!
DO YOU REALLY UNDERSTAND WHAT IT MEANS TO BE WEAK?
GOOW
"WEAK" IS THE PERSON WHO'S QUICK TO SAY, "I CAN'T!"
WHEN IT'S NOT THAT HE CAN'T!
IT'S JUST THAT HE WON'T!
RUSTLE
THERE'S NOTHING THAT YOU CAN'T DO! IF YOU WANT TO BE STRONG LIKE ME ...
...YOU CAN'T RUN AWAY FROM YOUR PROBLEMS! YOU HAVE TO STAND YOUR GROUND AND FIGHT!
JEANNE!

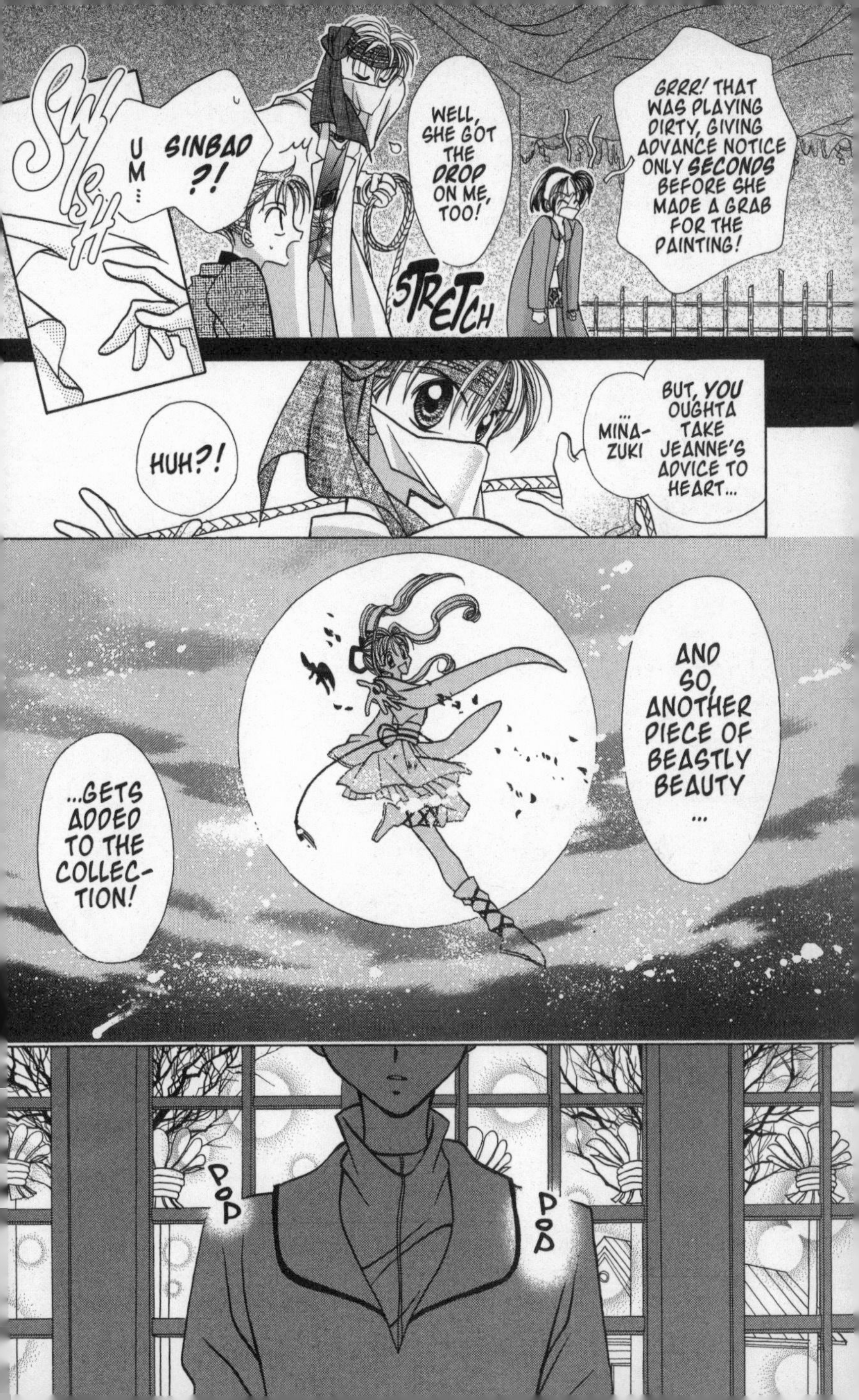
GRRR! THAT WAS PLAYING DIRTY, GIVING ADVANCE NOTICE ONLY **SECONDS** BEFORE SHE MADE A GRAB FOR THE PAINTING!
WELL, SHE GOT THE *DROP* ON ME, TOO!
STRETCH
SINBAD ?!
UM...
SWISH
BUT, *YOU* OUGHTA TAKE JEANNE'S ADVICE TO HEART...
...MINA-ZUKI
HUH?!
AND SO, ANOTHER PIECE OF BEASTLY BEAUTY ...
...GETS ADDED TO THE COLLEC-TION!
POP
POP

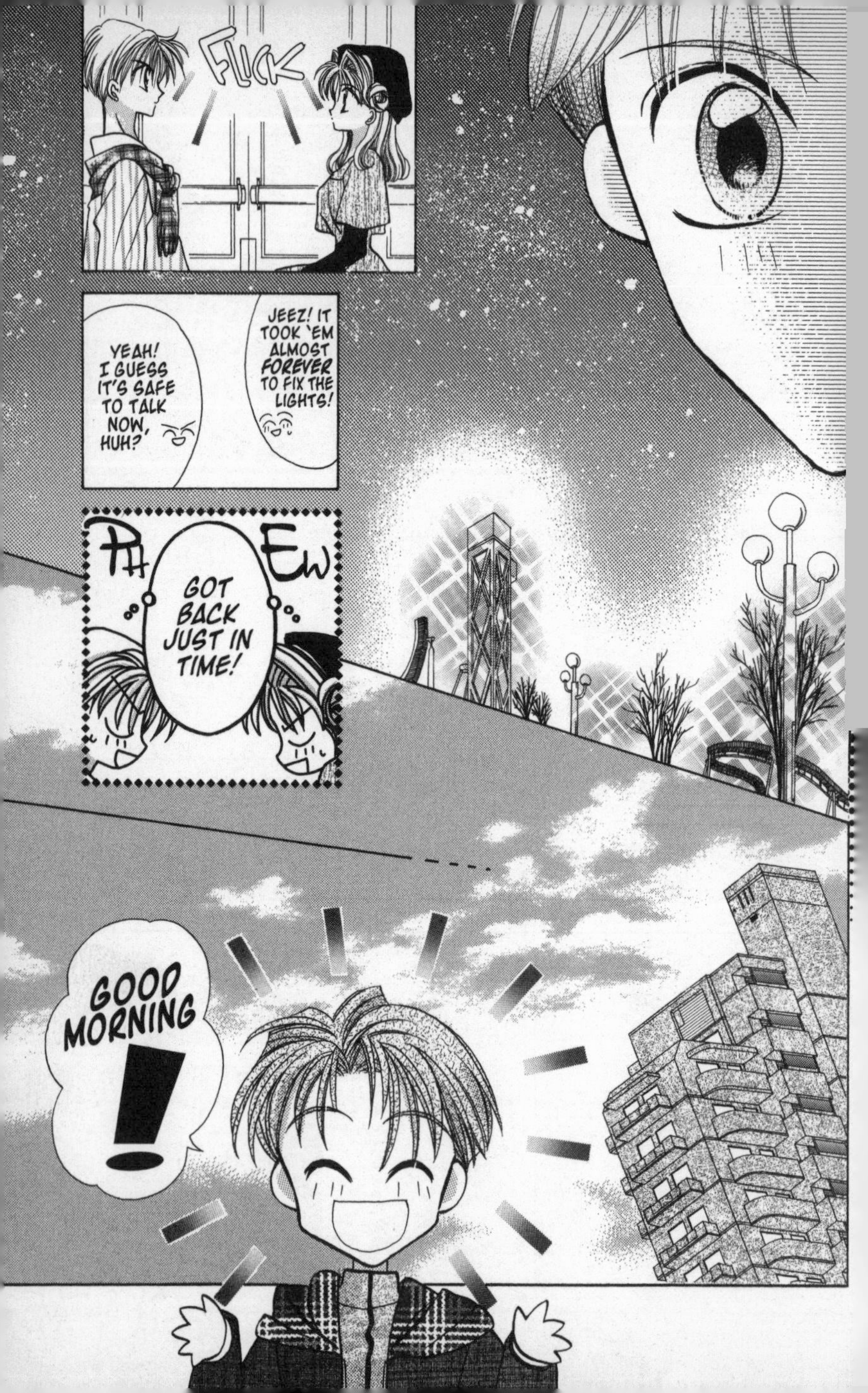
FLICK
JEEZ! IT TOOK 'EM ALMOST FOREVER TO FIX THE LIGHTS!
YEAH! I GUESS IT'S SAFE TO TALK NOW, HUH?
PHEW
GOT BACK JUST IN TIME!
GOOD MORNING!

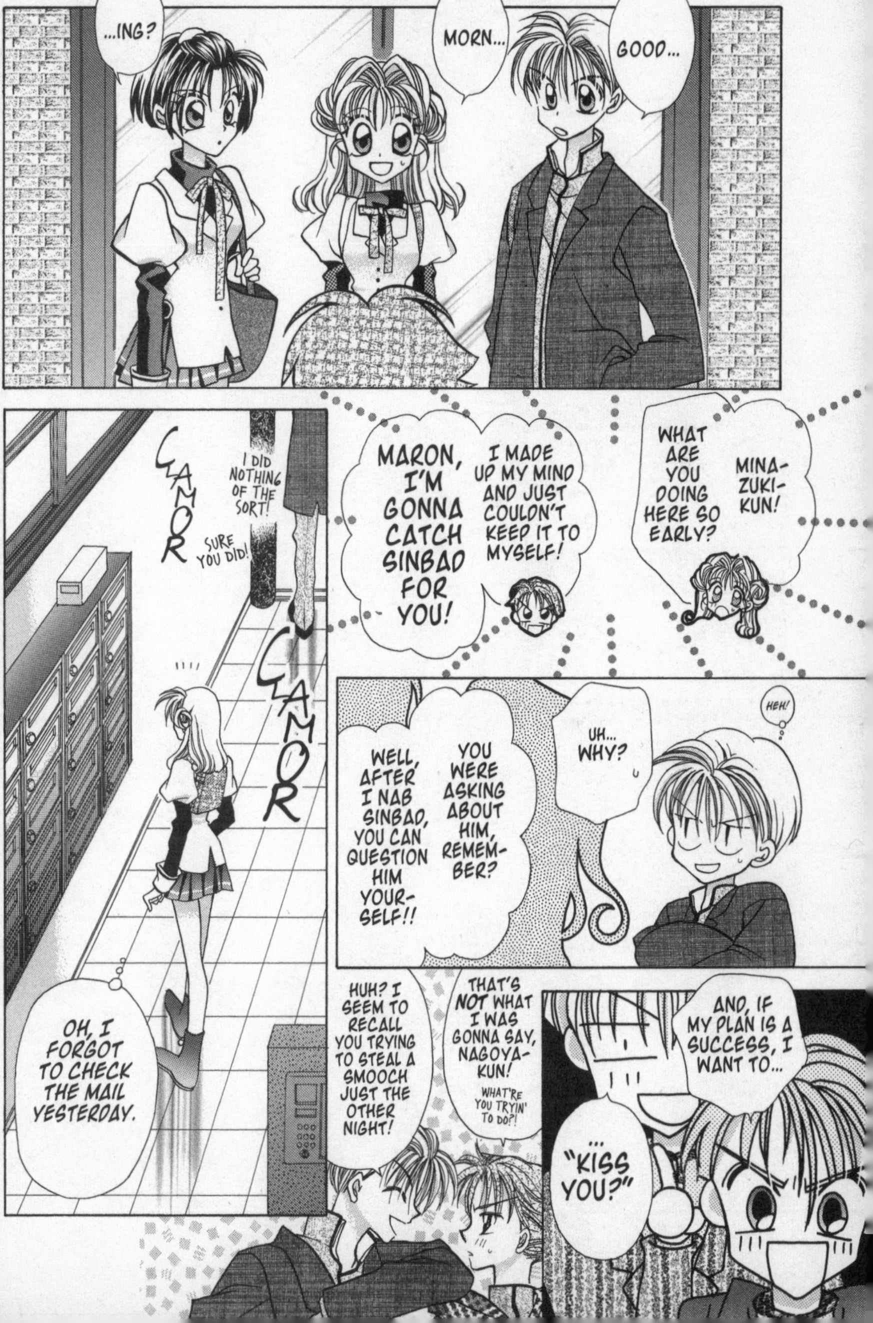
GOOD...
MORN...
...ING?
MINA-ZUKI-KUN!
WHAT ARE YOU DOING HERE SO EARLY?
I MADE UP MY MIND AND JUST COULDN'T KEEP IT TO MYSELF!
MARON, I'M GONNA CATCH SINBAD FOR YOU!
HEH!
UH... WHY?
YOU WERE ASKING ABOUT HIM, REMEMBER?
WELL, AFTER I NAB SINBAD, YOU CAN QUESTION HIM YOURSELF!!
AND, IF MY PLAN IS A SUCCESS, I WANT TO...
..."KISS YOU?"
THAT'S NOT WHAT I WAS GONNA SAY, NAGOYA-KUN!
WHAT'RE YOU TRYIN' TO DO?!
HUH? I SEEM TO RECALL YOU TRYING TO STEAL A SMOOCH JUST THE OTHER NIGHT!
I DID NOTHING OF THE SORT!
SURE YOU DID!
CLAMOR
CLAMOR
OH, I FORGOT TO CHECK THE MAIL YESTERDAY.

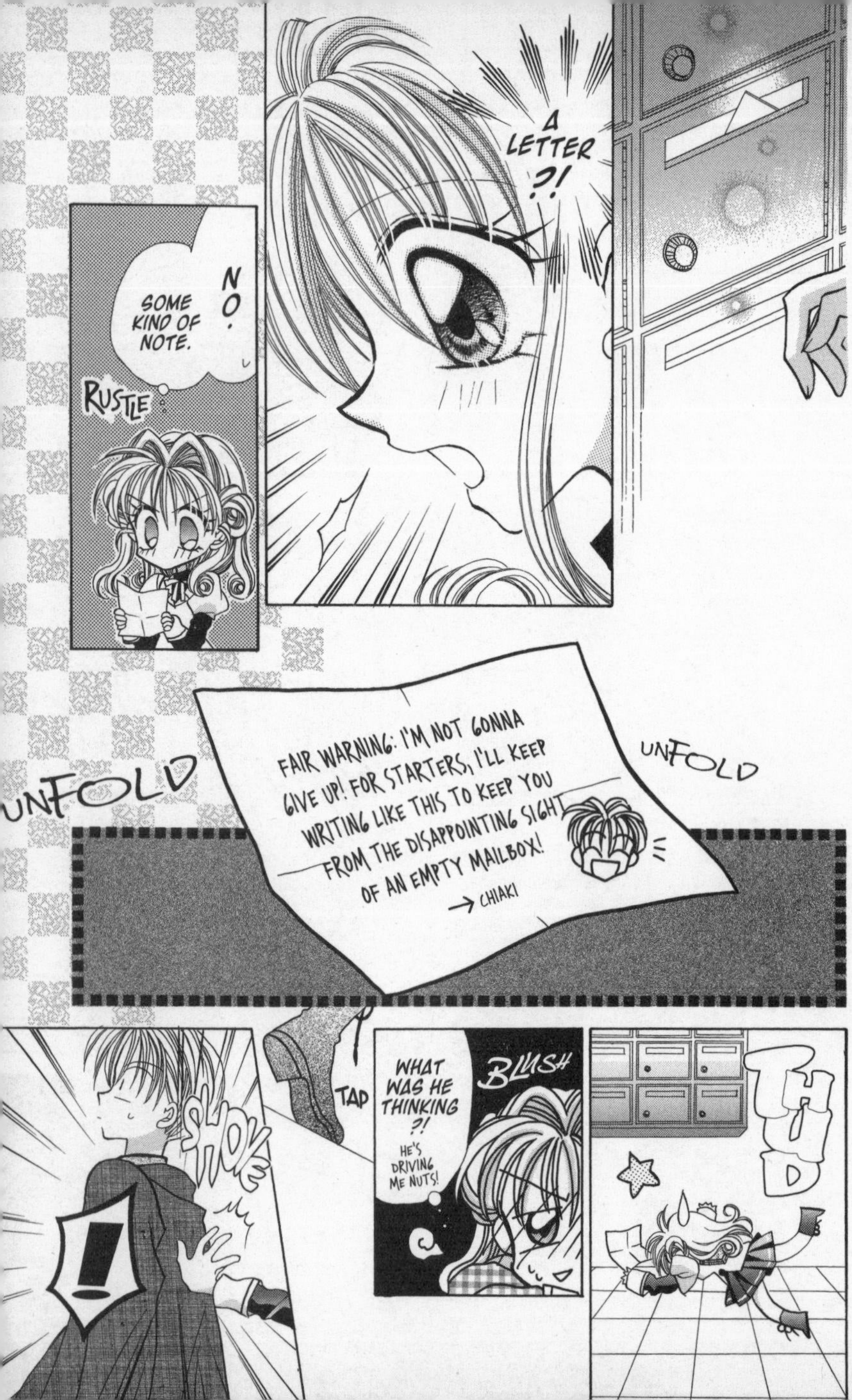
A LETTER ?!
NO.
SOME KIND OF NOTE.
RUSTLE
UNFOLD
FAIR WARNING: I'M NOT GONNA GIVE UP! FOR STARTERS, I'LL KEEP WRITING LIKE THIS TO KEEP YOU FROM THE DISAPPOINTING SIGHT OF AN EMPTY MAILBOX!
→ CHIAKI
UNFOLD
THUD
BLUSH
WHAT WAS HE THINKING ?!
HE'S DRIVING ME NUTS!
TAP
SHOVE
!

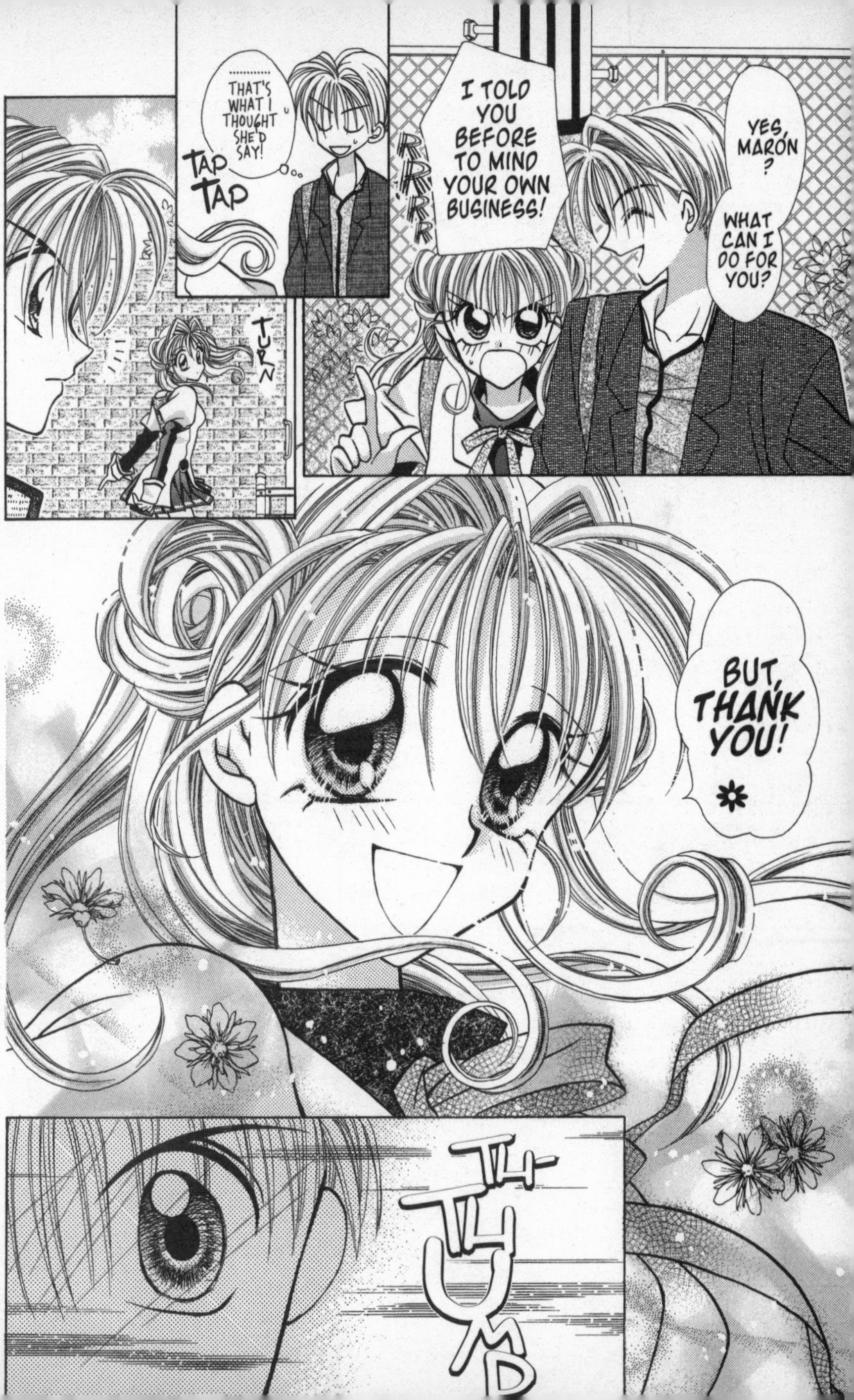
YES, MARON? WHAT CAN I DO FOR YOU?
RRRR
I TOLD YOU BEFORE TO MIND YOUR OWN BUSINESS!
THAT'S WHAT I THOUGHT SHE'D SAY!
TAP TAP
TURN
BUT, THANK YOU!
TH-THUMP

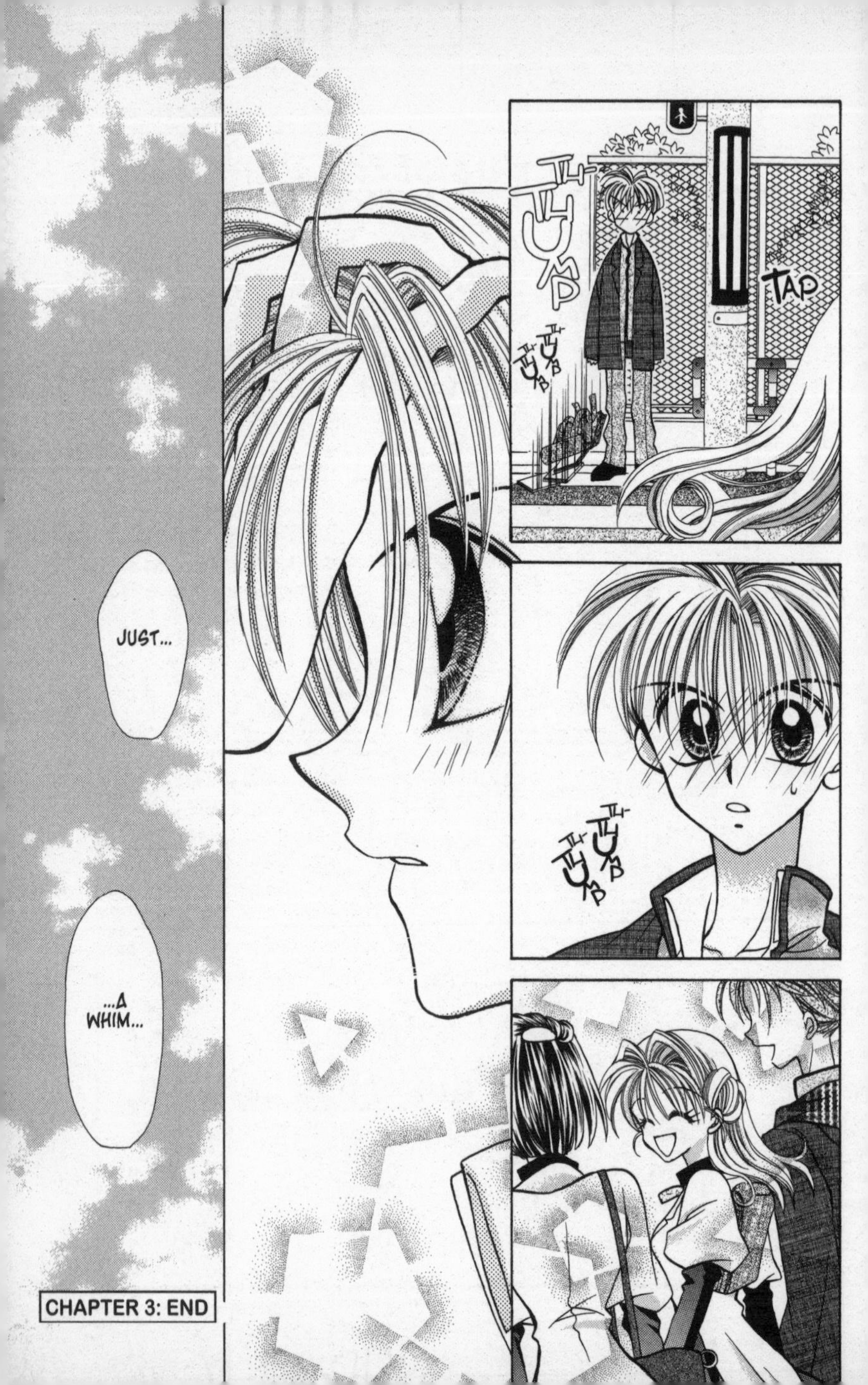
TH-THUMP
TH-THUMP
TH-THUMP
TAP
TH-THUMP
TH-THUMP
JUST...
...A WHIM...
CHAPTER 3: END

The Secrets of the Pendant

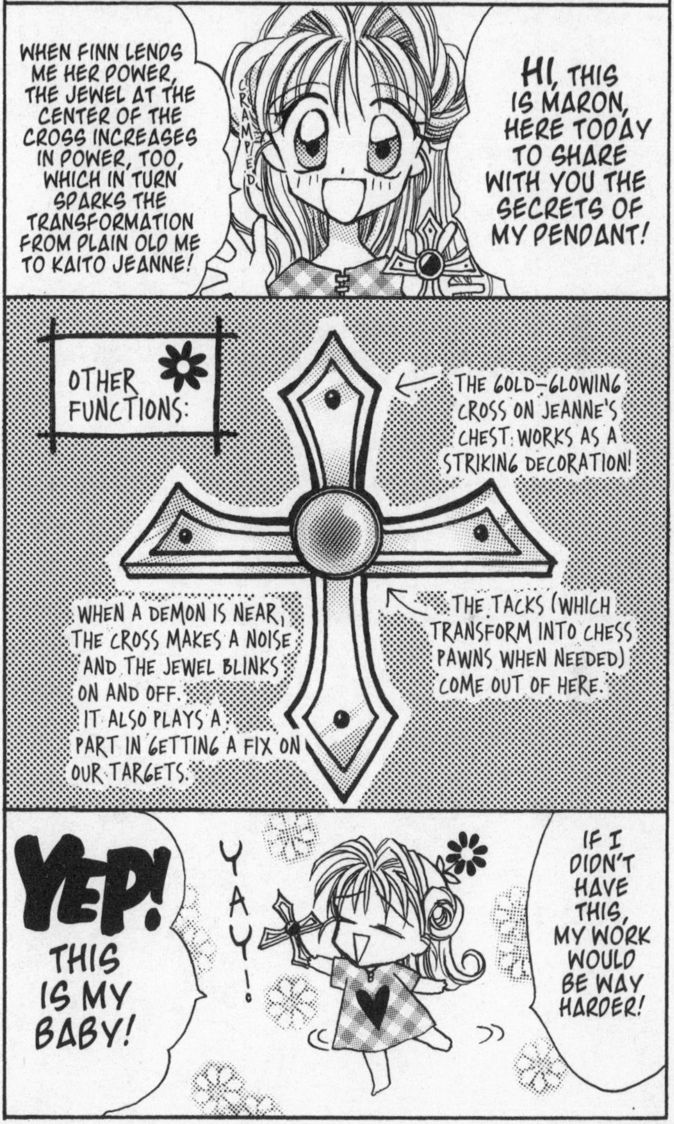
HI, THIS IS MARON, HERE TODAY TO SHARE WITH YOU THE SECRETS OF MY PENDANT!
CRAMPED
WHEN FINN LENDS ME HER POWER, THE JEWEL AT THE CENTER OF THE CROSS INCREASES IN POWER, TOO, WHICH IN TURN SPARKS THE TRANSFORMATION FROM PLAIN OLD ME TO KAITO JEANNE!
OTHER FUNCTIONS:
THE GOLD-GLOWING CROSS ON JEANNE'S CHEST WORKS AS A STRIKING DECORATION!
THE TACKS (WHICH TRANSFORM INTO CHESS PAWNS WHEN NEEDED) COME OUT OF HERE.
WHEN A DEMON IS NEAR, THE CROSS MAKES A NOISE AND THE JEWEL BLINKS ON AND OFF. IT ALSO PLAYS A PART IN GETTING A FIX ON OUR TARGETS.
IF I DIDN'T HAVE THIS, MY WORK WOULD BE WAY HARDER!
YAY!
YEP! THIS IS MY BABY!

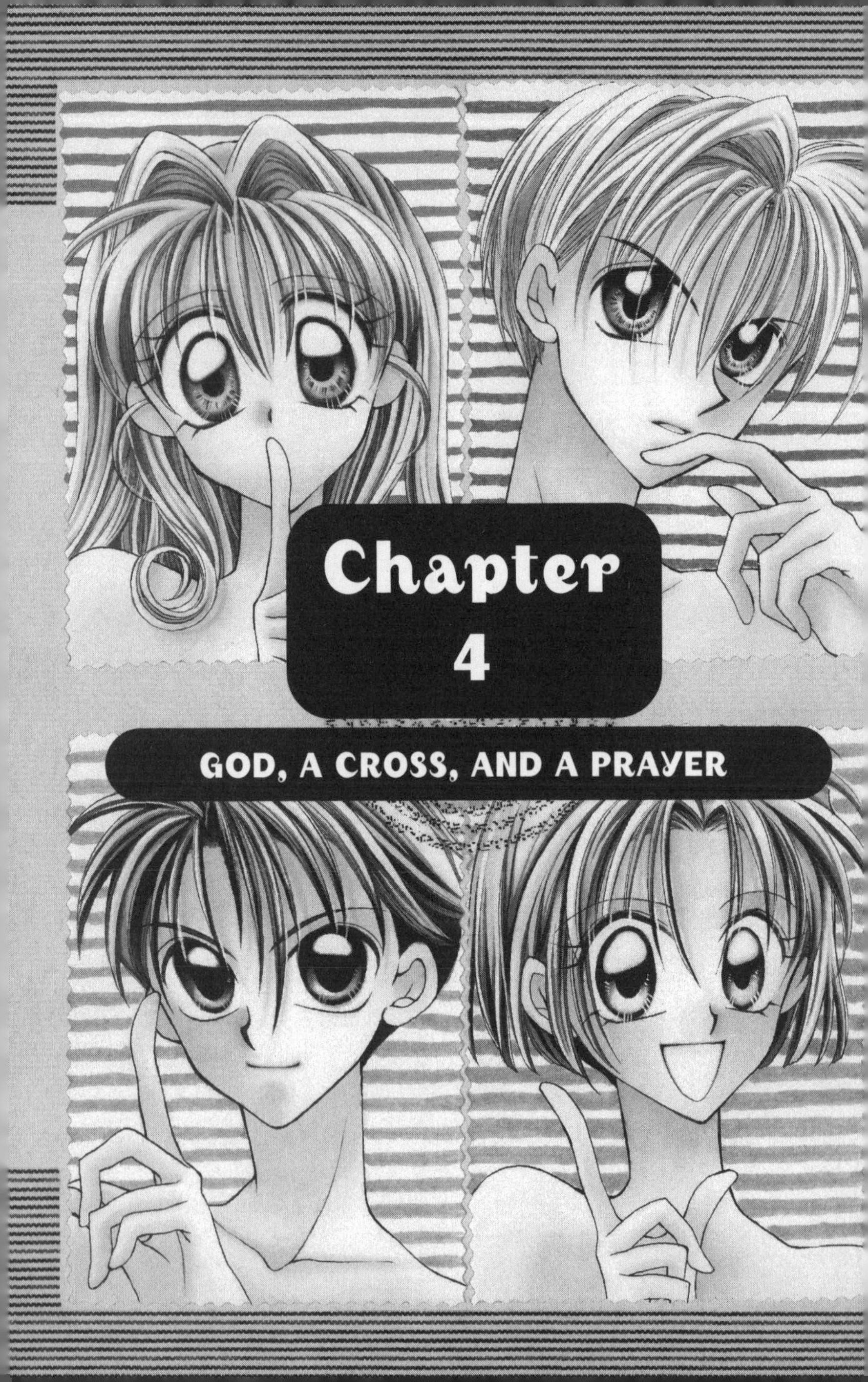
Chapter
4
GOD, A CROSS, AND A PRAYER

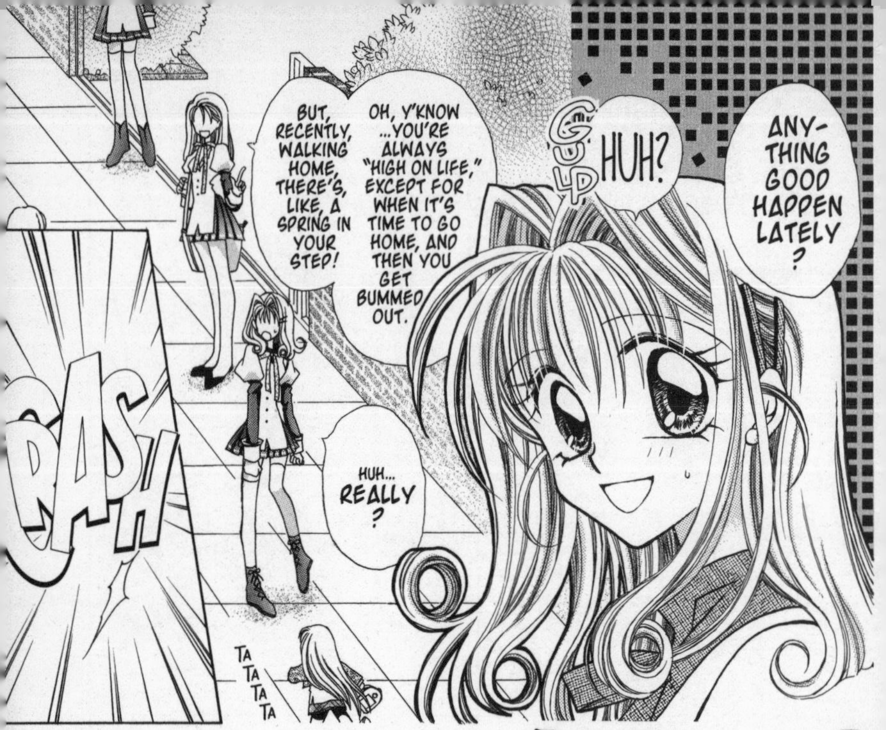
ANY-THING GOOD HAPPEN LATELY?
GULP
HUH?
OH, Y'KNOW ...YOU'RE ALWAYS "HIGH ON LIFE," EXCEPT FOR WHEN IT'S TIME TO GO HOME, AND THEN YOU GET BUMMED OUT.
BUT, RECENTLY, WALKING HOME, THERE'S, LIKE, A SPRING IN YOUR STEP!
HUH... REALLY?
CRASH
TA TA TA TA

CHAPTER 4: GOD, A CROSS, AND A PRAYER

"Who's your number one...?!"

I was shocked when I saw this tagline, thought up by my editor, because it perfectly captures the idea I was going for with the title page art, which is, "point to the person who is most dear to you"...except on the page, it seems that only Maron is having a hard time deciding the answer to that (or something...I kept her response unclear). Too bad for the other three characters, who are all pointing to their "number one" person, Maron. (Actually, it looks like Chiaki is also unsure about his answer.) Anyway, I always look forward to seeing the title page taglines that my editor comes up with; they're always spot on and really cool!

Regarding the story, this one is primarily action-oriented. Really, I want Sinbad to get in on the action more...umm, I love the last (kissing) scene.

WHOO-HOO!

→

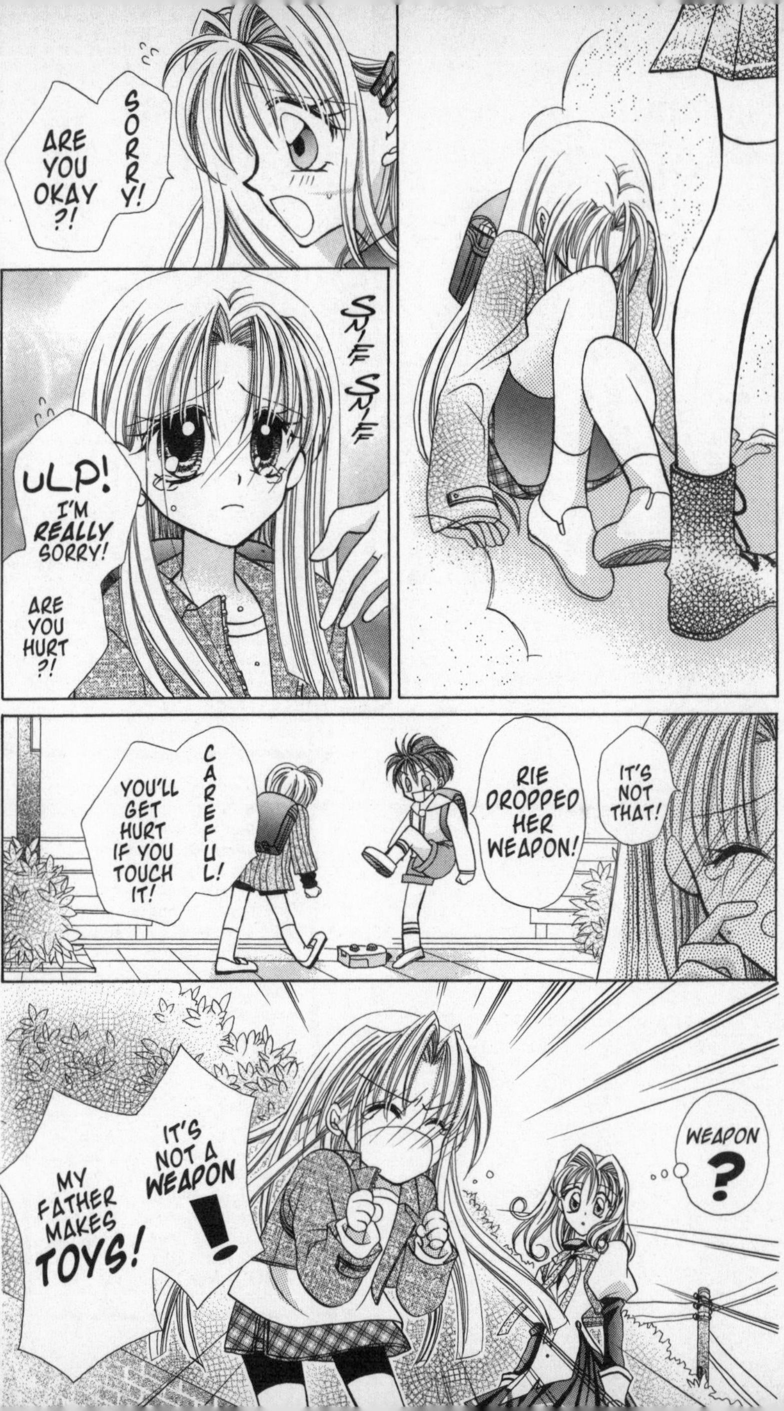
SORRY!
ARE YOU OKAY?!
SNIF SNIF
ULP! I'M REALLY SORRY!
ARE YOU HURT?!
IT'S NOT THAT!
RIE DROPPED HER WEAPON!
CAREFUL!
YOU'LL GET HURT IF YOU TOUCH IT!
WEAPON?
IT'S NOT A WEAPON!
MY FATHER MAKES TOYS!

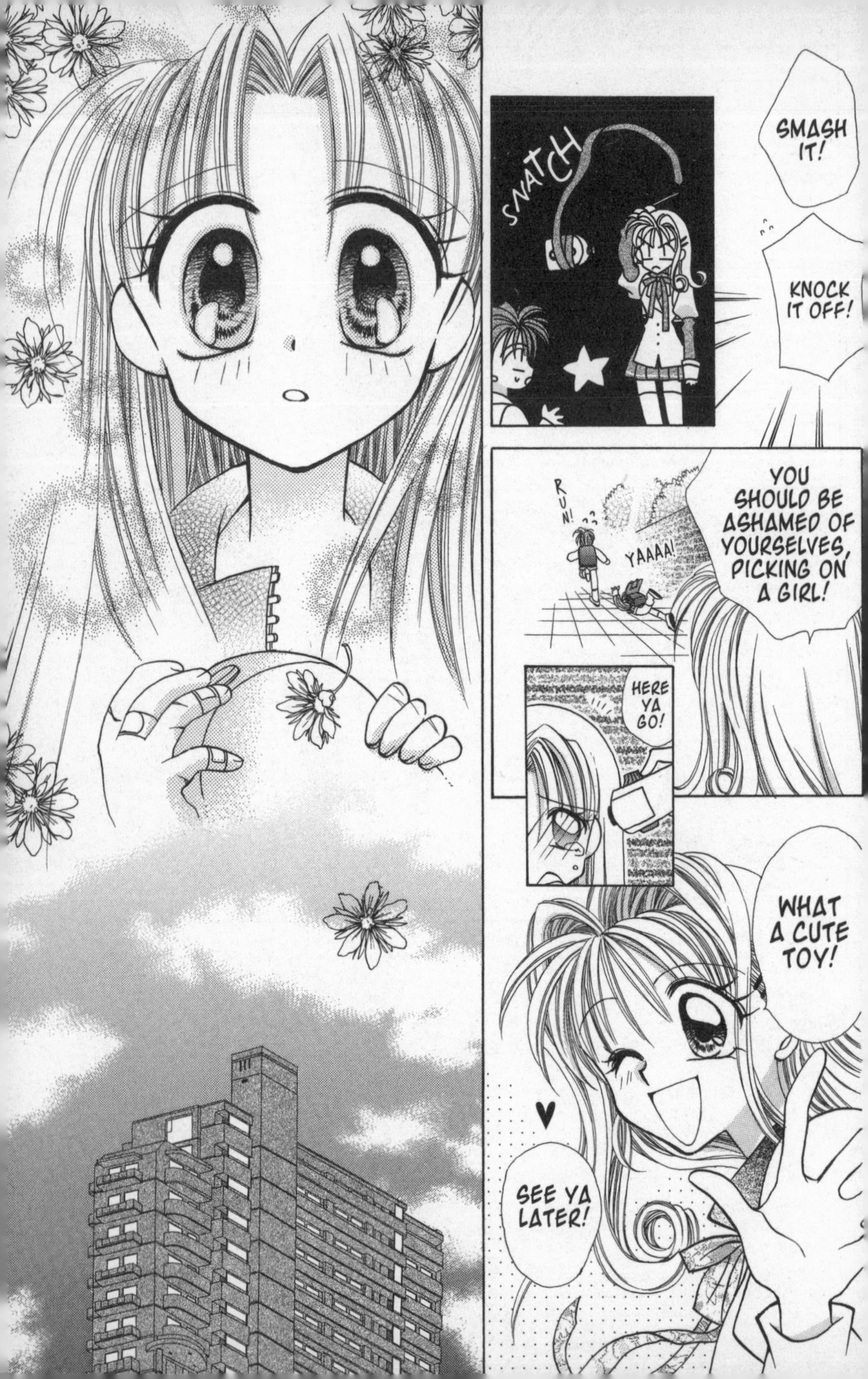
SMASH IT!
KNOCK IT OFF!
SNATCH
YOU SHOULD BE ASHAMED OF YOURSELVES, PICKING ON A GIRL!
RUN!
YAAAA!
HERE YA GO!
WHAT A CUTE TOY!
SEE YA LATER!

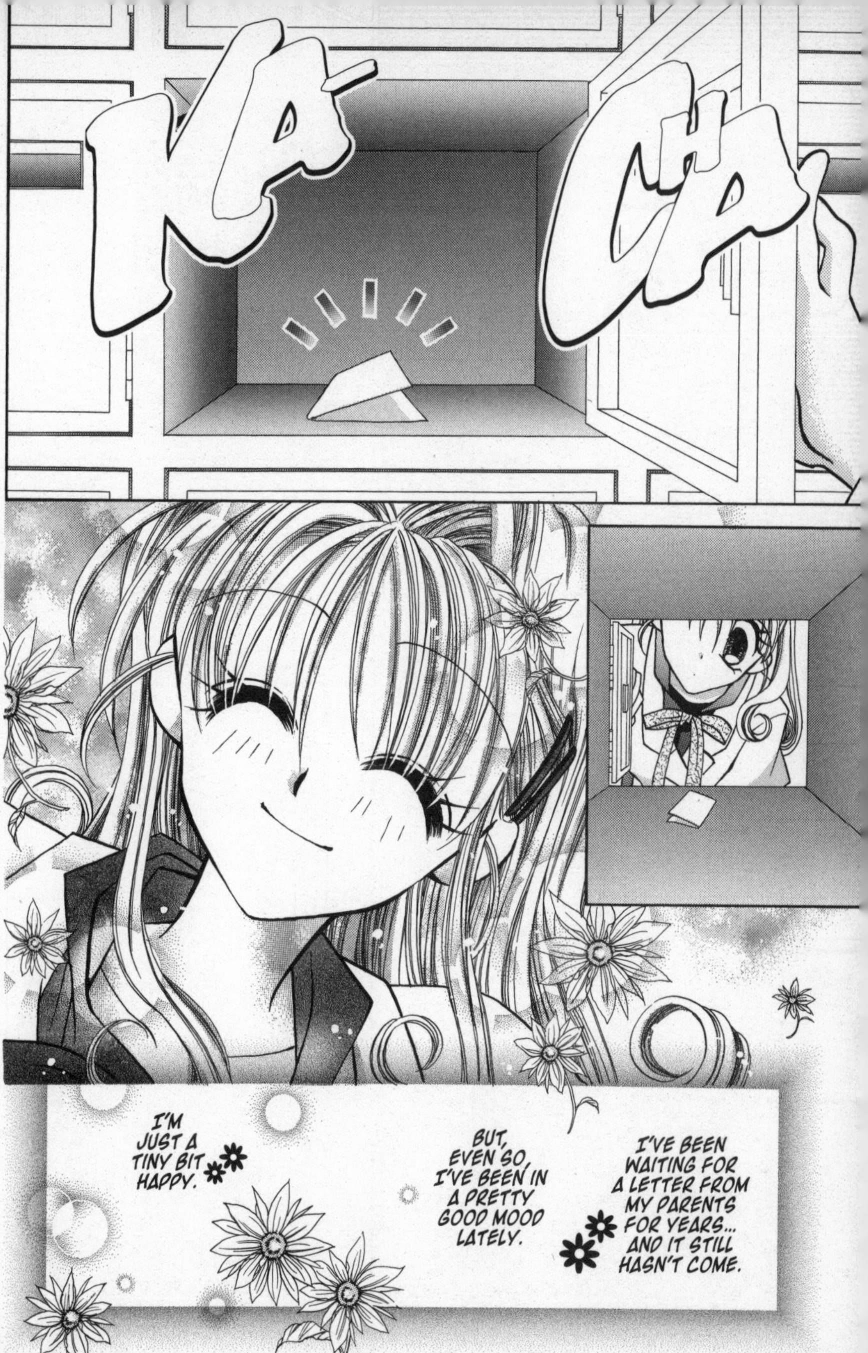
KA-
CHA
I'VE BEEN WAITING FOR A LETTER FROM MY PARENTS FOR YEARS... AND IT STILL HASN'T COME.
BUT, EVEN SO, I'VE BEEN IN A PRETTY GOOD MOOD LATELY.
I'M JUST A TINY BIT HAPPY.

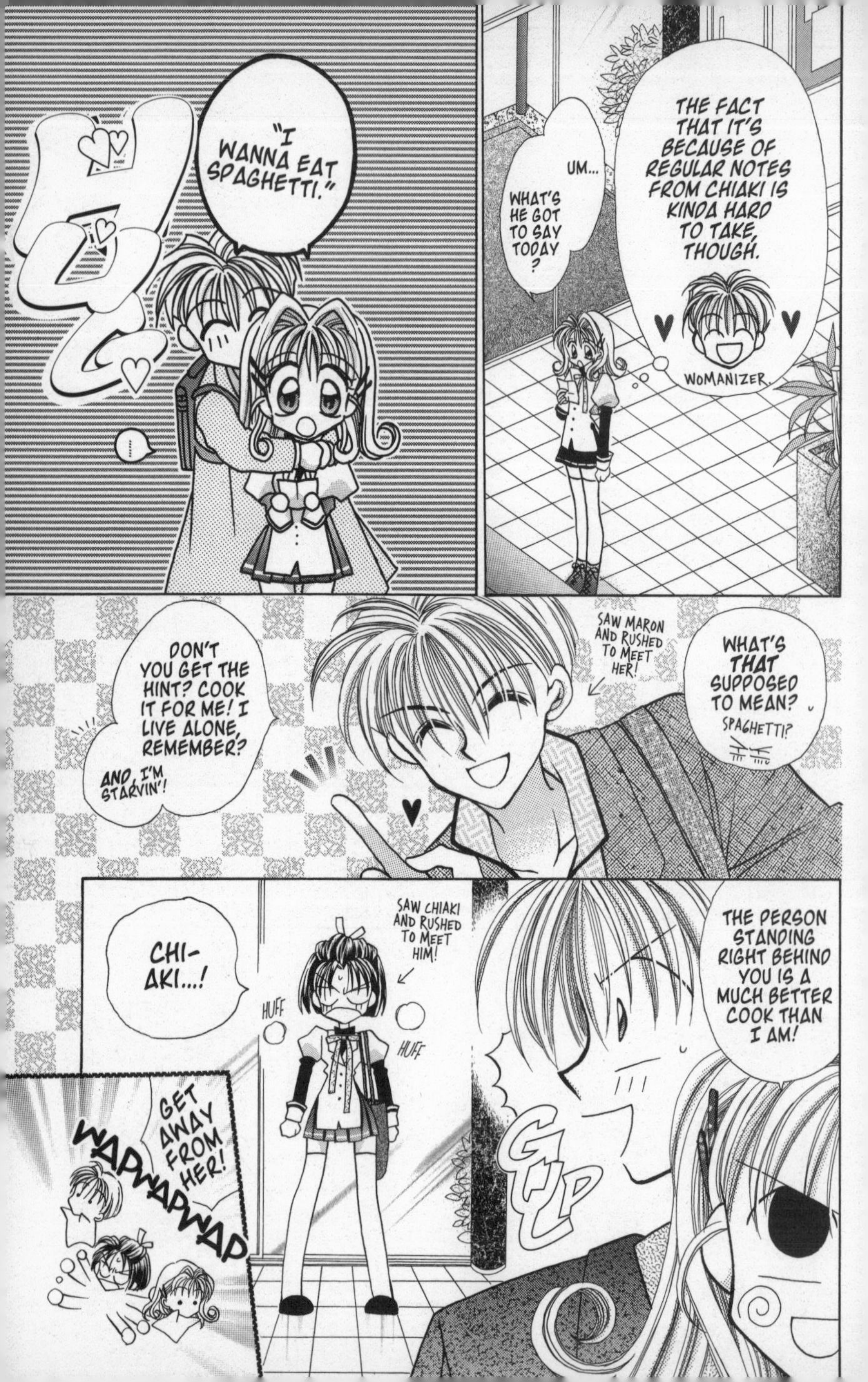
THE FACT THAT IT'S BECAUSE OF REGULAR NOTES FROM CHIAKI IS KINDA HARD TO TAKE, THOUGH.
WOMANIZER.
UM...
WHAT'S HE GOT TO SAY TODAY?
"I WANNA EAT SPAGHETTI."
...
WHAT'S THAT SUPPOSED TO MEAN?
SPAGHETTI?
SAW MARON AND RUSHED TO MEET HER!
DON'T YOU GET THE HINT? COOK IT FOR ME! I LIVE ALONE, REMEMBER?
AND, I'M STARVIN'!
THE PERSON STANDING RIGHT BEHIND YOU IS A MUCH BETTER COOK THAN I AM!
GULP
SAW CHIAKI AND RUSHED TO MEET HIM!
CHI-AKI...!
HUFF
HUFF
GET AWAY FROM HER!
WAPWAPWAP

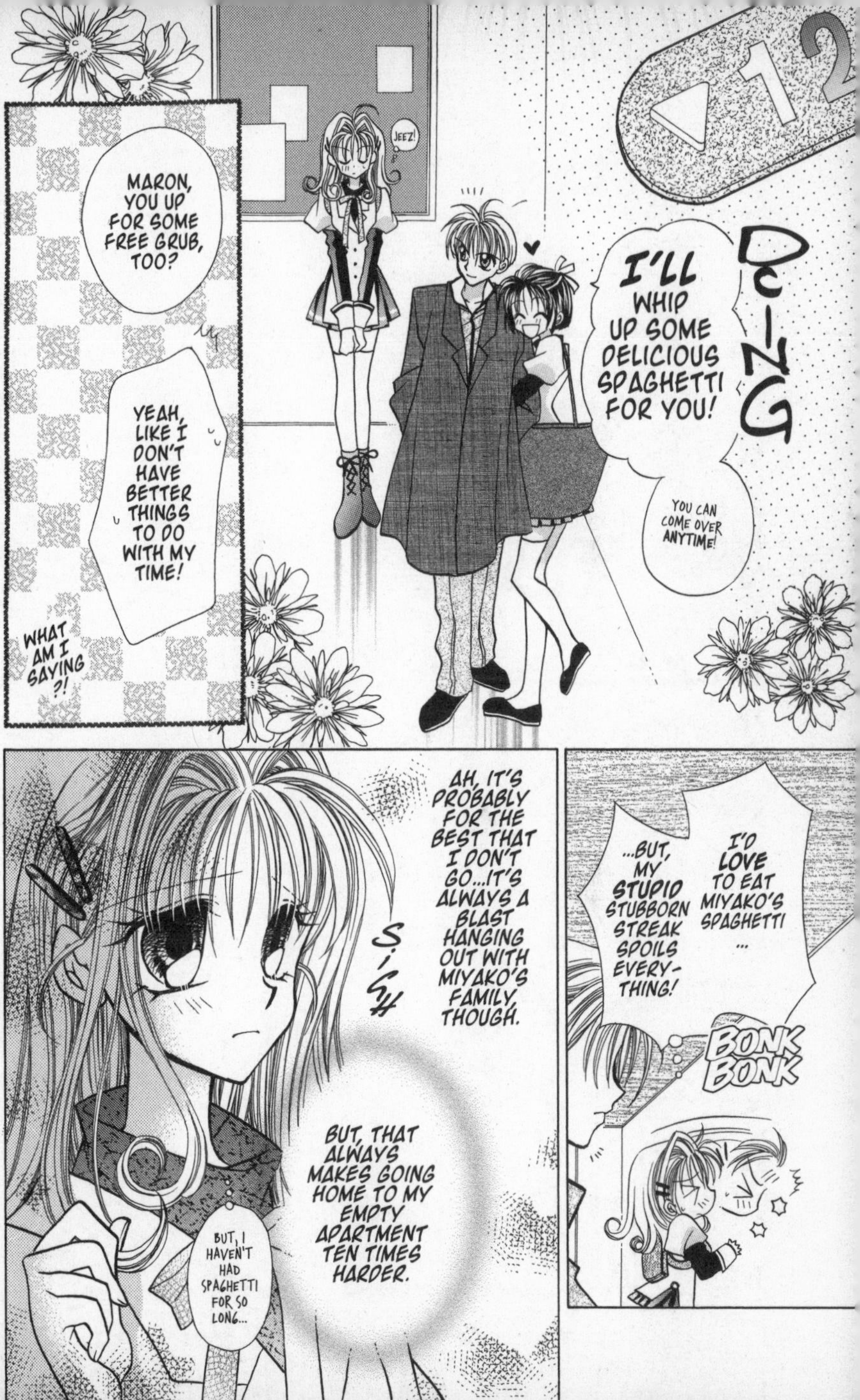
12
DING
I'LL WHIP UP SOME DELICIOUS SPAGHETTI FOR YOU!
YOU CAN COME OVER ANYTIME!
JEEZ!
MARON, YOU UP FOR SOME FREE GRUB, TOO?
YEAH, LIKE I DON'T HAVE BETTER THINGS TO DO WITH MY TIME!
WHAT AM I SAYING?!
I'D LOVE TO EAT MIYAKO'S SPAGHETTI...
...BUT, MY STUPID STUBBORN STREAK SPOILS EVERYTHING!
BONK BONK
AH, IT'S PROBABLY FOR THE BEST THAT I DON'T GO...IT'S ALWAYS A BLAST HANGING OUT WITH MIYAKO'S FAMILY, THOUGH.
SIGH
BUT, THAT ALWAYS MAKES GOING HOME TO MY EMPTY APARTMENT TEN TIMES HARDER.
BUT, I HAVEN'T HAD SPAGHETTI FOR SO LONG...

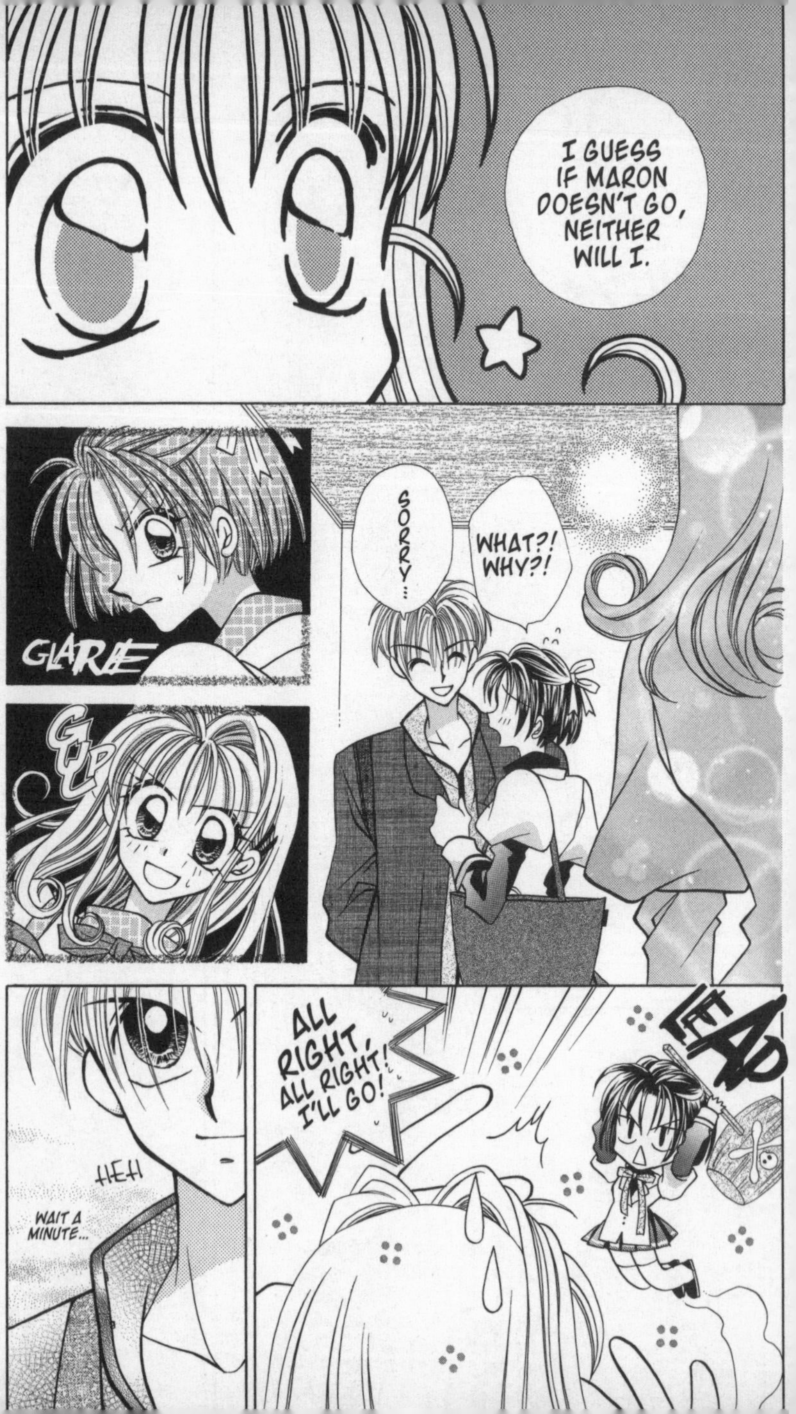
I GUESS IF MARON DOESN'T GO, NEITHER WILL I.
WHAT?! WHY?!
SORRY...
GLARE
GULP
ALL RIGHT, ALL RIGHT! I'LL GO!
HEH
WAIT A MINUTE...

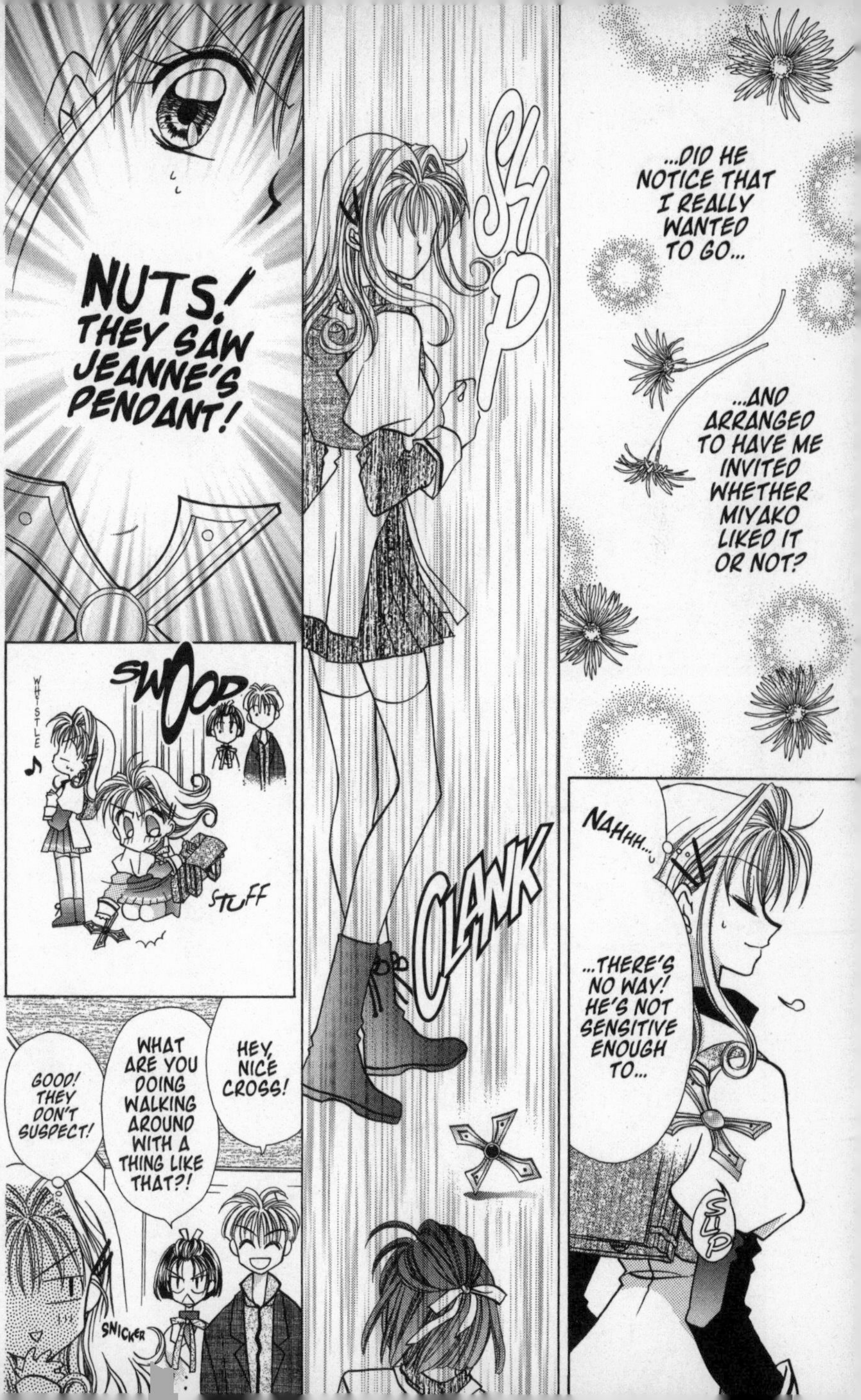
...DID HE NOTICE THAT I REALLY WANTED TO GO...
...AND ARRANGED TO HAVE ME INVITED WHETHER MIYAKO LIKED IT OR NOT?
NAHHH...
...THERE'S NO WAY! HE'S NOT SENSITIVE ENOUGH TO...
SLIP
SLIP
CLANK
NUTS! THEY SAW JEANNE'S PENDANT!
SWOOP
WHISTLE
STUFF
HEY, NICE CROSS!
WHAT ARE YOU DOING WALKING AROUND WITH A THING LIKE THAT?!
GOOD! THEY DON'T SUSPECT!
SNICKER

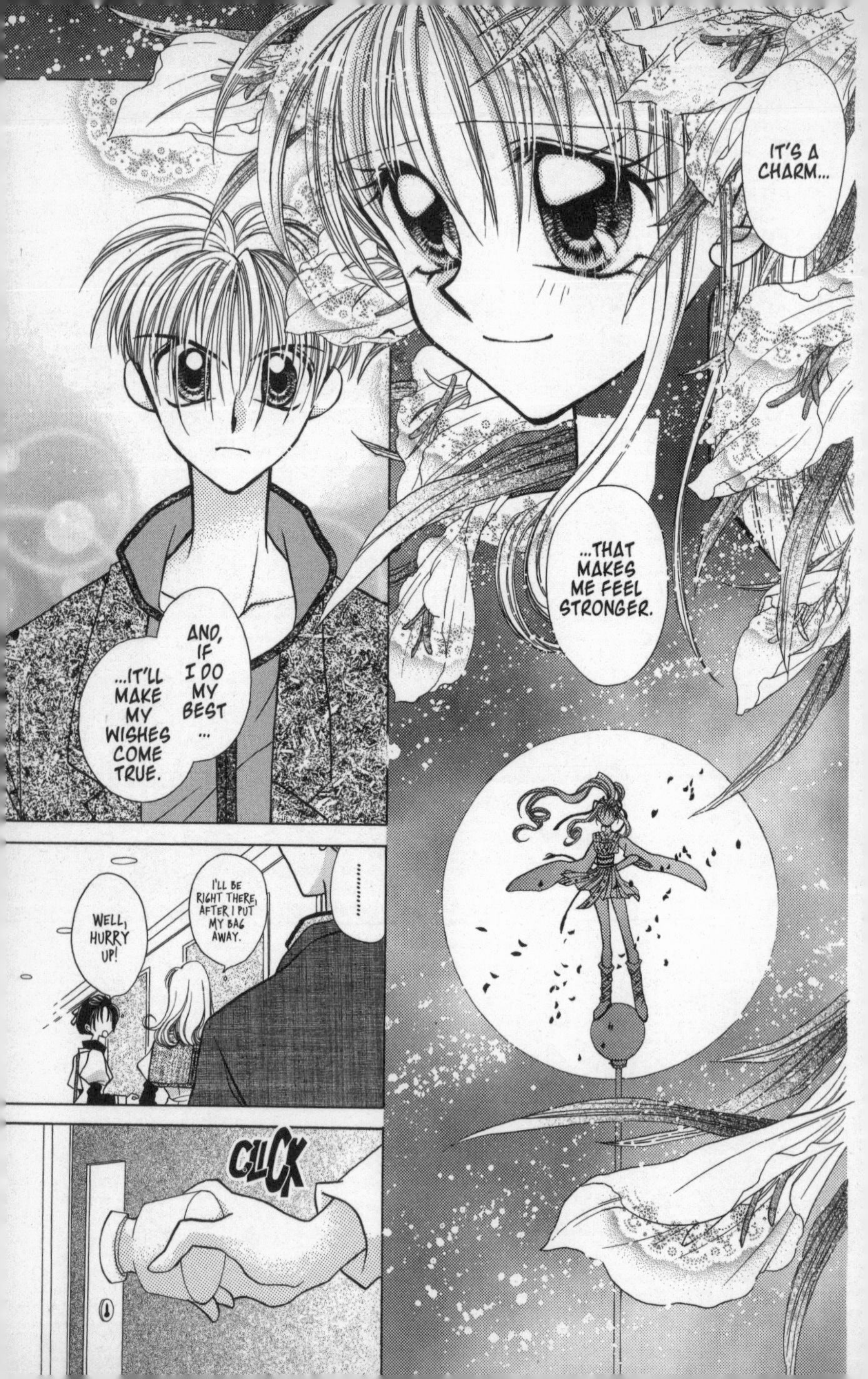
IT'S A CHARM...
...THAT MAKES ME FEEL STRONGER.
AND, IF I DO MY BEST...
...IT'LL MAKE MY WISHES COME TRUE.
......
I'LL BE RIGHT THERE, AFTER I PUT MY BAG AWAY.
WELL, HURRY UP!
CLICK

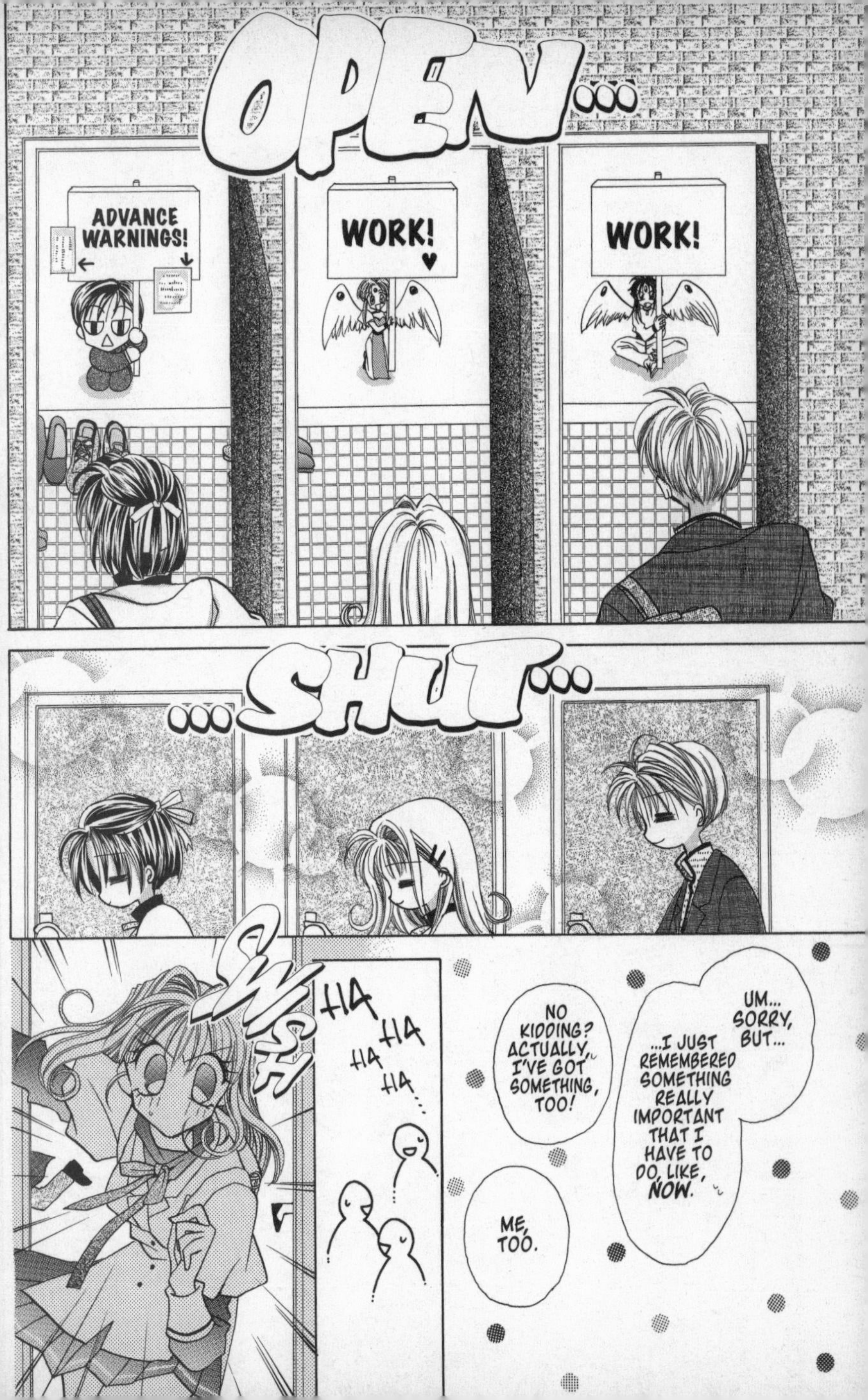
OPEN...
WORK!
WORK!
ADVANCE WARNINGS!
...SHUT...
UM... SORRY, BUT...
...I JUST REMEMBERED SOMETHING REALLY IMPORTANT THAT I HAVE TO DO, LIKE, NOW.
NO KIDDING? ACTUALLY, I'VE GOT SOMETHING, TOO!
ME, TOO.
HA HA HA HA...

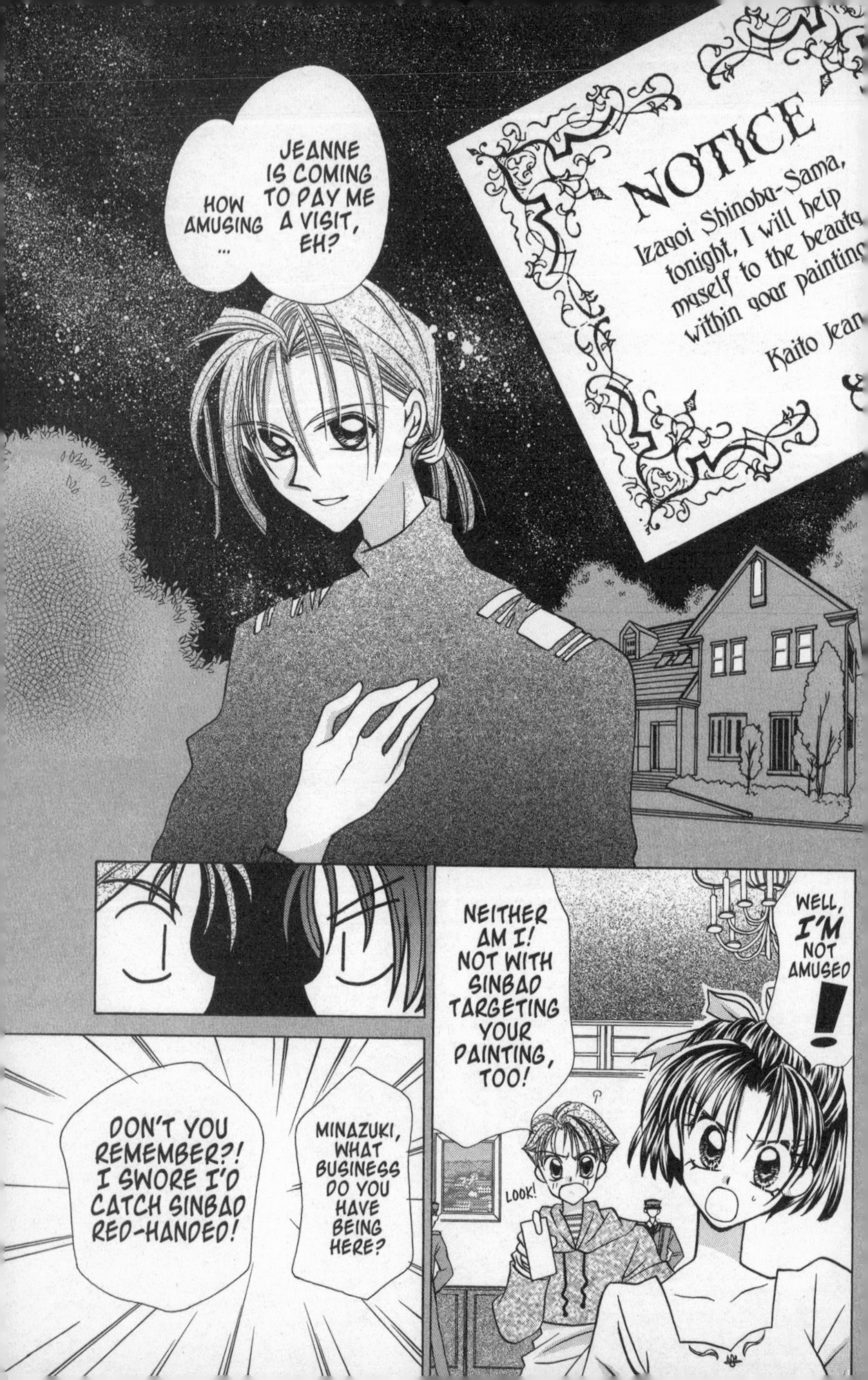
NOTICE
Izayoi Shinobu-Sama,
tonight, I will help
myself to the beaut
within your paintin
Kaito Jean
JEANNE IS COMING TO PAY ME A VISIT, EH?
HOW AMUSING ...
WELL, I'M NOT AMUSED!
NEITHER AM I! NOT WITH SINBAD TARGETING YOUR PAINTING, TOO!
?
LOOK!
MINAZUKI, WHAT BUSINESS DO YOU HAVE BEING HERE?
DON'T YOU REMEMBER?! I SWORE I'D CATCH SINBAD RED-HANDED!

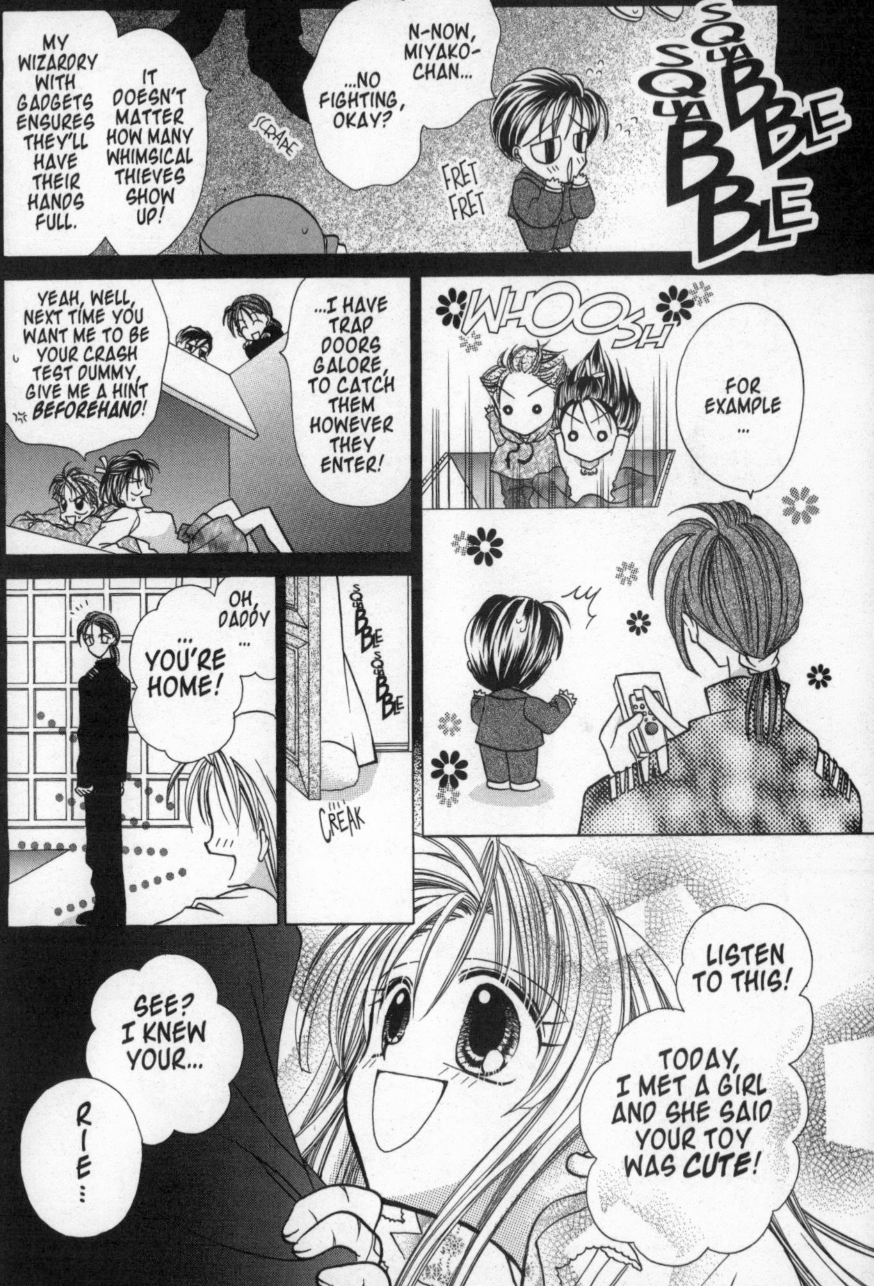
SQUABBLE SQUABBLE
FRET FRET
N-NOW, MIYAKO-CHAN...
...NO FIGHTING, OKAY?
SCRAPE
IT DOESN'T MATTER HOW MANY WHIMSICAL THIEVES SHOW UP!
MY WIZARDRY WITH GADGETS ENSURES THEY'LL HAVE THEIR HANDS FULL.
WHOOSH
FOR EXAMPLE ...
...I HAVE TRAP DOORS GALORE, TO CATCH THEM HOWEVER THEY ENTER!
YEAH, WELL, NEXT TIME YOU WANT ME TO BE YOUR CRASH TEST DUMMY, GIVE ME A HINT BEFOREHAND!
SQUABBLE SQUABBLE
CREAK
OH, DADDY ... YOU'RE HOME!
LISTEN TO THIS!
TODAY, I MET A GIRL AND SHE SAID YOUR TOY WAS CUTE!
SEE? I KNEW YOUR...
RIE...

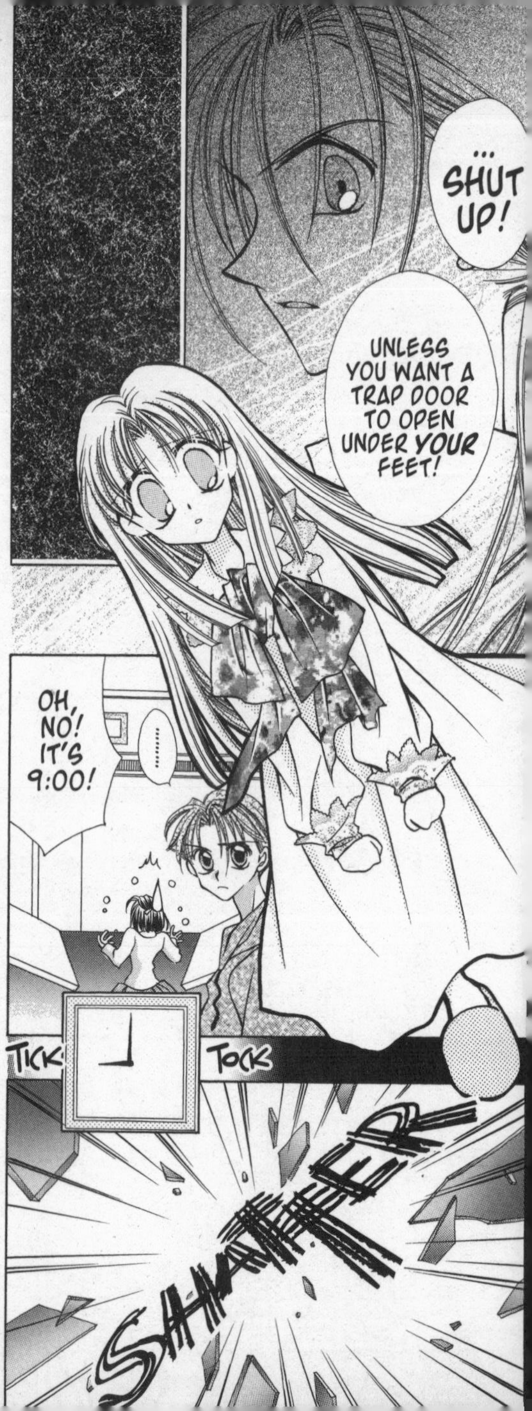
...SHUT UP!
UNLESS YOU WANT A TRAP DOOR TO OPEN UNDER YOUR FEET!
......
OH, NO! IT'S 9:00!
TICK
TOCK
SHATTER

AT A SIGNING: 5

So, anyway (I think I have a habit of saying this), I was relieved when my first autograph signing was all over (but my heart's going pitter-pat over the next one, in Nagoya.)

As I write this, it's August 4th...the Nagoya signing is on the 11th. During the signing, I was mega-nervous, but so were a lot of my fans. Still, their simple words of encouragement really made me feel all warm and fuzzy and also made me realize that I'm happy right now, doing what I'm doing. So, I want to thank all the fans so much for coming! Also, I'd like to thank the people in the editing department, who gave me the opportunity to take part in the event, and also the people in the promotions department, who had a tough job handling things after the signing turned out to be more successful than anyone imagined! Finally, I want to thank Obana Miho-Sensei; it was an honor to be at the same signing event with her. If I have the chance to do it again, I promise I'll be more professional and polished!

P.S. This is for the fans: are you still handling your autograph sheets with care? (After all, I **did** design 'em especially for the event.) I don't usually get the chance to use color, so treat 'em well; maybe even put it up on your wall! (Well, I'd be happy even if you put it away...as long as you hold onto it!)

This concludes "I went to a signing."

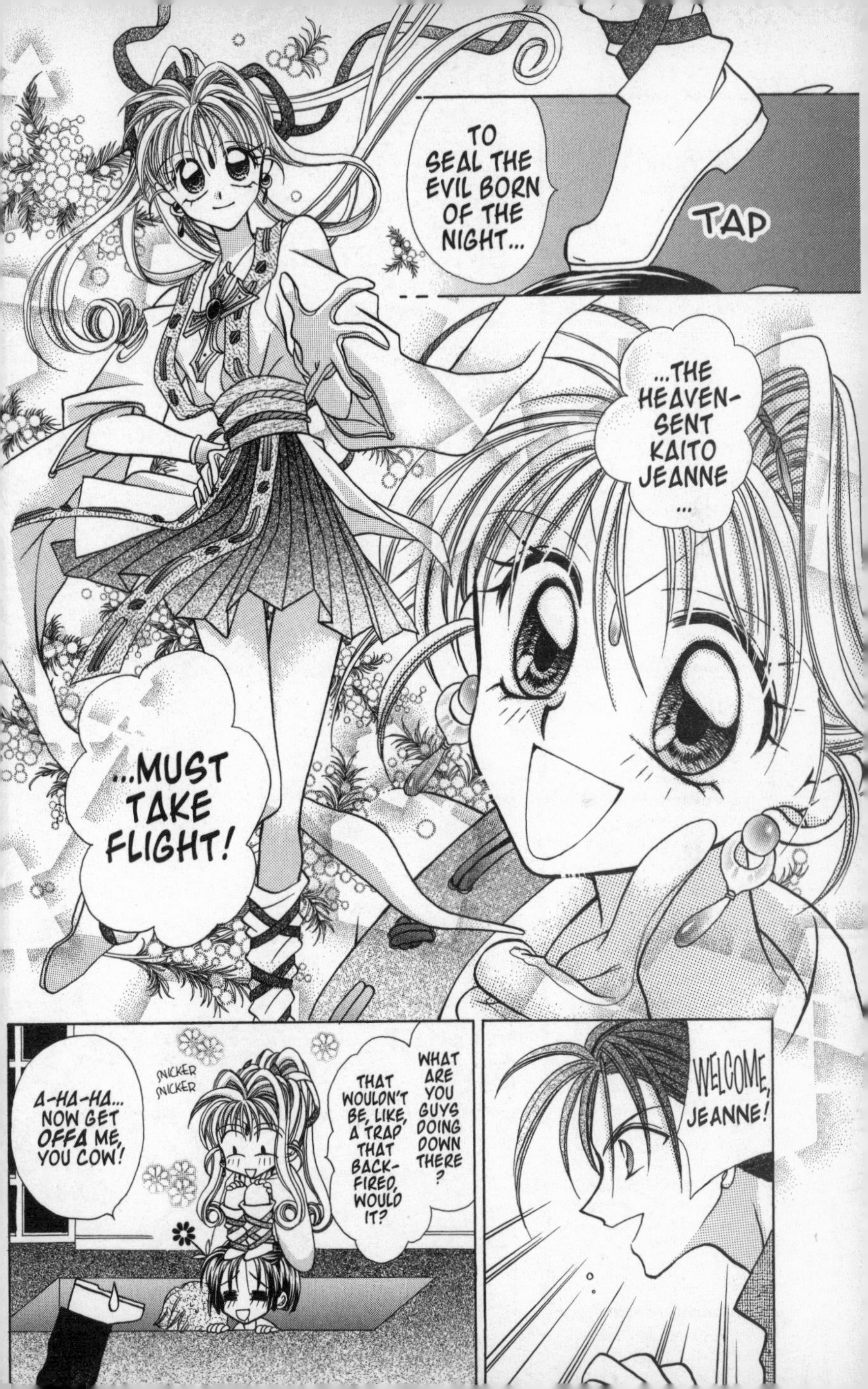
TO SEAL THE EVIL BORN OF THE NIGHT...
TAP
...THE HEAVEN-SENT KAITO JEANNE ...
...MUST TAKE FLIGHT!
WELCOME, JEANNE!
WHAT ARE YOU GUYS DOING DOWN THERE?
THAT WOULDN'T BE, LIKE, A TRAP THAT BACKFIRED, WOULD IT?
SNICKER SNICKER
A-HA-HA... NOW GET OFFA ME, YOU COW!

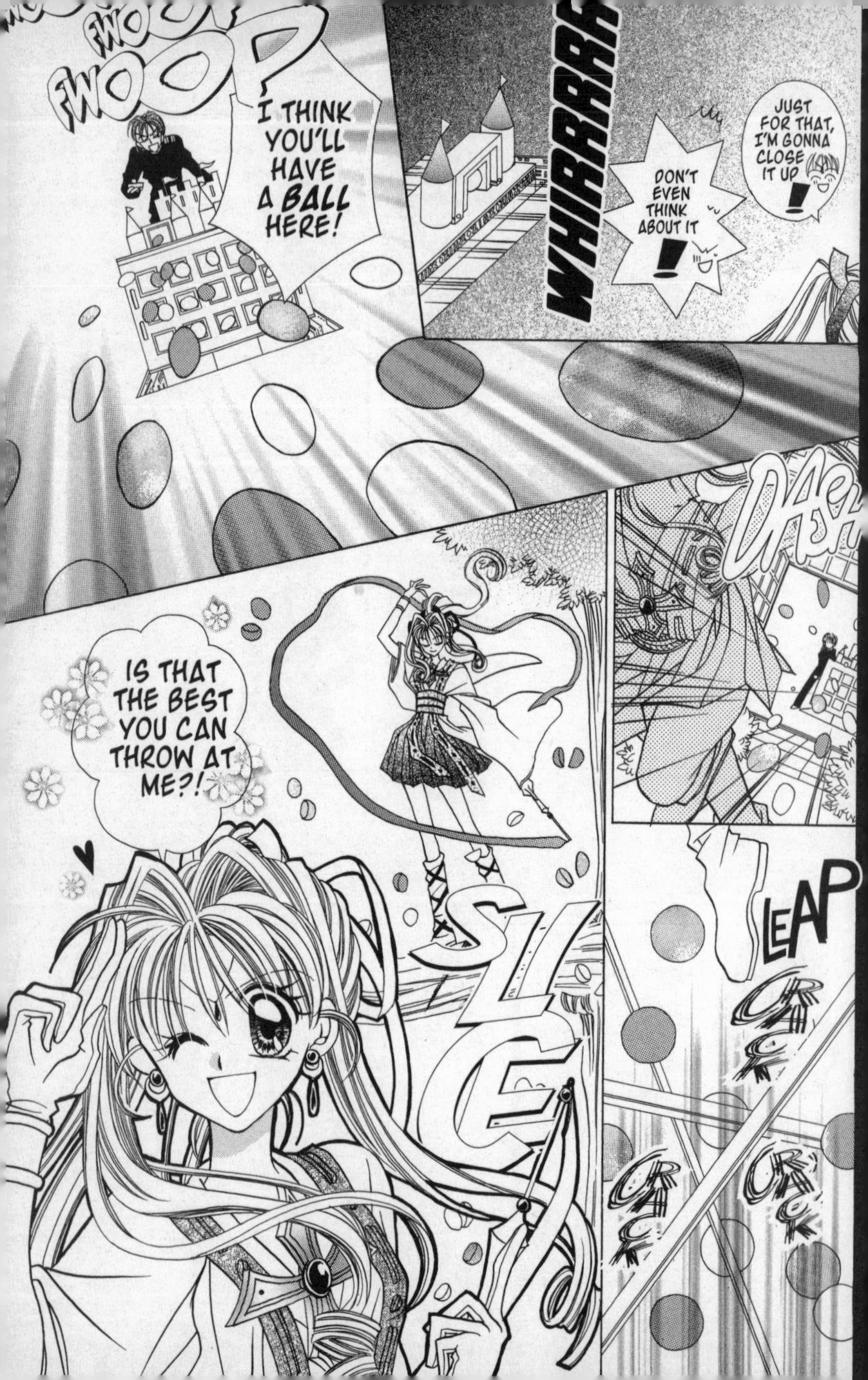
JUST FOR THAT, I'M GONNA CLOSE IT UP
DON'T EVEN THINK ABOUT IT
WHIRRRR
FWOOP FWOOP
I THINK YOU'LL HAVE A BALL HERE!
CRASH
LEAP
CRACK CRACK
CRACK CRACK
IS THAT THE BEST YOU CAN THROW AT ME?!
SLICE

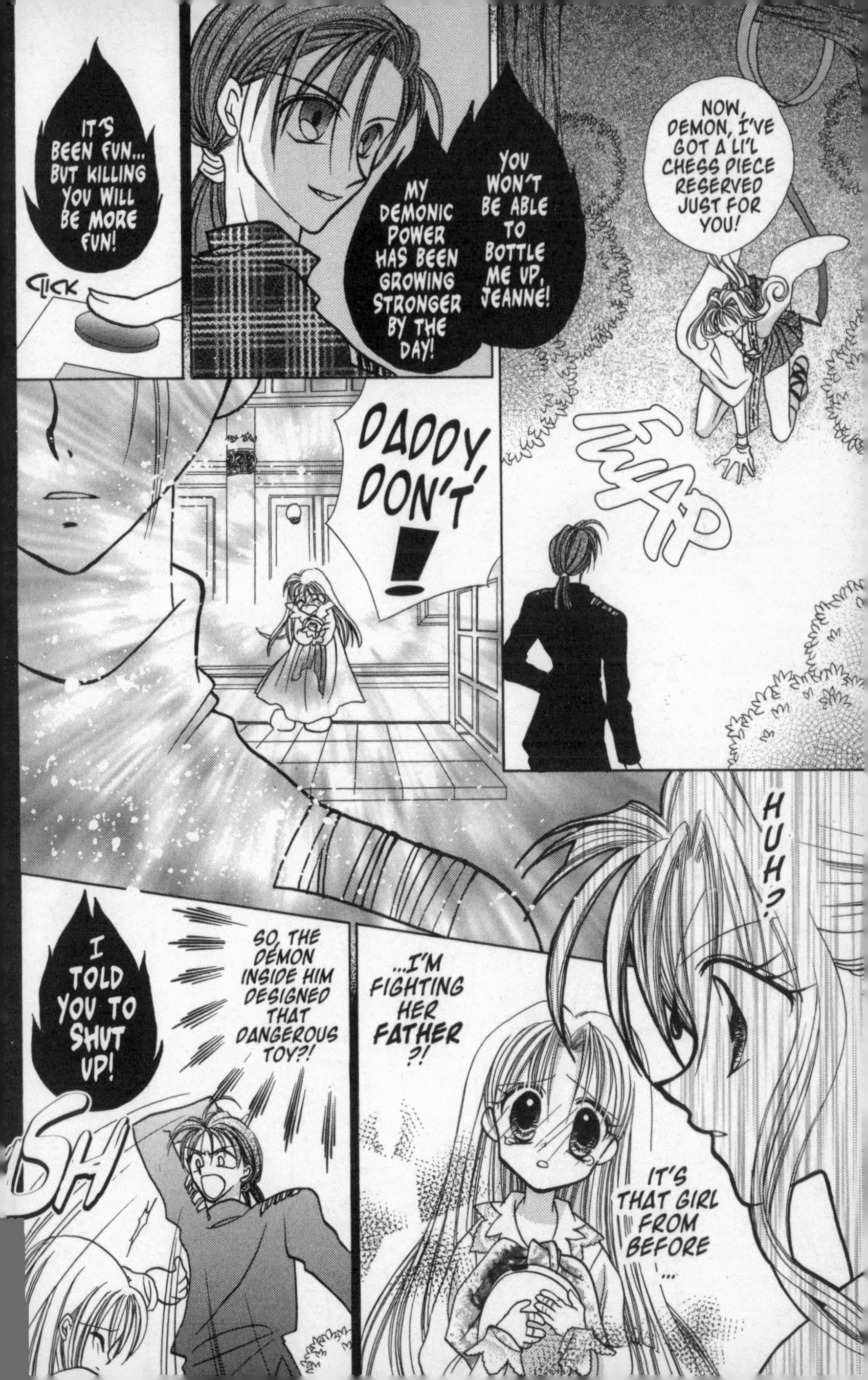

NOW, DEMON, I'VE GOT A LI'L CHESS PIECE RESERVED JUST FOR YOU!
FLAP
YOU WON'T BE ABLE TO BOTTLE ME UP, JEANNE!
MY DEMONIC POWER HAS BEEN GROWING STRONGER BY THE DAY!
IT'S BEEN FUN... BUT KILLING YOU WILL BE MORE FUN!
CLICK
DADDY, DON'T!
HUH?!
IT'S THAT GIRL FROM BEFORE...
...I'M FIGHTING HER FATHER?!
SO, THE DEMON INSIDE HIM DESIGNED THAT DANGEROUS TOY?!
I TOLD YOU TO SHUT UP!
SH

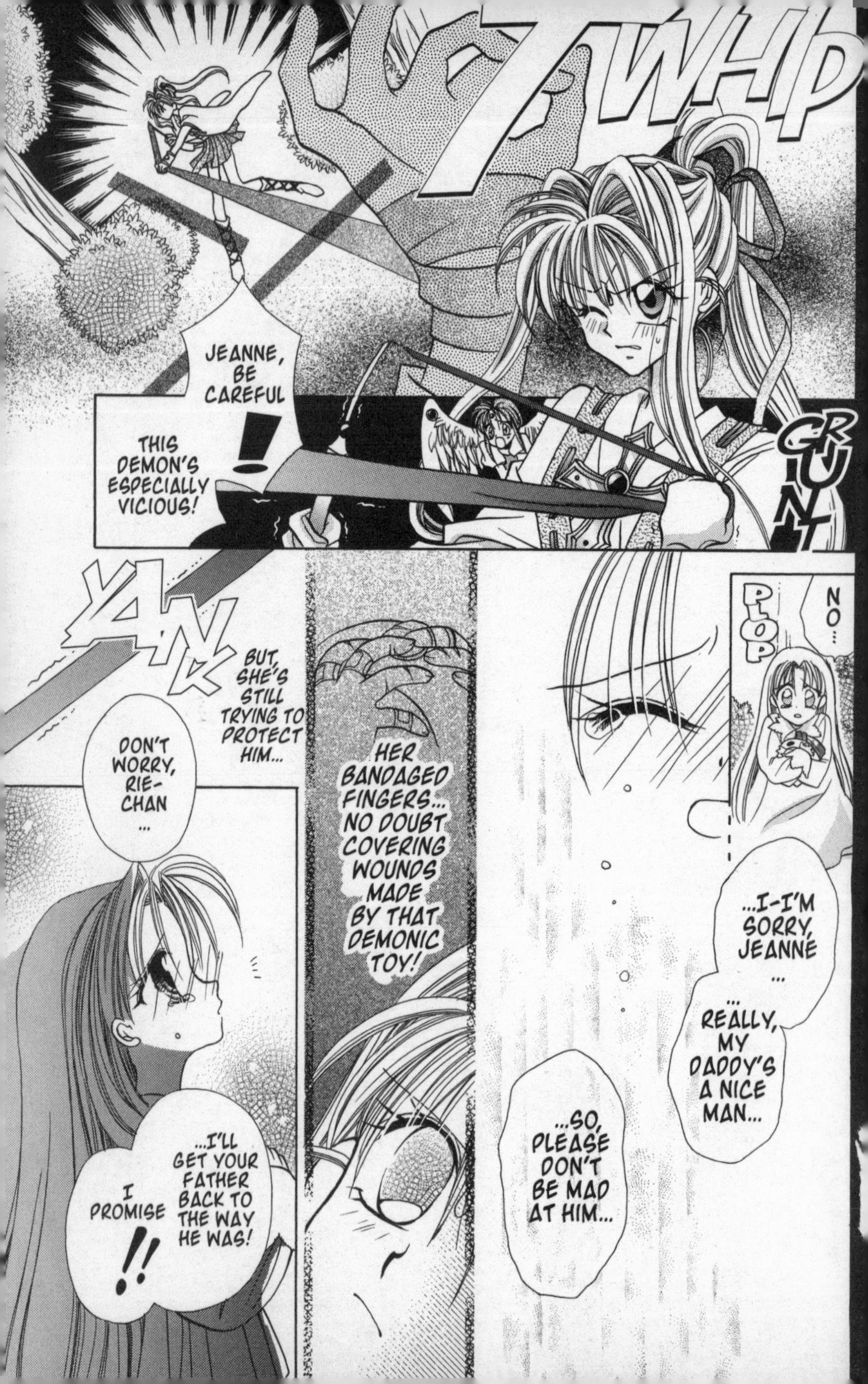
WHIP
GRUNT
JEANNE, BE CAREFUL!
THIS DEMON'S ESPECIALLY VICIOUS!
NO...
PLOP
...I-I'M SORRY, JEANNE...
...REALLY, MY DADDY'S A NICE MAN...
...SO, PLEASE DON'T BE MAD AT HIM...
HER BANDAGED FINGERS... NO DOUBT COVERING WOUNDS MADE BY THAT DEMONIC TOY!
YANK
BUT, SHE'S STILL TRYING TO PROTECT HIM...
DON'T WORRY, RIE-CHAN...
...I'LL GET YOUR FATHER BACK TO THE WAY HE WAS!
I PROMISE!!

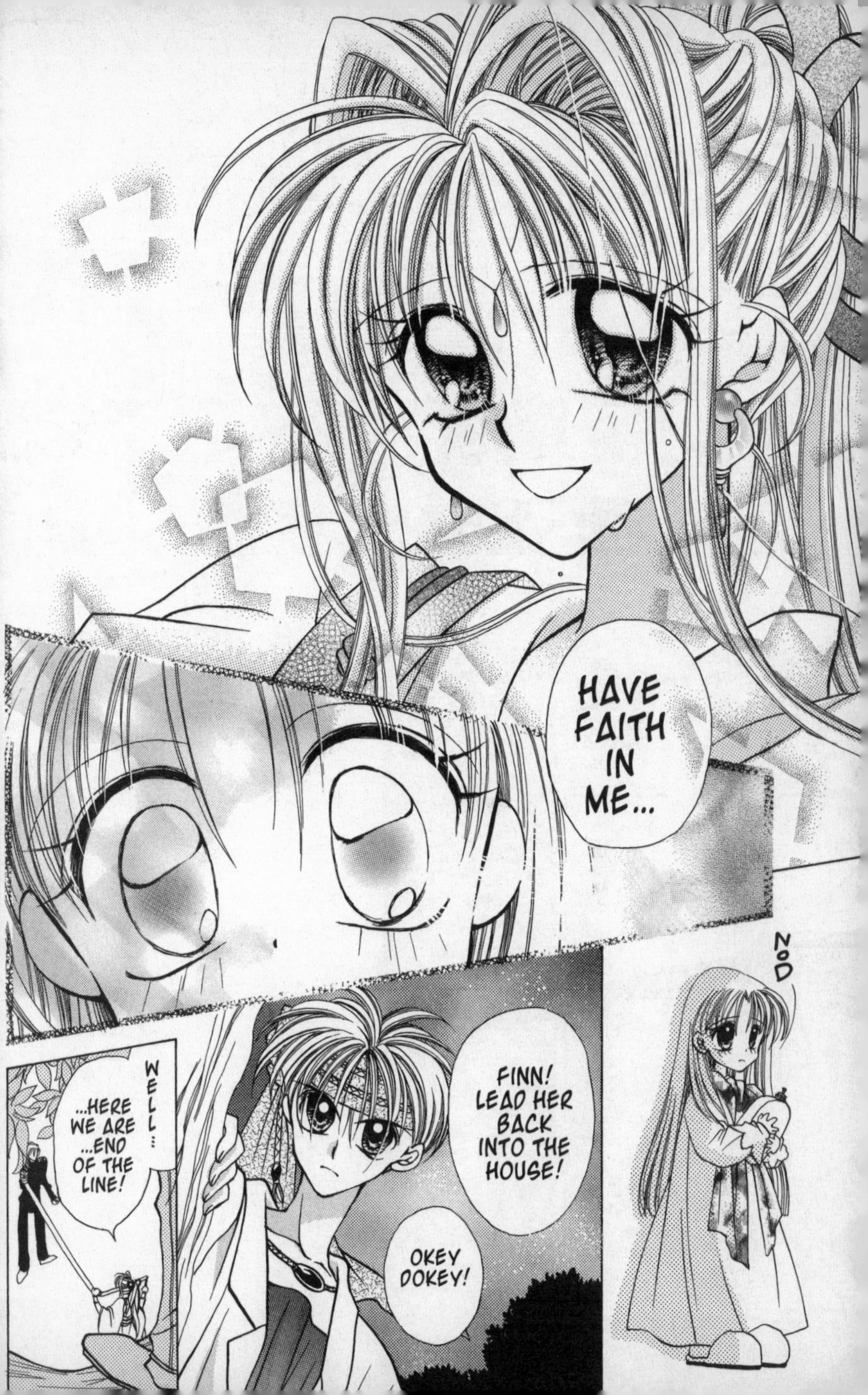
HAVE FAITH IN ME...
NOD
FINN! LEAD HER BACK INTO THE HOUSE!
OKEY DOKEY!
WELL...
...HERE WE ARE ...END OF THE LINE!

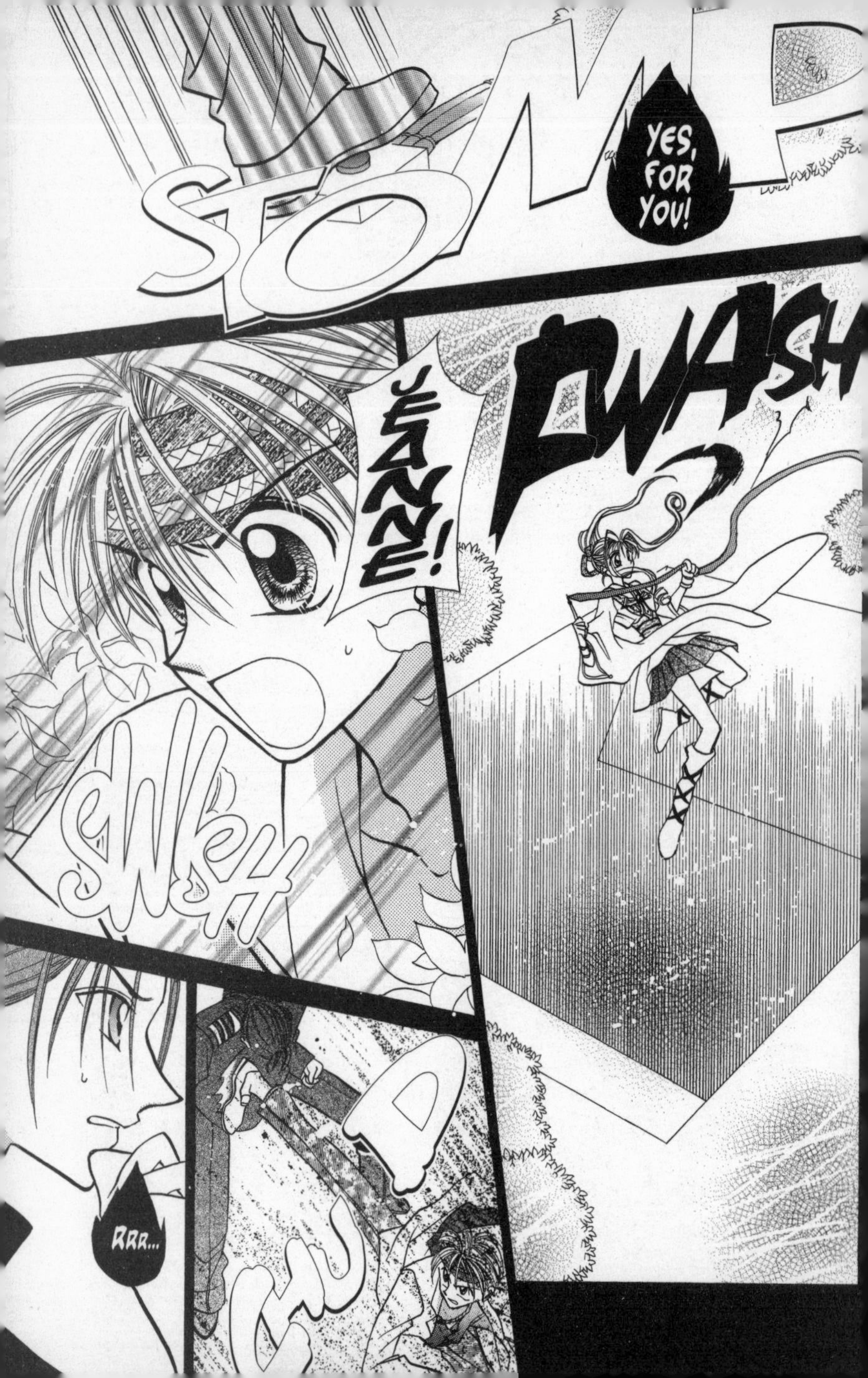
YES, FOR YOU!
STOMP
PWASH
JEANNE!
SWISH
RRR...

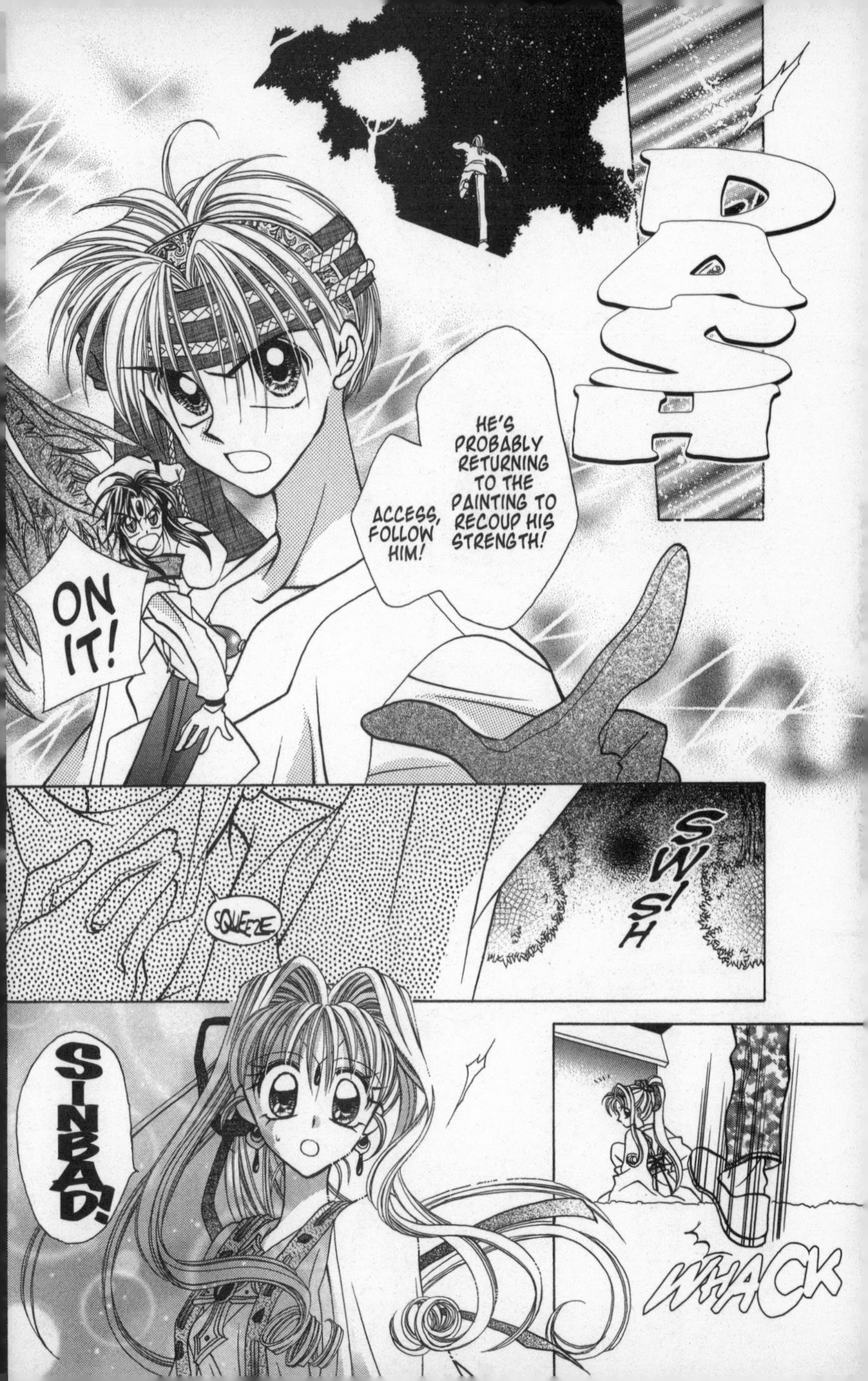
DASH
HE'S PROBABLY RETURNING TO THE PAINTING TO RECOUP HIS STRENGTH!
ACCESS, FOLLOW HIM!
ON IT!
SWISH
SQUEEZE
WHACK
SINBAD!

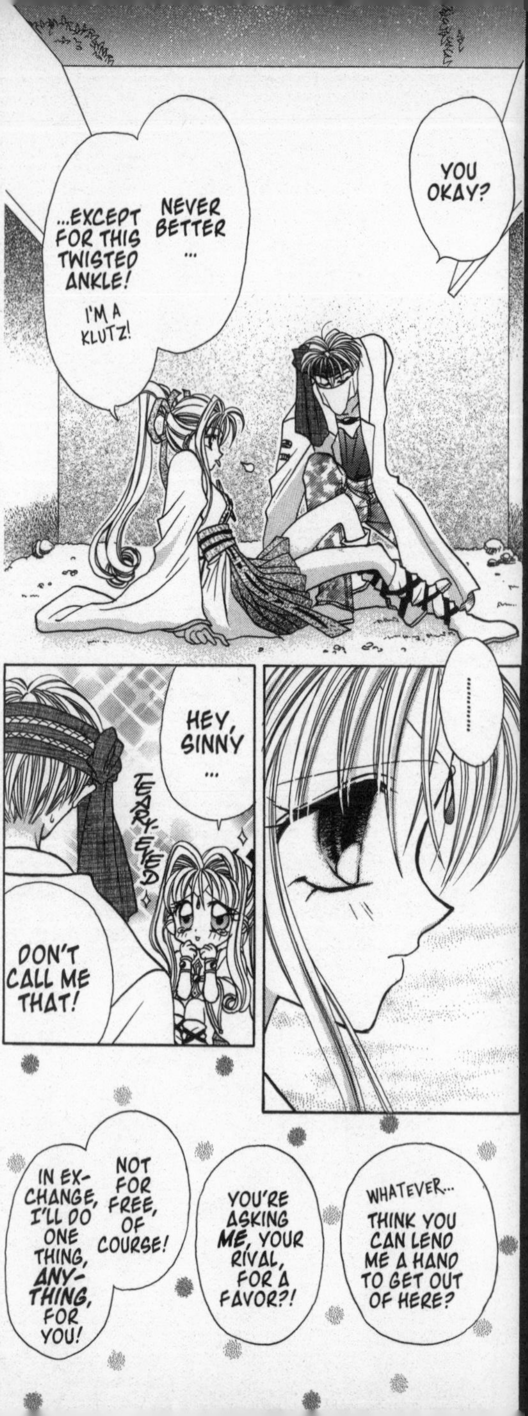
YOU OKAY?
NEVER BETTER...
...EXCEPT FOR THIS TWISTED ANKLE!
I'M A KLUTZ!
....
HEY, SINNY...
TEARY-EYED
DON'T CALL ME THAT!
WHATEVER... THINK YOU CAN LEND ME A HAND TO GET OUT OF HERE?
YOU'RE ASKING ME, YOUR RIVAL, FOR A FAVOR?!
NOT FOR FREE, OF COURSE!
IN EXCHANGE, I'LL DO ONE THING, ANYTHING, FOR YOU!

MUSIC THAT I LIKE

(I reserve the right to change the topic at any given moment though) (LOL) I'm a strange woman...I can't draw unless I'm listening to music. I especially like songs that stimulate my artistic endeavors. Anyway, I thought I'd take this space to talk a little about my favorite musicians and songs. Recently, I like Cocco's "Great, strong people," "Tsuyoku Erai Monotachi," the Brilliant Green's "There will be love there," and as always, anything by the B'z. But everyone already knows and loves these popular songs and artists, so this time I'll clue you in on a choice more off the beaten path. A lot of you probably know Komori Minami-san as a DJ for Lovelove Radio. But did you also know she's a voice actress and a singer? Anyway, if I had to recommend just one of her songs, it'd be "Angel Heart." Fantastic music, lyrics, arrangement...I can't get enough of it! If I may be so bold, I think the song fits Jeanne (Maron-chan) to a T! "Angel Heart" can be found on Minami-san's "Courage" album, which is so great that I'd definitely rank it as one of the top three cds I've ever bought! (I've got 80 cds in my collection, including singles.) All of her songs are well worth listening to!

↑ The genre is pop music, by the way!

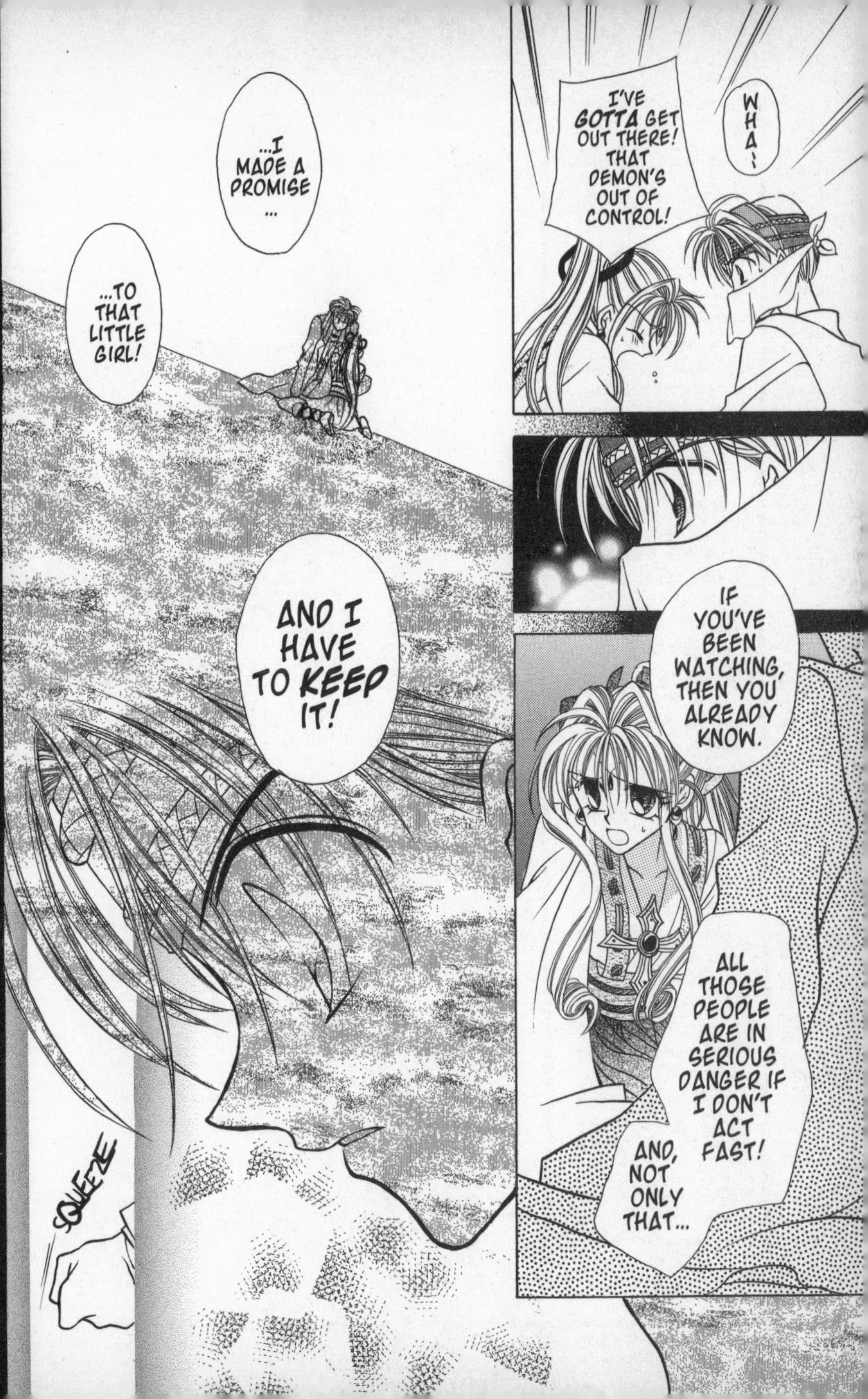
WHA...!
I'VE GOTTA GET OUT THERE! THAT DEMON'S OUT OF CONTROL!
IF YOU'VE BEEN WATCHING, THEN YOU ALREADY KNOW.
ALL THOSE PEOPLE ARE IN SERIOUS DANGER IF I DON'T ACT FAST!
AND, NOT ONLY THAT...
...I MADE A PROMISE...
...TO THAT LITTLE GIRL!
AND I HAVE TO KEEP IT!
SQUEEZE

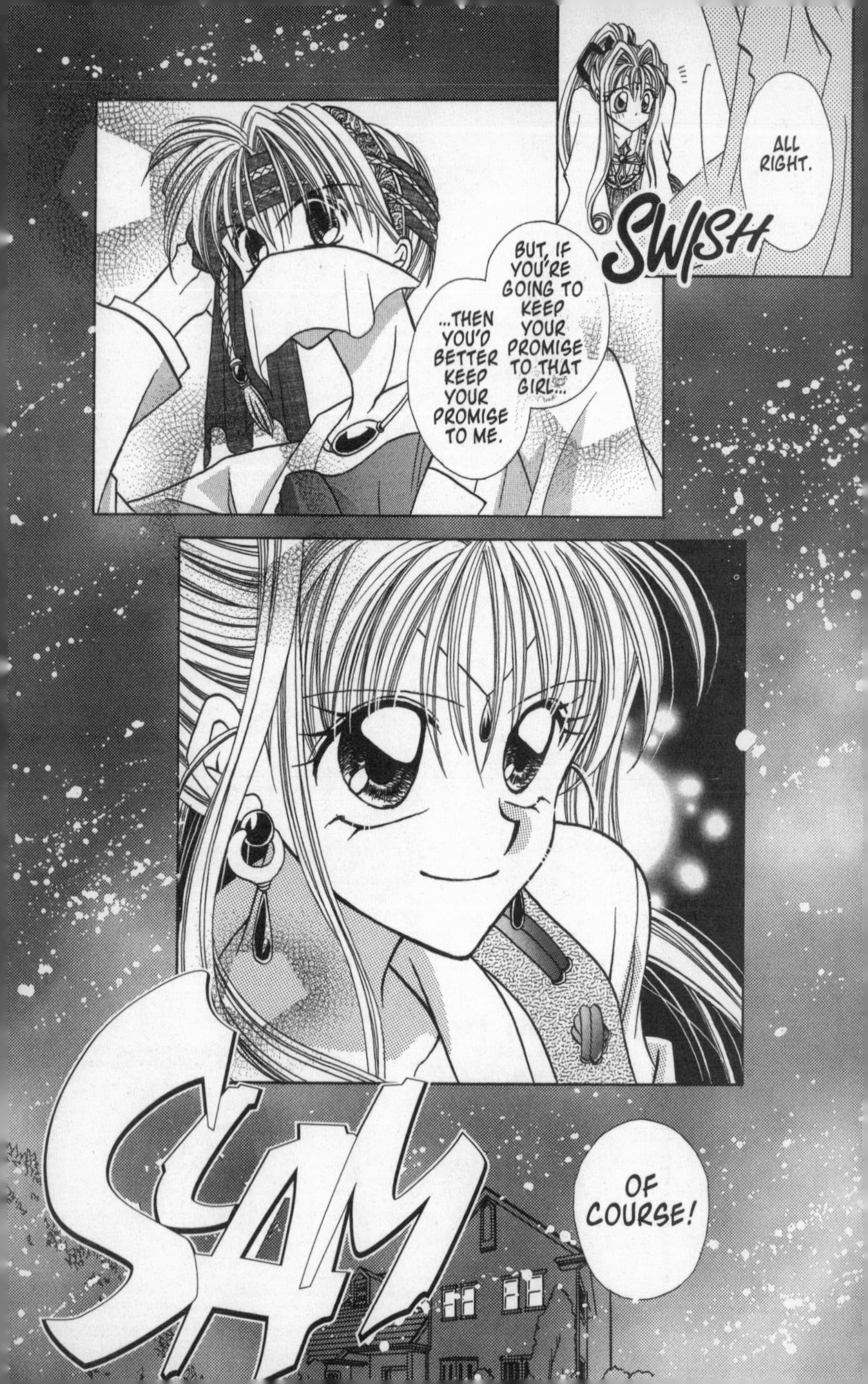
ALL RIGHT.
SWISH
BUT, IF YOU'RE GOING TO KEEP YOUR PROMISE TO THAT GIRL...
...THEN YOU'D BETTER KEEP YOUR PROMISE TO ME.
SLAM
OF COURSE!

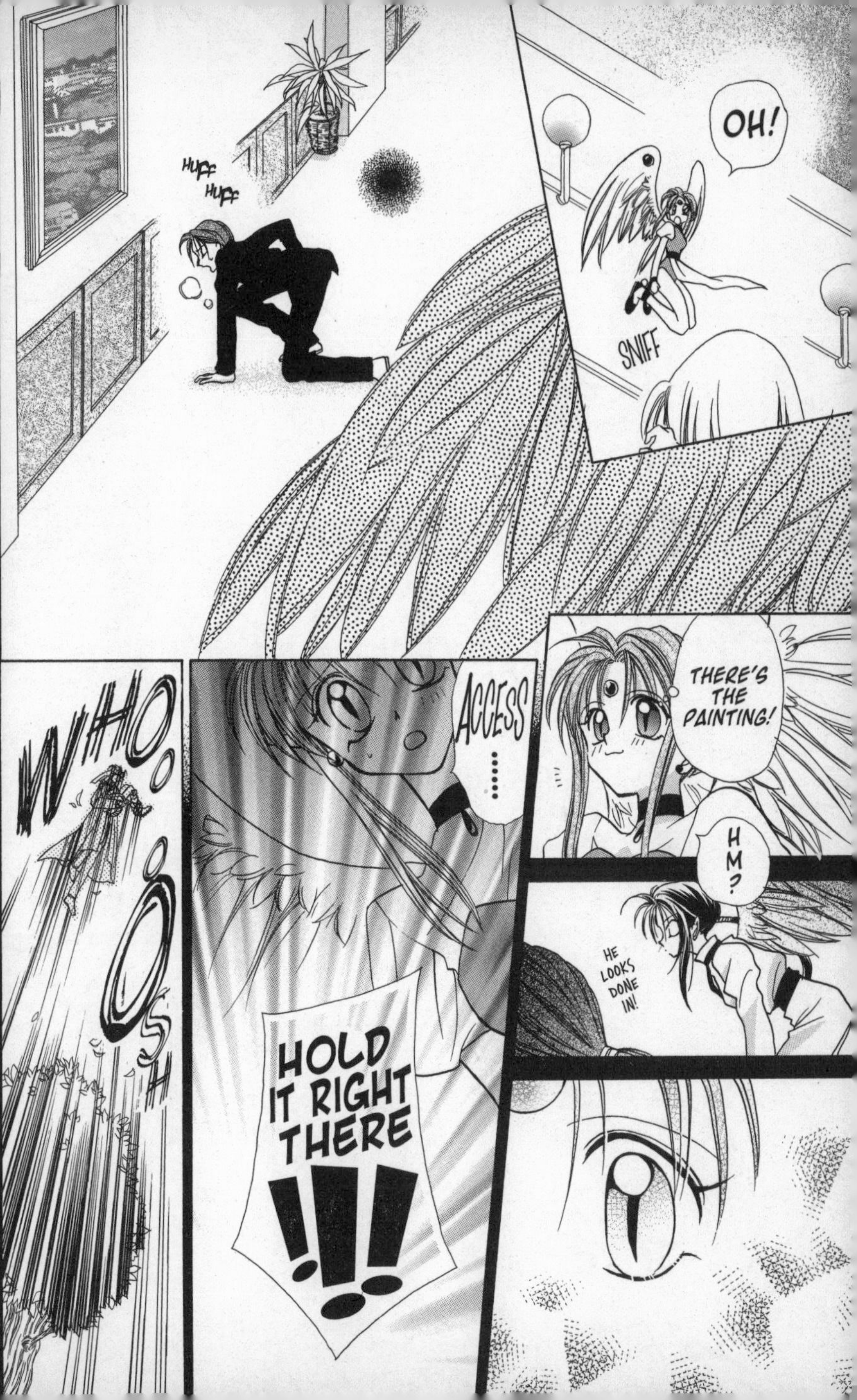
OH!
SNIFF
HUFF HUFF
THERE'S THE PAINTING!
HM?
HE LOOKS DONE IN!
ACCESS ......
HOLD IT RIGHT THERE!!!
WHOOOOSH

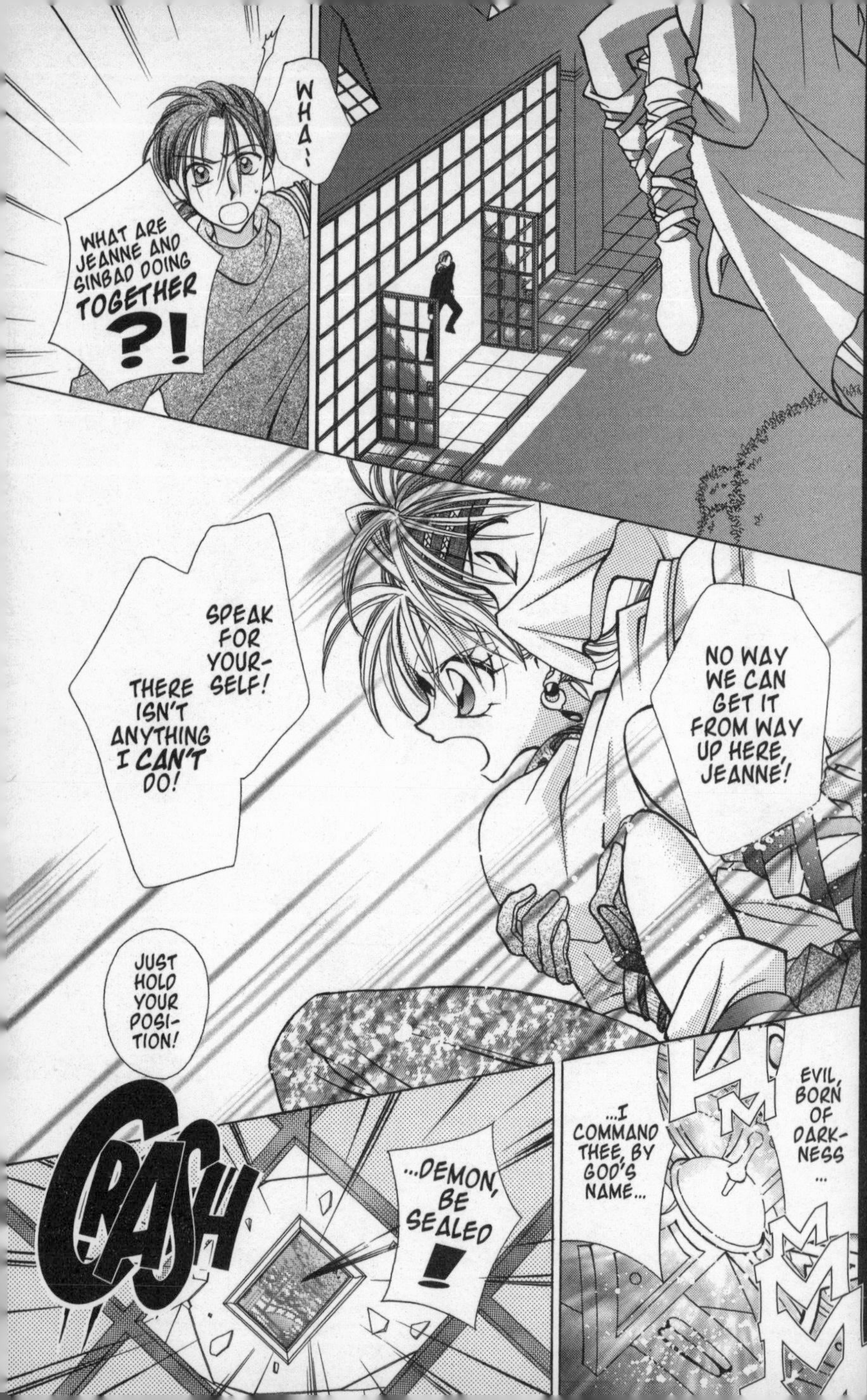
WHA...!
WHAT ARE JEANNE AND SINBAD DOING TOGETHER?!
NO WAY WE CAN GET IT FROM WAY UP HERE, JEANNE!
SPEAK FOR YOURSELF! THERE ISN'T ANYTHING I CAN'T DO!
JUST HOLD YOUR POSITION!
EVIL, BORN OF DARKNESS...
...I COMMAND THEE, BY GOD'S NAME...
HMMM
...DEMON, BE SEALED!
CRASH

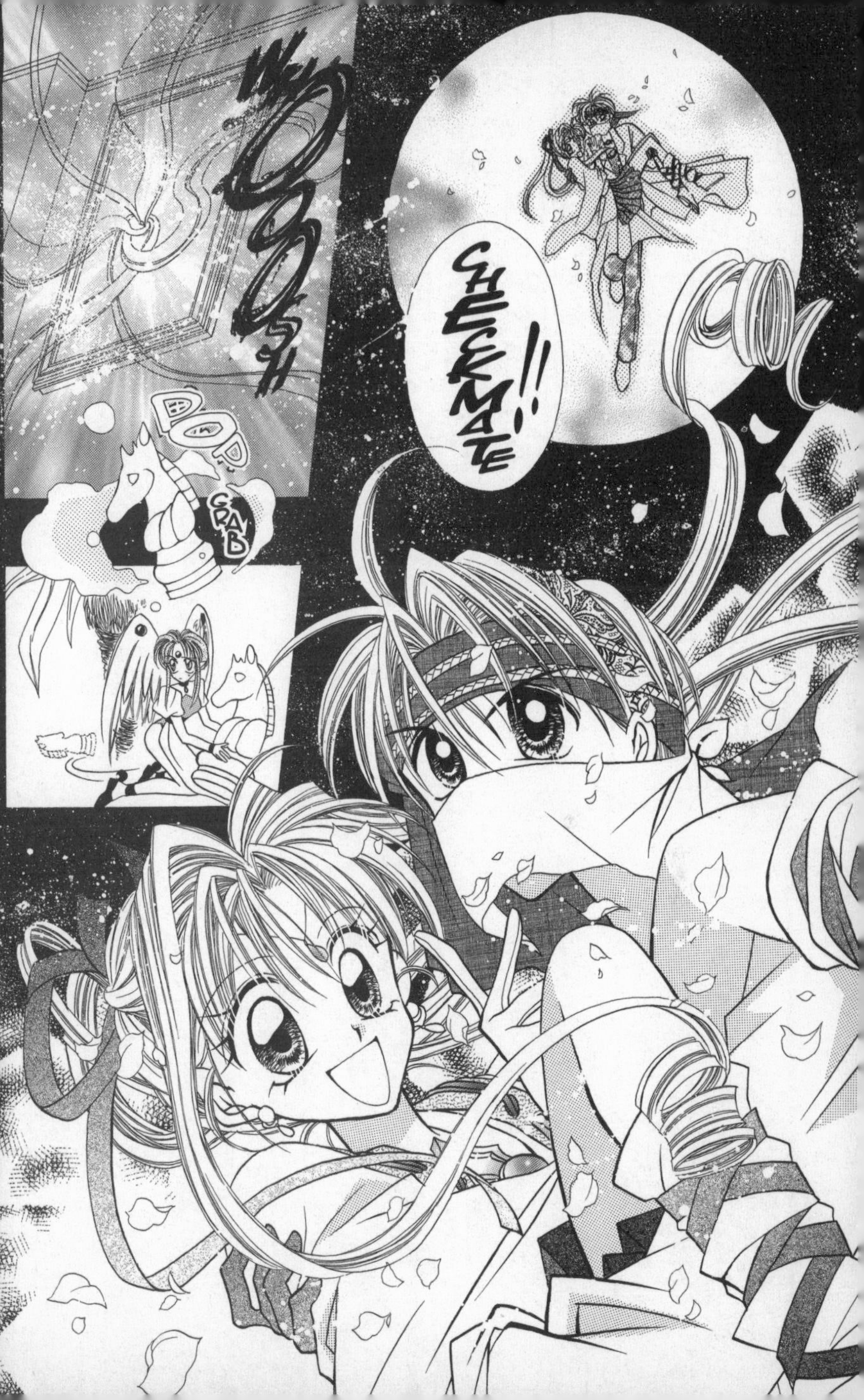
CHECKMATE!!
WHOOSH
POP
GRAB

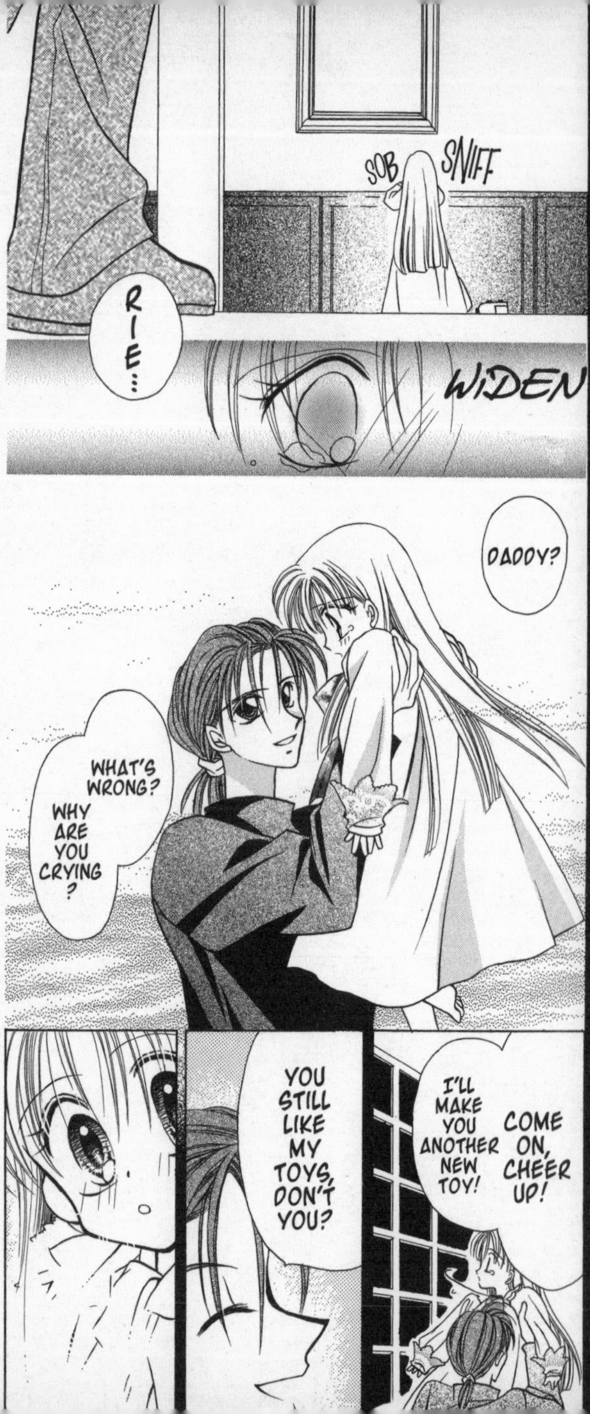
SNIFF
SOB
RIE...
WIDEN
DADDY?
WHAT'S WRONG? WHY ARE YOU CRYING?
COME ON, CHEER UP!
I'LL MAKE YOU ANOTHER NEW TOY!
YOU STILL LIKE MY TOYS, DON'T YOU?

SEE YOU!

Well, this is the last column. Thanks to everyone who's read this far. (I always write these things when I'm sleepy. Actually, I haven't had a decent sleep in a long time...) Anyway, regarding fan letters, because Jeanne is going to continue longer than I'd anticipated (I originally projected that about 12 episodes would do it) and seems to be more popular than my previous efforts (which I'm thrilled about), there's been a big spike in the number of fan letters I've been getting (which I'm even more thrilled about), which is why I haven't been able to reply to everyone recently. 'Til now, I've somehow managed to send responses to those readers who have included sases, but from now on, I can't even guarantee that. However, in the future, I'll use this space to answer readers' questions, so keep sending me mail! Also, I love to hear your thoughts for every episode, so if you're someone who thinks along the lines of "you don't have to answer me. Just listen to what I have to say!," please send me your opinion. If you do, you'll make me so happy I'll scream out at the top of my lungs.
Send to:

c/o CMX
888 PROSPECT ST #240
LA JOLLA, CA 92037

Oh, I'd also love it if you sent along fan comics featuring my characters!

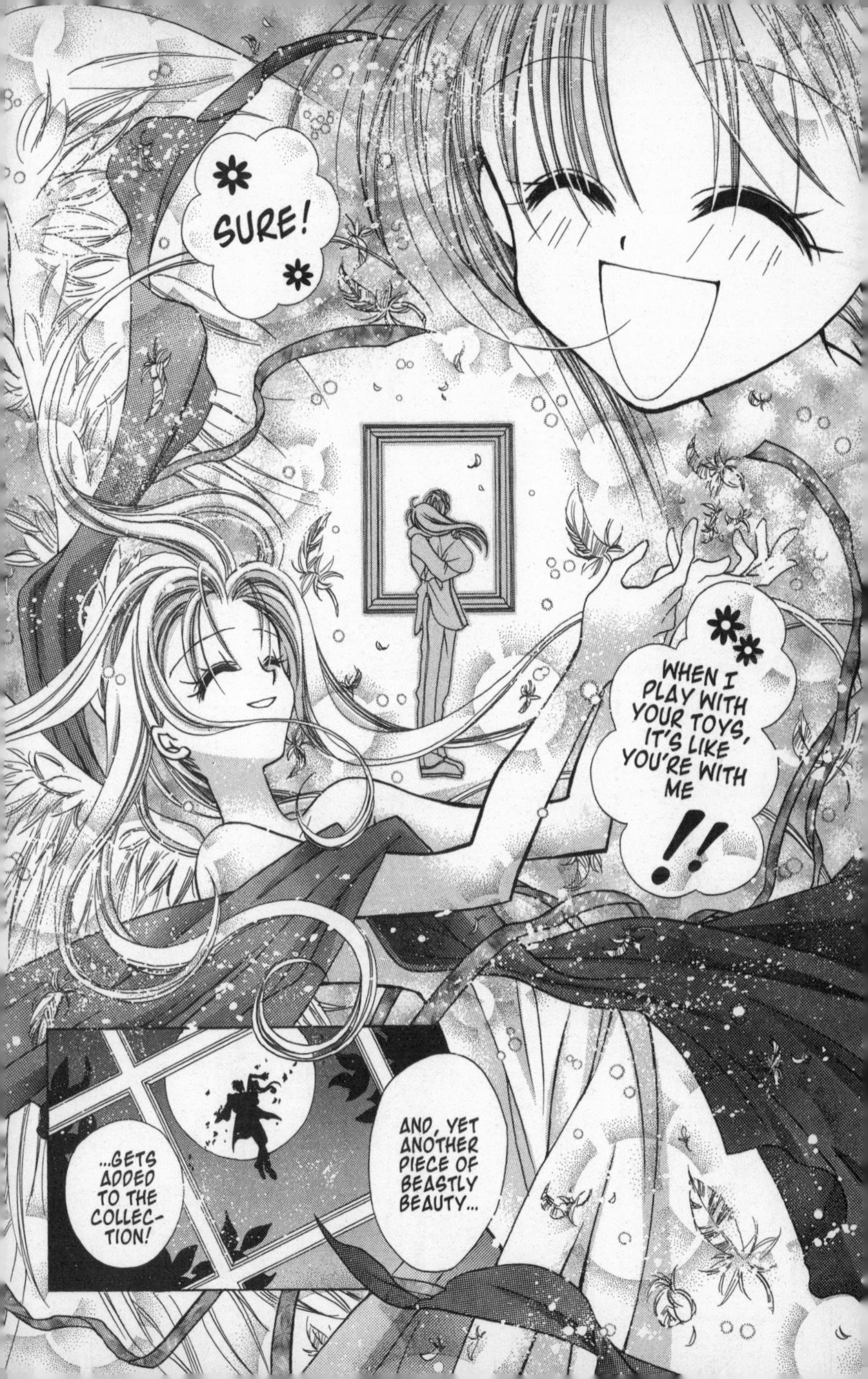
SURE!
WHEN I PLAY WITH YOUR TOYS, IT'S LIKE YOU'RE WITH ME !!
AND, YET ANOTHER PIECE OF BEASTLY BEAUTY...
...GETS ADDED TO THE COLLEC-TION!

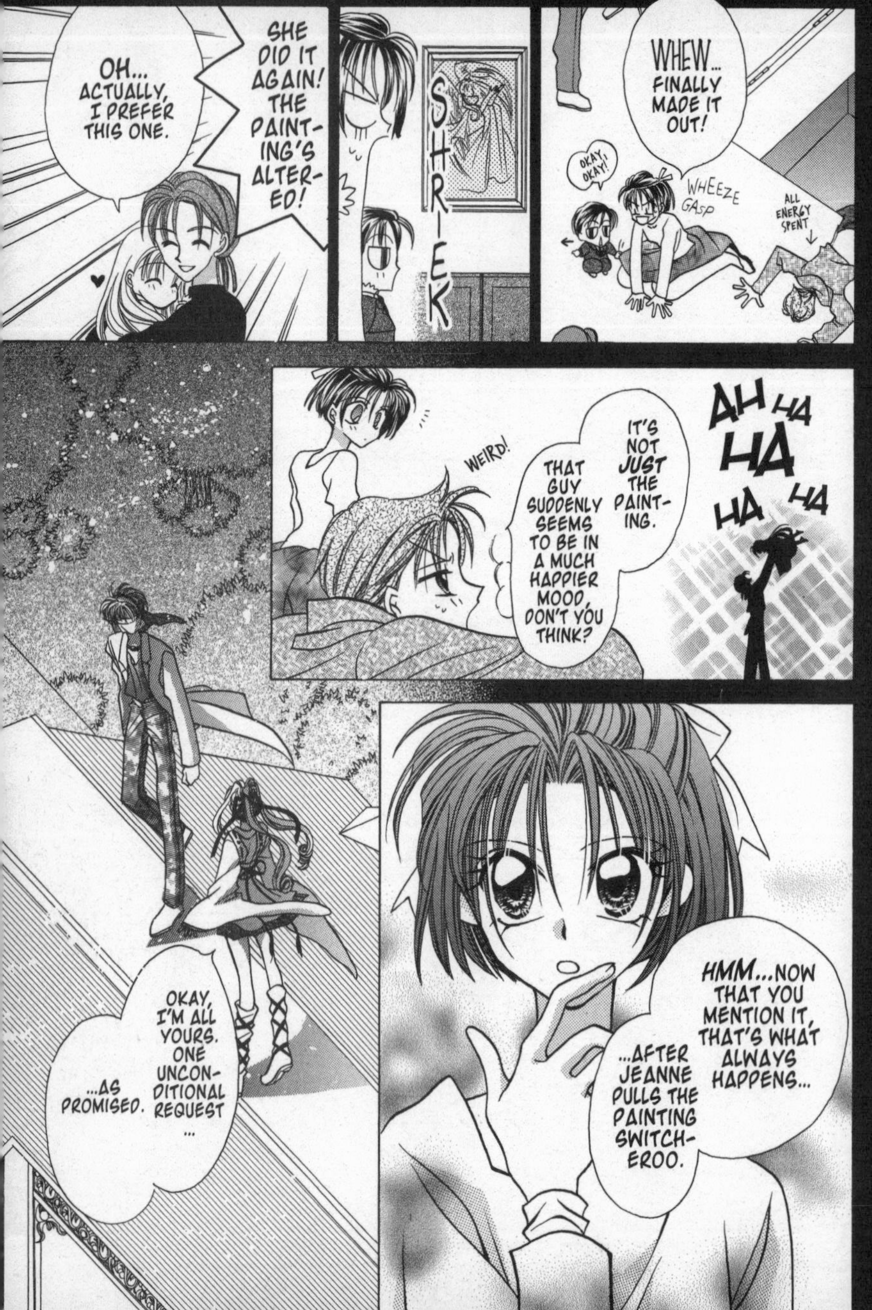
WHEW... FINALLY MADE IT OUT!
OKAY, OKAY!
WHEEZE GASP
ALL ENERGY SPENT
SHE DID IT AGAIN! THE PAINTING'S ALTERED!
SHRIEK
OH... ACTUALLY, I PREFER THIS ONE.
AH HA HA HA HA
IT'S NOT JUST THE PAINTING.
THAT GUY SUDDENLY SEEMS TO BE IN A MUCH HAPPIER MOOD, DON'T YOU THINK?
WEIRD!
HMM...NOW THAT YOU MENTION IT, THAT'S WHAT ALWAYS HAPPENS...
...AFTER JEANNE PULLS THE PAINTING SWITCHEROO.
OKAY, I'M ALL YOURS. ONE UNCONDITIONAL REQUEST...
...AS PROMISED.

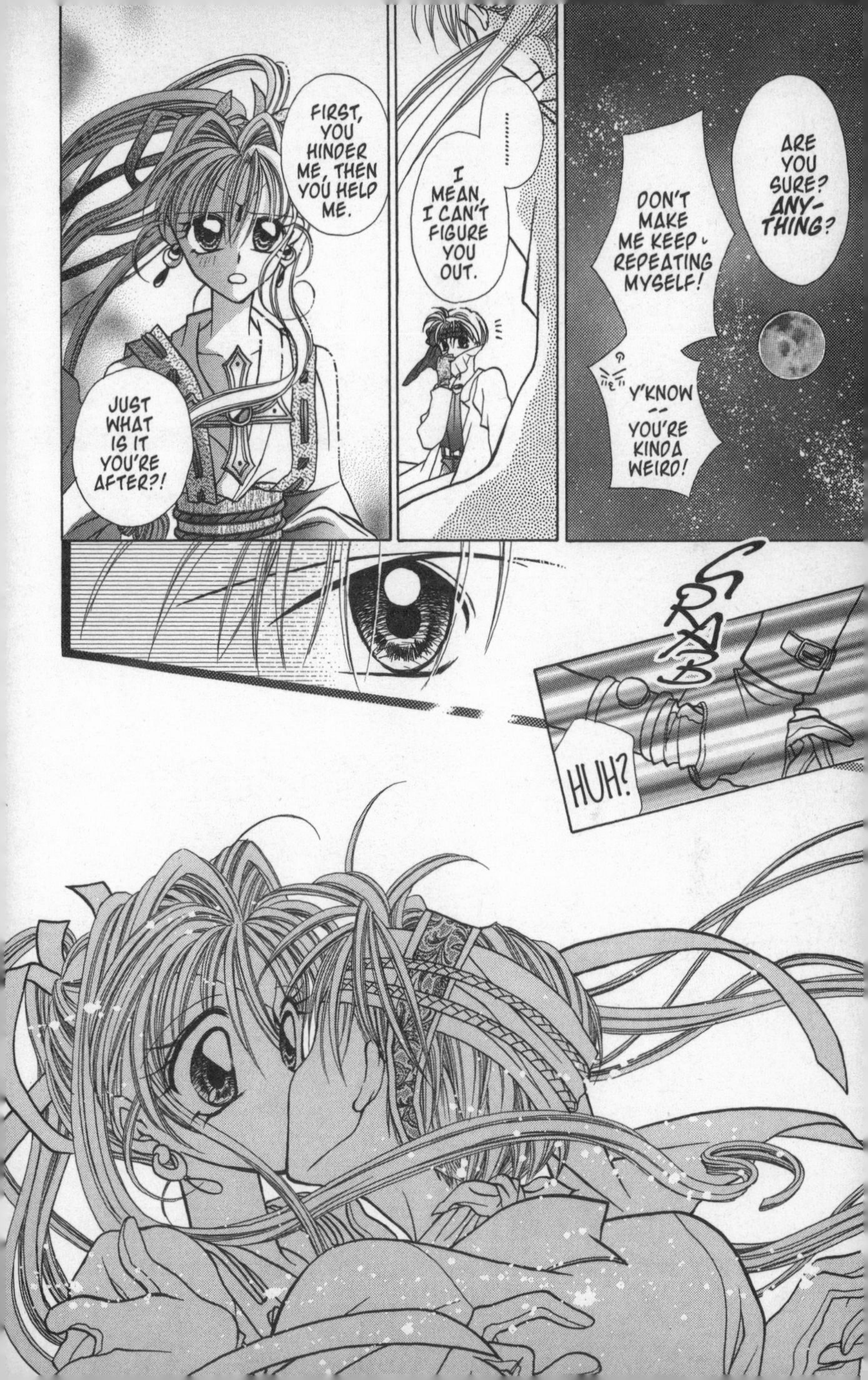
ARE YOU SURE? ANYTHING?
DON'T MAKE ME KEEP REPEATING MYSELF!
Y'KNOW -- YOU'RE KINDA WEIRD!
......
I MEAN, I CAN'T FIGURE YOU OUT.
FIRST, YOU HINDER ME, THEN YOU HELP ME.
JUST WHAT IS IT YOU'RE AFTER?!
GRAB
HUH?

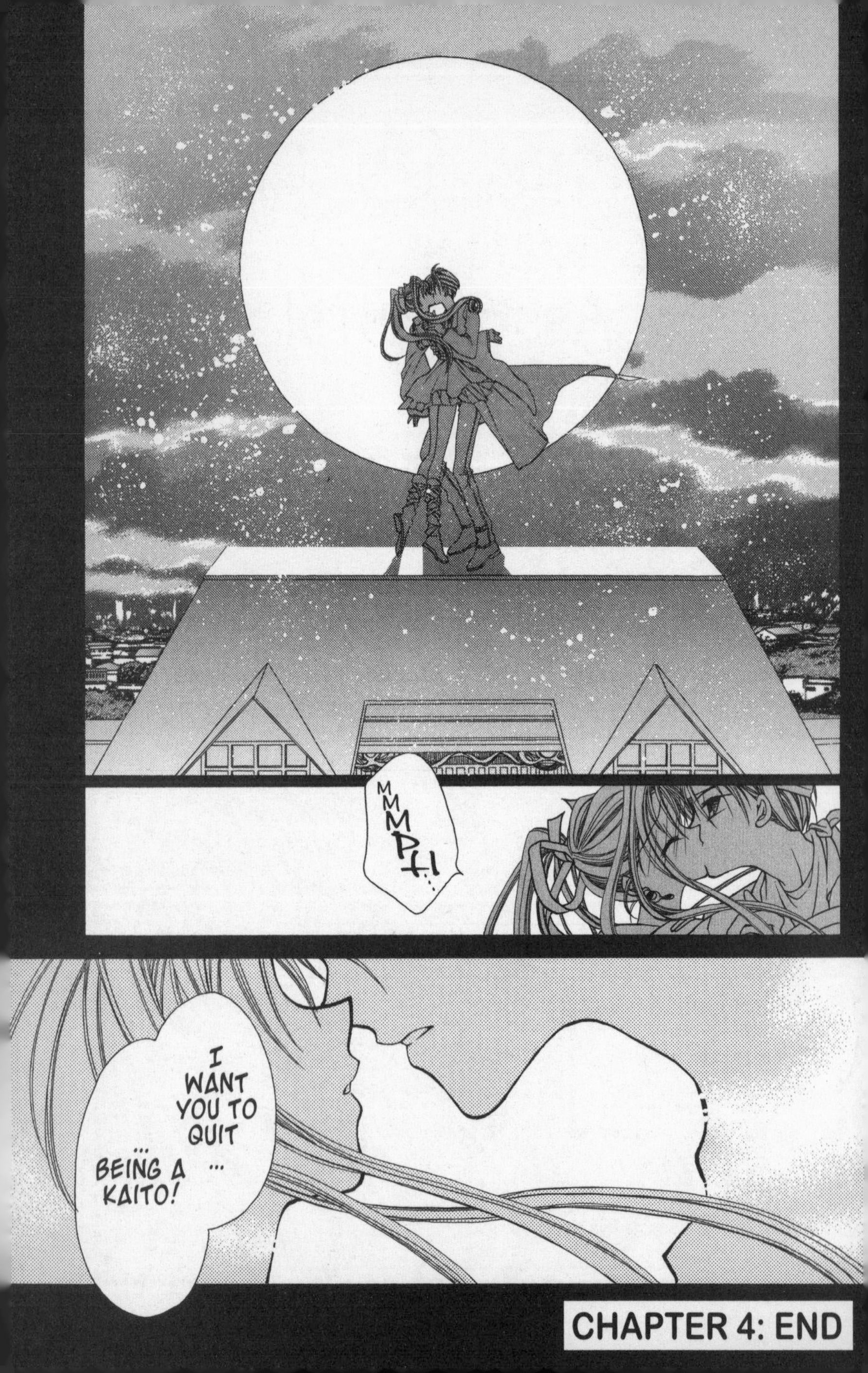
MMMPH!...
I WANT YOU TO QUIT... ...BEING A KAITO!
CHAPTER 4: END

PRESENTING... THE HEAVENLY ASSISTANTS!

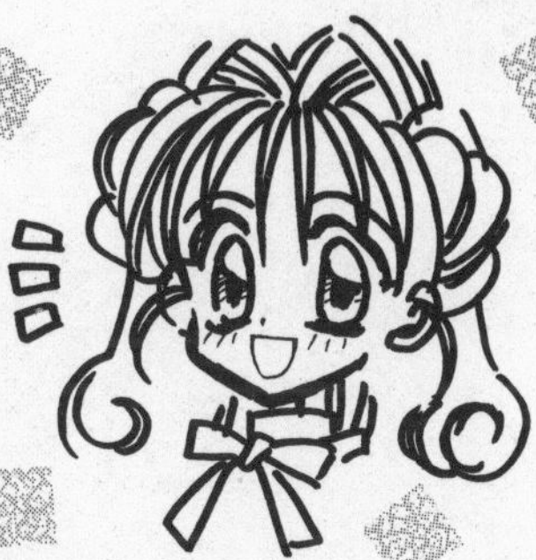

in these pages, my always supportive assistants (and friends) provide their p.o.v. about me. i'm lucky to have such talented staff on board!

TRULY, THANK YOU!

*By the way, i wrote the opening title intros for each assistant. There's no deep meaning attached.

Go/Go! HAPPY CHILDREN! Ai MINASE

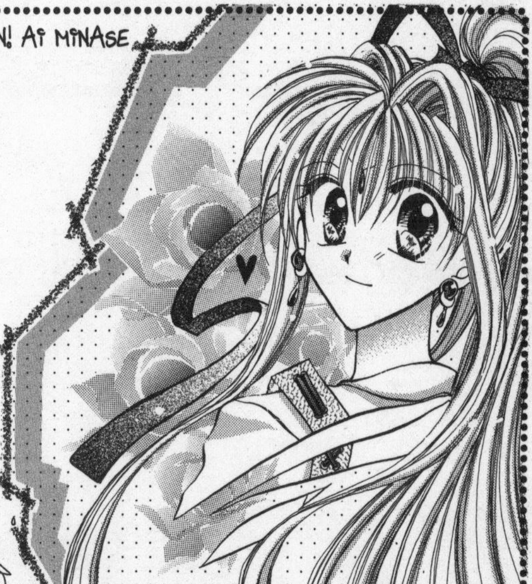
OK!

Nice to meet you. i'm Arina-sensei's assistant, Ai Minase! i've been friends with Arina-sensei since her debut ("2Love") and assistant since "NonFic." i loved "i.O.N," but, at the moment, i really, really love Jeanne, so it's such a blast for me to be able to help out with the series. So, of course, i'm going to stand by Jeanne and Arina-sensei for the long haul, as their number one fan! Arina-chi, keep fighting the good fight...next month...and beyond!

August 1998 Ai MINASE

LOVELY, DITZY ANGEL RUKA KAZUKI

Nice to meet you! I'm Arina-sensei's newest assistant, Ruka Kazuki! I've only had the opportunity to help on three stories so far, but already, I've learned so much! I have so much respect for Arina-sensei, because even working without much time or sleep, she always draws such beautiful art! I'm constantly blown away by it! Arina-sensei can count on my eternal support!

August 1998 RUKA KAZUKI

NON NON LOVELY GAL KYAKYA ASANO

Hello. Nice to meet you. I'm Arina-sensei's assistant, Kyakya Asano. I've been with Arina-sensei for about a year and a half. I have an immense amount of respect for her but, I highly value her friendship. I believe this manga has turned out so beautifully because Arina-sensei created it. I'm also a big fan of hers, so to all the other fans out there, I say, let's keep cheering Arina-sensei on and on and on! Oh, and keep your eyes peeled like oranges for volume 2!

August 1998 KYAKYA ASANO

P.S Of all the characters in Jeanne, I love Miyako-chan the best! Love ♡♡

↑ "EYES PEELED LIKE ORANGES!" WHAT'S THAT SUPPOSED TO MEAN! (LOL)

BY ARINA.

Ai Minase's Cutting with Scissors

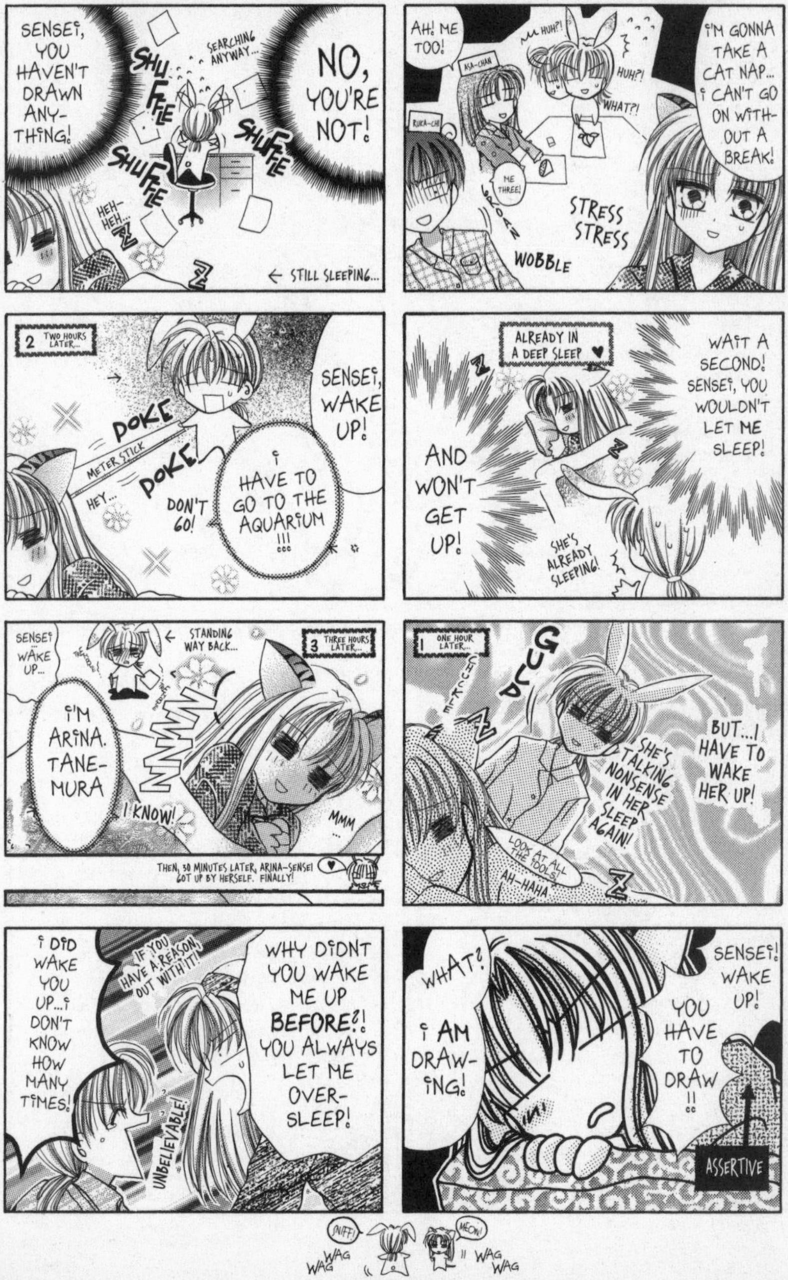
I'M GONNA TAKE A CAT NAP... I CAN'T GO ON WITHOUT A BREAK!
HUH?!
HUH?!
WHAT?!
AH! ME TOO!
ASA-CHAN
RUKA-CHI
ME THREE!
STRESS STRESS
WOBBLE
SENSEI, YOU HAVEN'T DRAWN ANYTHING!
SEARCHING ANYWAY...
SHUFFLE
SHUFFLE
SHUFFLE
NO, YOU'RE NOT!
HEH-HEH...
← STILL SLEEPING...
ALREADY IN A DEEP SLEEP ♥
WAIT A SECOND! SENSEI, YOU WOULDN'T LET ME SLEEP!
AND WON'T GET UP!
SHE'S ALREADY SLEEPING!
2 TWO HOURS LATER...
SENSEI, WAKE UP!
POKE
METER STICK
POKE
HEY...
I HAVE TO GO TO THE AQUARIUM!!!
DON'T GO!
1 ONE HOUR LATER...
GULP
CHUCKLE
BUT...I HAVE TO WAKE HER UP!
SHE'S TALKING NONSENSE IN HER SLEEP AGAIN!
LOOK AT ALL THE IDOLS!
AH-HAHA
3 THREE HOURS LATER...
← STANDING WAY BACK...
SENSEI... WAKE UP...
I'M ARINA TANEMURA
I KNOW!
MMM...
THEN, 30 MINUTES LATER, ARINA-SENSEI GOT UP BY HERSELF. FINALLY! ♥
SENSEI! WAKE UP!
YOU HAVE TO DRAW!!
WHAT?
I AM DRAWING!
ASSERTIVE
WHY DIDNT YOU WAKE ME UP BEFORE?! YOU ALWAYS LET ME OVERSLEEP!
IF YOU HAVE A REASON, OUT WITH IT!
I DID WAKE YOU UP...I DON'T KNOW HOW MANY TIMES!
UNBELIEVABLE!
SNIFF!
MEOW!
WAG WAG
WAG WAG

RUKA KAZUKI'S "LET ME TAKE A BREAK"

Arina-sensei is...
...great at impressions.
Sham-Poo from "Ranma 1/2"
AIYA!
SCRITCH SCRATCH
SOUNDS JUST LIKE HER!
CUTE!
ASA-CHAN
AI-NYAN
ME
Kaoru-Kun from "Eva"
NICE SONG...
SCRITCH SCRATCH
SOUNDS JUST LIKE THE REAL THING!
COOL!
Okkoto-Nusi from "Princess Mononoke"
I'VE COME BACK...FROM THE LAND OF THE DEAD...
SCRITCH SCRATCH
S-SOUNDS JUST LIKE HIM...
Deadline
SCRIBBLE SCRIBBLE
SCRITCH SCRATCH
SCRITCH SCRATCH
The day after deadline, when everyone can finally have a good time...
YAY! AFTER KARAOKE, LET'S PLAY... BADMINTON!
ME
ARINA-SENSEI
AI-NYAN
At first, it's a lot of fun...
HO HO HO! JUST TRY AND HIT MY MIRACLE SMASH!
OOH, WE'RE IN FOR IT NOW!
GYA HA HA!
...but 10 minutes later...
PANT
PANT
PANT
...the lack of any physical exercise during the usual grind catches up to our heroines...

KYAKYA ASANO'S SPACE BOY AND DOKKINKO ♪

SELF-CARICATURE →

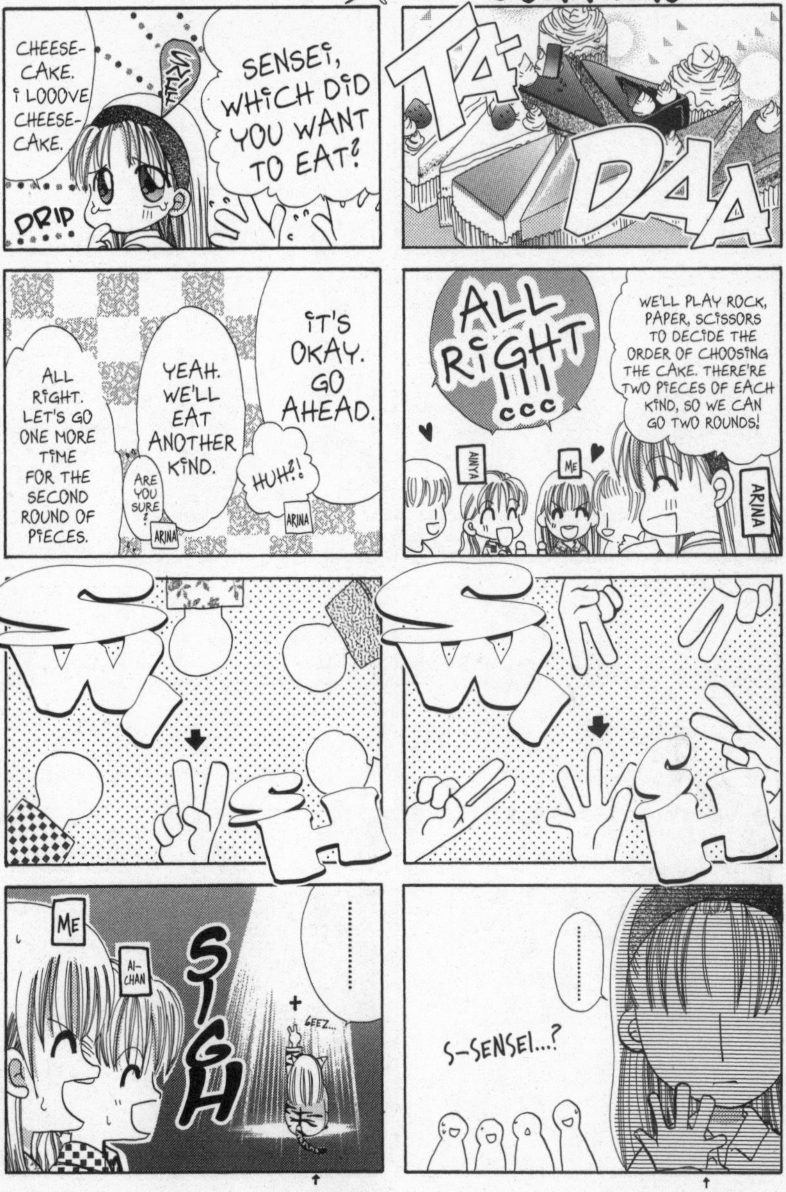

TA-DAA
SENSEI, WHICH DID YOU WANT TO EAT?
SNIFF
CHEESE-CAKE. I LOOOVE CHEESE-CAKE.
DRIP
WE'LL PLAY ROCK, PAPER, SCISSORS TO DECIDE THE ORDER OF CHOOSING THE CAKE. THERE'RE TWO PIECES OF EACH KIND, SO WE CAN GO TWO ROUNDS!
ALL RIGHT!!!
ARINA
ME
AINYA
IT'S OKAY. GO AHEAD.
HUH?!
ARINA
YEAH. WE'LL EAT ANOTHER KIND.
ARE YOU SURE?
ARINA
ALL RIGHT. LET'S GO ONE MORE TIME FOR THE SECOND ROUND OF PIECES.
SWISH
SWISH
......
S-SENSEI...?
......
GEEZ...
SIGH
ME
AI-CHAN

↑ SCISSORS

↑ PAPER